POLITICAL AWAKENING IN THE BELGIAN CONGO

# POLITICAL
# AWAKENING
# IN THE
# BELGIAN CONGO

## René Lemarchand

*University of California Press*
*Berkeley and Los Angeles*  1964

University of California Press
Berkeley and Los Angeles, California
Cambridge University Press
London, England
© 1964 by The Regents of the University of California
Library of Congress Catalog Card No.: 64-21774
Printed in the United States of America

For Pimme

# PREFACE

In this volume I am attempting to unravel the tangled skeins of nationalist developments in the Congo during the terminal phase of Belgian colonial rule. After the manuscript was completed, the Congo entered upon an entirely new and as yet uncertain phase of its political evolution. Indeed, the events that have taken place since independence form the substance of an altogether different chapter of the Congo's turbulent history, one in which the actors play different roles, reveal different motives, and move in a different sociopolitical environment. Nonetheless, I hope that the present study will provide at least part of the factual and analytical background necessary to an understanding of contemporary developments. If nothing else, the documentary evidence presented here should give the student of Congolese politics a starting point for further research, and for new or differing interpretations.

Sections of this book have already been published elsewhere in different form. Parts of chapter ii are borrowed from my article, "The Bases of Nationalism among the Bakongo," *Africa*, XXXI (Oct., 1961), 344–354; chapter xi is based largely on my article, "The Limits of Self-Determination: The Case of the Katanga Secession," *American Political Science Review*, LVI (June, 1962), 404–416; and chapter xii contains sections of my essay on Congolese political groups in James S. Coleman and Carl G. Rosberg, Jr., eds., *Political Parties and National Integration in Tropical Africa* (Berkeley and Los Angeles: University of California Press, 1964).

I did most of the basic research for this book in the Congo in 1960, before and after independence. To the Ford Foundation, which made my trip to Africa financially possible, I express my sincere gratitude. I also acknowledge my debt to the African Studies Center at the University of California, Los Angeles, for providing me with supplementary assistance while I was in the Congo and in Belgium.

I am grateful to the staff and the faculty of Lovanium University in Leopoldville, and in particular to Professor Jean Buchmann, then dean of the Faculty of Law, for their kindness and gracious hospitality during the first six months of my stay in the Congo.

I owe many thanks to the staff of the Institut de Sociologie in Brussels, and especially to its director, Professor Arthur Doucy, for his kind hospitality and for making available to me the research facilities of the institute. To M. Henri Rosy, research associate of the Institut de Sociologie, I express my appreciation for sharing with me so much of his time and personal knowledge. Acknowledgments are owing also to various Belgian officials and nonofficials for their coöperation, notably to Minister Auguste de Schrijver, Minister Auguste Van Hemelrijck, former Governor General Léo Pétillon, Professor Guy Malengrau, Aimé Lecointre, Guy Spitaels, Benoit Verhaegen, and Jules Gérard-Libois.

I am particularly conscious of my debt to Professor James S. Coleman, director of the African Studies Center at the University of California, Los Angeles, for his valuable comments on the manuscript as well as for his personal assistance during the troublesome circumstances that affected my work in the Congo and in Belgium. Among those who read the manuscript at various stages I would like to record my thanks to Professor Edouard Bustin and Professor Crawford Young for their detailed and constructive criticisms. Among those who improved the style and form of the manuscript I am especially indebted to my friends and colleagues at the University of Florida, David Chalmers and Russel Farnen.

Finally, I should add that this work could not have been written were it not for the many Congolese who went to much trouble to get me acquainted with the physical and political landscape of their country. As a matter of propriety I have decided not to mention their names, as many of them have occupied and continue to occupy responsible positions in the government and administration of the Congo; nonetheless, my debt to them is large.

For all the assistance I received from various quarters, the views expressed in this work are, of course, my sole responsibility. All errors of fact and interpretation herein contained are mine.

R. L.

# CONTENTS

x    *Contents*

# ILLUSTRATIONS (FOLLOWING PAGE 178)

1. The late Patrice Lumumba
2. Joseph Kasa-Vubu
3. Albert Kalondji
4. Cléophas Kamitatu
5. Antoine Gizenga
6. Paul Bolya
7. Albert Kalondji
8. A political meeting of the Union Kwangolaise pour l'Indépendance et la Liberté (Luka)
9. A group of Bangala warriors
10. A militant of the Alliance des Bakongo (Abako)
11. A Leopoldville voter
12. A Tshokwe dancer
13. A group of Baluba of Leopoldville
14. A Muyaka of Leopoldville
15. A patrol of Congolese soldiers
16. Albert Ndele
17. Moise Tshombe
18. Anicet Kashamura

# INTRODUCTION

The dramatic circumstances under which the former Belgian Congo acceded to self-government have focused public attention on an area of Central Africa which has since become one of the world's major trouble spots. The Congo has been the scene of events that had profound repercussions not only on the African continent but in the entire world. The state of political anarchy ushered in by independence has already confronted United States policy in Africa with issues of great urgency and complexity; it has endangered the very existence of the United Nations, and, in some quarters, has discredited its role; it has intensified the East-West struggle and thus has significantly increased the potential influence of the so-called "nonaligned" nations; finally, it has radically altered the political map of Africa and has nurtured strong doubts concerning the prospects of self-government for areas that are still under colonial rule. Yet, paradoxical as it may seem in view of the publicity given to these momentous developments, very little has been done so far in the way of a systematic investigation of the various factors and events that make up the background of the Congo crisis. The present study offers a tentative interpretation of political developments in the Congo during the brief transition from colonial rule to self-government.

Professor Ali Al'Amin Mazrui's comment that the Congolese, "in demanding self-government, . . . found out that the logical extreme of self-government meant too much 'self' and not enough 'government,' " [1] concisely sums up the essence of the problem posed by the advent of independence in the Congo. To be sure, the difficulties of creating an integrated national community from a multitude of ethnic "selves" are not unique to the Congo, as shown by the continuing efforts of African leaders to overcome the actual or potential threat of ethnic separatism. But in no other African territory have these difficulties assumed such magnitude, for in no other territory has the virulence of ethnic and regional particularisms been so pronounced. The history of Congolese nationalism is in large measure the story of an "unfinished revolution," for, although independence is now a reality, the task of national integration is only beginning.

My main objective, then, is to analyze the causes of political fragmentation in Congolese politics. As political parties are the principal media through which different brands of nationalism found expression,

1

primary emphasis must necessarily be placed on the social, economic, and political forces that predisposed certain groups of Africans to direct their allegiances toward specific parties, or to shift these allegiances from one party to another. In other words, beyond describing the ideological orientation and the formal structures of Congolese parties, one must seek to uncover the circumstances that have conditioned their growth and development. Only then is it possible to venture some general propositions about the elements of disunity which stand in the way of an integrated Congolese "nationality."

Although I have paid relatively little attention to the physical environment in which political groups have developed, the immensity of the area within the Congo's boundaries has an obvious bearing on the problem of national integration. Situated in the heart of the African continent, and stretching from the Nile-Congo divide in the east to the Atlantic Ocean in the west, the Congo covers some 905,380 square miles; it is about three times the size of Nigeria and one-third the size of continental United States. Next to the Sudan, it is the largest territory in the African continent. Included in its 13 million inhabitants are 10 to 11 million people of Bantu origins, 2 to 3 million Sudanic people, and about 40,000 Pygmies, mainly concentrated in the rain forests of the northeastern region. These groups are in turn divided into several hundred tribal groupings of varying size, unevenly distributed among the six provinces. Besides French, which is the lingua franca, four different vernacular languages—Kikongo, Kiswahili-Kingwana, Tshiluba, and Lingala—and about seventy-four tribal dialects are in active use. From the standpoint of size and ethnic diversity, therefore, the Congo occupies a unique position among other African territories.

Close ties exist between ethnic groups and political formations in the Congo, and the political parties that almost overnight mushroomed into existence reflect the ethnic diversity of the country. An exhaustive description of all these political groupings, however, would not only be tedious, but would probably add no significant insight to our analysis. Thus, although some references have been made to minor political groups, by and large I have restricted the scope of my inquiry to the parties that seem particularly significant in terms of their political orientation and following.

The question of what is meant here by "political party" is pertinent. According to Professor James S. Coleman, a political party is an "association that competes with other similar associations in periodic elections in order to participate in formal government institutions and thereby influence and control the personnel and policy of government." [2] Applied to the context of Congolese politics, however, this definition poses some difficulties. For example, the term "association" begs the question, for it does not tell us whether such semipolitical organizations as *évolués* clubs, friendly societies, tribal unions, and the like should be included. Even when the prospects of an electoral contest were in the distant future, some of these groups performed a variety of functions similar to those normally attributed to political parties. And when they finally had the opportunity to "participate in formal government institutions," some of them relied on methods other than those associated with electoral techniques. Clearly, the complexity of Congolese politics makes it difficult at this early stage to set forth a precise definition of "political party." For the time being, therefore, it is perhaps safer to adopt Thomas Hodgkin's tautological definition of parties as "all political organizations which regard themselves as parties and which are generally so regarded." [3]

Another caveat must be entered regarding the selection of a terminal date. Although this study is theoretically limited to preindependence developments, I have extended the time span to July 30, 1960, so as to include the Katanga secession. This decision is justified not only by the historical significance of the secession, but also because it is the logical outcome of a series of events which can be traced back to an early date, long before political parties even came into existence. On the whole, however, the main focus of inquiry is on the interplay of political forces on the Congolese scene until June 30, 1960, when the Congo became formally independent.

Finally, a few observations about the types of material used in this study are in order. Among the wide variety of materials dealing with the recent political history of the Congo,[4] the documents published by the Belgian Centre de Recherche et d'Information Socio-Politiques (CRISP) have been especially useful. Ruth Slade, *The Belgian Congo: Some Recent Changes,* and Alan P. Merriam, *Congo: Background to Conflict,* provided many provocative insights and thoughtful comments. On the history of Belgian colonization during and after the Free State period, the Archives of the Ministry of Colonies, in Brussels, were invaluable. Although most of the documents pertaining to the post-1913 phase are still in classified files, the several administrative reports that are presently available yield more information on the subject than any work in print which has appeared in recent times. But perhaps the most relevant source of documentation consists of the numerous African newspapers published during the preindependence period. In fact, I have drawn abundantly from the African press, including the vernacular press, to illustrate or buttress my arguments. Much of the information contained in this volume is drawn from unpublished documents furnished to me by both Africans and Europeans, and from personal interviews. Finally, whenever possible, I talked with the Africans themselves, in order to discover their interpretations of the phenomena discussed.

Part I of this study examines the traditional and historical setting in which Congolese groups operated. The main emphasis here is on those features of the traditional environment and historical evolution of the Congolese societies which have a bearing on subsequent developments. This survey, therefore, does not pretend to be complete; at best, it provides only a general sketch of the peoples and the cultures of the Congo, and of their history since their early contacts with European explorers. Part II considers the processes of social change initiated by the intrusion of Western influences, and the way in which they have affected the contemporary political scene. In this context the "colonial situation" refers to the broad range of situations that have stimulated, or delayed, the growth of nationalist sentiment and activity. Part III describes the rise and development of nationalist activities up to the time of independence. Part IV attempts to describe and analyze the structure and functioning of Congolese political parties, with special emphasis on their organization and leadership, and on the types of relationships they have established among themselves during the preindependence period.

# PART ONE

*Preliminary*

# I. THE PRECOLONIAL ENVIRONMENT

In few other parts of Africa are the links between modern political developments and precolonial societies more apparent than in the former Belgian Congo. Although there are wide variations in the degree to which traditional factors have influenced the growth of Congolese parties, nearly all of them have evidenced some sort of relationship to the traditional environment in which they grew. Indeed, even when this type of relationship would seem hardly compatible with the program and ideology of specific parties, the evidence shows that their leaders were fully aware of the advantages that might accrue from the exploitation of precolonial circumstances. Before we examine the way in which such circumstances have affected the development of political parties, something must be said of the major ethnic groups enclosed within the boundaries of the Congo. The main concern here is to identify the dominant groups, taking into account their modes of social and political organization and whatever historic and cultural relationships can be discerned among them.

## THE TRADITIONAL SOCIETY

The amazing variety of cultures and political systems encountered in the Congo makes it difficult to classify its peoples on the basis of commonly accepted criteria. Whereas some students have used linguistic differences, others have emphasized differences in the scale and type of political system associated with particular groups. Part of the difficulty in classifying Congolese societies on the basis of language is that the same language is sometimes spoken by different groups. The Kongo-speaking area, for example, encompasses a host of minor tribes besides the Bakongo—for example, Bayaka, Bambala, Bangongo—just as the Luba-Lunda speaking areas include within their linguistic boundaries many culturally and politically heterogeneous entities. Although the character of traditional political systems would seem more useful for an understanding of cultural differences, the classificatory devices used by Belgian scholars are not without certain limitations;[1] furthermore, the data available are still too scanty to permit a systematic analysis of the traditional political organization of Congolese societies. Perhaps a more fruitful

7

approach is to center upon the existence of common cultural traits, or "culture clusters," * among the peoples concerned.

In his study of "culture clusters" in the Belgian Congo, Alan P. Merriam distinguishes six major ethnic groups—Bakongo, Baluba, Mongo, Kuba, Mangbetu-Azande, and Warega—varying in size from the approximately 2,000,000 of the Mongo to the 73,000 of the Kuba.[2] Merriam's selection, based on "the literature available," excludes a number of significant groups—Lunda, Bayeke, and Bashi, to cite but a few—as well as many other groupings of lesser importance. Although these culture clusters constitute a fairly comprehensive cross section of the peoples and cultures of the Congo Basin, the scope of this study requires that certain other groups be taken into consideration.

The most important of these cultural aggregates, from the standpoint of subsequent political developments, is the Bakongo, presently divided among three different territories. While the vast majority of them inhabit the Republic of the Congo (1,200,000), they nevertheless form a sizable fraction of the population of Angola (350,000) and of the former Moyen-Congo (340,000). Four major tribal subgroups—Bantandu, Bandibu, Manianga, and Mayumbe—are located in Leopoldville Province, though some of them overlap on contiguous territories. Others, such as the Bansundi, the Bampangu, and the Bambata, are numerically less important. Despite considerable uncertainty as to their origins, recent historical research shows that the Bakongo must have originated in a small nuclear kingdom—the kingdom of Bungu—located on the northern bank of the Congo River, near the source of the Shiloango. They crossed the Congo in the twelfth or thirteenth century; after conquering the chiefdoms of Mpemba, Mpangu, and Mbata, they settled in the region of San Salvador, where Diogo Cão found them when he first landed in this part of Africa in 1482.[3]

Oral tradition substantiates historical sources on one major point: the Bakongo were originally divided into three kingdoms, Kakongo, Ngoyo, and Loango, with the former standing in relation to the others as a suzerain toward his vassal.[4] Bounded by the Congo River on the

---

* The concept of "culture cluster" is germane to the concept of "culture area" employed by the late Professor Melville J. Herskovits, but the two are not identical. As Alan P. Merriam points out, "two characteristics of the cluster tend to distinguish it from the area. The first of these is size; while it is conceivable that a culture cluster encompass as large a geographic distribution as an area, this would seldom be the case, for the cluster pertains most directly to smaller groups of peoples whose culture shows a degree of unity rather than simply similarity as in a culture area. This is further emphasized in the second difference between the two: the culture cluster involves a real commonality among the people concerned, with recognition of this commonality by the various groups" (see "The Concept of Culture Clusters Applied to the Belgian Congo," *Southwestern Journal of Anthropology,* XV (Winter, 1959), 373–395.

north and the Dande on the south, and by the Atlantic Ocean on the west and the Kwango on the east, the Kongo Kingdom* was itself divided into six provinces administered by local chiefs appointed by the king (*ntotila*). Elected from a royal clan by a council of noblemen, the king

MAP 1. *Major "culture clusters" in the Congo.* (Adapted in part from Alan P. Merriam, "The Concept of Culture Clusters Applied to the Belgian Congo," *Southwestern Journal of Anthropology*, XV [Winter, 1959], 377.)

was in theory an absolute monarch, appointing and dismissing councilors, court officers, and tax collectors at his discretion. But in practice his powers were limited by a council of elders which could depose him, and by the authority conferred upon the clan chiefs by tradition.

From his capital, Mbanza-Kongo, located in the vicinity of San Salvador (Angola), the king of Kongo at one time extended his rule over the neighboring kingdoms of Loango and Ngoyo, on the northern bank of the Congo. But his control over his vassals gradually diminished in the fifteenth and sixteenth centuries, until they became virtually independent. Although the king was at first treated as an equal by the Portuguese Crown, his authority rapidly dwindled under the influence of slave traders and tribal wars. Because slavery created vested interests among the chiefs, the period that followed the death of King Affonso, in 1540, was marked by internal strife and violent bickering among his successors.

---

* I have used the form "Kongo" to refer to the old Bakongo kingdom of San Salvador; the form "Congo" refers to the territory encompassed by the present boundaries of the Republic of the Congo.

In 1568 the Yaga, or Bayaka, moving westward from the Kwango, invaded the capital city and during the next two years raided the country and its inhabitants. As a result, less than two centuries after the Portuguese penetration "not even the chief of a good-sized village would have shed splendor on his position by assuming the title of the miserable kinglet of San Salvador, who was not even master in his own town and whose edicts carried no weight beyond a few slave hamlets in the vicinity of his farcical court." [5] Meanwhile, with the transfer of Portugal to the Spanish Crown in 1580, Portuguese influence began to recede, and in the following century the colonial authorities became almost exclusively concerned with the neighboring regions of Angola. Thus, although the Kongo Kingdom remained theoretically independent until its formal annexation by Portugal in 1883, it actually fell into a state of complete isolation, and when in 1857 the German explorer Bastian arrived at San Salvador he found "an ordinary native town, with a few scattered ruins of the Christian monuments of other days." [6]

Despite the cumulative impact of the slave trade, internal migrations, and tribal wars, the Bakongo have retained a strong sense of cultural unity. Their belief in a common origin, the continuity of their historic traditions, and the fact that they all share the same type of social organization, based on matrilineal, exogamous clans (*kanda*), all mark them off from neighboring groups. But probably the most powerful of all integrative factors is their common memory of the past splendor of their kingdom. Even to this day the words "Kongo Dia Ntotila" serve as a sort of cultural rallying cry for most Bakongo.

In the area lying east of the Bakongo cluster, between the Kwango and Kwilu rivers, there are a number of minor tribal groupings of different origins: Bayaka, Bambala, Bapende, Bahuana, Bangongo, and so on. With a population of 200,000, the Bayaka are by far the most important numerically. Scattered along the left bank of the Kwango, they occupy an area that stretches over the *territoires* of Popokabaka, Kasongo-Lunda, and Kenge. Despite obvious linguistic affinities with the Bakongo, the Bayaka have been influenced to a much greater degree by the Lunda, to whom they were nominally subject from the latter part of the seventeenth century until the beginning of the colonial period.[7] Like the Lunda, the Bayaka were organized into a centralized kingdom, and their paramount chief (*kiamfu*) was himself of Lunda origin. Although the kiamfu did manage to maintain effective control over the majority of the population, however, his subservience to the Lunda Kingdom was more apparent than real. Physically and culturally, the Bayaka resemble the Bambala, who inhabit an area lying south of Popokabaka. Politically, however, there are major differences between the two groups. The Bambala system of government "is extremely elementary; it might be described as communism with a strong flavoring of anarchy. . . . The unit is the village community at the head of which is the Fumu (chief)." [8] This observation would apply just as well to the Bahuana, the Bayanzi, the Bangongo, and many other tribal groupings of the area. Again, "the usual system of government throughout this part of the country seems to be by petty village chiefs, often independent, but sometimes under the suzerainty of a head chief who controls several villages." [9] Not only is there no trace of previous political unity, but equally striking is the absence of a common cultural heritage. Except for the Bayaka, whatever amount of cultural diffusion occurred among these peoples does not seem to have originated from any single major source. In brief, the Kwango-Kwilu area can perhaps best be pictured as a "shatter-zone" into which peoples of different traditions and origins moved in successive waves, under the joint pressures of the Kongo Kingdom on the west, the Lunda Kingdom on the south, and the Kuba Kingdom on the northeast.

The Kuba people, also known as Bushongo, are presently located in the territoire of Mweka, between the Sankuru and Kasai rivers.[10] Despite the evidence that the original Bushongo stock was physically, culturally, and linguistically related to the Baluba family, they now stand as a distinctive cultural group. Like the Bakongo, whose kingdom at one time exercised considerable influence on the Kuba, their kingdom was divided into several provinces administered by a governor appointed by the king (*nyimi*), and most other appointive offices—court dignitaries and officials—also tended to underwrite the authority of the king as the central figure in their political system. A distinctive feature of the political organization of the Kuba was a council of elders (*kolomo*) representing various crafts and arts, which served as an advisory body to the king. Because craft specialization among the Kuba coincided with a division of labor according to clan, guild representatives also acted as clan representatives. Just as oral tradition has preserved an accurate genealogy of more than 120 Kuba kings, the ancient ritual of the Kuba is still observed at the court of the nyimi. This type of conservatism is further illustrated by the survival of artistic traditions which continue to express the various aspects of the Kuba culture. That the Kuba people never felt the need to adapt themselves to Western acculturative influences—even though the proximity of the railroad would have permitted them to do so very easily—is in itself eloquent testimony to their attachment to their common cultural heritage.

With a population of approximately 1,500,000, the Baluba people form one of the largest cultural aggregations of the Congo. Although relatively little is known about their origins, oral traditions report that the first Baluba "empire" was founded in the fourteenth or fifteenth century by a Basonge chief named Nkongolo Mukulu.[11] At its height this empire stretched from Lake Tanganyika on the east to the Bushimaye River on the west, and from the Maniema in the north to the southern reaches of the Katanga. Beginning in the early part of the seventeenth century, however, partly as a result of successional disputes among the sons of Nkongolo, a number of Baluba subgroups—Bena Kanioka, Bena Konji, Bakwa Kalondji, Bakwa Dishi, and others—migrated in successive waves toward the Kasai. Some of these, like the Bena Lulua, settled in the northern part of the province, and others in the southern region, near Bakwanga. Meanwhile, a Bakunda chief by the name of Ilunga Mbidi is said to have founded the second Baluba "empire," which lasted from about 1550 to 1700. From then on, sporadic incursions by the Tshokwe and the Bayeke inaugurated a period of chronic instability which led to the division of Lubaland into competing chiefdoms, and by 1885 a fierce struggle opposed the paramount chief Kasongo Nyembo to his rival Kabongo, each drawing his support from different tribal subgroups—the former from the Shankadi, the latter from the Bena Samba. Once "pacified" by Belgium, what was left of the Baluba empire was divided into a number of independent chiefdoms, thereby furthering the disintegration of this once powerful political entity.

While the political organization of the Baluba is normally based on the extended family or the village group, at times they shared a consciousness of belonging to a wider political unit. But such consciousness, even when it did exist, was never strong enough to hold them together over a long period of time. The so-called Baluba "empire," aptly described as an "incorporative kingdom," [12] was in fact an amalgamation of different political units varying in size from the extended family to the tribe. There was a complete absence of political unity among the Baluba of the Kasai: "Partout c'est la même dispersion du pouvoir politique et la constitution de petites entités autonomes liées uniquement par le sentiment d'appartenir au groupe Luba et d'avoir une même langue." [13] The same observation applies to the Baluba population of the Katanga, whose traditional political system, like that of the Kasaian tribes, "ranges upward from the individual to the family, village, group of villages, province and tribe." [14] A similar diversity characterizes their social organization, which contains both patrilineal and matrilineal elements. The main countervailing influence to this variegated sociopolitical structure lies in the sense of cultural unity which permeates the attitude of the Baluba. Despite notable dialectical differences between the Kasaian tribes and those located in the Katanga, most Baluba are aware of belonging to a group higher than the village, the clan, or the province, mainly because they share a common history, during which they developed many cultural similarities.

The Lunda, presently divided among Katanga Province, Angola, and

Northern Rhodesia, settled in the area between the Bushimaye and the Lubilash rivers at some time before the Baluba occupied the country.[15] According to Northern Lunda traditions* the cradle of their "empire" was a relatively small kingdom located on the Bushimaye, in the territoire of Kapanga. Although the first large-scale emigration of the Lunda seems to have taken place at an earlier date, it was not until the reign of Mwata Yamvo (king) Maweji (*ca.* 1660–1675) that they undertook to subjugate neighboring tribes. Their westward expansion brought them into contact with the Bapende, Bayaka, Bakwese, Basuku, and Baholo peoples, and to the southeast they encountered the Luena, Tshokwe, and Luchazi peoples, whom they proceeded to organize into tributary kingdoms. Finally, a century or so later, a group of Lunda conquerors moved eastward to extend their hegemony over the Bemba, Tabwa, Bwile, Tumba, and Baluba populations. In practice, however, this eastern region never became part of the big Lunda kingdoms, such as the Mwata Yamvo's or Kazembe Kinkonle in the Luapula region.[16]

Between 1740 and 1850, while the Lunda conquered most of the territory comprised within the boundaries of the southern districts of the Katanga, the Bayeke organized themselves into a powerful kingdom. Under the leadership of their chief, Kalassa, they migrated from Unyamwezi (Tanganyika) to an area between the Lualaba and the Luapula, and from their stronghold at Bunkeia proceeded to establish their domination over the neighboring populations. Kalassa's son, Msiri, "became the master of a territory which had for boundaries on the west the Lualaba, on the north almost the ninth degree of latitude, in the east the Luapula, and on the south the Zambezi-Congo water parting. This vast country covered an extent of 63,000 square miles." [17] About 1883 Msiri attempted to extend his control to the Baluba tribes of the Lualaba. "Kikondja and other Baluba chiefs of the south," writes Torday, "recognized him as their overlord. The Balunda, fearing to see their country invaded, submitted, and the Bahusi and Balamba chiefs ended by repairing to Bunkeia to recognize the tyrant's authority." [18] The Lunda of Kazembe Kinkonle, located on the banks of the Luapula, opposed a vigorous resistance to Msiri's warriors, and, with the help of the Basanga and the Balamba, finally liberated themselves from the domination of the Bayeke.[19]

---

* Although the boundary between Northern and Southern Lunda is rather ill-defined, there are important linguistic and cultural differences between the two groups. The Northern Lunda are primarily located in the former Belgian Congo, while the southern tribes are found mainly in Angola and Northern Rhodesia. The Lunda population of the Congo has been estimated by C. M. N. White at 10,000, but the author concedes that this estimate is probably too low (see Merran McCulloch, *The Southern Lunda and Related Tribes* [London: Ethnographic Survey of Africa, International African Institute, 1951], p. 7).

Meanwhile, the Tshokwe took advantage of the situation to turn against their Lunda overlords. A first Tshokwe invasion is said to have taken place about 1852, but it was not until 1885 that they succeeded in asserting their independence from Mwata Yamvo. After invading his capital, at Mussamba, they killed Mwata Yamvo, and for the next ten years exercised their control over most of Lundaland. Shortly before the Belgian penetration, in 1895, the Lunda defeated the Tshokwe, who apparently had not fortified their villages, and thus momentarily regained control over their "lost territories" and former vassals.

As Mary Douglas points out, "most of the tribes which accepted Lunda suzerainty adopted Lunda titles and sent tributes back to the ruler, Mwata Yamvo, while at the same time the conquering newcomers were themselves assimilated linguistically and socially into the culture of their subjects." [20] From the Tshokwe, for example, the Northern Lunda borrowed a number of cultural and linguistic elements, including a matrilineal system of social organization. For this reason it is difficult to refer to a distinctive Lunda culture cluster. Yet their traditional political system, characterized by centralized chiefdoms more or less dependent upon the central authority of the Mwata Yamvo, and their common history have both contributed to give the Lunda a group consciousness of their own.

Very little is known about the Warega group, located in the Kivu.[21] While some authors have described their political system as primarily segmentary, composed of small independent units based on lineage affiliations, others contend that the Warega were once organized into a highly centralized kingdom. In any event, they have a fairly uniform social structure, characterized by an endogamous, virilocal, patrilineal clan organization which occasionally splinters into new groups. A distinctive feature of Warega society is the Bwame organization, a graded association that performs a variety of social and political functions. Perhaps the most important characteristic of the Warega culture cluster "is the emphasis placed on the system of social grading within the associations, as well as the importance and complexity of social relationships in general, coupled with a relative lack of interest in the supernatural world." [22]

The Azande, with a population of approximately 2 million, extend over an elongated strip of territory straddling the boundaries of the Central African Republic, the Sudan, and the Upper and Lower Uele districts of the Congo. They constitute an amalgam of invading Sudanic and indigenous tribes of different origins which developed a more or less common pattern of social and political organization. Under the leadership of the Avungura ruling clan, the Abomu conquerors established their overlordship over the neighboring peoples, and in the process founded a string of quasi-independent states ruled by members of the royal clan. This process of amalgamation by conquest "seems marked by the following characteristics: expansion under the direction of a popular hero; conservation and assimilation by the vanquished; death of the chief followed at once by anarchy and schism; fights between the would-be successors, followed by the ascendency of one (or more) and the reassembling of the people accordingly; resumption of expansion and acquisition of new territories." [23] Many tribes that are today considered to belong to the Zande family at one time or another constituted entirely separate entities. For example, the Banginda, Ngbaya, Abwameli, Tokpwo, and other peoples are now completely Zandeized. Others, like the Abarembo and the Amadi, though not completely assimilated, have nevertheless been greatly influenced, politically and culturally, by the Azande. Still others, like the Mangbetu, though partially Zandeized, constitute politically and linguistically distinct entities. In practice, however, the sociopolitical organization of the Mangbetu is very similar to that of the Azande. The formal political structures in both are pyramidal in organization, with the king representing the supreme power holder. At the lower levels, authority is divided among chiefs and subchiefs appointed by the king to administer his provinces, and these in turn appoint "deputies" to buttress their power among the people. Thus, from their centralized political structure and common clan organization the Azande derived at one time a strong sense of cultural unity.

The Mongo, who form the largest single culture cluster of the Congo, are found in all the provinces except the Katanga. In its widest acceptance the term Mongo refers to three major subcategories: (1) the Mongo restricted, which represent the nucleus of the Mongo tribes and comprise such groups as Ntombe, Nkundu, Ekota; (2) the Mongo extended, which applies to Mongandu, Bambole, Bakutu, and Bakusu; and (3) the Batetela Mongo, made up primarily of Ankutshu, or Batetela.[24] Unlike the former groupings, the Mongo have little or no tradition of political unity. They constitute a congeries of minor tribes organized into small autonomous entities whose boundaries are usually coterminous with the village group. There are no kingdoms or other large political entities, and "political fragmentation seems to be the rule." [25] Despite the absence of a unifying political focus, however, these different tribal groupings evince a relatively strong Mongo-consciousness, perhaps less noticeably among the tribes that are farthest from the nuclear groups, the Mongo extended and the Batetela Mongo. This sense of commonality is owing not only to the preservation of genealogical relationships among some of the constituent groups, but also to their common historical traditions and belief in a common origin; all Mongo trace their ancestry back to a mystical figure, or god, called Mongo, and many of them take special pride in calling themselves "the children of Mongo."

The area stretching between the Congo and Ubangui rivers, corresponding roughly to the northern half of Equateur Province, is inhabited by a host of smaller tribes of Sudanic origins which together have a population of 736,000.[26] The main groups are Ngbandi, Ngbaka, Banda, Ngombe, and the so-called "Gens d'Eau," a generic term coined by H. Burssens to designate a subracial mixture which includes such groups as Bondjo, Lobala, Baloi, Ngiri.* Except for the Ngbaka, who seem to have come from the Lake Tchad area, most of these groups trace their origins to the regions of Darfur and Kordofan (Sudan). During the fifteenth and sixteenth centuries, under the pressure of such conquering groups as the Asundia and the Abara, they migrated in a southwestern direction, toward the Ubangui Basin. The Ngbandi settled on the northern fringe of Equateur Province about the seventeenth century, while the Ngombe and the Ngbaka moved southward across the Mongala River until they came in contact with the Mongo populations. Like the Mongo, each of these groups formed a congeries of small autonomous communities—villages or groups of villages—with no formal political bonds connecting them. Political authority was normally vested in a village chief whose office was hereditary within the senior lineage of the clan or extended family, but his powers were checked by a council of notables: "Le chef du village gouverne partout avec l'aide du conseil des notables (les vieux, les seigneurs du village, les *wan* chez les Ngbaka). Des assemblées aux quelles assistent tous les adultes se tiennent régulièrement sous un abri public (en général une grande hutte sans parois) et on y discute les questions et les problèmes les plus divers." [27] Relations among neighboring communities are still primarily based on bonds of kinship and marriage, but these rarely transcend ethnic boundaries. Thus, while their Sudanic origins undoubtedly tend to mark them off from the Bantu tribes, each group nevertheless retains some awareness of its cultural distinctiveness.

It appears from the foregoing survey of the peoples of the Congo

---

* In *Les Bangala* (Bruxelles, 1907), C. Van Overberghe and E. De Jonghe have lumped these people together, along with many other tribes of the Equateur, as Bangala. Using the term in a more restricted sense, John H. Weeks designates as Bangala "those natives who lived at, and in the vicinity of Diboko (Nouvelle Anvers)" ("Notes of the Bangala of the Upper Congo River," *Journal of the Royal Anthropological Institute*, XL [1910], 398). It has been established, however, that no tribe or group of tribes ever claimed the appellation of Bangala: "Il n'existe aucune tribu ou peuplade portant le nom ethnique de baNgala, bamangala, ou maNgala, ni aucune langue vernaculaire du nom de Lingala" (G. Van Bulck, "Mission Linguistique 1949–1951," *Institut Royal Colonial Belge, Mémoires*, XXXI, fasc. 5 [Bruxelles, 1954], p. 43).

Basin that a single "culture area" [28] does not necessarily possess the degree of uniformity that the phrase tends to convey. Indeed, depending on the level of generality which one wishes to adopt, one may discern a number of different cultural aggregates within the Congo cultural area. Equally striking is the diversity of traditional political systems, varying in size from the small autonomous communities found among the Bambuti Pygmies of the Ituri forest to the large-scale kingdoms of Bakongo, Baluba, Lunda, and Azande. Even among the latter one may distinguish further variations in the degree of centralization of formal political structures. The contrasting patterns of political organization in the "despotic" kingdom of Kongo, on the one hand, and the "incorporative" kingdoms of the Baluba and Lunda peoples on the other, are an illustration.[29] What needs to be stressed here, however, is the prevalence of large-scale entities which, despite their variant forms of political organization, have retained certain basic cultural uniformities. In some areas the very multiplicity of small tribal groupings seemed to favor political integration, but where local tribes were not so numerous or so small they tended to form insoluble lumps in the Congolese body politic. In other words, the ethnic diversity of the Congo population does not exclude some measure of ethnic homogeneity at the local or regional level, and the process of amalgamation becomes all the more problematic.

## THE INFLUENCE OF TRADITIONAL FACTORS ON MODERN POLITICAL MOVEMENTS

The comment that "Nigeria is notoriously a precarious lumping together of peoples whose separate identity is at least as real a matter as their acceptance of national unity" seems even more appropriate to the problem of national unification in the Congo.[30] Both countries were given artificial boundaries by European colonizers, but Belgian policies and institutions made it infinitely more difficult for the Congolese to fit themselves, organizationally and psychologically, into the new territorial framework. Although in modern times the leaders of both countries have depended upon precolonial loyalties and institutions to meet the requirements of the new political order, most observers would agree that such dependence has been far more pronounced among the Congolese than among the Nigerians.

Central to an understanding of the nature of this relationship is the inclination of some Congolese politicians to conceptualize nationhood in terms of linguistic and cultural affinities, with the result that in their minds "nation" and "tribe" tend to become synonymous. Drawing attention to "the solid and natural ties" that unite the members of certain "tribes," a Muluba journalist of Elisabethville explained: "Many tribes would have deserved the appellation of nation if one had taken into account the ethnic affinities of their members, and, above all, if our tribes had not lost their political and administrative unity long before the penetration of the whites." The logical conclusion is that "tribalisme et nationalisme sont synonymes en ce sens que tribu égale nation." [31] Strictly speaking, however, national consciousness is rarely identified with the tribe—used in its more restricted sense to designate a relatively small social group primarily based on kinship and lineage affiliations— but with certain "peoples," or "nationality groups," composed of cul- turally or linguistically related tribes.* It is among peoples with common historical traditions and a common language, who at one time formed a single political unit, that one finds this embryonic sense of nationhood; among the Bakongo, whose common language, culture, and history pro- vide a major focus for the crystallization of a pantribal consciousness, this feeling has reached its highest level of intensity. But it is also found, in a more diluted form, among societies that have no tradition of political unity, such as the Mongo.

It follows that where "nationality" is still the most obvious reference group, ethnic boundaries have set important limitations on the scope of political party activities, the latter tending to reflect the ties of culture, history, and language in existence before the imposition of Belgian rule. The case for identifying modern political parties with such ties was argued by the Bakongo leaders in these terms: "Since the true union of the Congolese can only be realized by way of a political evolution . . . this evolution must begin first on an existing foundation. That means that groups historically, ethnically and linguistically united or allied organize themselves to form as many political parties." [32] That this con- ception of the nation, as an aggregate of distinctive loyalties based on tradition, was widely shared by Congolese politicians is attested by the phenomenal growth of "ethnic" parties in the period preceding inde- pendence. The most notable of these in Leopoldville Province was Joseph Kasa-Vubu's Abako (Alliance des Bakongo), constructed around a Ba- kongo cultural association which had as its stated objective the "preserva- tion, unification, and expansion of the Kikongo language." Like the Abako, the Luka (Union Kwangolaise pour l'Indépendance et la Liberté) in the Kwango District, the Unimo (Union Mongo) in the Equateur, the Balubakat (Association des Baluba du Katanga) in the Katanga, and the

---

* This distinction is based on Professor Coleman's definition of the concepts of "tribe" and "nationality." "The tribe," writes Coleman, "is the largest social group defined primarily in terms of kinship, and is normally an aggregation of clans," whereas a "nationality" is the largest traditional African group above a tribe which can be distinguished from other groups by one or more objective criteria (normally language)" (*Nigeria: Background to Nationalism* [Berkeley and Los Angeles: Uni- versity of California Press, 1958], pp. 423–424).

MSM (Mouvement Solidaire Muluba) in the Kasai restricted their membership to specific "nationality groups"—the Unimo to the Mongo of the Equateur, the Luka to the Bayaka of Leopoldville Province, the Balubakat to the Baluba of the Katanga, and the MSM to the Baluba of the Kasai.

Furthermore, the traditional culture has not only tended to restrict the field of operation of certain parties, but has also conditioned the political objectives of their leaders, especially if the traditional political structures provided a unifying focus for a people's loyalties. A fundamental aspect of the pantribalist ideal of the Abako is the revival of the historic kingdom of Kongo, not as it existed before the European conquest, but encompassing in its jurisdiction the kingdoms of Loango and Ngoyo.[33] The cultural identity of the Bakongo makes it necessary, in the eyes of their leaders, to overlook the different acculturative influences that have operated under the tutelage of French, Belgians, and Portuguese, and assign immediate priority to the reconstruction of the precolonial political community. In the words of a prominent member of the Central Committee of the Abako, "L'Abakisme est une tendence nationaliste qui cherche à grouper des personnes ayant une même origine, même histoire, et des traditions, des coutumes communes, patrimoine des ancêtres, afin de sauvegarder la culture Africaine et de l'ameliorer." [34] Or, more succinctly: "L'Abako c'est l'union rétablie." [35]

Even in the absence of previous political unity, a conscious effort was made to give certain nationality groups a larger measure of political cohesion than actually existed. For example, addressing a group of Mongo of Leopoldville, Justin Bomboko, the Unimo leader, expressed his desire to restore the unity of the "Mongo Kingdom": "Si les choses marchent très bien, nous allons reconstituer notre royaume Mongo, sans tenir compte des barrières territoriales, invention de l'administration colonialiste pour mieux administrer le pays. Nos ancêtres ne connaissaient ni territoire ni district." [36] Similarly, the efforts of Sylvain Mangole (better known as Kalamba) to create a Lulua kingdom were clearly aimed at fostering a common political consciousness among the Lulua.[37] In each instance the effort was motivated by a desire to create an artificial political structure through which power could be secured. It is noteworthy, however, that these attempts, though dictated by considerations of opportunism, were largely inspired by the traditional political folklore of African societies.

The tendency to seek in the past a justification for contemporary political objectives is not a feature of ethnic parties alone. For the leadership of the Parti Solidaire Africain (PSA) African socialism was nothing more than the modern political expression of the communal solidarity that once prevailed in some traditional societies. Antoine Gizenga, when asked if his party had any affinity with Marxist doctrines, replied that its "social program . . . draws its inspiration from traditional African structures. Our populations have never known anything approaching a capitalist regime. Tribal life is based on a communal system, according to which the land and its resources are the collective property of the family, the clan, or the tribe. Our present objective is to adapt our traditions to modern forms of civilization."[38] The same kind of eclecticism characterized Lumumba's attitude toward traditional African values. As conscious as he was of the need to transcend the purview of ethnic particularisms, he also realized that the future could not, and should not, be separated from the past, and that the new political order could not be entirely divorced from the context of African culture. What Lumumba sought to achieve was the "transformation of the typically African cultures of the past into a new, Neo-African culture, drawing its inspiration from the old principles, and retaining the distinctive genius [*le génie propre*] of the African peoples." As he explained, "we do not want these ancestral traditions to remain fixed in their archaic mold, but on the other hand we do not want a slavish copy of European civilization. What we want is to improve and perfect our own culture by adding to it certain elements of European civilization."[39]

Third, some traditional authority systems have influenced the angle of political vision of the Congolese, their political perspectives as well as their conception of authority. Nowhere is this influence more clearly seen than among the Bakongo. The range of values identified with Kasa-Vubu's personality is deeply rooted in the traditional authority structure of the Bakongo. His role is not only reminiscent of the king's; it is consciously recognized as a modern version of the king's omnipotence.[40] The Bakongo display a wide measure of deference and esteem, sometimes verging on the mystical, toward their surrogate monarch.[41] Furthermore, Bakongo leaders have tended to revive the authority of the clan as the basic sociopolitical unit of their society. For example, to the question as to how power would be organized after independence, an editorialist answered that in the first place "one has to understand how things were in the ancient Kongo Kingdom"; after explaining how certain clans migrated from Mbanza-Kongo to the surrounding areas, the writer emphasized that they had all had a similar organization, and that membership in a clan was the only badge of citizenship among the Bakongo:

Du prétendu citoyen qui veut se faire blanc, quel sera son clan dans cette communauté? Car le blanc n'a pas de clan! C'est la raison pour laquelle il ignore notre savoir-vivre. Tous les Bakongo ont leur autorité car ils appartiennent à l'un ou l'autre clan. Quiconque n'a pas de clan est-il réellement citoyen? Est-il l'habitant du pays?[42]

Again, late in 1959 the same newspaper stated that the true meaning of independence was that it would restore the authority of the clan chief: "L'indépendance amie des tribus vous annonce qu'il faut observer l'autorité du chef de clan—elle organise les villages, respecte les lois des ancêtres, guide l'ignorant, commande le respect envers tout le monde." [43] This theme, however, was largely overshadowed by the litanies devoted to "King Kasa," whose "courage, tenacity, wisdom, calm, intelligence, comprehension" conferred upon him infallibility.

In contrast with this elitist conception of authority, certain leaders have shown a clear propensity toward "collective leadership," especially where the traditional patterns of authority of their group of origin tended in this direction. In a speech to a group of political leaders of the Equateur, the Mongo leader Jean-François Iyeki insisted on the need to preserve the traditional pattern of decision making: "Naguère dans nos villages, quand il y avait un problème grave à résoudre, tous les notables se réunissaient autour du chef et examinaient la situation. Il doit en être de même maintenant." [44] On the whole, however, the incidence of other variables—the personality of certain leaders and the degree to which they have been conditioned by the traditional milieu—makes any attempt at generalization unrealistic. Certainly there is no such thing as a Bantu philosophy of authority, let alone a Bantu concept of chieftaincy, for there are in fact many variations in the way that traditional authority systems shape the political orientation of African leaders.

Closely related to the traditional political culture is the use of certain symbols of authority, of what Charles Merriam called the "miranda" and "credenda" of power, as well as the mode of cognition through which political phenomena are perceived and interpreted. The use of traditional symbols by the Abako is best exemplified in the ubiquitous display of the so-called "Kodia," which is both the emblem of the party and the symbol of ancestral virtues.* The magico-religious properties attributed to the Kodia were defined by the official organ of the Abako: "The Kodia has no property of its own since its powers come from God, in whom all decision-making powers rest; it merely executes divine prescriptions." [45] Implicit in this definition of the role of the Kodia is the identification of political success with divine will, in a manner somewhat reminiscent of Calvinist ethics. Another property ascribed to the Kodia is the preservation of party orthodoxy. It serves to prevent the occurrence of "deviationist" and "heretic" tendencies: "It is the vigilant guardian of strict orthodoxy. The slightest infraction to the rule may bring a terrible punishment,

---

* The Kodia, meaning literally "shell," was often invoked in the course of "judicial songs" (*nkunga mambu*) whenever a litigation of some sort arose. Its propitiating virtues were supposed to bring about the most favorable set of circumstances that could possibly be wished for.

in particular sterility, sickness, and death." [46] The Kodia called up emotional reactions far more powerful than did an ordinary nationalistic symbol, as it stood for a complex of attitudes and beliefs deeply rooted in the religious consciousness of the Bakongo.

The retention of traditional cognitive symbols is illustrated by the Abako's explanation for its victory in the general elections. Reminding its readers that the Abako list had received, as a distinctive sign, the number 3, the party organ attributed the electoral success of Abako candidates to the magic properties of the number. Symbolically related to the origins of the Kongo Kingdom, the magic number brought a victory in which "God and the memory of our ancestors have been a powerful aid." [47] A similar explanation was offered to account for the Abako's success in the boycott of the 1959 elections, which in the eyes of its leaders were merely meant to retard the accession of the Congo to independence. As the polling date fell precisely on Nsona-Nsona, or "Ancestors' Day," such a coincidence was presumably an ill omen for the Belgian administration and a presage of success for the Abako.[48] Although the Abako draws heavily from the traditional belief system of the Bakongo, its official interpretations and predictions of political phenomena are not based exclusively on traditional modes of cognition. Rather, they must be viewed as particular techniques used by the party elites to strengthen the appeal of the Abako.

In parties that were organized and led by individuals who claimed a position of prestige and authority in the traditional order, much of the impetus came from the leaders' ability to identify themselves with the ancestral values of their societies. For example, the success of the Lulua-Frères among the Lulua was owing in part to Chief Kalamba's personal prestige; as grandson of the famous Kalamba Mukenge, paramount chief of the Lulua, Kalamba resuscitated the vision of an imaginary kingdom and thus greatly enhanced the party's appeal. As early as 1955 several chiefs had recognized him as their supreme ruler (*mwannangana*), and in August of that year Kalamba reportedly declared "before an immense crowd" that "all the chiefs and their subjects seem to remember the distant past and recognize what they had almost forgotten. . . . If this could happen, you must recall that it is thanks to the Lulua-Frères association, whose members have gone through all kinds of trouble [*se sont donnés toutes les peines du monde*] to inculcate this idea in the hearts of your people." [49] As Kalamba already held a position of authority in the colonial society (*chef de secteur* of the Bakwa Katawa in the territoire of Luluabourg), one is tempted to associate these efforts to promote a renaissance of traditional institutions with the proliferation of smaller parties that came into being through the initiative of customary or appointed chiefs. The very size of the party's membership, however, coupled with its decidedly anti-European orientation, suggests that we are dealing here with an entirely different type of phenomenon.

In fact, identification with the precolonial culture was even more effective for party leaders whose traditional claim to high rank was denied in the colonial society. Because they had no vested interest in the colonial status quo they could legitimately pose at the same time as the defenders of nationalist* ideas and the custodians of tradition. A man like Rémy Mwamba, secretary-general of the Balubakat, could stress his direct descent from the "first Muluba, Mutombo Mukulu," [50] and could use this connection to fortify his party's appeal among the Baluba. As the grandson of Msiri, Godefroid Munongo could use his prestige and influence to spread the ideas of the Confédération des Associations Tribales du Katanga (Conakat) among the Bayeke. And Justin Bomboko's chiefly origins were a valuable asset for the Unimo. Like Sékou Touré in Guinea and Modibo Keita in Mali, these men were so situated that they could relate their people's future hopes to the past, and thus magnify the appeal of their parties among the masses.

A final aspect of the relationship between traditional factors and modern developments concerns the degree to which precolonial hostilities have influenced contemporary divisions. Heinrich von Treitschke's statement that "it is war that turns a people into a nation" is probably too simple a formula to explain the persistence of ethnic particularisms among the Congolese. For one thing, the factor of common interests has undoubtedly served to mitigate ancestral rivalries, as evidenced, for example, by the absence of perceptible antagonisms between the Lunda and the Bayeke, the Bayeke and the Batabwa, the Lunda and the Bayaka. Moreover, the fact that certain groups lived in peace and harmony before the intrusion of European forces did not prevent the occurrence of irreconcilable conflicts among them, such as the deadly struggle that continues to oppose the Lulua to the Baluba in the Kasai. Nonetheless, it would be a mistake to underestimate the strength of secular animosities.

We have seen how, through conquest and accretion, the Luba, Lunda, Bayeke, and Kuba kingdoms evolved from small nuclear units into broader political entities. In the process their rulers established their hegemony over different tribes, sometimes assimilating them into their

---

* In this study the term "nationalist," unless otherwise qualified, applies to any group consciously attempting to cast off the yoke of colonialism regardless of its ultimate objective, size, or ethnic composition. The same negative connotation is suggested by Thomas Hodgkin: "My own inclination is to use the term nationalist in a broad sense to describe any organization or group that explicitly asserts the rights, claims and aspirations of a given African society (from the level of the language group to that of Pan-Africa) in opposition to European authority, whatever its institutional form and objectives" (*Nationalism in Colonial Africa* [New York, 1956], p. 23).

own culture, sometimes organizing them into semiautonomous depend-
encies. Whatever the form and extent of the conquest, many of these
conflicts have left a legacy of mutual fear and suspicion. Even though
the Baluba suffered less from the incursions of Msiri's warriors than other
tribes, to this very day the memory of the Bayeke chief conjures up feelings of revulsion among them; that Msiri "maintained himself in power
only through countless and unqualifiable massacres, cruelties, and feroci-
ties," and that his grandson is "the descendant of a bloodthirsty poten-
tate," are matters of common knowledge.[51] Similarly, the occasional raids
launched by Baluba elements against the Sanga clans and related tribes,
and their periodic clashes with the Lunda of Kazembe, have probably
sharpened antagonisms between the southern tribes of the Katanga and
the Baluba populations. The present hostility between Tschokwe and
Lunda can be explained only by reference to the sequence of tribal wars
unleashed by the Tshokwe against their Lunda overlords in the period
immediately preceding the European occupation of the Katanga. Finally,
part of the opposition between Bayaka and Bakongo must be viewed
against the background of the Bayaka invasion of the Kongo Kingdom in
the seventeenth century. In each instance, memories of past onslaughts
tend to fuse with recent experience, thereby intensifying contemporary
political cleavages.

Emphasis on the existence of certain ties between precolonial societies and modern political developments does not suggest that Congolese
parties are unique in this respect; although the nature of such ties may
differ from country to country, many African parties "must be understood
in their relations with precolonial systems." [52] It must be stressed that
during the centuries that preceded the colonial period certain groups
developed a cultural identity of their own, and that such an identity is
still the most enduring and most cohesive basis for the organization of
political groups in the Congo.

# II. HISTORICAL BACKGROUND

Just as the precolonial past offers insight into the problem of national unification in the Congo, the welter of change and crisis which has confronted the Congolese since the penetration of European colonizers provides the indispensable backdrop to an understanding of recent political developments.

As elsewhere on the African continent, the imperial power introduced common administrative institutions, a common language, a common system of communications and transportation. All of them tended to weaken, if not obliterate, ethnic particularisms. What is not always realized, however, is that while Belgian colonial policies undoubtedly played a part in welding together people of different stocks, the coastal populations had been in contact with Western civilization for centuries before Belgium even existed as a nation. During the four centuries preceding the "scramble for Africa" the Portuguese established formal political links with these people, brought them Christianity, and, through the slave trade, introduced a semicommercialized economy. Although these ties became increasingly tenuous as time went on, the effect of Portuguese domination on subsequent generations of Africans cannot be ignored. Equally instrumental in shaping present-day attitudes toward non-Africans, and among African groups, were the early contacts of the eastern populations with Arab slave traders. The domination of the Arabs, who came more recently than the Portuguese and affected more people, is more directly relevant to an understanding of contemporary politics. Yet both influences have left their imprint on the minds of Africans. This fact is as much a reflection on what Belgium failed to accomplish as an indication of the pervasiveness of the forces operative before the annexation of the Congo.

## EARLY EUROPEAN INFLUENCES

The first recorded expedition to the Congo may be traced back to 1482, when the Portuguese explorer Diogo Cão discovered the estuary of the Congo River, which he named Zaïre, after the Kikongo term *nzadi*, or *nzari*, for "river." [1] Upon hearing of the existence of the Kongo Kingdom, Cão dispatched an embassy to the king, the famous Manicongo. But when he learned that his fellow companions were held in custody at the King's court, Cão took an equal number of Africans as hostages and sailed back to Lisbon. While in Lisbon the African captives were apparently treated with exceptional benevolence by the Portuguese king, for when they returned to the Kongo, in 1485, they acted as messengers of goodwill on behalf of John II, thus preparing the way for the establishment of formal diplomatic relations between Lisbon and Mbanza-Kongo.[2]

It is important to stress at the outset that the motives that then inspired Lusitanian policy in Africa were quite different from those of the Portuguese colonizers. To spread the gospel among the heathen, and, for this purpose, to establish friendly relationships with the King of Kongo, were the immediate goals of the Portuguese Crown. The ultimate objective was the discovery of the Ethiopian kingdom of Prester John, a legendary figure who combined the qualities of king and priest.

From the very beginning the King of Kongo was treated by his European counterpart as an equal. In 1491, after the arrival of a Portuguese embassy at San Salvador, the King was converted to Catholicism, along with a number of African notables. After his death in 1506, his successor, Affonso, became an ardent supporter of Christianity, repeatedly insisting on having more priests sent to the Kongo, and in 1520 his son Henrique was consecrated Bishop of Utica, *in partibus infidelium,* by Pope Leo X. Meanwhile, the etiquette of the Portuguese court was gradually accepted by Affonso and his entourage; members of the royal family were sent to Portugal to study; ambassadors were sent to Rome and Lisbon; and the King, like most European monarchs, paid allegiance to the Pope.

That the intentions of the Portuguese Crown were essentially peaceful is further indicated by the set of instructions (*regimento*) given by King Manuel to his emissary, Simão da Silva, in 1529. The instructions covered a variety of subjects, ranging from the conditions under which Portuguese law could be applied in the Kongo to commercial and religious matters, but there was no "suggestion of authoritarian restraint on the people of the Congo."[3] The sanctions prescribed by the regimento, however, do suggest that the use of compulsion had already left its mark on at least some elements of the African population: "Priests who had abused the population were to be sent immediately to Lisbon," and "any slaves they possessed were to be sent to Portugal on another ship at the owners' expense."[4]

Once rendered licit by the clergy, the slave trade grew rapidly, engendering mutual distrust between Affonso and the Portuguese while profoundly affecting the social and political institutions of African society. Upon the arrival in São Tomé of Fernão de Mello, who represented the interests of the Portuguese Crown in the early days of Affonso's reign, the Portuguese slave traders along the coast began to send their agents to the interior. The slave traffic, growing by leaps and bounds, became a matter of personal concern to Affonso. In 1526 he appointed a commission of three chiefs to ascertain whether the slaves bought were really captives of war or his own subjects, and appealed to the Portuguese king to impose some restraint on the companies. His efforts were in vain, and in subsequent years thousands of slaves were shipped annually to São Tomé, Brazil, or the West Indies. "Since the conquest of these kingdoms began," wrote the Portuguese historian Cardonega in 1680, "there have been dispatched [from Mpinda] in most years [*um anno por otro*] about eight to ten thousand units of slaves, which sum up to almost a million souls." [5] When Great Britain abolished the slave trade in 1807, the Portuguese dealers became the main procurers of slave labor; therefore the demand for slaves was largely met by the export of Congolese. It was not until 1878, when Portugal finally prohibited the slave trade, that the traffic came to an end.

Behind the tribal wars and human sufferings caused by the slave trade lies a fact of considerable psychological importance. To a large extent, the suspicion and resentment that to this day permeate the attitude of the Congolese toward non-Africans must be attributed to slavery. And the fact that the Bakongo, because of their geographical position, were more severely affected than the populations of the interior may be one reason that some of them regard the Portuguese, rather than the Belgians, as their "real enemies."

The effect of the Portuguese presence on the Bakongo was no less devastating than the impact of slave-trading activities on the populations of the coast of Guinea. But the association of Portugal with the Kongo Kingdom was distinctive in that it initially stood for something quite different from the ruthless and predatory spirit of latter-day colonizers. This "unique European experiment . . . stands for the pacific good intentions, seldom realized, of the Portuguese Crown, and it stands for the faith of an African prince in his alliance with a European power." [6] The mutual respect and deference which first characterized the relations of Portugal with the King of Kongo may help to explain why the Bakongo "have always preserved a strong sense of independence." [7] To pretend that the Kongo Kingdom "never became a tributary state" is probably inaccurate—even if some Bakongo nationalists still identify the early phase of Portuguese domination with a state of "natural freedom" [8]—for at one point it did become, in fact if not in theory, politically dependent upon Portugal. But it may reasonably be argued that the degree of freedom initially enjoyed by the kings of Kongo has fostered among the Bakongo a more intense desire for independence than would otherwise have developed.

For many years after Cão's expedition the Kongo Kingdom possessed all the trappings of a sovereign nation-state. Not only were diplomatic ties established with Lisbon and Rome, but within the boundaries of his territory the king of Kongo was allowed ample scope for his powers. For eighty years "the Manicongo was political ruler of his kingdom, with authority which frequently extended over the Portuguese residing there. Portuguese intervention was officially limited to commerce and religion. There is no suggestion of official Portuguese tyranny or occupation during these years." [9] The Kongo Kingdom continued to be administered as a separate administrative entity at least until 1883. This historical experience gave a legitimate basis to the "myth" of the Kongo Kingdom, on which Bakongo nationalists stake their claims.

## The Arab Domination

Beginning in the mid-nineteenth century, as Portuguese influence was rapidly fading in the Lower Congo, came the thrust of Arab slave traders from the east. Fanning out from a thin strip of territory extending from Cape Delgado to Lamy, on the East African coast, the Zanzibar Arabs were already engaged in important trading activities with the peoples of the Tanganyika and Nyasa lake shores. In their quest for slaves and ivory, they expanded westward across Lake Tanganyika into the Maniema region, and about 1860 founded a trading station on the Lualaba, at Nyangwe. By 1885, when the Congo Free State came into being, the Arabs controlled most of the area between the Lualaba and Lomami rivers.

Unlike the Portuguese in the west, the Arabs were not interested in converting the Africans to their faith, nor did they seek to establish formal political bonds with the local chiefs. They were "first and foremost traders, and when they turned their attention to the African interior, they were interested not in political but in commercial occupation." [10] Their sole objective was to ensure a regular flow of slaves and ivory to Zanzibar, which at that time was the main commercial entrepôt on the East African coast. The common view that Arab domination in the Congo was accompanied by brutal atrocities and wholesale plunder conveys a grossly distorted picture of Afro-Arab relationships. The Arabs certainly were responsible for sufferings caused by the slave trade, but such effects were rarely intentional. Their policy was to obtain their slaves and ivory by peaceful bargaining rather than by force; their normal practice was to use the local chiefs as middlemen for procuring the human commodity, as the Portuguese had done a few centuries earlier. "They armed the chiefs, and the chiefs did the rest." [11]

As they expanded farther inland, the Arab chiefs* set up a fairly

---

\* In this context the term "Arab" is used to designate not only Arabs of pure race, but half-caste Arabs and Arab-influenced Bantus who took part in the trade.

elaborate system of administration. Their territories were usually divided into a number of districts administered by lieutenants, who in turn appointed local officials to act as intermediaries between the African chiefs and their immediate superiors.[12] Arabs like Mohammed Ben Junna (better

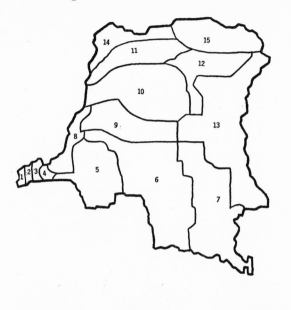

| | | |
|---|---|---|
| 1. Banana District | 6. Kasai District | 11. Bangala District |
| 2. Boma District | 7. Lualaba District | 12. Aruwimi District |
| 3. Matadi District | 8. Stanley Pool District | 13. Stanley Falls District |
| 4. Cataracts District | 9. Lac Leopold District | 14. Ubangui District |
| 5. Kwango District | 10. Equateur District | 15. Uele District |

MAP 2. *Administrative boundaries of the Congo Free State, 1895.* (Adapted from *Atlas du Congo Belge* [Bruxelles, 1945].)

known as Tippo-Tip), Munie-Mohara, and Kibonge managed to exercise considerable influence over the local tribes. Tippo-Tip, in particular, the most famous of all the Arab chiefs, whose domain stretched over a vast territory to the west of the Lualaba, between Kasongo in the south and Isangi in the north, became so powerful that he was in reality "an uncrowned king of the region between Stanley Falls and Tanganyika Lake, commanding many thousands of men inured to fighting and wild Equatorial life." [13] Although the Arabs had the means to coerce the African chiefs, as a rule coercion was unnecessary, for the commercial interests of the two parties were usually complementary. It was only when Europeans began to compete with the Arabs for allies among the indigenous population that the latter had to use force to retain their control.

Although the Arabs made no conscious effort to inculcate their own habits and religious beliefs upon the Africans, and allowed the chiefs to retain as much political freedom as they deemed compatible with the preservation of their commercial interests, their influence became a pervasive reality in the whole eastern part of the Congo. The influence of Arab culture was apparent in the style of dress and the mannerisms of the African chiefs, as well as in their professed attachment to Islam.[14] Another sign of the Arab presence was the attention paid to agricultural improvement through the introduction of new crops and new methods of cultivation: "In the midst of savage Africa, if you come across fertile rice plantations, the cultivation of wheat, lemons, and guavas, and splendid plantations of bananas, it is entirely owing to the Arabs."[15] In general, however, it was in the vicinity of the trading stations at Nyangwe, Riba-Riba, Kirundu, Kasongo, and Isangi that the Arabs left their most durable imprint. Stanleyville was a "large and thriving township in every sense of the word Arab, peopled by the imported tribes and under the general headship of a bonafide Arab. The scene might well be laid in Morocco."[16] Even to this day the so-called "Arabisés" of Stanleyville are distinctively Arab in their dress, customs, and religion. The Arabs must also be credited with the introduction of Swahili, which today serves as a vehicular language for hundreds of thousands of Africans in the Katanga, Kivu, and Orientale provinces.

Although the Arab domination did not lead to a degree of political and cultural assimilation comparable to that which may be observed among the predominantly Islamized peoples of West Africa, its impact upon the indigenous population was extremely significant. The slave trade produced a widespread disruption of traditional institutions among the peoples of the eastern region. At the same time, however, new cultural ties and institutions were introduced which tended to supersede the old ones. Through the diffusion of a new vehicular language the Arabs provided an important unifying bond among the local populations, and Islam, wherever it found acceptance either as a creed or as a ritual, also played a part in bringing together peoples of different ethnic stocks. Furthermore, by organizing trading centers and markets and by developing lines of communication between the coast and the interior, the Arabs facilitated and accelerated contacts among the different tribes. In other words, within a few decades the Arabs introduced a number of important integrative forces which continued to operate long after they relinquished control over the area. Nationalist movements organized along tribal lines therefore encountered little success in this region, even though in some instances, as among the Azande, the traditional political structure could conceivably have provided a basis for such movements.[17]

THE LEGACY OF THE CONGO FREE STATE

In November, 1884, as the participants in the Berlin West African Conference proceeded to set the ground rules for the partition of the

African continent, the king of the Belgians, Leopold II, had already gained a strong position in the Congo. His desire to acquire an overseas empire led him to summon an international geographical conference at Brussels, in 1876, for the purpose of "opening to civilization the only part of the globe where it has not yet penetrated"; in the same year, to cover up his colonial ambitions, Leopold created the African International Association "to build up hospitable and scientific stations up the Congo, to discountenance the slave-trade, to survey, inquire, analyze the land, people, and resources." [18] What gave the association a decisive impetus was the news of Henry M. Stanley's celebrated journey down the Congo River, from Nyangwe to the Atlantic. In November, 1878, Leopold formed the Comité d'Etudes du Haut Congo (later known as the Association Internationale du Congo) to investigate the possibility of establishing a railroad communication between Stanley Pool and the Atlantic, and the following year Stanley was commissioned by the King to lead the Comité's first expedition to the Lower Congo. It was clear from the very beginning, however, that the intentions of the Belgian king were not entirely altruistic. His ultimate objective, as revealed by the instructions given to Stanley by Colonel Stauch, president of the Comité, was to organize "a republican confederation of free negroes, . . . such confederation to be independent, except that the King . . . reserved the right to appoint the President who should reside in Europe." [19] Instead, the Congo was converted into the personal property of King Leopold, and remained so until its annexation by Belgium in 1908.

By 1885, when the Congo Free State received international recognition, the authority of the Comité d'Etudes du Haut Congo was established on each bank of the Congo, some 1,350 miles upriver. Forty "hospitable and scientific" stations had been erected above and below the lower river cataracts; five steamers had been launched on Stanley Pool; and some 450 treaties had been concluded with more than 2,000 chiefs. On the basis of these treaties the association claimed sovereignty over more than 1 million square miles:

We are already a state according to International Law, a state extending 1,350 miles inland from our lower station in the Congo, with a breadth varying from 20 to 450 miles, with means to influence all the tribes from the sea to Tanganyika, a distance 1,250 miles from the source of the Kasai to the sources of the Timbiri, a distance of 1,100 miles from San Salvador to the shores of Muta-Nzige—a clear 1,300,000 square English miles, containing a population of about 40,000 million souls.[20]

The validity of these territorial claims, though naturally open to question, was accepted by the parties to the Berlin Conference, where the assumption that "European powers had the right to annex African territory for their own advantage as long as the nominal consent of a certain number of African chiefs had been obtained" was unquestioned.[21] But once the association had won recognition as a sovereign state, it became necessary to ensure "the establishing of authority in the regions occupied" in order that "its new occupations may be held effective." [22]

While the Berlin Conference entrusted Leopold with absolute powers to carry out this task, the Belgian parliament was unwilling to take any responsibility. It authorized King Leopold to become the sovereign of the Congo Free State on the condition that "the union . . . [between Belgium] and the new state of the Congo be exclusively personal." [23] Furthermore, if the King wanted to retain personal control of the Free State, he alone was to bear the financial cost of the enterprise. To meet this responsibility, which imposed a heavy strain on the royal resources, Leopold made ever-increasing demands for prestations from the African population. The resulting flood of international criticism ultimately forced Leopold to terminate this "personal union."

Because of the financial burden, Leopold welcomed the assistance of private enterprise and missionary societies in carrying out the "civilizing" of the Free State. Between 1884 and 1886 Catholic and Protestant missionaries did a great deal of exploring, most of which must be credited to George Grenfell, a Baptist. Missionary efforts were matched by the explorations of Von Wissmann in the Kasai, Roget in the Uele, Van de Velde in the Kwango, Van Gèle in the Ubangui, and many others. In 1887 two expeditions were organized by the Compagnie du Congo pour le Commerce et l'Industrie, and in 1891 the Compagnie du Katanga set out to penetrate the area south of Stanley Falls in order to establish trading posts on the Lomami and Lualaba rivers. The expedition, which ended in disaster at Riba-Riba in 1892, brought the state into open conflict with the Arabs. Initially, however, the balance of forces between the Free State and the Arabs dictated a policy of conciliation. As the state had neither the men nor the money to emerge victorious from a trial of strength with the Arabs, Captain Van Gèle, acting on behalf of the association, persuaded Tippo-Tip to recognize the rights of the Free State between Banana and Stanley Falls,[24] and in 1887, after an agreement with Stanley at Zanzibar, Tippo-Tip was appointed governor of the Falls.

While these arrangements allowed the Free State forces to gather strength, Tippo-Tip's conciliatory attitude antagonized his followers. They became increasingly hostile to the state, as the export duties on ivory made trade less and less profitable. Moreover, state agents, whose commission was calculated on the amount of ivory collected, competed with the Arabs to monopolize the trade. Although these pressures led to frequent clashes between Arabs and Europeans, the Free State nevertheless insisted on "the absolute necessity of continuing a temporizing policy towards the Arabs." [25] After the Riba-Riba incident, however, Dhanis, believing that the policy had outlived its usefulness, decided to engage in hostilities.

The campaign, which lasted nineteen months and caused an estimated 70,000 casualties, was in fact a war of conquest waged by Africans against Africans on behalf of alien powers. According to Sidney L. Hinde, who served as an officer, the campaign involved "a dozen white officers and four hundred regular troops on one side and a couple of hundred Arab chiefs supported by a few hundred half-Arabs and commanding large numbers of irregular soldiery on the other." Only "extraordinary luck, together with good leadership, was the cause of our first success." [26] Aside from the fact that the Free State forces were better equipped and organized, though smaller, the unexpected switch of allegiance of some of Tippo-Tip's former vassals proved equally decisive. But the potential advantage resulting from these defections was acknowledged only insofar as it served immediate military purposes. An example is the fate that befell the Batetela chief Ngongo Lutete, remembered today by his people as the former ally of the Free State who became its victim as well. His execution upon his return from the Dhanis expedition against Tippo-Tip's son, in 1892, illustrates the arbitrary methods employed by Free State agents in their dealings with African chiefs. Its main significance, however, is that it created a deep and lasting resentment among the Batetela, culminating in a series of military revolts at Luluabourg in 1895, at Darfi in 1897, and at Shinkakasa in 1900.[27]

The pacification of the Arab zone enabled the Free State to extend its authority over the territory between the Lualaba and the Great Lakes. Its immediate result, however, was to place an additional burden on the state's financial resources. As a remedy for the financial difficulties that by 1890 were threatening his colonial enterprise, Leopold sought an alternative source of revenue by creating a state monopoly on rubber and ivory. In September, 1891, a secret decree informed the district commissioners of the Aruwimi-Uele and Ubangui to "take urgent and necessary measures to place at the disposal of the state the produce of the domain, especially rubber and ivory." [28] In 1892 about half of the state's territory was reserved as *domaine privé*, for exclusive exploitation by Free State agents. In 1896 the *domaine de la couronne*, covering some 289,000 square kilometers in the Lake Leopold II region, was added. By 1896 the systematic exploitation of this vast domain, over which Leopold claimed absolute ownership, had substantially improved the state's financial position. On the other hand, the harassing system of prestations enforced upon the African population—officially referred to as "labor tax" —led to the abuses and atrocities that were publicly denounced a few years later by the Congo Reform Association.

The most resented aspect of the economic system introduced by the Free State was the incessant demands made on the Africans for the collection of rubber. After 1894 there was a phenomenal increase in the production of rubber: "Up to that time no year has produced as much as 5% of the rubber which since 1900 has figured as the annual yield." [29] This spectacular increase was accompanied by a profound alteration in traditional African institutions. Hundreds of Africans were taken away from their villages and compelled to work under the supervision of *capitas* chosen from different tribes, who behaved like so many local tyrants.[30] The regular quotas imposed by the state were seldom taken into consideration, and because of the vested interests inherent in the system, the *chefs de poste* and the capitas coöperated to obtain a maximum output. The exactions were met with resistance, and resistance was met with repression.[31] "Madness is the only hypothesis for explaining the insensate cruelty and bestiality which figure so prominently in the charges made, and because of the madness it has developed the present system stands condemned." [32]

Protestant missionaries were the first to give evidence of the cruelties inflicted upon the African population. In 1895 the American Baptist missionary J. B. Murphy publicly criticized the state for the extreme methods associated with the "rubber system," and in the following year similar criticisms were voiced by the Swedish missionary Sjøblom. But it was not until 1904, when Edmund D. Morel decided to form the Congo Reform Association, that the reform movement began to gather momentum. The publicity given the stories of Protestant missionaries in the association's journal, the *Official Organ,* caused a considerable stir in both England and the United States, and the publication of a report by the British consul in Boma, Sir Roger Casement, further substantiated Morel's charges against the Free State.

The repercussions on Belgian public opinion were not immediately noticeable, and it was not until 1906, when Félicien Cattier published his *Etude sur la situation de l'état indépendant du Congo,* that the Belgian public began to appreciate the full significance of the charges. In *La Question congolaise,* published the same year, the Jesuit theologian Arthur Vermeersch echoed Cattier's criticisms of the Leopoldian system, and suggested that Belgium annex the Congo in order to get out of the difficulties created by the reform movement. In the parliamentary arena these views were largely shared by the Catholic deputies, who thought that Belgium was morally obligated to annex the Congo. A more persuasive argument was advanced by the future minister of colonies, Jules Renkin, who declared in April, 1908: "The Congo will constitute for Belgium an excellent colony; . . . its ivory, rubber, and mineral deposits . . . will provide an inexhaustible source of riches." [33] In August, after a long-drawn-out debate, the Chamber of Representatives, by a vote of 83 to 54, with 9 abstentions, and the Senate, by a vote of 63 to 24, with 11 abstentions, voted in favor of annexation.

This brief survey offers only a glimpse into the difficulties, both internal and external, which finally compelled Leopold to surrender the Congo to Belgium. The weight of external pressures was a decisive factor, but the Leopoldian system could hardly have aroused so much criticism had it not itself engendered abuses. For almost the entire period of the Free State the Congolese were subjected to a staggering sequence of wars, repression, and regimentation. Of course, the Congo was not the only part of Africa where abuses were committed, for "France has allowed concessionaire companies to do things quite as bad as those attributed to the Leopoldian regime in the hinterland of the French Congo and Gabon. Charges of the same kind have been leveled against the Portuguese in the far interior of Angola, and it was actions of this kind that provoked the first risings against the Germans in 1885 and 1889." [34] Yet the scale of violence and bloodshed in the Congo was without precedent in other parts of Africa.

Indeed, the impact of the Free State was so devastating, and its aftereffects were so disruptive, because the initial shock of European intrusion was followed almost immediately by a systematic exploitation of human and natural resources. Even after pacification, the exactions of Free State officials caused a number of sporadic revolts which in turn led to punitive expeditions, such as those ordered against the Budja in 1898, 1901, and 1905. Elsewhere, retaliation occurred in haphazard fashion, thereby causing new disturbances among innocent tribes.[35] In retrospect, the social and political disruption resulting from the application of physical violence seems to be the main reason for delaying the establishment of a uniform and viable system of administration until the early 1930's. Meanwhile, however, the erosive effects of the earlier system had seriously compromised the chances of future success in the field of local administration.

In terms of its psychological impact, the Free State left a legacy of latent hostility on which subsequent generations of nationalist leaders could capitalize to gain popular support for their cause. On the other hand, the ruthlessness of the methods employed under the Leopoldian regime left a legacy of fear and hopelessness which, initially at least, discouraged the emergence of nationalist activities.

THE EVOLUTION OF BELGIAN POLICY

In the years that followed annexation most of the abuses associated with the Free State were abolished. The monopoly exercised by the administration on native produce was brought to an end; a more reasonable system of taxation was substituted for the labor tax; and ultimate control over the affairs of the colony was formally vested in the Belgian Chambers. But these reforms, however meritorious, did not bring about a complete reversal of policy. Indeed, writing in 1919, a Belgian observer went so far as to suggest that the goals of Belgian policy had undergone no basic transformation since the days of the Free State, and that under the cloak of philanthropy the policy of the government tended as before toward "the debasement [*avilissement*] of a race, not its emancipation." [36] The analogy here suggested does not imply identity of administrative methods, but rather a similarity of attitudes and assumptions regarding the aims of colonization, as well as certain parallel trends in the policies adopted to fulfill those aims.

First, the humanitarian ideals that Leopold so loudly professed were continually emphasized in later years by Belgian officials. The opening sentence of a celebrated work by a former governor general—"Dominer pour servir: C'est la seule excuse à la conquête coloniale, c'en est aussi sa pleine justification"—concisely sums up the humanitarian aspect of Belgian colonial enterprise.[37] Paternalism implied a moral obligation to further the "moral and material well being" of the Africans, but so long as the obligation was only moral there was no room left for reciprocal rights and duties.[38] The assumption that governed the attitude of the Belgian government until 1959 was that political rights could legitimately be denied to the Congolese so long as their social and economic needs were properly met.

Second, the change of emphasis from economic exploitation to benevolent paternalism did not bring a fundamental change in the Belgian policy toward the mass of the Congolese. While Belgian policy aimed at preserving traditional institutions in order to use them as instruments of local government, from the very beginning the tendency was to substitute the authority of Belgian-inspired legislation for the authority of the African chiefs, thereby violating the very principle of indirect rule. The seeds of this contradiction were already present in the terms of a decree of 1906: "Le chef exerce son autorité sur les membres de la chefferie conformément à la coutume indigène, pourvu qu'elle ne soit pas contraire aux règles d'ordre public universel ni aux lois de l'Etat qui ont pour but de substituer d'autres règles aux principes de la coutume indigène." [39] The same principle was embodied in the decrees of 1910 and 1933 on "customary authorities," and since the distinction between the powers of the chief qua chief and those of the chief qua functionary was never made clear, the role and functions of the chiefs continued to be identified with those of a functionary appointed by, and subservient to, the administration.

Third, the attitude of the Belgian government toward the educated elite reflected a similar tendency to accommodate legal precedents to the new conditions created by social and economic changes. Until 1952 the status of the so-called "civilized" Africans was regulated by a decree of 1895, which provided for the juridical assimilation of certain categories of people. But in spite of its promising implications, the decree remained a dead letter, and after annexation the attention of the Belgian government was centered exclusively on the organization of the *chefferies indigènes.* In 1952, when the Belgian government recognized that "a number of individuals had emancipated themselves from their tribal conceptions," and therefore deserved to be treated on equal terms with Europeans, a fresh attempt was made to give educated Congolese a special juridical status. The decree of 1952 on "immatriculation" aimed at the assimilation of the African elite, but in fact did little more than revert to the system envisaged by the decree of 1895. Moreover, as juridical assimilation did not imply equality of educational and economic opportunities, the status of the elite remained virtually unchanged.

Finally, in the absence of meaningful concessions regarding freedom of the press and the right of association, Belgian rule tended to operate in a climate of authoritarian constraint reminiscent of the Free State. Because of the rigorous censorship and surveillance exercised by the Belgian government, popular discontent found an outlet in sporadic revolts and religious movements which were inevitably met by repression; as in the days of the Free State, the local authorities found the use of armed force a convenient solution to their problems.[40] It was not until August, 1959, less than a year before independence, that the Belgian government formally consented to grant civil liberties.

One is inclined to agree with the statement of a Belgian official that "Belgian colonial policy was pursued with a remarkable continuity by the Independent State first, and then by Belgium." [41] For purposes of analysis, however, one may distinguish at least three phases in the evolution of Belgian policy. In a first period, extending roughly from 1908 to 1952, Belgian policy was almost wholly centered on the notion of "native autonomy"; from 1952 to 1958, Belgian official thinking became mainly concerned with the concept of "Belgo-Congolese Community" and the way in which it ought to be put into practice; finally, with the declaration of January 13, 1959, in which the metropolitan authorities formally committed themselves to the principle of self-government, Belgian colonial policy entered its third and final phase. The distinction among these three phases is not made with reference to all aspects of Belgian policy, but merely on the basis of certain innovations introduced in 1952 and 1959.

### The Theory of "Native Autonomy"

The Belgian government, relying on the assumption that the Congolese should remain subject to Belgium's tutelage "as long as a substantial part [of the African community] proves incapable of exercising political control over the management of public affairs," [42] but offering little or no opportunity in the way of training toward that end, was logically unable to envisage any line of development other than protracted bondage. It did make allowance, however, for some degree of autonomy in the sphere of native administration. Native autonomy did not mean that "native society should be entrusted with the direction of the administrative and judicial organization established by the colonizing power," but merely "autonomy within the framework of native institutions." [43] Insofar as it aimed at preserving the existing indigenous political institutions, the theory of native autonomy had much in common with the British system of indirect rule. Partly because of the way in which it was applied, however, this policy never attained the measure of success achieved by indirect rule in some parts of British Africa.

Although the Free State theoretically recognized the authority of traditional chiefs, in practice every effort was made to replace them with "trustworthy elements" whose only claim to authority was their personal loyalty to the state. Even where the authority of the chiefs was formally acknowledged, primary reliance was placed on "native messengers" who were expected to "coöperate with the administration and act as intermediaries between the chiefs and the administration," but whose functions were in fact similar to those of the capitas and the *gardes-forestiers*.[44] After annexation, a halfhearted attempt was made to restore the authority of the chiefs through a system of *chefferies* and *sous-chefferies* headed by chiefs who were identified by the district commissioners as the "lawful rulers of their people." According to the *exposé des motifs* of the decree of 1910, the objective of the administration was "de créer dans toute l'étendue de la colonie des groupements animés d'une vie propre et munis de moyens d'action traditionnels destinés à pourvoir aux intérêts communs des membres des groupements dans le cadre de l'administration politique et administrative générale." [45] Actually, the main innovation introduced by the decree was that the native messengers were to act as lower-ranking functionaries, entirely subject to the authority of the chiefs, while the latter continued as before to be little more than functionaries acting on behalf of the local authorities.

The way in which this policy was implemented defeated its purpose: "Some of the chiefs have been invested out of complacency or lassitude, or for immediate practicality, in spite of the fact that they lacked all

qualification. The chefferies have been fragmented in violation of tradition. Groups of natives have been constituted into chefferies and errone-
ously considered as separate entities." [46] One reason for this state of
affairs was the red tape involved in the everyday tasks of administration,
which left little time for other duties.[47] Some territorial agents laid the
blame on concessionaire companies; in the Katanga the agents of the
Comité Spécial du Katanga were held responsible for the lack of progress
in the organization of chiefdoms.[48] Elsewhere, as in the Kongolo, the
methods adopted by Africans to elect their chiefs were regarded as "un
dissolvant inévitable des chefferies." [49] An additional factor, which few
administrators would admit, was that most of them lacked the qualifications to inquire into the political organization of the local tribes.

Regardless of the underlying causes, a universal consequence of
this policy was to further the process of administrative disintegration
which began under the Free State. The greatest difficulties were encountered in the Orientale and Equateur provinces, where the sheer number
and fragmentation of tribal entities led to a phenomenal proliferation
of chefferies and sous-chefferies. In the Equateur, for example, 2,710
chefferies were reported in 1921; and in the Stanleyville District, in Orientale Province, no less than 840 chefferies and 170 sous-chefferies were
registered in 1928 for a total of 122,000 adult males. In the territory of
Elila, in the Maniema District, half of the chefferies included less than
fifty adult males each, and some had as few as twenty or twenty-five.[50]
By 1930, a total of 4,970 chefferies and sous-chefferies had been officially
recognized.

Beginning in 1921, under the ministry of Louis Frank, elaborate
instructions were given to local administrators to reduce the number of
sous-chefferies. After making appropriate inquiries, district commissioners
were to single out the "most intelligent, influential, and understanding"
of the several chiefs and dismiss the others—but only when "the minds
of his colleagues will be sufficiently prepared for this innovation." [51] It
was not until 1933, however, that specific legislative measures were taken
to consolidate the existing units into more manageable entities. The most
significant of these was the introduction of a system of *secteurs* incorporating within their boundaries the chefferies that were too numerous
or too weak to serve as administrative units. Between 1933 and 1945 the
number of recognized units dropped from 3,189 to 595, and by 1950 only
476 chefferies and 571 secteurs were functioning in the colony.

The social and political dislocation engendered by the amalgamation
of previously autonomous units, and the heritage of administrative confusion bequeathed by the Free State, are not the only reasons for the
limited success of Belgian policy in the field of native administration. In
the first place, the investiture of the chiefs continued to be based on

criteria that were often at variance with those prevailing in the traditional society. Article 27 of the decree of 1933 stipulated that "customary norms determine who is qualified to exercise the functions of chief," but in practice the selection of chiefs was often based on other criteria. The decree was sidestepped not only because of the difficulty of determining customary qualifications and the lack of competent administrators to do so, but also because of the high order of priority accorded to the personal skills and ability of the aspirants.

Furthermore, there was a fundamental contradiction between the functions devolved upon customary chiefs and the role they were expected to play in the traditional society. According to the decree of 1933, the invested chief was to communicate to his subjects the instructions issued by the administration, collect taxes according to the rates prescribed in local ordinances, recruit militia for the *force publique*, arrest all "natives" guilty of contravening the laws, and discharge other duties as requested by the administration. A major source of difficulty, in other words, lay in the attempt to integrate within the same legal framework basically different, and conflicting, sources of authority:

Indirect rule, as conceived by Belgium, had in it the germs of the development of a society under its own rulers whose authority should be sanctioned by the maintenance of traditional relationships with their subjects. Once the chief is transformed by one and the same process into a despot and a puppet, the relationship becomes so distorted that it remains doubtful whether there remains advantage in casting the traditional chief for the part.[52]

Finally, in only a few instances did the traditional authority systems provide a basis for the application of indirect rule. In those areas of Equateur, Orientale, and Kivu provinces where small-scale political entities predominate, indirect rule led to so phenomenal a fragmentation of authority that even the most fervent advocates of the system did not hesitate to admit its shortcomings. Elsewhere, the deliberate application of a policy of "divide and rule"—as among the Azande and the Mangbetu of Orientale Province—created similar difficulties. The division of certain regions into a multitude of artificial administrative units spelled inefficiency or anarchy, or both.

An overall appraisal of the consequences of the Belgian version of indirect rule is rendered especially difficult by the empiricism that governed its application, and by the great diversity of the traditional systems encountered in the Congo. In the few areas where the structure of indigenous societies permitted effective use of indirect rule, as among the Lunda, the Bayaka, and the Warega, it has provided ethnic or regional movements with traditional bases of support. Elsewhere, however, as in some parts of Orientale Province, where the administration's methods tended to destroy the unity of the larger tribal groupings, the Belgian system has undoubtedly discouraged the formation of such movements. In some instances the displacement of chiefly authorities and the division of preëxisting political units have tended to perpetuate natural cleavages, as between the Tschokwe and the Lunda once the former were removed from the latter's overlordship, or to create new ones, as among the Baluba after the relegation of the Paramount Chief Kasongo Nyembo.[53] On the whole, however, the divisive effects of Belgian policy seem to overshadow its other aspects.

### The Belgo-Congolese Community

Beginning in 1952, in response to the economic and social changes that took place during the postwar years, the Belgian government oriented its policy toward the attainment of a new ideal, the Belgo-Congolese community. This ideal did not imply a radical change in the constitutional relationships between the colony and the metropolis, but rather a shift in human relations between Europeans and Africans. Cautioning his audience against possible confusion, Governor General Pétillon stated in 1956:

Let us not confuse what might be called a Belgo-Congolese union with the Belgo-Congolese community. The Belgo-Congolese union is concerned with the constitutional relationships that will some day be established between Belgium and the Congo. Today's major problem is a different one. It is related to the implementation of an internal Belgo-Congolese community through a policy of association, taking into account the whole and the parts, principles and contingencies, convergences and divergences.[54]

In fact, the new doctrine reflected an uneasy balance between the *évolués'* * demands for equality and the settlers' insistence on retaining their privileges. The inescapable contradictions of a formula that, in Pétillon's own words, pretended to be at the same time "idealist and realist, clear and *nuancée*, cautious and bold," [55] are further illustrated by the following declaration:

We have rejected (1) the policy of juxtaposition because it is incompatible with the creation of organic ties and the promotion of a new society; and (2) the policy of assimilation because it would end up in a simplistic substitution of Western civilization for Bantu customs. . . . A policy of association, on the other hand, need not take numbers into account; it tends toward a community of interests, aspirations, and good human relations between . . . the natives and the Belgians established in the Congo.[56]

---

* In the Congo the term "évolué" referred to a class of Africans who had achieved literacy and showed other evidences of Westernization. In this study, however, the term does not necessarily imply disaffiliation from traditional membership groups.

As a first step toward this goal, the 1952 decree on immatriculation provided for the juridical assimilation of Africans who were able to show "by their upbringing and way of life" that they had reached an adequate "state of civilization." [57] This condition lay at the heart of the dilemmas created by the procedure of immatriculation; for those Congolese who wished to preserve certain aspects of their traditional culture and at the same time benefit from the privileges accorded to Europeans, the conflict of values could hardly resolve itself through the acquisition of an immatriculation card. The basic error underlying the Belgian policy was to assume that the adoption of Western standards of behavior was the sole criterion by which to evaluate the "state of civilization." [58]

Reflecting on the conflict of values created by immatriculation, one Congolese commented:

Sometimes the procedure of immatriculation demands from the applicant a false [*empruntée*] and hypocritical life. We have on several occasions seen holders of a *carte de mérite civique* who felt obliged to marry religiously but who otherwise would not have displayed an ardent desire to enter this contract; their only motive is to please the missionaries for fear that they might otherwise make unfavorable comments to the consultative commissions.[59]

Many Congolese saw in the procedure of immatriculation a Belgian stratagem designed to make them subject to higher taxes. Arguing on behalf of the *immatriculés,* Father Joseph Van Wing declared before the Colonial Council in 1955:

Immatriculation is a trick [*attrape-nigaud*], an item of Belgian propaganda in the United Nations. Yet we have had the courage to apply for immatriculation, but we are sorry we did, for it did not bring us any advantage; on the contrary, the whites and the *non-immatriculés* scoff at us. The only advantage is that of being obliged to pay fines three times higher when we are caught by the police.[60]

Most évolués clearly realized that the attitude of mutual tolerance which might have prevailed between Africans and Europeans could not be brought about through legal action.

The decree on immatriculation was followed by a series of piecemeal measures designed to break down the barrier of racial discrimination between Africans, whether matriculated or not, and Europeans. A decree of February, 1953, allowed Africans to own land in rural and urban areas, and in 1955 they were given free access to public establishments and permission to buy and consume alcoholic beverages. A few years later, in 1958, substantial changes were introduced in the judicial system of the colony, the most significant being that offenses committed by Africans were to be justiciable in all courts instead of only in *tribunaux de police.* All these reforms were predicated on the questionable assumption that racial discrimination could be legislated out of existence.

Perhaps the most disappointing aspect of the Belgo-Congolese community concept was that it paid virtually no attention to the political future of the Congo. The only line of political development envisaged in 1952 was the extension of native autonomy to urban areas. As Governor Pétillon stated in 1952, "Far from abandoning our traditional policy, what I have actually in mind is a reversion to our former concept of indirect administration, which, as timid as it may have been at the outset, has become increasingly attenuated under the pressure of economic circumstances." [61] His view was that the "apprenticeship of self-government" should start at the local level. In both rural and urban areas conciliar organs were to be elected by and from an electorate composed of "notables"; higher councils, presumably provincial assemblies, would then be elected by the lower organs. Restrictive qualifications later added to this declaration of intent indicated, however, that the prospects of meaningful political participation remained extremely distant. Evoking the possibility of limited self-government, Pétillon declared in 1954:

For our councils to remain advisory for a long time to come is a fundamental necessity so long as the education of the natives still has to become a reality, and so long as the composition and the method of designation of our assemblies do not reflect the whole of the Congolese population. The Belgian nation, seat and source of all powers, cannot remain faithful to its colonial conceptions and contemplate a delegation of decision-making powers to African councils.[62]

This last sentence suggests that the approach of the Belgian government to colonial problems has not always been so empirical as some observers believe. Indeed, a convincing case could be made for the view that its failure to prepare the Congolese for the responsibilities of self-government was owing primarily to its commitment to the doctrine of paternalism. The idea that the Belgian nation was "the seat and source of all powers," and should remain so "for a long time to come," explains the impatience displayed by Congolese nationalists when the possibility of "full independence" finally entered their vision.

### The Declaration of January 13, 1959

This possibility presented itself in the early days of January, 1959, with the issuance of two official statements, one from Prime Minister Gaston Eyskens and the other from the Crown. "It is our firm intention," stated the King's message, "without undue procrastination, but also without fatal haste, to lead the Congolese populations forward toward independence in prosperity and peace." [63] Although there has been some speculation that this abrupt shift of policy had actually been forced upon the government by the rioting that broke out in Leopoldville on January 4, the concessions envisaged in these declarations grew out of the recommendations made by the *groupe de travail* appointed in August, 1958, by the Minister of Colonies to examine "the views and aspirations of the inhabitants of the Congo concerning the way in which the political and administrative evolution of the country should be conducted." [64] Yet, even if the government declaration of January 13 had long been planned for that particular date, the Leopoldville riots were a determining factor in the use of the word "independence." [65]

Despite its momentous implications, however, the declaration of January 13 was not entirely free of ambiguity. First, no mention was made of a specific target date for independence. Although the royal message openly recognized the need to "lead the Congolese . . . toward independence," the government's statement merely noted that "in order to organize a democracy capable of exercising its sovereign prerogatives . . . decision-making powers must be progressively devolved [upon all the inhabitants of the Congo] with increasing competence and in a democratic manner, according to institutional changes."

Second, the royal message favored "original adaptations which respond to the proper character and the traditions that are dear [to the Congolese people]," but the government seemed to favor a different approach. Its declaration provided for the election of territorial and communal councils by direct and universal suffrage, which would in turn elect provincial assemblies. An indirectly elected *conseil général* would be ultimately substituted for the Conseil de Gouvernement to form the House of Representatives, and a *conseil de législation*, composed of two delegates from each province, would form the Senate. Far from being an "original adaptation," this new governmental structure had all the appurtenances of a Belgian import.

Finally, as no specific measures were envisaged to enlarge civil liberties, the promises contained in the government's declaration were likely to remain unfulfilled. Until August, 1959, freedom of association was regulated by an ordinance of February 11, 1926, which allowed district commissioners "to dissolve all associations deemed contrary to civilization or likely to constitute a threat to public safety." Article 1 of the ordinance provided that "no association may be formed unless it is authorized by the district commissioner";[66] before such authorization could be issued, the applicant had to submit the names and addresses of the association and its *dirigeants*, its objectives and insignia, the frequency of its meetings, and a statement of its financial resources. These prescriptions were supplemented by periodic circulars from the Governor

General concerning the prophylactic measures that should be used against the spread of "subversive movements."

It might have been expected that by 1959 some of these restrictions would have been lifted. In some respects, however, they were made even more crippling. In July, 1959, the text of a draft decree on freedom of association and reunion was submitted to the Conseil de Législation (formerly the Conseil Colonial); it provided that "every association must, within thirty days of its constitution, be declared to the district commissioner or the *premier bourgmestre* of the town in which its headquarters are located." [67] An association had to give most of the information required by the ordinance of 1926 on its aims, leadership, and sources of financial support. In addition, to make things even more complicated, a distinction was made between indoor and outdoor meetings; a meeting could be held behind closed doors only after a permit had been secured from the local authorities. Aside from technical deficiencies and obvious loopholes, the text of the decree clearly demonstrated that, in the words of a Congolese observer, "the real motive behind this distinction between indoor and outdoor reunions is to allow the administration to keep fully informed of what goes on." [68]

No less disappointing were the legislative proposals concerning the freedom of the press. Early in 1959 a draft decree submitted to the Conseil de Législation made it mandatory for anyone wanting to publish a newspaper or a periodical to give advance notice to the provincial governor. Meanwhile, the governor general retained the right to "prohibit or suspend the introduction or circulation within the Congo of all material he deemed likely to disturb the public order." [69] It was not until August 4, 1959, when nationalist forces were already at flood tide, that the regime of civil liberties underwent significant alterations. A communiqué issued on that date by the Governor General announced that the right to associate depended only on a simple declaration of intent.[70]

Even then, every effort was made by the administration to retain control of the situation. On August 4, 1959, the very day that the Governor General lifted the restrictions imposed by the decree of 1926, Vice-Governor General André Schoeller sent secret instructions to the provincial governors on the measures to be taken against "public and militant actions involving the development of one or several subversive themes." [71] Nonnatives who failed to heed the warning of the local functionary in charge of relations with political movements were to be immediately expelled, natives were to be placed under arrest, and the associations they were connected with were to be dissolved or suspended. In brief, what seemed on the surface to be a major step toward the enlargement of civil liberties was largely nullified by the role the administration continued to play behind the scenes.

Legal controls over public expression and association doubtless inhibited the rise of nationalist movements, but they were not always applied with equal rigor throughout the Congo. Depending on the attitude of district commissioners toward Africans, meetings held in some places would not have been tolerated elsewhere. By January, 1959, a number of political groups had been recognized by the administration, even though some of them could conceivably be regarded as "subversive." Until then, however, the strict surveillance maintained over the African population was certainly the main factor in delaying the emergence of organized political groups. For the same reason, at least until 1958, the Belgians were remarkably confident of their ability to insulate the Congo from the tide of nationalist sentiment.

## THE ROAD TO SELF-GOVERNMENT

The rapid sequence of events that led to independence must be viewed in the three-dimensional perspective of (1) the development of nationalist assertions in the Congo, (2) the settlers' reaction to the policy of the Belgian government, and (3) the role of opposition forces in the Belgian parliament. While the ever-increasing tempo of nationalist assertions obviously played a dominant part in accelerating the process of emancipation, these were by no means the only forces that impinged upon the metropolitan government. Equally decisive were the cross-pressures resulting from the combination of domestic and colonial influences, which ultimately played into the hands of the nationalists.

Even though there is no evidence that it had been instigated by the Abako, the sudden outbreak of violence in Leopoldville on January 4, 1959, gave the Belgians a full measure of the intense nationalist feelings of the Bakongo population. What precipitated the rioting was the decision of the premier bourgmestre, Mr. Tombeur, to prevent the Abako leaders of the Kalamu Commune from holding a meeting in the premises of the YMCA. This decision and the popular excitement caused by the news that the African bourgmestre of Kalamu, Mr. Penzi, would seize the occasion to report on his recent trip to Belgium, were enough to spark a violent reaction among the Africans. It resulted in a wholesale plunder of European property; cars were stoned, windows were broken, shops were looted, and Catholic missions were sacked. To prevent the rioting from spreading to European quarters the local police force was authorized to make use of its arms. The next day the force publique was called from Thysville, and later it was joined by a battalion of Belgian paratroopers from Kamina. Order was finally restored, but only after an exceedingly brutal repression. The official figures cited by the Belgian government said that 49 Congolese were killed and 101 were wounded, and that 140 "slightly wounded" were "not taken to the hospital." [72] On the other hand, a Bakongo tract mentioned "at least 600 Africans killed," and another 540. In the words of a Belgian commentator, "never had any riot in the Belgian Congo had such proportions, nor had any repression resulted in so many deaths." [73]

The first reaction of the Belgian government was to dissolve the Abako and arrest its leaders, three of whom (Joseph Kasa-Vubu, Daniel Kanza, and Simon Nzeza) were subsequently sent to Belgium. Shortly thereafter, on January 16, an order issued by the Provincial Governor enjoined the "floating" population of Leopoldville to return to their villages; in the following weeks an estimated 15,000 unemployed left the capital.[74] Thanks to this last measure, the ferment of nationalist ideas spread to the countryside, creating a climate of unrest in the Lower Congo and in neighboring regions. In April, 1959, further violence erupted among the workers of the Huileries du Congo Belge, in Leverville.[75] A few months later, in August, 1959, Luluabourg became the scene of a bloody rioting, directed in part against the stand of the local authorities on the Lulua-Baluba tangle. The next trouble spot was Stanleyville, where, on October 30, 1959, after Lumumba addressed a meeting of the Mouvement National Congolais (MNC), a violent uprising caused the death of twenty-six Africans. Lumumba, who was thought responsible for staging the riots, was arrested along with the provincial cadres of the MNC, and held in "preventive custody" until January 18, 1960.

Regardless of the immediate factors behind these manifestations, they added considerable weight to the demands of party leaders. On February 14, 1959, the MNC issued a statement urging the Belgian government "to define its new policy as well as the spirit in which it will be applied." On March 26, on the inauguration of the MNC's provincial headquarters, Lumumba declared in Leopoldville that although his party agreed with the government declaration in principle, it could only be regarded as "an invitation to further negotiations." As it became increasingly clear that such an invitation would not be forthcoming, the delegates to the Luluabourg Congress, held in April, 1959, unanimously endorsed a proposal sponsored by the MNC for the election of a Congolese government in January, 1961. Not to be outdone by their competitors, the Abako leaders issued a communiqué demanding the election of provincial governments in January, 1960, and the formation of a central government in March, 1960. As each party sought to emulate the demands of its rivals, the promises contained in the government declaration largely lost their appeal.

In the meantime, lacking the domestic support to implement his policy, the Social Christian minister, Van Hemelrijck, adopted a temporizing attitude which only added to the impatience of the Congolese masses. While drawing increasingly heavy fire from the more conservative members of his cabinet for giving in too fast to the desiderata of the nationalists, Van Hemelrijck was faced with mounting criticisms from the Socialist deputies. As early as March, 1959, his decision to order the transfer of the Abako leaders to Brussels had been the subject of a violent controversy in the Belgian Chambers. Members of the opposition had criticized the Minister for acting on his own initiative, without consulting the other members of the cabinet or even attempting to secure the consent of parliament. They also questioned his decision on its own merits; if it was the government's intention to negotiate with the leaders of the Abako, the Socialists argued, the latter would automatically be recognized as *interlocuteurs valables;* but as they represented only a small fraction of the Congolese population, this result was clearly unacceptable. On the other hand, if the government denied the Abako leaders the right to speak on behalf of the entire Congolese population, what purpose did it seek to achieve by retaining them in Belgium? The Minister's reply that his sole concern was to prevent further outbursts of violence in Leopoldville was received with skepticism by the opposition, and on April 11, 1959, the Belgian Socialist Party (PSB) adopted a resolution recording the party's disapproval of the government's policy and urging that "all necessary steps be taken to lead the Congo rapidly to independence."[76] A few days later, on April 21, the Liberal deputy Lahaye warned the Minister against the possibility of a trial of strength on the Algerian model: "La politique de force à l'heure d'Accra est la pire des politiques, car elle mènerait à un bain de sang, et plus loin à la perte du Congo, à la perte totale. ... [La politique de force] procède du plus incontestable racisme: Elle est irraisonée, affective; elle est de plus imbécile dans sa conception et son application."[77]

Actually, Van Hemelrijck realized that the success of the policy outlined in the statement of January 13 depended on a rapid and effective transfer of authority. It depended, according to him, on the establishment of a provisional government in late 1959, or early 1960. General elections would be held after a transitional period of approximately four years, during which the Belgian government would closely collaborate with the Congolese authorities in setting up the institutional framework of the country. But it presupposed, above all, that the feelings of animosity which until then had governed the attitude of the European population toward the Africans would eventually give way to a climate of mutual tolerance. In June, 1959, Van Hemelrijck visited the Congo, intending to do his best to realize this objective. But his presence widened the gap between positions that had already become irreconcilable; in each province he visited the manifestations of hostility staged by the white settlers were paralleled by enthusiastic reactions from the Africans. Caught between the inertia of the colonial administration and the overt hostility of the settlers on the one hand, and the cross fire of partisan attacks on the other, the Minister obviously lacked the leverage to impose his policy.

New difficulties cropped up in the month of August, when several members of the cabinet—Wigny, Lilar, de Vleeschauer, and Eyskens, among others—voiced their opposition to Van Hemelrijck's decision to accelerate the process of political transfer. Although his decision was based on recommendations made by Vice-Governor General Schoeller, the *chef de cabinet* of Prime Minister Eyskens, Count d'Aspremont-Lynden, was sent on a secret mission to Leopoldville, over the head of the Minister, to check the situation.[78] Faced with this breach in the normal chain of command, Van Hemelrijck handed his resignation to the King on September 3. Meanwhile, blissfully indifferent to the political convulsions in the Congo, Governor General Hendrick Cornélis took off on his vacation, leaving all responsibilities to the Vice-Governor.

After the former president of the Social Christian Party (PSC), Auguste de Schrijver, was appointed to succeed Van Hemelrijck, a fresh attempt was made to come to terms with the Congolese leaders. In his broadcast of September 4, 1959, the Minister confirmed that popular elections would be held in the month of December at the level of the *commune* and *territoire,* and that central and provincial assemblies would be set up by 1960. In a second message, on October 16, de Schrijver elaborated on the government's proposals. Sixty per cent of the provincial councilors were to be indirectly elected by the territorial and communal councils, 30 per cent were to be coöpted by the elected members, and 10 per cent were to be appointed by the administration. Two central organs —the General Council and the Legislative Council—were to be elected in 1960 and endowed with "substantial powers." By August or September, 1960, a council of ministers presided over by the Governor General would be functioning.[79] The last measure represented an important step toward self-government, but its psychological effect was largely nullified by the Minister's refusal to extend the principle of popular representation to the provincial assemblies.

In a joint memorandum issued on September 27, 1959, the Abako and the PSA notified the Belgian government of their intention to boycott the December elections "as long as the electoral procedures proposed by Belgium will remain antidemocratic." On September 19 Lumumba announced that his party would not participate in the elections "as long as the structure of the legislative councils will not be revised along democratic lines." The MNC-Kalondji and the Parti du Peuple followed suit on November 23 and 25, respectively. With a few exceptions, the Congolese leaders felt that the December elections were nothing but a dilatory maneuver invented by the Belgian government to retard the accession of the Congo to independence. As a nationalist newspaper explained, all the government wanted to do was put a group of African puppets into office.[80]

Meanwhile, on November 5, a group of Socialist deputies, taking up an idea that had already been expressed by the Parti Travailliste, and later by the MNC-Kalondji during its Elisabethville Congress, proposed that a round-table conference be held in Brussels for the purpose of negotiating the terms of a settlement between the Congo and Belgium. The representatives of all Congolese parties would be invited to the conference, and the Belgian parliament would be fully associated with it.[81] Instead, however, the Minister insisted that informal talks be conducted in Leopoldville between the Congolese leaders and the government, possibly with the "assistance" of parliamentary members designated by the Chambers.[82] Predictably, the Socialist group formally rejected the Minister's suggestion on the grounds that it minimized the role of the Chambers to the extreme and would in no way serve as a substitute for a round table.[83] Under the pressure of events, with the Congolese leaders repeatedly insisting on the need for a negotiated settlement, de Schrijver finally accepted the Socialists' formula and on November 26, 1959, announced before the Congo Press Association, in Leopoldville, that "a grand conference" would be held in the month of January for the purpose of elaborating the future political structures of the Congo.[84]

The Brussels Round Table lasted from January 20 to February 20, 1960, and was attended by some ninety-six Congolese representing thirteen different political groups. Although from the very beginning the government sought to control the agenda, reserving the issue of a target date for independence for ultimate consideration, the Congolese quickly formed a united front on the critical issue of independence. The delegates of all parties unanimously agreed that the promise of independence must come before they would further consider the machinery of government. On January 27, after a brief exchange of views between the Minister and the delegates, the date of independence for the Congo was fixed for June 30, 1960. The next day, to allay all possible doubts about Belgium's honoring her commitment, a Socialist senator, Henri Rollin, assured the Congolese that on this date they would be handed "all the keys" to their household.[85]

This momentous decision was embodied in the second resolution adopted by the conference: "As of June 30 next the Congo, within its present frontiers, shall become an independent state whose inhabitants shall, under conditions to be enacted by law, have the same nationality." Another set of resolutions defined the future character of the Congolese polity, pending the drafting of a basic constitutional document. Finally, provision was made for the establishment of transitional organs; until

June 30, executive authority was to be shared by the governor general and the Collège Exécutif Général, composed of six Congolese appointed on the basis of one from each province. Similar organs were set up at the provincial level, in the form of *collèges exécutifs provinciaux*, each to be composed of three Congolese chosen from among the dominant political groups. In addition, a commission of six members was appointed to the staff of the ministry, in Brussels, to assist the government in the drafting of laws, decrees, and conventions.

It is clear that Belgium's precipitate break with her colony was not prompted by any single set of factors. Aside from the intolerable pressures that were brought to bear upon the colonial authorities by the sudden thrust of nationalist activities, several other elements must be taken into consideration. The previously mentioned fact that the Belgian government was largely the captive of the parliamentary opposition not only precluded the possibility of a colonial war but also helped to accelerate the trend toward independence. Another explanatory factor was the economic repercussions of the outbreaks of January 4, 1959. While the Congo had long ceased to be a profitable enterprise, the insecurity created by the Leopoldville riots resulted in a massive flight of capital, which made the prospects of economic recovery all the more distant. Indeed, one conclusion that emerges from the report of the De Voghel Commission, appointed in 1959 to inquire into Congolese economic problems, is that a promise of independence was the price that had to be paid to restore confidence in the economic future of the country. Finally, in some places at least, the basic administrative structures of the colony had virtually disintegrated. In the absence of trained Congolese administrators, the Belgian authorities could not possibly hope to retain effective control over the situation, even if they wished to do so; on the other hand, subsequent events demonstrated that an abrupt withdrawal of authority would not solve problems created by decades of political miscalculation. The hand-washing response of the Belgians led the *Economist* of January 30, 1960, to comment that the "Belgian government has evidently decided it is better to risk administrative chaos, with Africans in charge of it, than to risk more fighting between Belgians and Africans by seeking to put the brake even slightly on."

From the standpoint of subsequent political developments, the implications of this move can hardly be overestimated. Briefly stated, it meant that independence was thrust upon the Congolese before they had even had a chance to habituate themselves to the responsibilities of self-government. In the meantime, the approach of independence released a host of ethnic and regional animosities which had long been held in check by imperial controls.

PART TWO

*The Colonial Situation*

# III. THE ADMINISTRATIVE FRAMEWORK

It is generally recognized that the impress left upon the African society by the imposition of a common administrative framework has been instrumental in fostering a sense of nationhood among the different peoples within a given territory, but it must be added that the extent to which Africans actually share this feeling is likely to reflect the patterns and style of administration introduced by the colonizing power.

In view of the centralizing and uniform system of administration introduced by Belgium, one would therefore expect a greater sense of national unity than presently exists among the Congolese. What appears at first sight as a paradox is owing in part to the fact that relatively little attention has been paid to the changes that occurred in the Congo between 1908 and 1933, when the administrative structure devised by Belgium was given its final shape. During these twenty-five years different patterns of administration evolved in different parts of the colony, and continued to affect the attitude of Belgian officials long after 1933. Furthermore, the division of the Congolese territory into provinces and districts has in some instances accentuated the individuality of certain regions. Finally, assuming that the central organs set up in the Congo could provide a unifying political structure, it must be remembered that their functions remained strictly advisory throughout the colonial period. This advisory role and the fact that the Congolese were given only token representation in the central institutions of the colony undoubtedly lessened the prospects of political integration.

Other features of the Belgian superstructure have operated in the opposite direction. The Belgian system has been a source of unity or disunity depending on whether we focus our attention on the regional or the territorial level, and whether we consider one policy period or another. In this chapter we attempt to evaluate the relative significance of these different aspects of the Belgian administrative framework in terms of their influence on the growth and shape of nationalist developments.

The Administrative Superstructure

The Colonial Charter, which until its abrogation in 1960 remained the basic constitutional document for the colony, reflects an interesting compromise between its authors' desire to bring the weight of public

55

opinion to bear on colonial matters, and their fear of parliamentary inter-ference.[1] Although the right of the Chambers to exercise control over the administration was explicitly recognized by the charter, the right to legislate for the colony was vested in the king, who exercised his preroga-tives through the minister of colonies by way of royal decrees with the advice of the Colonial Council. In practice, however, and largely through the Chambers' default, the minister of colonies acquired a central position in the conduct of colonial affairs.

The isolation of the Congo from the sphere of metropolitan politics, and the resulting lack of parliamentary interest in colonial problems, were primarily responsible for the attenuation of the Chambers' prerogatives.[2] The most significant of these lay in the provision that the budget of the colony had to be approved by parliament before it could be enacted.[3] Yet the estimates prepared by the governor general and reviewed by the minister seldom reached the floor of parliament before the beginning of the fiscal year, thus rendering inoperative the provision of the charter stipulating that "at least four months prior to the beginning of the fiscal year a draft project of the budget will be printed and distributed to the members of the Legislative Chambers." The yearly submission of a so-called *budget extraordinaire* allowed the minister to supplement the funds already approved by the Chambers in accordance with his current needs. Finally, he enjoyed discretionary powers to transfer budgetary allocations from one item to another. In short, although technically re-sponsible to the Chambers for the administration of the colony, the minister was left with wide discretion in the regulation of his policy.[4]

The Colonial Council, appointed partly by the king and partly by the Chambers, provided a more effective check on ministerial decisions. Although its members could only advise the minister or draw attention to their *voeux,* their relative detachment from domestic issues enabled them to acquire a reputation of impartiality which added considerable weight to their recommendations. As the late O. Louwers observed, "The Colonial Council has two merits: one is that it is never swayed by the passions or the influence of domestic politics, and the other is that it is concerned only with the general interest." [5] Nevertheless, although the views of members of the Colonial Council may have been taken into consideration, there is reason to believe that their influence was more apparent than real. Their outlook on colonial matters was inevitably affected by their patrician origins, and their occupational backgrounds tended to reflect the entrenched prerogatives, privileges, and powers of colonial interest groups. In 1933, for example, of the fourteen members of the Colonial Council, twelve had served in the colony as administra-tors, missionaries, lawyers, or industrialists.[6] This pattern of social and economic affinities, which remained fairly constant throughout the colonial period, meant that the council's members rarely questioned the principles, if not the details, of the legislative proposals submitted to their attention.

As the foregoing considerations suggest, the minister enjoyed considerable, though not unlimited, authority in the conduct of colonial policy. It does not follow that the views of colonial officials had no bearing whatsoever on metropolitan decisions. Indeed, depending on the personality of the officeholders and the way in which they visualized their roles, colonial governors had on some occasions considerable control over the formulation of Belgian colonial policy: "The extent to which colonial policy can be said to be initiated locally or to be controlled from Brussels would appear to depend largely on the personality of the minister and of the governor at any given time." [7]

This uncertain relationship lay at the root of the tensions that arose between the metropolitan and colonial bureaucracies. Against the efforts of the metropolitan government to retain unfettered control over the affairs of the colony, there was a tendency on the part of some governors to claim an equal share of responsibility in the formulation of Belgian colonial policy. An early step in this direction was taken in 1922, when Governor Maurice Lippens submitted a memorandum to the Minister of Colonies in which he argued for the decentralization of authority from Brussels to Boma, and from Boma to the provinces.[8] The Governor believed that the sheer size of the colony, the diversity of its populations, and the lack of adequate communications necessitated an increased delegation of executive powers at all levels of the administrative hierarchy.[9] In response to his demands, a decree issued on July 6, 1922, stipulated that the governor general was to be consulted on all draft decrees before they were submitted to the Colonial Council.[10] In fact, however, the governor general continued to be subject to the remote control of the minister of colonies, and in January, 1923, Governor Lippens resigned in protest against what he considered to be an unwarranted intervention of the metropolitan authorities in the affairs of the colony.[11]

More recently, Governor Pétillon's move to force upon the metropolitan government his own definition of the Belgo-Congolese community created new tensions between Brussels and Leopoldville. Beginning in 1954 with the appointment of Auguste Buisseret as minister of colonies, the Governor General played an increasingly important part in the formulation of Belgian policy. This reversal of administrative relationships, motivated in part by the Governor's opposition to certain aspects of the Minister's policy, found its clearest expression in Pétillon's definition of the Belgo-Congolese community, in his address of July, 1956, to the Conseil de Gouvernement.[12] His apparent infringement of the Minister's authority led to considerable friction, and in June, 1957, Buisseret reminded the Governor that he alone was responsible for defining Belgium's policy in Africa. As a further indication of his prerogatives he expunged several passages from the speech prepared by the Governor for the opening session of the Conseil de Gouvernement. Although the Minister's reminder was never made public, the metropolitan and the colonial press gave a clear hint of its contents and implications.[13] Even more significant, perhaps, were the conspicuous blanks that appeared in the printed version of the Governor's speech. In any event, the publicity given to the incident, and the fact that it occurred at a time when nationalist forces were beginning to gather strength, undoubtedly helped to discredit the authority of Belgian officialdom among the Congolese.

Further evidence of administrative disharmony appeared in the early part of 1959, when the Crown opposed the policy advocated by Van Hemelrijck. The conflict between the Crown and the Minister, initially centered on what became known in Belgium as "l'affaire du Gouverneur Général," was in fact the symptom of a deeper and more fundamental conflict between the colonial and metropolitan bureaucracies. After the Leopoldville riots Van Hemelrijck gained the distinct impression that Cornélis, who succeeded Pétillon as governor general in 1958, lacked the foresight and initiative to implement his policy. About the same time the private declarations made by Cornélis to the Minister reinforced the latter's conviction that Cornélis should be "called to other functions." But the Minister did not feel that he should disclose his intentions until a candidate had been found to fill the vacancy, and until the approval of his cabinet had been secured. Meanwhile, however, rumors began to gain currency that all was not well between Brussels and Leopoldville, and on April 10, 1959, a Leopoldville group addressed a petition to the King, expressing loyalty to the Governor General and calling attention to the disastrous consequences that would result from further attempts to discredit Cornélis' authority.[14] This appeal to the Crown, combined with pressure from trusted members of the King's entourage, led the King to veto the candidacy of Raymond Scheyven to the post of governor general, against the decision of the Council of Ministers. The full circumstances of the royal veto were never disclosed to the press, but the mere fact that Van Hemelrijck felt the need to assert publicly his "perfect identity of views" with the Governor General indicated a change in the state of affairs.[15]

These various tensions decisively aided the development of nationalist sentiment and activity in the Congo. Not only did it make the Congolese elites aware of internal divisions among Belgian officials, but it also reinforced their conviction that these divisions could be exploited to their own advantage.

In theory, at least, the limitations imposed on the powers of the governor general by the metropolitan authorities implied similar limitations on the provincial governors. But the theory did not necessarily imply a corresponding subordination of the provincial authorities to the governor general. Although the general trend from 1914 to 1947 was toward an increased centralization of responsibility from the provincial headquarters to the capital, the initial position of the governor general in relation to the provincial governors was one of *primus inter pares*. This situation, which made for a wide measure of provincial autonomy, accounts for the subsequent resistance encountered by the central government when it sought to tighten control over the provinces.

The changes that took place in the administrative status of the Katanga illustrate the point. The province was initially administered as a separate entity, first by the Compagnie du Katanga, a chartered company founded by King Leopold in 1891, and from 1900 by the Comité Spécial du Katanga, a semipublic organism enjoying unfettered control over local affairs. Because of the lack of adequate communications between the capital and the interior, and also because the industrial development of the province required a large measure of decentralization, the administration of the Katanga was entrusted in 1910 to a vice-governor general whose powers were similar to those of the governor general. According to a royal decree of March 22, 1910, the vice-governor was to exercise executive powers "under the authority of the governor general," but the implied limitation on his powers remained a dead letter. In practice the governor general had virtually no control over the provincial authorities. In 1911 it was said that the "Minister of Colonies deserves his title more than he did in 1908, for we have not one but two colonies, although many in Belgium are not aware of it." [16]

At the time the official point of view of Minister Renkin was that "the organization of an autonomous administration was justified in the Katanga . . . but not elsewhere, at least for the time being." [17] In 1913, however, a similar status was given to Orientale Province. After 1914 the system was extended to the four provinces then in existence, but the vice-governors assumed a somewhat subordinate position vis-à-vis the governor general. While they retained the "haute direction" of their provinces, and shared with the governor general the right to exercise legislative powers in emergencies, the governor general was the fount of all executive powers; he alone represented the king in the colony, and as such assumed the "haute direction" of "all the administrative and military services established in the colony." [18] It was also explained that the royal decree of 1914 "drew its inspiration from a desire to give the provincial governments a simple and uniform organization and to subordinate them to the governor general for all matters of common interest." [19]

Actually, the effect of this reorganization on the relationships between the central and the provincial governments remained uncertain. While the vice-governors were theoretically reduced in status, the nature and scope of their powers depended ultimately on the attitude of the governor general at any given time. During the brief term of office of Governor Lippens, for example, the vice-governors enjoyed as broad a delegation of authority as they could possibly hope for. According to a famous circular issued by Governor Lippens in March, 1922, they were given "full responsibility" to "govern and administer their provinces." [20] But there was a widespread feeling among Belgian officials, especially in Brussels, that the reform was unsatisfactory because it obviously failed to attain the degree of administrative uniformity and coherence which was to be expected. Consequently, in March, 1930, an *ad hoc* commission of seven members was appointed by the Minister to "study the question of administrative decentralization of the colony." [21] On the basis of the commission's recommendations, a new system was established in 1933 under the governorship of General Tilkens, which provided for the replacement of the vice-governors by provincial commissioners and the transfer of their prerogatives—notably their emergency powers—to the governor general. In addition, a group of senior officials (*inspecteurs d'état*), responsible for local and provincial administration, was attached to the governor general.[22] Despite the violent criticism voiced by some Belgian deputies against the centralist character of the reform, the situation remained unchanged until July 1, 1947.[23] A decree of that date restored to the vice-governors (now called provincial governors) the powers they had held before the decree of 1933.[24]

Undoubtedly, the separate administrative status enjoyed by the Katanga from 1910 to 1914 is one of the factors that stimulated the emergence of separatist sentiment in that part of the Congo. As early as 1920 a reorganization plan, submitted to the Minister of Colonies by Monsignor de Hemptinne, M. de Meulemeester, president of the Court of Appeals of Elisabethville, M. Wangermée, formerly vice-governor of the Katanga, and several other prominent personalities, demanded (1) "a larger share of provincial autonomy"; (2) "the transfer of the government general to Brussels and the integration of the colonial and metropolitan services"; (3) "a more rational organization of the Ministry of Colonies" through "the abolition of all the special services . . . [attached to] the ministry"; and (4) "an administrative reorganization of the colony" based on "an effective, yet discreet, representation of private interests" and "the adaptation of the administrative services to the real needs of the colony." [25] Except for the last point, these proposals were never seriously considered by the metropolitan government. Yet, as will be seen later, they formed the basis of the program adopted by the European oligarchy of the Katanga in the years preceding independence.

After the reform of 1933 vehement protests were raised by the European population of the Katanga against what an Elisabethville newspaper, *L'Essor du Congo,* termed "une entreprise de démolition." [26] In 1958 Jean Sépulchre, editor of *L'Essor,* referred to the "stupid and retrograde impulse given by General Tilkens to his administration by his rigorous and centralizing reform of 1933," but he emphatically praised Governor Lippens, "the most intelligent and the greatest of our governors," for the "audacious and noble instructions contained in his circular of 1922." [27] These strictures not only illustrate a local reaction to the *capitis deminutio* inflicted by the decree of 1933 on the provincial governments, but also throw a revealing light on the subsequent operations of European and African political groups in the Katanga.

But the effect of these reforms on Belgian policy as a whole was by no means limited to the Katanga. Between 1910 and 1933 native policies were largely regulated on the basis of directives issued by the vice-governors, with little coördination, and in the most empirical fashion. The detailed instructions contained in the 1920 edition of the *Recueil à l'usage des fonctionnaires et agents du service territorial,* though precisely intended to remedy the situation, proved ineffectual. In 1928, for example, Monsignor de Hemptinne noted that "the reading of the reports from the four provinces [left] a painful impression of uncertainty, hesitation, incoherence, and disagreement in the field of native policy," and about a year later Governor Tilkens expressed his "conviction that the instructions of the government . . . [were] not observed, because frequently misinterpreted or even ignored." [28]

This confusion must be attributed essentially to the different conceptions and methods adopted by the provincial governments in the early stages of Belgian administration. But it also reflects the resistance of the district commissioners to the tendency of the provincial authorities to supervise every detail of native policy, as if they did not trust their "experience" or feared their "insubordination." [29] In 1921 a district commissioner of the Katanga, André van Iseghem, remarked that the vice-governors claimed for themselves the broadest scope of authority but adamantly refused to surrender any part of it to their subordinates.[30] Again, in 1931 the Association des Fonctionnaires et Agents de la Colonie, a professional organization representing the interests of the *fonctionnaires* employed in the colony, publicly criticized the "personal" and "particularistic" policy of the vice-governors. As a possible alternative to the existing organization, which allegedly ran counter to "the moral and material interests of the natives," the spokesmen of the association advocated the suppression of the provinces and their replacement by nine districts "whose boundaries will be determined on the basis of geographic, economic, and demographic factors." [31] Apparently, at least until 1933, the separate administrative development of the provinces was a source of friction among the various echelons of the administrative hierarchy as well as of administrative disunity, both among and within the provinces. Meanwhile, the successive adjustments of the territorial organization to the changes in the administrative superstructure produced further divisions among the African population.

### TERRITORIAL ORGANIZATION

The Free State was divided into fifteen districts, varying in size from a hundred to several thousand square miles. The district of Stanley Falls, for example, embracing a huge expanse of territory east of the Lomami River, covered some 270,000 square miles, whereas the tiny district of Banana covered only 120 square miles.[32] For purposes of local govern-

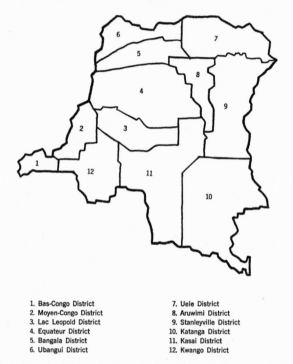

| | |
|---|---|
| 1. Bas-Congo District | 7. Uele District |
| 2. Moyen-Congo District | 8. Aruwimi District |
| 3. Lac Leopold District | 9. Stanleyville District |
| 4. Equateur District | 10. Katanga District |
| 5. Bangala District | 11. Kasai District |
| 6. Ubangui District | 12. Kwango District |

MAP 3. *Administrative boundaries of the Belgian Congo, 1910.* (Adapted from *Atlas du Congo Belge* [Bruxelles, 1945].)

ment, the larger districts were divided into zones, the zones into secteurs, and the secteurs into *postes*.

In 1910, as a result of the consolidation of the districts of Banana, Boma, Matadi, and Cataracts into a single administrative unit, the number of districts dropped from fifteen to twelve. At the same time parts of the Stanley Falls and Lualaba districts were welded into a single district, henceforth known as the Katanga. Except for the Katanga, now made a vice-government general, the administrative subdivisions adopted by the Free State were maintained until March 28, 1912. On that date

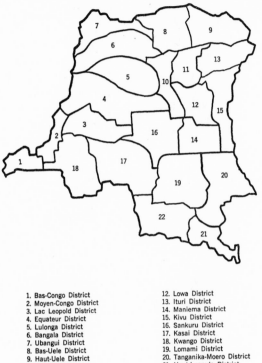

1. Bas-Congo District
2. Moyen-Congo District
3. Lac Leopold District
4. Equateur District
5. Lulonga District
6. Bangala District
7. Ubangui District
8. Bas-Uele District
9. Haut-Uele District
10. Aruwimi District
11. Stanleyville District
12. Lowa District
13. Ituri District
14. Maniema District
15. Kivu District
16. Sankuru District
17. Kasai District
18. Kwango District
19. Lomami District
20. Tanganika-Moero District
21. Haut-Luapula District
22. Lulua District

MAP 4. *Administrative boundaries of the Belgian Congo, 1912.* (Adapted from *Atlas du Congo Belge* [Bruxelles, 1945].)

an *arrêté royal* divided the Congo into twenty-two districts and in turn subdivided these districts into a multitude of territoires whose boundaries were fixed by the governor general.

This organization underwent a major change in 1914 with the incorporation of the existing districts into four provinces: Congo-Kasai, Equateur, Orientale, and Katanga. This measure was viewed by the metropolitan government as the corollary of the administrative reform introduced by the arrêté royal of July 28, 1914. As the exposé des motifs pointed out, the "division of the (Congolese) territory into provinces will greatly facilitate decentralization; control over the districts will be more immediate and more effective; there will be a greater sense of initiative and responsibility; the higher authorities will be more quickly and better informed; their action will adapt itself with greater flexibility to the local circumstances." [33] In fact, however, the process of amalgamation had been effective in the Katanga since 1912, and in Orientale Province since 1913, but it was not until 1919, when the Congo-Kasai was for-

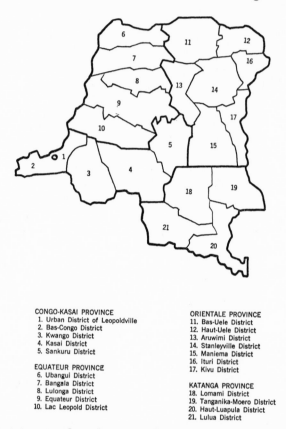

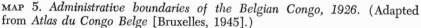

CONGO-KASAI PROVINCE
1. Urban District of Leopoldville
2. Bas-Congo District
3. Kwango District
4. Kasai District
5. Sankuru District

EQUATEUR PROVINCE
6. Ubangui District
7. Bangala District
8. Lulonga District
9. Equateur District
10. Lac Leopold District

ORIENTALE PROVINCE
11. Bas-Uele District
12. Haut-Uele District
13. Aruwimi District
14. Stanleyville District
15. Maniema District
16. Ituri District
17. Kivu District

KATANGA PROVINCE
18. Lomami District
19. Tanganika-Moero District
20. Haut-Luapula District
21. Lulua District

MAP 5. *Administrative boundaries of the Belgian Congo, 1926.* (Adapted from *Atlas du Congo Belge* [Bruxelles, 1945].)

mally constituted into a vice-government, that the setup envisaged by the arrêté royal of 1914 was finally translated into reality.[34]

In 1933, in order to achieve what Minister Tschoffen described as a "more harmonious grouping of the provinces," [35] the Congo-Kasai and Orientale provinces were divided into four units, thus bringing the total number of provinces to six: Leopoldville, Lusambo (Kasai), Costermansville (Kivu), Elisabethville (Katanga), Stanleyville (Orientale), and Coquilhatville (Equateur). Meanwhile, the number of districts was reduced from 21 to 15 and the number of territoires from 180 to 102. Athough the provincial boundaries remained fairly stable in subsequent years, the

boundaries of districts and territoires underwent frequent transformations, most of them intended to accommodate sectional and tribal divisions.[36] By 1956, as a result of the various changes, 26 districts and 135
territoires were officially registered.

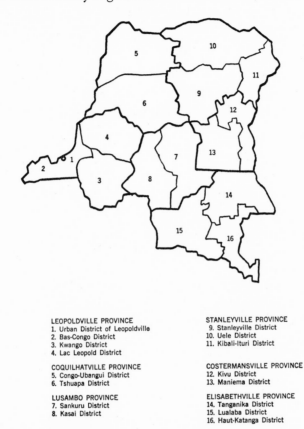

LEOPOLDVILLE PROVINCE
1. Urban District of Leopoldville
2. Bas-Congo District
3. Kwango District
4. Lac Leopold District

COQUILHATVILLE PROVINCE
5. Congo-Ubangui District
6. Tshuapa District

LUSAMBO PROVINCE
7. Sankuru District
8. Kasai District

STANLEYVILLE PROVINCE
9. Stanleyville District
10. Uele District
11. Kibali-Ituri District

COSTERMANSVILLE PROVINCE
12. Kivu District
13. Maniema District

ELISABETHVILLE PROVINCE
14. Tanganika District
15. Lualaba District
16. Haut-Katanga District

MAP 6. *Administrative boundaries of the Belgian Congo, 1933.* (Adapted
from *Atlas du Congo Belge* [Bruxelles, 1945].)

These successive adjustments, mostly dictated by administrative con-
venience, emphasize the artificiality of the Congo's administrative boundaries. As in other parts of Africa, "European rule was imposed like a
great steel grid over the amorphous cellular tissue of tribal Africa."[37]
This grid, however, did not leave a permanent impress on the African
communities, and today the majority of the Congolese seldom identify
themselves with the name of any province but with the tribe located
within the province. The efforts made by Belgian administrators, especially after 1933, to adapt district boundaries to tribal divisions sometimes encouraged this type of identification. Yet the extreme diversity of

ethnic patterns did not always permit the application of this policy, and in some instances administrative entities became the foci of new loyalties. This phenomenon is best illustrated by the predisposition of certain tribes of the Katanga to identify themselves as Katangese rather than Batabwa, Bayeke, Lunda, or the like. The fact that the boundaries of the Katanga remained comparatively stable after 1910 provides a partial explanation for its distinct political personality.

Territorial divisions have set certain limitations on the scope of political activities, even to the point of favoring the emergence of a separate regional consciousness among Africans. According to one Congolese, "One need only look at the territorial organization to realize that the administration has been especially careful to divide rather than to unite. . . . Thus the Congolese of one province are treated as foreigners by the inhabitants of another province." [38] The form and the character of the representative institutions established in the colony have also contributed, albeit indirectly, to the maintenance of tribal and sectional particularisms.

### THE INSTITUTIONAL FRAMEWORK

The lack of opportunities afforded the African population for effective participation in the government of the colony is quite certainly one of the factors that impeded the formation of Congolese political groups:

The really decisive factor—the precipitant—in the formation of political parties has been constitutional reform providing for (1) the devolution by the imperial government of a sufficiently *meaningful* and *attractive* measure of power to induce or to provoke nationalist leaders to convert their movements into political parties, and (2) the introduction or refinement of institutions and procedures, such as an electoral system, which would make it technically possible for parties to seek power constitutionally.[39]

The fact that at least until December, 1957, neither of these conditions was satisfied largely accounts for the delayed appearance of Congolese parties.[40] It does not follow, however, that there were no representative institutions in the Congo until 1957, but those that did exist were never endowed with a "meaningful and attractive" measure of power, and their members were all handpicked by the governor general, the provincial governors, or the district commissioners. Consequently, in the absence of a truly representative central institution that could serve as a training ground for future political leaders, Africans had little or no opportunity to develop a sense of national unity.

### Central and Provincial Organs

In order to ensure coördination among the different echelons of the administrative hierarchy, the arrêté royal of 1914 provided for the institution of advisory organs at the central and provincial levels, which were exclusively composed of official members. Under the system introduced in 1933 the Conseil de Gouvernement and the *conseils de province*, previously known as *comités régionaux*, were enlarged to include both official and unofficial members. Until 1947, however, when two Africans were admitted to the Conseil de Gouvernement, the members were all Europeans.

Between 1951 and 1957 the number of "regular" African members appointed to the central and provincial councils increased respectively from eight to twelve and from three to six, and in 1957, as a symbolic gesture toward attainment of the Belgo-Congolese community, African and European councilors were integrated into four categories: (1) middle classes, (2) employers' associations, (3) notables, and (4) rural and extrarural classes. At the same time the ratio of Africans to Europeans was increased from approximately one-third to one-half of the unofficial membership of the Conseil de Gouvernement, which meant that in terms of its overall membership Europeans were still in the majority.

As African councilors were generally chosen from among "local personalities" whose rank and prestige depended upon the maintenance of the colonial status quo, their attitude was usually strongly conservative. In 1955, for example, "native interests" were represented by six "native authorities," including two chefs, three chefs de secteurs, one *chef de centre extra-coutumier*, and two clerks.[41] In spite of the changes introduced in 1957, native authorities retained a predominant voice in the Conseil de Gouvernement; the clerks became more important numerically but less so proportionately, representing only one-fifth of the African membership as against one-third under the previous arrangement. Moreover, once they had become the spokesmen of the middle classes, the notables, the rural and extrarural classes, and so on, instead of merely posing as the representatives of native interests, the symbolic significance of their new titles somewhat reinforced their conservatism.

As a provisional measure pending the introduction of electoral processes, the Conseil de Gouvernement could have served a useful purpose had it been vested with genuine responsibilities. But its powers were wholly advisory. It met every three months to examine the fiscal proposals issued by the Minister of Colonies, and to "give its advice on draft decrees and draft ordinances submitted to its attention by the governor general, on the execution and planning of public works, and on all questions presented by the governor general."[42] Similarly, the powers devolved upon the provincial councils were limited to "examination of the moral and material conditions of the native population" and to such matters as "the development of public works and the economic infrastructure of the districts," the "general administration of the districts," and the "defense and police of the districts." As a consequence, there was a notable lack of popular interest in the debates of the councils. As one évolué put it,

Whether one turns to the Commissions du Travail et du Progrès Social Indigène (TEPSI), the Conseil de Cité, the provincial councils, or the Conseil de Gouvernement, the representative character of the Congolese institutions is as ridiculous as it is undemocratic. . . . The Congolese members seated on these councils never consult the mass of the natives, and the majority of the population does not even know their names.[43]

Several arguments have been advanced by Belgian officials to rationalize this situation. One, which has been repeatedly emphasized in metropolitan spheres, is that so long as political rights were denied to Europeans there were no legitimate grounds for extending them to the Congolese. It has also been suggested that the protective implications of paternalism would inevitably disappear once the Africans had to compete with Europeans for positions of influence. As Pétillon explained,

The regime which we have until now applied to the Congolese was based on benevolence, favor, and, *pour dire le mot,* paternalism. With the opening of opportunities for Africans, they will enter a regime of selection and competition. . . . As soon as they enter into competition with the Europeans . . . they will no longer benefit from this kind of paternalist protection.[44]

Finally, it has been argued that, because the rural populations lacked the requisite political maturity, a progressive democratization of the existing organs must necessarily be deferred to a distant future. The notion that preparation for the responsibilities of legislative government must start at the grass roots, with the domestication of parliamentary institutions at the level of the chefferie, was expressed by a former governor general, P. Ermens:

It is far more urgent to initiate the African elites to the management of the *chefferie* rather than to invite them to sit on the central and provincial councils. . . . The majority of the inhabitants of the Belgian Congo has not acquired, and is far from acquiring, the political maturity which would permit and justify the introduction of parliamentary government in the colony.[45]

Yet, even if more active participation in chefferie affairs would have given the Congolese a sense of public responsibility, the question still remains as to whether or not the existing organs of local government could have been used effectively for that purpose.

### Local Organs

In contrast with the system of local government established in certain parts of British Africa, where the district councils gradually took over from the district commissioners a wide range of administrative functions, the local institutions introduced by Belgium allowed for only a limited measure of self-government. The general features of the Belgian system have been compared with its British counterpart in Uganda:

In the Congo, the machinery of African participation in local government at the District level is discontinuous and without effective responsibility. It therefore fails to involve the participation or to engage the interest of the ordinary man. In Uganda, the African Local Government has a permanent secretariat of its own, occupies its own imposing edifice, disposes of considerable financial resources, and makes resolutions which can acquire the force of law.[46]

Up to a point this broad characterization also applies to the situation that prevailed in the urban areas of the Congo. For analytical purposes, however, a distinction must be drawn between the so-called "customary" and "extracustomary centers"—in other words, between rural and urban areas.

The Belgian version of indirect rule was not systematically applied until 1933, and even then it left considerable room for local variations. Yet as early as 1920 Minister Frank intimated that Belgian policy should seek not only to "support traditional authority," but also to "develop the participation of the natives in the administration of the colony." [47] For this purpose the district commissioners were instructed to group the native authorities of their chefferies or secteurs into a council, known as *conseil de chefferie* or *conseil de secteur*. This organ, "constituant une sorte de tribunal des palabres," was primarily intended to serve a judicial function; but it could also discuss such matters as compulsory crops, porterage, and taxation. In the end, the degree to which either of these functions was given precedence over the other depended on local authorities.

In Orientale Province, for example, the deliberative function of these councils was quickly overshadowed by adjudication, and in 1922 they were legally transformed into native tribunals. The official viewpoint of the provincial authorities, as expressed in a circular of February 22, 1922, was that "the renaissance of native tribunals" would provide the means whereby the authority of the African chiefs could be restored and strengthened.[48] In practice, however, their principal function was not so much to ensure the settlement of disputes according to customary law as to enforce the administration's policy. A decree of April 15, 1926, formalized and extended the system of *juridictions indigènes* to the other provinces.[49]

The concentration of judicial and executive powers in the same legal structure led to many abuses. In Orientale Province, where this policy was first inaugurated, the native tribunals were converted into powerful instruments of coercion; their jurisdiction overstepped the bounds of custom and their sentences, though exceptionally harsh and usually awarded on the flimsiest grounds, were never revised by the administration. The chefs de secteurs, officially regarded as "the custodians of custom," exercised quasi-dictatorial powers in their *circonscriptions* in violation of all customary prescriptions. As a rule, petty offenders paid heavy fines to provide revenue for the native treasuries or suffered severe corporal punishment. More important, perhaps, these measures were often directed against traditional chiefs, whether or not they happened to be located in the secteur. On several counts the evidence gathered by Monsignor de Hemptinne is extensive and crushing; after citing specific cases of abuse, he concludes that "this rule, although supposedly indirect, is actually the worst form of direct government." [50] In this respect the part played by the *tribunaux de secteurs* in Orientale Province provides a revealing insight into subsequent political developments; these courts dealt a telling blow to the authority and prestige of the chiefs and prepared the ground for the emergence of radical sentiments among the rural masses.

The structure of the native court system established by the decree of 1926 remained basically unchanged in later years, but an effort was made in 1933 to introduce a more effective separation of powers. The tribunaux de chefferies and the tribunaux de secteurs continued to adjudicate and enforce the rules of the administration, sometimes in the same arbitrary fashion,[51] but their functions and organization, if not always their membership, were kept separate from those of the consultative councils introduced by the decree of December 5, 1933.[52] These councils, consisting of "notables" chosen by the district commissioner from the groups included in the secteurs or the chefferies, were allowed to discuss "all matters of local interest." In fact, however, their activities remained highly perfunctory, because the territorial agent or the district commissioner could suspend or prohibit their deliberations, and because they enjoyed only limited financial responsibility. It has been observed in connection with the Conseil de Territoire of Mahagi, in Belgian Alurland, that these councils only "offered a means whereby the Belgian administration . . . [could] sound the chief on any measures which he . . . [proposed] to take, and in theory . . . [provided] the chiefs with an opportunity of reporting the opinions of their subjects." [53] Furthermore, because resolutions could not pass from the conseil de chefferie or the conseil de secteur to the conseil de province and ultimately to the Conseil de Gouvernement, it seems unlikely that local councils could ever contribute to even a limited measure of national integration.

Except for Leopoldville, where European and African areas were jointly administered as a *district urbain,* African centers of mixed tribal origins were until 1931 usually administered through special ordinances issued by the provincial governments. These regulations, however stringently applied, did not always prove satisfactory, and the new conditions created by the growth of European centers increased the problems of urban administration. In 1930 the Permanent Committee of the Congrès Colonial National suggested a series of measures which served as a foundation for the decree of 1931 on the centres extra-coutumiers. Its underlying principle was that the administration of Africans living outside their customary areas should be entrusted to an African acting on behalf, and under the supervision, of European officials.[54]

Under the system introduced in 1931 the centres extra-coutumiers were administered by a chef de centre assisted by a *conseil de centre* whose members were appointed by the district commissioner. Their activities, limited to the discussion of all matters of local interest not regulated by local ordinances, were in turn subject to the supervision of a comité protecteur composed exclusively of European members. Between 1932 and 1952, however, the number of centres extra-coutumiers increased only from twenty-one to thirty-five, and in subsequent years, owing to "the difficulty of finding Africans capable of exercising the functions of chief, or of acting effectively as members of a council," [55] the tendency was to resort to a form of direct administration associated with the term *cité indigène*. Under this type of administration, first inaugurated in Leopoldville in 1945, African areas were directly controlled by the territorial agent or the district commissioner, assisted if necessary by a *chef de cité* and a council, both "appointed and dismissed by the district commissioner." [56] Actually, the change of policy was more apparent than real, because ultimate control always rested with the European administration.

A common feature of the Belgian system of administration was the division of African centers into separate *zones* or *quartiers,* each having its own consultative council headed by a *chef de zone* or a *chef de quartier,* known in Leopoldville as *capita ya balabala*.[57] In some places, as in Matadi, the organization of these councils was envisaged as a preliminary step before the constitution of a conseil de centre. Elsewhere, as in Leopoldville, the measure was adopted as an experiment designed to prepare Africans for the municipal reform announced by the Statut des Villes.[58] On the whole, this structural innovation did not prove a very effective means of inducing popular participation in local government; but insofar as it did generate a certain amount of interest, as it apparently did in Leopoldville, it certainly favored the emergence of communal sentiments.[59] Moreover, where African quarters were tribally homogeneous, this type of administration reinforced the tribal individuality of urban dwellers.

In terms of its political implications, the municipal reform introduced by the decree of March 26, 1957, known as the Statut des Villes, was one of the most important measures taken by the Belgian government in postwar years.[60] The text of the decree underwent numerous alterations during the nine years that elapsed after it was first submitted to the Colonial Council; by the time it was finally enacted much of its content had already been outstripped by the evolution of African opinion. Nevertheless, its effect on the development of Congolese political groups is significant.

Broadly speaking, the Statut des Villes had a twofold objective: (1) to integrate the African and European quarters of Leopoldville, Elisabethville, and Jadotville into a new administrative unit, officially designated as *ville* (town), and (2) to give Africans the means of taking part in the administration of urban affairs. In areas given the status of town by the governor general, provision was made for the institution of communal councils whose members would then select their own bourgmestres. At a higher level, a municipal council, presided over by a premier bourgmestre, would provide the means for integrating African and European councilors into the same legal framework.

In theory, communal councilors were to be appointed by the premier bourgmestre after consultation, but in practice, "from the very beginning . . . consultation meant elections as was recommended by the Colonial Council, and appointments [were] made on the results of the poll." [61] Similarly, the overwhelming majority of bourgmestres, though in theory appointed by the governor general, were coöpted by the communal councilors from their own membership. Their powers, however, like those of the premier bourgmestre, were those of a fonctionnaire acting "within the limits of the *ordonnances d'administration générale* and *arrêtés provinciaux*." [62] The governor general could dissolve the communal and municipal councils, or suspend their proceedings, and he alone was authorized to "institute into towns those areas of justifiable importance." As of December, 1957, only Leopoldville, Elisabethville, and Jadotville obtained the status of town. Stanleyville, oddly enough, failed to qualify, although its African population was more numerous than that of Jadotville.

In spite of its restrictive features, the reform of 1957 had several important consequences. First, it stimulated the growth of parties, not only because electoral processes called for the organization of a party apparatus to enlist popular support, but also because they invited competition among various contestants. But the right to organize political groups was not automatically recognized by the colonial authorities. In fact, the maintenance of statutory limitations on the right to organize explains in part why electoral competition was in most instances conducted on a tribal basis and through the medium of ethnic or regional associations. In a sense, therefore, the circumstances under which the elections were contested legitimized the development of Congolese parties along tribal lines.

Moreover, the effect of elections on the development of political groups was necessarily limited to areas where political activities were considered legitimate. In contrast with French West Africa, where "elections synchronized political development among territories where political pressure was unequal," [63] the 1957 elections in the Congo accentuated the unevenness of political pressure among the different provinces. The immediate result was a polarization of political activity around Leopoldville and Katanga provinces.

From a psychological standpoint, however, the concessions accorded by the decree of 1957 profoundly influenced the whole population of the Congo. Among the Congolese elites, they encouraged further demands and created new expectations. In a joint motion introduced on the floor of the Conseil de Gouvernement in June, 1958, Gaston Diomi, Arthur Pinzi, and Sébastien Kini insisted on a "veritable democratization of the new institutions." [64] Among the proposed reforms were (1) the extension of the Statut des Villes to other urban areas, (2) the elimination of the prerogatives held by the governor general, and (3) the enlargement of the powers devolved upon the bourgmestres, so as "to allow them to administer their communes independently with the help of their councils, whose powers should also be enlarged." The same motion finally concluded: "In the eyes of the Congolese, the development of political institutions and their democratization must in all logic lead as rapidly as possible to internal autonomy, and, depending on the degree of evolution attained, to full independence." [65]

In December, 1958, the status of town was extended to Bukavu, Stanleyville, Luluabourg, and Coquilhatville, but nothing was done to reinforce the position of the bourgmestres vis-à-vis the administration. Not until January, 1959, with the announcement that communal elections, as distinct from consultations, would soon be held by universal suffrage, was a more significant share of political responsibility finally offered to the Congolese. At this point, however, few among the Congolese nationalists were willing to settle for less than full independence.

Evaluating the general significance of Belgian administrative policy, a Belgian scholar and former administrator notes that "the Belgian colonial administration strongly encouraged the building of an autonomous self-ruling system of local government—similar to the British system of native authorities—while the establishment of an autonomous self-ruling Central Government was persistently discouraged."[66] This generalization, at least in theory, seems correct. But the analogy between the Belgian and the British versions of indirect rule calls for certain reservations, for in fact the Belgians were far less consistent and determined than the British in their efforts to adapt existing traditional structures to the needs of local government. Although Belgian policy repeatedly emphasized the importance of indigenous political institutions, they were frequently ignored or suppressed. Indeed, even after 1933, when the Belgian government consciously endeavored to reinforce the authority of the chiefs through the institution of local councils, in only a few instances did the real traditional authorities enjoy recognition. The result has been a general weakening of traditional political units, to an extent that is paralleled in only a few areas in British territories. Insofar as it failed to develop a strong system of local government, Belgian policy prepared the ground, albeit unwittingly, for political integration at the territorial level—much more so, for example, than British policy in places like northern Nigeria, the northern territories of Ghana, or Uganda. On the other hand, the central institutions devised by Belgium, unlike their British counterparts, were, for all intents and purposes, a monopoly of the European administration. The paradox is that while the Belgian government stubbornly insisted on the need to maintain the unity of the Congo, nothing positive was done, in terms of political participation and loyalty, to translate this aim into reality.

# IV. GOALS AND ORGANIZATION OF THE "COLONAT"

Owing in part to the official attitude of the Belgian government toward European settlement, until the postwar period the Congo attracted only a small number of Europeans. In 1908 only 3,000 whites lived in the Congo; between 1920 and 1940 their number increased from 6,971 to 27,791. In the decade following World War II, on the other hand, the non-African population almost trebled, from 34,789 in 1946 to 98,804, in 1956. By 1959, 114,341 non-Africans lived in the Congo, of whom 88,913 were Belgian, 1,582 were Asian, and the rest were of diverse origins; the total represented a ratio of 1.50 to 160 in proportion to the total African population.[1] Less than 10 per cent of the nonindigenous population were really bona fide settlers. As a consequence, relatively few Belgians living in the Congo were inclined to identify their future with that of the colony. In 1921 Governor Lippens pleaded for the idea of a "Greater Belgium":

The time has come for us to teach our children in primary schools to look upon the colony as an integral part of the Fatherland, and to identify "Congo" with "Belgium." Let us inculcate in their minds the idea of a "Greater Belgium." Let us cultivate and exalt in them the feelings of patriotic pride inspired by the sovereignty that we exercise in Africa.[2]

Despite these exhortations, only a tiny fraction of the Belgian population came to look upon the colony as "an integral part of the Fatherland." Yet, according to all the evidence, European settlers have played a significant, and in some instances a decisive, role in shaping the course of Congolese politics.

Their physical presence and their repeated efforts to propagate and legitimize the myth of white supremacy were critical factors in the growth of racial consciousness among the Africans. And at one point the sense of injury and frustration which grew from racial discrimination found an outlet in nationalist activity. At this stage, however, organized settler interests were in a position to exert a powerful influence on the direction and outcome of the political struggle between the metropolitan government and the Congolese nationalists, and, at a later date, among the nationalists themselves. Before turning to an examination of the potential strength, the aims, and the strategies pursued by organized settler interests in their efforts to accommodate themselves to the changing political situation, we must consider the social, economic, cultural, and regional variables that have affected settler behavior.

## THE CHARACTER AND DISTRIBUTION OF SETTLER INTERESTS

As early as 1920 a Belgian writer invoked the example of Rhodesia, "where thousands of British families have established themselves," to advocate an increased influx of "landed" settlers whose presence would leave an "indelible imprint" on the colony.[3] In the same year a former colonial civil servant saw in the "discovery of vast areas habitable by Europeans one of the most remarkable events of our time," and regarded it as "a presage of the establishment in the heart of Africa of numerous industries and important agricultural enterprises."[4]

Such views, however, could hardly be reconciled with the official thinking of the Belgian government. Drawing a distinction between the *colonie de peuplement,* "where immigrants bring along with themselves their own laws and institutions," and the *colonie d'encadrement,* "where the metropolis has established its sovereignty over a numerous native population, and where local government merely exercises delegated powers," the late Professor Marzorati unambiguously identified the Belgian Congo with the latter type of dependency. Its distinctive constitutional feature was that "government was not controlled from below, as in a colonie de peuplement, but from the top, that is, by the metropolitan authorities and institutions."[5]

This distinction assisted the Belgian government in its efforts to withhold political rights from both Africans and Europeans. But it also provided a rationale for allowing into the colony only a limited number of immigrants, and only those who, according to official standards, seemed sufficiently capable or resourceful not to become "public burdens" or embittered agitators. The Belgian conception of a *colon* involved a set of assumptions that differed markedly from those generally associated with the term "settler." The Belgian idea of a colon was mainly "that of a professional man, or one who has a guaranteed employment of some kind; no immigration is countenanced of persons merely seeking employment, or whose interest is that of 'settling' in the sense that this term might be used in Rhodesia."[6]

Official concern over the dangers that would presumably result from the implantation of a "poor white" class in the Congo found expression in the use of certain control devices designed to regulate the flow of prospective immigrants. One of these was the power granted to the governor general by a decree of 1948 to establish quotas of alien immigrants as he deemed fit to protect "the public interest."[7] Another was the *caution,* or deposit, which applicants had to pay before they were admitted

into the colony, and which was forfeited if they failed to establish themselves.[8] Equally instrumental was the extension or denial of credit facilities through the Société du Crédit au Colonat et à l'Industrie (SCCI), a
semigovernmental corporation set up after the war as a substitute for the
Office de Colonisation. In effect, the relative distribution of financial aid

TABLE 1

RELATIVE ALLOCATION OF SCCI FUNDS, 1948–1957

| Recipient | Number | Per cent | Net sum[a] | Per cent |
|---|---|---|---|---|
| Industry | 389 | 19.7 | 347,318 | 26.3 |
| Agriculture | 509 | 25.8 | 297,285 | 22.5 |
| Crafts | 314 | 15.9 | 162,299 | 12.3 |
| Commerce | 257 | 13.0 | 128,056 | 9.7 |
| Professions | 73 | 3.7 | 29,120 | 2.3 |
| Others | 71 | 3.6 | 26,765 | 2.3 |
| Total | 1,613 | 81.7 | 990,843 | 75.5[b] |

[a] In thousands of Belgian francs ($1 = 50BF).
[b] The remaining 24.5 per cent went to the Congolese middle classes.
SOURCE: *Le Congo Belge* (Bruxelles: Infor-Congo, 1959), II, 141.

by the SCCI between 1948 and 1957, as shown in table 1, largely accounts
for the proportionate growth of certain economic categories during this
period.

One of the significant facts revealed by table 2 is the striking diver-

TABLE 2

CHANGING PATTERNS OF EMPLOYMENT OF THE SETTLER POPULATION, 1950–1957

| Category | Belgians 1950 | Belgians 1957 | Aliens 1950 | Aliens 1957 | Total 1950 | Total 1957 | Relative percentage 1950 | Relative percentage 1957 |
|---|---|---|---|---|---|---|---|---|
| Agriculture | 804 | 1,463 | 267 | 320 | 1,071 | 1,783 | 21.7 | 19.2 |
| Commerce | 547 | 1,120 | 1,439 | 2,412 | 1,986 | 3,532 | 40.3 | 38.0 |
| Industry | 461 | 920 | 429 | 580 | 890 | 1,500 | 17.9 | 16.2 |
| Crafts | 170 | 673 | 104 | 487 | 274 | 1,160 | 5.5 | 12.5 |
| Professions | 127 | 515 | 51 | 222 | 178 | 737 | 3.8 | 7.9 |
| Retired | 47 | 27 | 10 | 6 | 57 | 33 | 1.2 | 0.4 |
| Others | 234 | 335 | 238 | 204 | 472 | 539 | 9.6 | 5.8 |
| Total | 2,390 | 5,053 | 2,538 | 4,231 | 4,928 | 9,284 | 100.0 | 100.0 |

SOURCE: *Le Congo Belge* (Bruxelles: Infor-Congo, 1959), II, 139.

sity of economic interests represented by the *colonat*. While the settler population almost doubled between 1950 and 1957, its occupational distribution among the different sectors of the Congo's economy remained virtually unchanged. In 1957 approximately 38 per cent of the economically active settler population was engaged in commercial activities; 19 per cent, in agriculture; and 16 per cent, in industry.

There were several important areal variations in the distribution of settler interests. The heavy concentration of *commerçants* (middlemen, traders, shopkeepers, etc.) in Leopoldville and Katanga provinces, with a clear majority of aliens falling into this category, seems especially significant in view of the hostility among the Congolese toward the *petits blancs*. They assumed, however, a significantly more threatening position in Leopoldville Province, where they were viewed as a direct source of economic competition by the African population, than in the Katanga, where alternative sources of employment were always available.

Another characteristic feature was the prevalence of industrial activities in Leopoldville and Katanga provinces. As the figures in table 3 indicate, the proportion of industrial settlers was noticeably higher in Leopoldville Province, but it must be remembered that the material stake held by the European industrialists of the Katanga was out of all proportion to their numerical strength. The mere fact that the net profits derived from exploitation of the mineral wealth of the Katanga should have accounted for nearly one-half of the colonial revenue of the colony is eloquent testimony to the potential power and influence of its European population.

Finally, the high percentage of landed settlers in Orientale and Kivu provinces is noteworthy. True, the colons who belonged to a landholding class represented but a small fraction of the European population; only 1,200 were actually registered as farmers in 1954,[9] and, under existing regulations, no settler could take up more than 500 hectares of land.[10] On the other hand, the scarcity of cultivable land in Orientale Province, coupled with the highly arbitrary system of concessions enforced by the Belgian government, generated hostility among the local African population toward landed settlers. The same holds true of Kivu Province, where the antagonism between the African and the European communities expressed itself in extremely racialistic terms. The comparatively high population density in the north and south Kivu districts, areas where the concentration of agricultural settlers was the heaviest, also helped to sharpen racial antagonisms.

Another factor revealed by table 2, which also accounts for the lack of strong social cohesion among the settler population, is the high proportion of aliens in the colonat. Approximately one-half of the colons established in the Congo in 1957 could claim Belgian nationality; the

TABLE 3

PROVINCIAL DISTRIBUTION OF THE SETTLER POPULATION, 1958

| Occupation | Leopoldville | | Equateur | | Orientale | | Kivu | | Katanga | | Kasai | | Total | |
|---|---|---|---|---|---|---|---|---|---|---|---|---|---|---|
| | Belgians | Aliens | Belgians | Aliens | Belgians | Aliens | Belgians | Aliens | Belgians | Aliens | Belgians | Aliens | Belgians | Aliens |
| Agriculture | 103 | 23 | 123 | 30 | 477 | 99 | 615 | 121 | 207 | 42 | 50 | 9 | 1,575 | 324 |
| Crafts | 198 | 166 | 19 | 9 | 92 | 56 | 63 | 23 | 263 | 183 | 36 | 15 | 671 | 452 |
| Commerce | 377 | 762 | 53 | 204 | 135 | 466 | 182 | 245 | 353 | 693 | 88 | 128 | 1,178 | 2,498 |
| Industry | 342 | 245 | 31 | 26 | 109 | 52 | 140 | 42 | 240 | 143 | 54 | 44 | 916 | 522 |
| Professions | 196 | 124 | 14 | 13 | 51 | 39 | 73 | 23 | 145 | 41 | 23 | 10 | 502 | 250 |
| Other | 47 | 55 | 25 | 30 | 99 | 79 | 148 | 66 | — | — | 17 | 5 | 336 | 235 |
| Retired | 9 | — | — | — | — | — | — | — | — | — | 15 | 3 | 24 | 3 |
| Provincial total | 1,272 | 1,375 | 255 | 312 | 963 | 791 | 1,221 | 520 | 1,208 | 1,102 | 283 | 214 | 5,202 | 4,284 |
| Per cent | 48.05 | 51.95 | 44.97 | 55.03 | 54.90 | 45.10 | 70.13 | 29.87 | 52.29 | 47.71 | 56.94 | 43.06 | 54.55 | 45.45 |

SOURCE: *Rapport annuel sur l'administration du Congo Belge* (Bruxelles, 1959), p. 290.

other half were of Greek, Italian, Portuguese, or other nationality. The Portuguese, who numbered 4,878 in 1958, were one of the most sizable of these minorities. Because of their inferior economic position they had low prestige relative to the Belgian community. Moreover, their concentration in a few urban areas, Leopoldville in particular, where they monopolized most of the retail trade, led to continued friction with urban Africans, who regarded them as a major obstacle to their own vocational advancement.

Another factor explaining the lack of cohesion among the European population in general, and among the colons in particular, was the linguistic and cultural cleavages within the Belgian population itself. In 1958 approximately 53 per cent of the colonial civil servants, 83 per cent of the Belgian missionaries, and a substantial, yet undetermined, proportion of the settler population were of Flemish extraction.[11] In short, from 60 to 63 per cent of the total Belgian population residing in the Congo belonged to a cultural minority identified with one of the most burning issues of Belgian politics.

The cultural and occupational heterogeneity of the non-African population was not the only factor that lessened the prospects of monolithic solidarity in the face of nationalist pressures. The settlers' tendency to identify their future, socially, politically, and emotionally, with that of the Congo varied from one province to another, and from one socioeconomic category to another. The willingness to consider the Congo as their home was far more noticeable, for example, among the landed colons of the Kivu than among the businessmen and industrialists of Leopoldville Province. But it was in the Katanga, where the influx of European elements was encouraged by the sudden opening of apparently unlimited economic opportunities, that this tendency was the most evident. From the very beginning, the colons of the Katanga displayed a distinctive kind of parochialism, characterized by a strong sentimental attachment to their province and a marked hostility toward all measures or institutions that smacked of centralization.

The special administrative status enjoyed by the Katanga in the early days of Belgian colonization was a powerful stimulus to the growth of separatist sentiment in that part of the Congo. The rankling memories left among the settlers of the Katanga by the centralizing measures of 1933 explained in part the animosity they consistently harbored toward Leopoldville—"hydre insatiable," as the editor of an Elisabethville newspaper, A. Decoster, described it, "cité pourrie par l'ambition mégalomanique [sic] des buildings." [12] This hostility became more intense with the economic growth of the province, and stemmed from the fact that the proportion of public expenditures devoted to the Katanga appeared minute when compared with the overall contribution of its taxpayers to colonial revenues.[13] They felt that they alone supported the debt charges of the other provinces as well as the operating costs of the colonial bureaucracy at Kalina.

Another factor that solidified settler cohesion in the Katanga related to the circumstances under which settlement was carried out. Unlike other provinces, the Katanga was colonized under the auspices of a quasi-independent agency, the Comité Spécial du Katanga (CSK), which until 1910 enjoyed full administrative control over the territory then included within the Katanga's boundaries. The CSK was responsible not only for the granting of freehold property and of mining concessions, but also for the administration of the Colonization Department, whose principal function was to promote, in every possible way, the development of an agricultural colonat. To serve this purpose the Syndicat Foncier du Katanga was set up in 1920, thanks to the financial backing of the Union Minière du Haut Katanga (UMHK), the Compagnie du Congo pour le Commerce et l'Industrie (CCCI), and several other large-scale capitalist enterprises. It proved to be a valuable source of financial assistance for prospective settlers, and performed as well an important aggregative function by serving as a connecting link among various settler interests.[14]

The propinquity of South Africa, together with the fact that the Flemish and the Afrikaans "are linked by the ties of race and language," [15] also influenced the outlook and ambitions of the Katanga settlers. "Whether we like it or not," wrote the editor of *L'Essor du Congo* in 1944, "our own evolution from the stage of simple colonization to the stage of a more solid and denser European implantation will be increasingly conditioned by that of South Africa." [16] Long before these lines were written, the form of government and the policies of the Union of South Africa provided a source of inspiration for the social, economic, and political demands voiced by the European oligarchy of the Katanga. As early as 1911, for example, *L'Etoile du Congo,* one of the first newspapers to be published in Elisabethville, cited the Union as a model which the governor general should emulate: "If Katanga is to become a credit to South Africa, a very different state of affairs from that which presently exists must be inaugurated in the country. . . . If our new governor is to be a success, he will not consult any man holding an official position; he must put aside officialdom altogether and must call together real businessmen who understand the true inwardness of affairs." [17] The influence of the Union of South Africa on the settler community of the Katanga was also reflected in the suggestion made by a delegate to the Comité Régional du Katanga in 1924 that a system of native reserves "similar to that which prevails in the Union of South Africa" be adopted in order to satisfy the demands of the colons,[18] and in the resolution adopted in 1936 by a settler organization of Elisabethville that the decree of July 15, 1934, on the concession of native lands, be revised along the lines of the South African settlement act of 1912.[19] The proximity of South Africa and the Rhodesias also affected the settlers' concept of the future character of the Katangese polity. If nothing else, it accelerated the movement for dominion status under white domination in the years preceding independence.

### ORGANIZATIONAL DEVELOPMENT

It is not unnatural that the Katanga, in view of the social, economic, and political forces at work there, was at the forefront of prosettler activities. In point of fact, one of the earliest settler organizations formed in the Congo was the Fédération des Groupements et Associations du Katanga, founded in Elisabethville on February 14, 1934.[20] As its name indicates, the organization incorporated within its membership several associations, or *groupements,* which until then had operated independently. These were the Association Agricole du Katanga, the Association des Colons Belges au Katanga, and the Groupement des Intérêts Immobiliers, founded respectively in 1921, 1923, and 1932.[21]

The economic depression that hit the Congo in the early 1930's was an important factor behind the merging of these associations. The threat of unemployment, the devaluation of landed property, and the burden of increased taxation all contributed to the unification of settler interests. Regardless of their occupational status, the colons of the Katanga unanimously criticized the monopolization of economic activities by "powerful capitalist organisms," the absence of adequate credit facilities, and the failure of the metropolitan government to ease the burden of taxation.[22] Faced with the prospect of a worsening economic situation, they felt the urge to pool their strength in order to maximize their influence:

C'est dans ces circonstances critiques et angoissantes que les Groupements et Associations du Katanga, animés par un sentiment de solidarité étroite, voyant le fruit de toute une vie de labeur compromis, ont décidé de s'allier et de constituer une Fédération. Celle-ci défendra avec fermeté les intérêts de ses membres; elle combattra avec vigueur toute mesure inconsiderée qui tendrait à produire le désordre au Katanga, ou à aggraver la situation pénible de ses membres.[23]

The centralizing measures of 1933 were equally instrumental in fostering a sense of solidarity among the Katanga settlers. In their minds the decision of the metropolitan government was wholly unjustified and contrary to the interest of the Katanga, for it deprived the local authorities of a prestige they felt was "necessary to the maintenance of their relations with [their] southern neighbors, and indispensable in [their] relations with the native population." [24]

Partly because the Katanga settlers realized that their grievances were shared by settlers in the other provinces, and also because they wished to acquire a broader territorial base, the Fédération des Groupements et Associations du Katanga decided in 1935 to extend its membership to the rest of the colony. The organization consequently changed its name to Fédération des Groupements et Associations du Congo Belge, but its objectives remained essentially the same. According to Article II of its statutes, the object of the federation is "to defend the moral and material interests of its members; to collaborate with the organisms seeking the economic renovation of the colony and the well-being of its inhabitants; to encourage a rational colonization of the territories of the Belgian Congo which are amenable to white settlement." [25] Provision was made, however, for a coördinating apparatus, composed of a general council, an executive council, and a yearly congress to be held, on a rotating basis, in each of the provincial capitals.[26] In 1939 the federation organized a permanent secretariat in Elisabethville which not only facilitated coördination among its member associations but also collaborated on the publication of a monthly bulletin, the *Bulletin Mensuel de la Fédération des Groupements et Associations du Congo Belge.*[27]

The outbreak of World War II, although temporarily suspending the activities of the federation, did not destroy its hopes. On the contrary, the end of hostilities allowed the colons to make a fresh start in defending the "position of the whites against all external and internal threats" and in giving an "opportunity to those suffering from the oppression of the Nazis to find in the Congo a country of adoption where they can re-create a better future for themselves." [28] In May, 1944, a group of Katanga settlers founded the Union pour la Colonisation (Ucol) to replace the now-defunct Fédération des Groupements et Associations du Congo Belge. Its explicit goals were "to deploy all possible efforts to obtain for the white population of the Congo the liberties granted by the Belgian constitution to its nationals, and to promote, by all available means, the growth of European colonization." [29] The organization had representatives in each of the six provinces and in Ruanda-Urundi, but its administrative seat was in Elisabethville, and most of the 400 dues-paying members registered in 1947 were drawn from the Katanga. An effort was made to achieve a certain measure of political and social cohesion through periodical assemblies and the publication of *Ucol,* an official monthly organ. But there was in fact little or no coördination among the several branches of the organization.

The awareness of growing threats to their respective interests induced the European settlers to close their ranks behind a new organization, the

Fédération des Associations des Colons du Congo Belge et du Ruanda-Urundi, better known as the Fedacol. This organization, set up early in 1950, was the settlers' response to the introduction of a draft decree on the "immatriculation and assimilation of civilized natives" on the floor of the Conseil de Gouvernement.[30] The principal objectives of the Fedacol were "defense of the colonat" and "promotion of a rapid and harmonious development of European settlement in the Congo." [31] The chairmanship of the organization was assigned to a different provincial delegate every year, and the organizational structure included a permanent executive committee and a delegate in Brussels. Through the appointment of representatives of the colonat to metropolitan agencies, and lobbying activities designed to enlist the support of Belgian deputies, the Fedacol became a powerful pressure group.[32] Its spokesmen seized the opportunities offered by the colonial press to make their voices heard, and its official organ, the monthly *Eurafrica,* helped to mobilize support for its ideas among the European population. The delegates of the Fedacol to the Conseil de Gouvernement were fully conscious of their pressure-group functions, as evidenced by the number of settler-sponsored voeux introduced at its yearly sessions.

Yet, for all its efforts to achieve solidarity among the whites, the Fedacol won the effective support of only a small fraction of the settler population in the Congo. Table 4 reveals that only one-fourth of the

TABLE 4

PROVINCIAL DISTRIBUTION OF THE FEDACOL MEMBERSHIP, 1959

| Province | Non-African population | Settler population | Fedacol membership | |
| --- | --- | --- | --- | --- |
| | | | Affiliated members | Per cent of settler population |
| Leopoldville | 32,143 | 1,966 | 148 | 7.5 |
| Equateur | 6,501 | 599 | 110 | 18.3 |
| Orientale | 15,473 | 1,850 | 607 | 32.8 |
| Kivu | 12,788 | 1,397 | 470 | 29.4 |
| Katanga | 33,918 | 3,065 | 975 | 31.8 |
| Kasai | 8,634 | 544 | 174 | 31.9 |
| Total | 109,457 | 9,421 | 2,484 | 25.8 |

SOURCE: *Courrier Africain* (CRISP), No. 25 (July, 1959), p. 3.

colonat belonged to the Fedacol. But, significantly enough, the Katanga made the heaviest contribution. Symptomatic of area discontinuities in terms of settler solidarity is the fact only 7.5 per cent of the total settler population of Leopoldville Province was affiliated with the Fedacol, as against 31.8 per cent in the Katanga.

## POLITICAL OBJECTIVES

The search for some kind of modus vivendi between the African and European communities remained at the forefront of the settlers' preoccupations in the decades preceding independence. But the centralization of decision-making processes in the hands of the metropolitan government left hardly any room for local initiative. Equally compelling, therefore, was the question of metropolitan-colonial relationships, and the way in which they might affect the position of the colonat in relation to the African population.

From the very beginning, the acquisition of political rights identical with those enjoyed by Belgians of metropolitan status was viewed by the colons as an essential precondition to the attainment of mutually satisfactory relationships between the metropolis and the colony.[33] This objective, prompted by the settlers' intense desire to arrogate unto themselves as much freedom as they thought compatible with "the defense of colonial interests," reflects the attraction of the idea of dominion status for the settler population. Speaking on behalf of the Ucol before the Commission du Colonat in 1946, M. Deschamps stated that the "Belgian colons do not want to be regarded as foreigners in a country which is now theirs. The Congo must therefore remain a Belgian entity, perhaps in a form comparable to a British dominion." [34] It was recommended that a parliament be set up in the colony which would have the authority to initiate and enact laws, and to which the colonial government would remain accountable. The natives would not be granted representation until they acquired a "sufficient degree of political maturity." In the meantime all appropriate measures would be taken to encourage "a massive influx" of settlers into the colony. The granting of visas for the Congo was to be liberalized; the caution was to be eliminated from the list of requirements to be met by prospective settlers; there were to be substantial tax exemptions and a more efficient procedure for the concession of freehold property.

There were few disagreements among the colons as to the nature of their ultimate political goals, but they did not always see eye to eye on the methods to be adopted. The Katanga settlers believed that only through a separate and autonomous status could the provincial authorities achieve the degree of prestige and political freedom which, they insisted, was indispensable in their relations with the Africans. As early as 1931, for example, a petition submitted to the Belgian government by the Association des Colons Belges au Katanga urged the metropolitan authorities to grant home rule to the Katanga. In substance it argued that

The Katanga wants home rule. A petition signed by Belgian colonists urges that Katanga should have its own parliament and that the sons of the colonists, men born in the country, should be chosen as officials rather than young, inexperienced men from Belgium.

The petition states that while these officials are full of ardor, they are also full of conceit and disdain for the old colonists, whom they want to teach how to colonize and who come there batch after batch to make the same errors.[35]

The Belgian government turned a deaf ear to the association's demands, but its members nevertheless persisted in their efforts to wrest political control from the metropolis. After the reform of 1933 they became increasingly critical of the centralist character of Belgian policy; as a first step toward the acquisition of provincial autonomy they urged the metropolitan government to "give back to the heads of the provinces their former titles and legislative powers, and to grant them an even greater latitude than they had before the last reorganization."[36] The Belgian settlers also demanded adequate representation in the Colonial Council and the Belgian Chambers. Finally, the decree of January 12, 1923, pertaining to the organization of urban districts, was to be revised in order to "allow Europeans living in urban centers to take an active part in their administration."[37] These preliminary steps would ultimately lead to dominion status for the Katanga.

In contrast with the Katanga settlers, others favored a gradualist approach to colonial problems. For example, the essentials of the constitutional reform advocated by de Maleingreau d'Hembise before the Commission du Colonat in 1946 consisted in transferring the seat of the Colonial Council from Brussels to Leopoldville and altering its membership so as to give stronger representation to the settler element. But the council's prerogatives would have remained unchanged, at least for the time being.[38] Similarly, M. Dubois, speaking a few years later on behalf of the Fedacol before the Congrès Colonial National, admitted that "the installation of legislative, executive, and judicial authorities in the Congo" was the immediate goal of the colonat, but added that "the principle on which it based its views was the formation of a single state, indissolubly linked with Belgium, composed of a European and a native community," and that the colonat "tended toward a progressive transfer [*un glissment progressif*] of legislative powers from Belgium to the Congo."[39]

A fundamental assumption underlying these proposals was that the African community in the social and political structure of the Congo was to remain subordinate to, and separate from, the European community. In 1950, in response to measures suggested by the Belgian government to improve the status of "civilized" Africans, the spokesmen of the

Fedacol expressed their opposition to all attempts at social integration: "The European community is too much aware of the excellence of Western civilization to let it run the slightest risk of being submerged under the flood of a hybrid combination of civilization and barbarity." [40] In an effort to justify their position they contended that "the most intelligent among the natives did not seek satisfactions of a sentimental order, but material, tangible, and useful gratifications, such as better housing, education, and medical care." [41] They also argued that the extension of judicial "assimilation" to qualified Congolese would inevitably result in a "castelike system" with all the "regrettable consequences" that such a system would entail.[42]

When the decree on immatriculation came into force in 1952, the Fedacol felt the need to pay lip service to the principles sanctioned by the new legislation, but adamantly refused to retreat from its initial position. At the ninth session of the Congrès Colonial National, held in Brussels in 1953, the Fedacol delegate stated in the same breath that the organization favored "total rejection of all racial discrimination and adoption of the formula 'equal rights and duties to equal degrees of civilization,'" and "the maintenance of a political system characterized by the presence of two parallel and distinct communities." [43]

A limited attempt was made by one section of the Fedacol to put integration into practice in 1953, when Maus, Marrès, and de Maleingreau invited "African middle classes" to join the various settlers' unions. But this move, which was fully consonant with the manifesto adopted by the General Council of the Fedacol in July, 1952,[44] was violently criticized by another group of colons, represented by M. Bonté, chairman of the Union des Colons de la Province Orientale (Unicol) and M. Ballageer, chairman of the Associations Professionnelles de la Province de Leopold-ville (Aprocolin). They strongly objected to the views of the integrationists, and suggested instead that African middle classes form their own separate organizations.

This suggestion led to the emergence in 1954 of several African middle-class associations, known as the Associations des Classes Moyennes Africaines (ACMAF), which paralleled the white settlers' unions. But the absence of organic ties between the two lessened the prospects of genuine coöperation among their members. Moreover, the siege mentality that characterized European settlers, with its undercurrents of defiance and insecurity, made these prospects all the more distant. And yet the African middle classes were viewed in some European quarters as prospective allies, or at least as a stabilizing element whose influence would help to counter the threat of nationalist upheavals. On March 3, 1955, the Fedacol delegate in Brussels addressed a confidential note to the Minister of Colonies emphatically stressing the need to organize a class of native évolués who will agree with the ideals and principles of our Western civilization. . . . Less numerous than the native masses, yet powerful and influential, they will be our indispensable allies among the native communities. These middle classes will be the black bourgeoisie which we shall provide with wealth and organization, and which, like all the bourgeois in the world, will be opposed to all internal and external changes.[45]

The limited extent to which this policy was carried out explains in part why these optimistic hopes did not materialize. But it would be incorrect to dismiss the foregoing considerations as mere evidence of wishful thinking. They are, on the contrary, directly relevant to an understanding of the processes of adjustment which took place in certain areas of the Congo during the ultimate phase of Belgian colonialism.

PATTERNS OF ACCOMMODATION

Discussing the problem of "native participation in governmental councils," a Leopoldville newspaper stated in 1944: "The European element will never accept a downgrading in favor of the native element and will always demand to be kept ahead [*exigera toujours le maintien de son advance*]. In so doing it repudiates the principle of democratic equality, and the political organization of the colony cannot, therefore, be based on this precept." [46] With the social and economic transformations of the postwar period, however, the possibilities of serious political tensions could not be indefinitely ignored. In 1954, already anticipating the transformation of consultative organs into lawmaking bodies, the representatives of the colonat introduced before the Conseil de Gouvernement several reform proposals designed to alter the existing system of representation.

Their first objective was to reinforce their position vis-à-vis the African councilors. At the same time they faced the difficult task of reconciling the principle of "functional representation" with that of multiracial representation. They consequently suggested (1) that native interests, which had hitherto stood as a separate group, be integrated into the existing categories; (2) that native interests be so apportioned as to keep them numerically inferior to each European membership group; and (3) that their number be augmented through the addition of new categories of interests.

According to the scheme advocated by de Maleingreau in 1954, three broad classes of interests were to be seated in the Conseil de Gouvernement: (1) general interests, (2) private interests, and (3) political interests. Each of these categories was to be subdivided into (1) officials and notables; (2) societies, independent middle classes, and labor; and (3) rural and urban areas. Each subcategory, with the exception of "officials and notables" was to be given equal representation.[47] The fact that private interests would have an absolute majority over each of the remaining categories, in the event of an effective transfer of authority, would place the colons in a singularly advantageous position. Although the proportion of Africans to be included in the categories mentioned was never specified, the author of the proposals nevertheless emphasized that there would never be a "preponderant representation of native interests . . . in any of the categories of councilors. The whites are the sole guides and carriers of the civilization of this country." [48] And besides, argued the proponent of the scheme, an eventual *capitis deminutio* of the white element would undoubtedly be regarded by the natives as an attempt on the part of the settler population to shirk its responsibilities. [49]

The introduction of limited democratic processes in 1957 led the colonat to make a new attempt to resist political change. Early in 1958, referring to the Statut des Villes, the chairman of the Fedacol declared before the Commission du Colonat that "this unfortunate decision was premature under the prevailing circumstances," and that "a rigid parity between native and European interests should be maintained in all Congolese political institutions." [50] Only a few months earlier, however, equal representation of African and European interests had been strongly criticized by a spokesman of the colonat on the grounds that disagreements among the white councilors might induce some of them to side with the Congolese. It was therefore suggested that the African delegates to the municipal councils be "designated by appropriate means by the administration without resorting to electoral processes." [51]

In the meantime the European population of the Katanga had become increasingly committed to the idea of dominion status under white supremacy as a solution to the dilemmas posed by the first manifestations of Congolese nationalism. In an article entitled "Pour un Statut de dominion au Katanga," an anonymous defender of settler interests wrote in the October 26, 1956, issue of *L'Essor du Congo:* "The Katanga should immediately form a distinct political entity, administered by a vice-governor general appointed by the King, and assisted in his functions by a council whose members would be chosen from among individuals proposed by economic corporations that take part in the economic life of the country."

A few months later, in April, 1957, the Central Committee of the Katanga section of the Fedacol, the Ucol-Katanga, issued a political program which contained more than a hint of separatism. Recalling at the outset that the Congolese tribes—"once plunged in the darkness of ignorance, superstition, and fetishism"—owed their "present peace and happiness" to "our administrators, missionaries, and settlers," the dirigeants of the Ucol clearly indicated their desire to oppose all nationalist tendencies, which, they maintained, were nothing but racist manifestations: "C'est contre ces tendances et ces nationalismes, qui ne sont en réalité que du racisme sciemment débaptisé, et qui sont aux antipodes d'une saine collaboration mondiale, que l'Ucol s'élève en établissant la doctrine politique dont les grandes lignes sont reprises ci-dessus." [52] They argued that "a Congolese nationality does not exist in the narrow sense that some would like to ascribe to the word, no more than there exists a European or an Asian nationality," and that the Congo is only a congeries of political units "composed of a union of tribes of the same race, or of an amalgam of conquering tribes and submitted races." Above "tribal hostilities and racial differences," however, they acknowledged the existence of a community of interests between "the autochthons and the European immigrants," based on the economic development of the country and conditioned by an increased immigration of European elements, a fiscal policy intended to protect infant industries through tax exemptions, and the maintenance of private enterprise. In order to maintain harmonious relations between the metropolis and the colony, they recommended a broad decentralization of all administrative services, "the granting of a certain degree of autonomy to the provinces," and the "reëstablishment of provincial vice-governors." The higher organs of the colony, they added, should limit their intervention to a broad definition of colonial policy and to "the coördination and harmonization of the rights and duties of each region."

This statement of principles was elaborated in a mimeographed document, also released in April, 1957, which contained a detailed outline of the constitutional reforms advocated by the Ucol-Katanga.[53] The substance of these proposals was directly borrowed from the ideas of Arthur Doucy, director of the Solvay Institute. Focusing his analysis on the social and anthropological context of the colonial situation, Doucy argued convincingly for an administrative reorganization that would take into account the cultural diversity of the Congolese populations, their different stages of evolution, and their variant modes of social and political organization. "The solution to many problems," he concluded, "may be found only in a bold policy of decentralization." [54] In practice, it meant the transfer of the government general from Leopoldville to Brussels and the delegation of some of its prerogatives to a new provincial functionary, the royal commissioner. The royal commissioner would represent the king in each of the provinces, exercising all executive powers within the limits stipulated by laws, decrees, and arrêtés royaux; he would exercise ultimate control over the "administrative and military services established in the province"; he would submit the annual budget of the province to the Minister of Colonies and would report directly to Brussels. For purposes of coördination, a high commissioner would act as liaison between the provinces and the metropolis, but under no circumstances would he claim administrative control over the provinces: "Il remplit essentiellement une mission de coordination et de représentation. ... Il ne détient aucun pouvoir administratif direct." [55]

Doucy's theme had already been expressed, with some variations, in the reorganization plan submitted to the Belgian government in 1920 by a group of Europeans living in the Katanga;[56] the Ucol-Katanga therefore responded with remarkable enthusiasm to the proposals contained in the "plan Doucy." As the editor of *L'Essor du Congo* admitted, "Ce sont les idées générales et les suggestions de Mr. Doucy qui nous semblent se rapprocher le plus de nos façons de concevoir les choses. Comme la plupart d'entre nous il perçoit l'impossibilité d'appliquer à notre immense Congo une politique unique." [57] Also, the Ucol-Katanga leaders could rest their case on the authority of a well-known metropolitan observer whose judgment and objectivity, they thought, constituted an important psychological asset. Moreover, the personal and ideological affinities that existed between Auguste Buisseret, the Liberal minister of colonies, and certain persons associated with the Université Libre de Bruxelles led them to expect a favorable hearing in government spheres. But the response of the metropolitan government was not quite what they anticipated. Speaking before the Chamber of Representatives in July, 1957, the Minister of Colonies unambiguously reaffirmed his intention to maintain the unity of the Congo against all fanaticisms and chauvinisms: "Le Ministre se refuse à contribuer à semer la division, à édifier outre-mer un ou plusieurs états racistes voués à une décadence rapide, à mentir ainsi à l'idéal de nos pères, ruiner les fondements mêmes de leur oeuvre africaine." [58] Without making a specific allusion to the "plan Doucy," the Minister of Colonies nevertheless dispelled all hopes that it would serve as a basis for future reforms.

Thus rebuked, the Ucol-Katanga decided to opt for an independent course of action centered on a "specifically Katangese policy." In 1958 Achille Gavage, a leading member of its Central Committee, made a strong plea for a multiracial political organization that would aggregate within its ranks the interests of the Katanga settlers and of "all the Congolese born in the Katanga and all the Africans who are definitely integrated within the Katangese population." "Ce groupement," he added, "devrait penser Katanga d'abord, Congo ensuite, car le Katanga, de par ses caracteristiques climatiques et ethnographiques doit former une entité distincte des autres régions congolaises. Le Katanga doit jouir au plus tôt de son autonomie interne." [59] In the following months "Katangese autonomy" became the leitmotiv that set the tone of the editorials published in the local press, and when in May, 1958, the president of the Ucol-Katanga announced the formation of the Union Katangaise, there were few doubts about the nature of its political objectives or the identity of its leaders. In fact, the platform of the party was largely a duplication of the "political doctrine" elaborated a year earlier by the Central Committee of the Ucol-Katanga,[60] and the president of its Provisional Committee was Achille Gavage, the European settler who played so active a role in the promotion of a "specifically Katangese policy." Local branches of the Union Katangaise were organized in Kolwezi, Jadotville, and other places in the Upper Katanga, and by the end of 1958 the party could claim the overwhelming support of the settler population, including that of such powerful corporate interests as the Union Minière du Haut Katanga.

Despite the efforts of the Union Katangaise to crystallize support around the issue of Katangese autonomy, the Belgian government's declaration of January 13, 1959, made it quite plain that the Congo would accede to independence as a single geographical and political unit. This decision, which excluded the possibility of dominion status for the Katanga, naturally influenced the strategy of the colonat, but did not cause a fundamental revision of its political objectives. As we shall see in a subsequent chapter, the tactics employed by the colonat consisted of communicating its ideas and conceptions to those Africans who claimed to be genuine Katangese, so as to make the prospects of secession both economically attractive and politically meaningful.

In the meantime, the Fedacol felt the need to reconcile the principles acknowledged by the metropolitan authorities with the interests of its members. Apparently unperturbed by the doctrinal deviation of its Katangese branch, the Fedacol defined its official position in a declaration that appeared under the misleading title, "Loyal Collaboration with the Declaration of January 13." After paying lip service to "the way in which the Belgian government intends to reach the conditions that are essential to the establishment of a genuine democracy," the declaration called attention to "the perplexity and the intense fears" of the Belgian population. With the obvious intention of allaying these fears, the Fedacol enumerated the steps that would presumably lead toward a "genuine democracy." One of these steps was to maintain an equal representation of European and African interests in all conciliar organs. Rhetorically stressing the need for a dialogue, the author of the declaration stated that politics "is the art of choosing a goal and a means. The goal is the multiracial, modern nation; the means is the dialogue. The principle of equal representation aims only at rendering the dialogue useful, fruitful, and durable." [61] The second step was the appointment of traditional authorities—"to which the government's declaration unfortunately omitted to pay homage"—to all councils as de jure members. Third, all legislative organs at both provincial and territorial levels were to be indirectly elected. Finally, there was to be a high proportion of appointed delegates, representing the existing functional categories. At this stage of the Congo's political evolution, however, the idea of a dialogue, no matter how "fruitful" or "durable," was no substitute for the idea of self-government, and in the eyes of many thoughtful Congolese these proposals represented little more than an eleventh-hour attempt on the part of the colons to hold on to their positions.

A close observer of the Congolese scene has recently stated that "few Belgians thought seriously of the future of the Congo . . . and few were prepared to come forth with concrete proposals and suggestions when the emerging fact of independence came to be realized."[62] This view, however, cannot be accepted without reservation, for in principle most settlers were committed to the idea of dominion status under white supremacy, and in practice all their efforts were directed toward the achievement of this goal. But there were fundamental differences of opinion over the methods to be employed. In contrast with the attitude of the settlers in other provinces, the European community of the Katanga always tended to regard provincial autonomy as a precondition for the attainment of dominion status, partly because of the historical and ecological factors operative in the Katanga, and partly because of the economic advantages they hoped to derive from this change of relationships. But this factor, as we shall see, was also a source of separatist sentiment among some of the tribes located in the Katanga. These differences and similarities in the attitudes of Europeans and Africans were important elements in the pattern of alliances formed in the months preceding independence.

# V. THE IMPACT OF WESTERN
## ECONOMIC FORCES

The settler's image of himself in relation to the African, invariably colored by a sense of racial superiority, found expression in a mood of racial and cultural arrogance which in turn generated a widespread feeling of humiliation and revolt among the Congolese. But the existence of this feeling does not alone explain the emergence of nationalist forces. Before such forces can become operative, nationalist sentiment must crystallize in organizational form and around appropriate issues. Nationalism is not only the manifestation of a "united will," but the result of the social and economic transformations that have attended the penetration of Western influences.[1]

The first point to stress, therefore, in considering the impact of Western economic forces on the growth of nationalist sentiment in the Congo is their close relatedness. It is doubtful that nationalism could have expressed itself otherwise than through sporadic resistance movements unless new values and ideas had already altered traditional structures. The penetration of modern, secular influences, and the resulting weakening of tribal bonds, caused a restratification of Congolese societies. A new class of évolués emerged, composed of clerks, medical assistants, traders, artisans, and so on, which gradually estranged itself from the traditional order and became increasingly susceptible to the appeals of nationalism. Along with the economic opportunities offered by the introduction of a money economy and the development of industry, a host of racial, social, and economic grievances were created which found an outlet in nationalist activities.

Second, the same forces that set the stage for the emergence of nationalist assertions were of critical importance in creating or preserving antagonisms among groups, partly because the response of Congolese societies varied considerably depending on the character of their traditional political systems. The fact that the Baluba adapted themselves to urban conditions with far greater ease than the Bakuba or the Bateke, and eventually managed to control the commercialized sector of the economy of certain provinces, is an illustration. Another factor of disunity was the uneven incidence of modernizing forces. As will be recalled, certain coastal groups, such as the Bakongo, maintained episodic rela-

94

tions with Europeans many centuries before the imposition of the *pax belgica,* whereas the populations of the interior did not come in contact with Western civilization before the last quarter of the nineteenth century. Finally, these temporal variations in the exposure of indigenous societies to Western influences were matched by important area differences in the scale of urbanization and industrialization. The high level of industrialization attained by the Congo does not detract from the fact that only a small part of its territory became industrialized, and that the agricultural sector continued to be important in the economy of the country.

Although the penetration of Western economic forces may have been a prerequisite to the ascendency of Congolese nationalism, it is equally true that some of the present political cleavages might not have been so acute—and, indeed, might not even exist—if all parts of the Congo had been industrialized simultaneously and uniformly. The main concern here is to analyze the effects of urbanization and commercialization, not only in terms of their positive contribution to the growth of nationalist sentiment and activity, but also in terms of their divisive implications.

THE CONSEQUENCES OF URBANIZATION

The steady flow of rural Africans into urban areas is perhaps the most significant feature of the postwar social transformation. In 1940 only 1,617,899 Congolese lived in towns, but 3,047,734, or 23.12 per cent of the population, were no longer living in their tribal areas in 1957.[2] Leopoldville, which had 46,500 inhabitants in 1939, claimed 282,765 in 1954. Between 1946 and 1954 the population of Elisabethville increased from 65,397 to 119,997, and that of Stanleyville from 22,374 to 54,365.

This spectacular growth of urban centers, though frequently encouraged by the use of official pressure to recruit labor for European enterprises, reflects the seduction exerted upon the Congolese by the economic and social advantages of city life. With the increase of mobility between urban and rural areas, village inhabitants became more aware of these advantages and consequently more sensitive to the acquisition of achieved status. In other words, they became increasingly anxious to improve their status position by their own efforts. As one évolué vividly explained,

In the beginning, tribal and other prohibitions, and also the fear of life in European towns—fear of hunger and the forced labor one imagines must exist there—operated against the rural exodus. But the inhabitants of these towns, coming back on holiday or passing through their villages—mostly ex-soldiers, "boys," and the subjects of foreign colonies—transform the village mentality. These people of the towns make a good impression. They are well dressed. . . . They reveal the secret of their condition: Money, the white man's God.[3]

The rush of population toward urban areas also reflected the conditions that prevailed in the *centres coutumiers,* and, in particular, the desire of the Congolese to escape the arbitrary authority of appointed chiefs as well as the physical exactions resulting from the imposition of the *corvée,* or "customary labor" (*travaux coutumiers*).[4] A determinative factor, according to Lumumba, was "the transformation of traditional modes of social organization, caused by the appointment of chiefs who are unfamiliar with customary ways of life."[5] In general, the efforts of urbanized Africans to escape customary sanctions were paralleled by a desire to attain status and prestige through the acquisition of wealth and education. The gradual weakening of traditional ties was therefore accompanied by the introjection of new values. But as these processes took place simultaneously, the Congolese made ambivalent, schizoid responses to the acculturative influences of urban life.

Reflecting upon the tendency of the évolués to emulate European ways, Antoine-Roger Bolamba, the editor of *La Voix du Congolais,* observed in 1945:

The évolués are well dressed and wear fashionable clothes. They meet in front of bookshops and look for new books. They read Georges Duhamel, Henri Bordeaux, Roland Dorgelès, and all the modern writers. They discuss, rightly or wrongly, current affairs. You meet them in cafés exchanging ideas on current problems with a rare exuberance.[6]

This portrayal aptly conveys the intellectual curiosity of urbanized Africans. Yet it is somewhat misleading, for in many respects the évolués tended to retain a strong sense of identity with their respective cultures.

The hold of cultural affinities was clearly reflected in the presence of tribally homogeneous sectors within the same town. To be sure, there were certain exceptions to the rule, depending on the tribal background and the degree of Westernization of urban dwellers; in the patterns of urban settlement in Stanleyville, for example, "ethnic origins continue to play an important role in determining the residence of the 'less civilized' inhabitants, but lose some of their importance among the 'more civilized.'"[7] Elsewhere the degree of civilization of the Congolese had little or no influence on the tribal solidarity of urban dwellers, and cultural and linguistic affinities often prompted the members of the same tribe to settle in the same quarter regardless of individual differences in wealth or education. This brings us to a consideration of the cultural and historical variables that conditioned the responses of Congolese societies to the impact of urbanization.

The relative consequences of urbanization are perhaps best illustrated by the different reactions of the populations of the Kasai to the penetration of Western influences. While some societies, such as the

Bakuba, have consistently opposed all forms of innovation, others, such as the Baluba, have shown a far stronger inclination to come into contact with modernizing influences.

The Bakuba are better known for the richness of their artistic traditions than for any other aspect of their culture. As a form of expression, these traditions reflect the strong attachment of the Bakuba to the ultimate values and standards of their society. Their traditional authority system, culminating in the person of the king, from whom all powers are derived, has undergone very few changes since the inception of colonial rule. The fact that polygamy remains the most tangible sign of the king's authority shows that the traditional customs and beliefs of the Bakuba remained largely immune to the influence of Christianity. Their political system, in short, closely approximates David Apter's "consummatory model": "Society, the state, authority and the like are all part of an elaborately sustained, high-solidarity system in which religion as a cognitive guide is pervasive." [8] The crucial point is that these structural features conspired to make the Bakuba society averse to innovation, for innovation meant the destruction of the traditional society. As one administrative report succinctly put it, "Les Bakuba végètent toujours dans leur apathie séculaire. Ils vivent de peu et se contentent de produire strictement ce qui leur est nécessaire." [9]

In sharp contrast with this static, tradition-bound society, the Baluba have responded much more enthusiastically to the impact of urbanization. Beginning in 1909, with the foundation of the Catholic mission of Mikalayi, near Luluabourg, they gradually drifted from the Bakwanga region to the other urban centers of the province. From 1912 to 1931 their territorial expansion was accelerated by the demand for labor created by the construction of the Chemin de Fer du Bas-Congo au Katanga (BCK), linking Port-Francqui with Sakania, and by 1922 the territoire of Mweka was reported to be "on the verge of becoming an immense refuge of Baluba." [10] In postwar years Baluba elements moved in increasing numbers into the major urban centers of Kasai and Katanga provinces, and by 1954 accounted for about 57 per cent of the cité indigène of Luluabourg and 35 per cent of the centre extra-coutumier of Elisabethville.[11] They formed a sizable part of the labor force employed by the Union Minière and the Forminière, and supplied the vast majority of the seasonal workers employed by the BCK. Furthermore, by taking full advantage of the educational opportunities offered by Catholic missionary schools, they managed to obtain most of the jobs available. As a result, while expanding territorially, they aroused a considerable amount of anti-Baluba feeling among the indigenous tribes. This resentment against the growing threat of Baluba domination lay at the root of the tribal rivalries that envenomed the political scene of the Kasai.

It may be that the resourcefulness and the dynamism of the Baluba, sometimes attributed to intrinsic behavioral traits, were encouraged by the shortage of land in south Kasai. But it is equally plausible to ascribe these predispositions to historical and cultural factors. Their long subservience during the precolonial period to the neighboring Bakuba, and the democratic character of their traditional political institutions, both helped to alleviate the weight of primordial structures.

The greater adaptability of certain tribes to urban conditions is also exemplified by the Bakongo population of Leopoldville. Their heavy concentration in the Lower Congo, and the sociopolitical changes that occurred during the course of precolonial migrations, allowed them to absorb the impact of urbanization with relative ease. Furthermore, their early exposure to Western influences mitigated the strain of rapid social changes. As Professor Maquet has stated,

The rate of change varies throughout the Congo area. Among the Bakongo, who have been in contact for a long time with Europeans, the changes in the culture as a whole are most noticeable. Many Bakongo pagans are now said to consider magic as a superstition and polygamy as a savage custom. Further, the young generations seem to have an attitude toward Western culture very different from that prevailing 20 or 30 years ago. Now they think that the European level is attainable.[12]

The ability of the Bakongo to adapt themselves to modernizing influences offers a striking contrast to that of certain neighboring tribes, such as the Bateke. The Bateke people "were never well disposed toward the European. . . . After several attempts at futile risings the remnant of the south Stanley-Pool Bateke returned to the lands north of the Stanley-Pool from which they had come."[13] More recently it has been noted that "the Bateke, in spite of their proximity to Brazzaville, and their poverty, systematically reject urban life; whereas among the Bakongo the social climate is favorable to the travels of the young which are regarded as a source of wealth for their families."[14] This peculiar attitude, deeply rooted in the value structure of their society, explains why the Bateke, even to this day, generally tend to withdraw from their urban environment.

The more intensive urbanization of certain tribes does not necessarily imply a greater receptivity to "national" symbols of authority. Although the Baluba who lived in Katanga and Leopoldville provinces were an exception, those who migrated toward the urban centers of the Kasai have been overwhelmingly disinclined to transcend their tribal perspectives. Similarly, the intensive urbanization of the Bakongo did not prevent them from retaining an acute sense of their own cultural identity. In each instance urban conditions have positively encouraged the development of ethnic group activity involving the participation of culturally related tribes. The presence of different ethnic minorities in the same town made them all the more aware of their mutual differences, thereby favoring the growth of ethnic nationalisms:

Ethnic nationalisms are born in large urban centers where Congolese of different origins, who speak different languages, intermingle. These contacts, instead of bringing hearts closer together, often have the opposite effect. It makes them conscious of their differences and strengthens feelings of mutual alienation. The alien is always more or less an enemy among people who are still impregnated with clan sentiments.[15]

On the whole, this is a valid assessment of the situation that prevailed in many urban centers in the years preceding independence. Urban conditions have undoubtedly sharpened cultural cleavages between Bangala and Bakongo in Leopoldville, Baluba and Lulua in Luluabourg, Baluba and Lunda in Elisabethville, and to a lesser extent, between Ngombe and Mongo in Coquilhatville. And these antagonisms have in turn provided the basis for varying degrees of ethnic nationalism among some of the groups concerned. Sometimes, however, the tribal heterogeneity of the urban population has operated to diminish the strength of ethnic particularisms. The ethnic diversity of the Stanleyville population is certainly the main reason for its conspicuous indifference to the appeals of ethnic nationalism; of sixty-six different tribal groupings that made up the population of Stanleyville in 1954, fifty were represented by groups of less than 500 people, only five by groups of more than 2,000, and not a single one by more than 6,000.[16] The significance of this factor was clearly perceived by one African, who explained the absence of tribalism in Stanleyville by pointing out, "Nous avons trop de tribus."

On the other hand, the presence of a numerically preponderant nationality group has frequently acted as a catalytic agent among otherwise unrelated tribes. It was the threat of Bakongo domination which caused the so-called "Bangala" of Leopoldville to acquire a sense of group consciousness, in spite of the fact that one can hardly speak of a "Bangala" tribe. The term Bangala, "in its widest meaning . . . includes about half of the total population of the Congo-Ubangui and the Tshuapa districts, viz. also many people who for a major part belong to the Sudanese tribes of Ubangui, or the Ngombe group." [17] In Leopoldville, however, it is principally used to designate the members of tribes other than the Bakongo who lived and worked in the city. And yet, however vague and arbitrary, the term Bangala gradually became identified with an embryonic nationality feeling among urbanized Africans of diverse tribal origins.

This phenomenon, sometimes referred to as "ethnogenesis by census redefinition," is not unique to the Congo. It is also found in Libreville (Gabon), for example, where Togolese and Dahoman immigrants have acquired over a period of years a new and artificial ethnic identity, expressed by the term "Popo." But in no other territory is there so great a proliferation of artificially—one might say "semantically"—created ethnic groups as in the Congo. Although by no means solely responsible, the official use of such terms as "Bangala," "Lulua," and "Kasaians" to refer to particular groups of tribes has undoubtedly contributed to the growth of a separate "ethnic" consciousness among the peoples concerned.

The tensions produced by tribal variations in the scale of urbanization are not the only factor that has inhibited political integration in the Congo. Geopolitical factors have also played an important part in limiting the scope and the speed of social change throughout the country. By 1955, of fourteen cities with a population of more than 20,000, six were located in the Katanga, three in Leopoldville Province, two in the Kasai, and one in each of the remaining provinces. This uneven distribution of Congolese cities largely reflects the circumstances that caused their growth. Some, like Leopoldville, Matadi, Stanleyville, and Luluabourg,

TABLE 5

POPULATION OF THE PRINCIPAL URBAN CENTERS OF THE CONGO, 1955

| Province and city | Resident African population | Percentage of total population of province |
|---|---|---|
| *Leopoldville Province* | | 14.5 |
| Leopoldville | 322,230 | |
| Boma | 28,724 | |
| Matadi | 69,945 | |
| *Equateur Province* | | 1.7 |
| Coquilhatville | 29,805 | |
| *Orientale Province* | | 2.5 |
| Stanleyville | 60,742 | |
| *Kivu Province* | | 1.5 |
| Bukavu | 30,584 | |
| *Katanga Province* | | 21.7 |
| Elisabethville | 131,184 | |
| Albertville | 26,198 | |
| Jadotville | 60,363 | |
| Kamina | 27,553 | |
| Kolwezi | 51,230 | |
| Manono | 28,021 | |
| *Kasai Province* | | 3.5 |
| Luluabourg | 47,049 | |
| Bakwanga | 24,253 | |

SOURCE: L. Baeck, "Léopoldville, Phénomène Urbain Africain," *Zaïre* (June, 1956), p. 615.

served as connecting links between inland waterways and railroads; others, like Elisabethville, Jadotville, and Kolwezi, owe their recent growth to the copper-mining industry of the Katanga. But most of the provincial capitals, the so-called *chefs lieux de province*, also served as administrative and commercial centers. Of these, Leopoldville, which is both the capital city and the chef lieu de province, and Elisabethville deserve special mention.

In 1946 Leopoldville and Elisabethville were the only two cities with a population of more than 40,000. But because of the increasing centralization of administrative services in the capital city, and because of its strategic location, Leopoldville underwent a much faster growth than Elisabethville. In 1935 the population of Leopoldville was 26,622, and that of Elisabethville was 22,858. Between 1935 and 1950, however, Leopoldville's rate of growth doubled in comparison with Elisabeth-ville's, and by 1958, with a total of 367,979, Leopoldville was the most densely populated city in the Congo. The degree of urban concentration in Leopoldville is shown by table 5; almost three-fourths of the urban population of the province lived in the capital city, while approximately two-thirds of the urban population of the Katanga were disseminated among five different cities.

Another element that distinguishes the population of Leopoldville from that of Elisabethville is its tribal diversity (see table 6). The comparatively large influx of immigrants from the Moyen-Congo and Bas-

TABLE 6

GEOGRAPHIC ORIGINS OF THE POPULATION
OF LEOPOLDVILLE, 1955

| Origin | | Total |
|---|---|---|
| Leopoldville Province | | 191,861 |
| Leopoldville District | 57,923 | |
| Moyen-Congo District | 38,904 | |
| Bas-Congo District | 51,762 | |
| Lac Leopold II District | 14,860 | |
| Kwilu District | 5,899 | |
| Kwango District | 22,513 | |
| Equateur Province | | 24,142 |
| Orientale Province | | 5,176 |
| Kivu Province | | 1,308 |
| Katanga Province | | 1,241 |
| Kasai Province | | 12,883 |
| Ruanda-Urundi | | 63 |
| Other territories | | 48,843 |

SOURCE: L. Baeck, "Léopoldville, Phénomène Urbain Africain," *Zaïre* (June, 1956), p. 628.

Congo districts accounts for the high degree of urbanization of the Bakongo. But one must also note the heavy proportion of immigrants from the other districts of the province, and from the other provinces. The contribution made by Equateur Province to the flow of immigrants, which emphasizes the role of the Congo River as a major line of communication between the capital and the hinterland, accounts for the presence of a sizable Bangala minority in Leopoldville. Finally, a substantial fraction of the population of the capital was made up of Africans who came from neighboring territories. A rather different pattern of urbanization is exemplified by Elisabethville, where 65 per cent of the population of the centre extra-coutumier originated in the Katanga, 35 per cent in the Kasai, and only 1 per cent in the other provinces.

The foregoing considerations partly explain why Leopoldville became the scene of the first manifestations of Congolese nationalism. The concentration of Africans of different origins in a single urban area created the fears and grievances that initially motivated nationalist activities. At this stage, however, the geographical dispersion of Congolese cities, and the limited expansion of facilities for transportation and communication between them, raised a serious obstacle to the development of a unified nationalist movement. In retrospect, it seems that the peripheral location of Leopoldville and Elisabethville, and the fact that they are diametrically situated in relation to each other, were potential handicaps in the organization of a territorial nationalist movement, and valuable assets in the hands of the Katangese separatists. But these factors alone do not explain the existence of tribal and sectional particularisms. Just as the strains produced by urban conditions often tended to reinforce these particularisms, the problems created by the commercialization of African labor also tended to aggravate latent hostilities among tribal groups.

### THE GROWTH OF A WAGE-LABOR FORCE

So long as compulsion remained the principal means of securing human labor, and payment in kind was the principal reward for such labor, one could hardly speak of a permanent wage-earning class. Actually, for many years after annexation, and for the vast majority of the Congolese population, "fiscal work" was the only form of wage employment. Individual earnings derived from compulsory communal labor were used to meet fiscal obligations, and few workers, therefore, depended on a money wage, or salary, for a living.

In subsequent years, however, the development of the mining industry of the Katanga, and the concomitant growth of large-scale expatriate enterprises, opened up a major field of wage employment. At the same time the improvement of facilities for transportation expanded trading activities and brought new industries and new opportunities. The result was a rapid increase of the commercialization of labor, a process that was further accelerated during World War II by the rising demand for strategic raw materials. Between 1942 and 1944 the production of rubber increased from 2,000 to 9,263 tons; the production of copper rose from 122,000 tons in 1939 to 165,500 in 1944, while the production of tin rose from 11,150 to 22,300 tons; and during the same years the total output of cadmium increased sevenfold, jumping from 3,086 to 21,544 kilograms.[18] As individuals moved into urban centers in ever-increasing numbers, dependence on a money economy was extended to new strata of the population. By 1955, 1,183,000 Congolese—or 9.4 per cent of the total population and 38.9 per cent of the adult able-bodied male population—were engaged in wage employment, which meant that approximately 69 per cent of the total money income of the native population went to salaried workers, the remaining 31 per cent going to independent agricultural producers, artisans, and entrepreneurs.[19] Although primarily concentrated in the more industrialized areas of the colony—Katanga and Leopoldville provinces—these new occupations brought a host of social and economic changes which finally spread into the rural areas.

It could be argued that the rapid proletarianization of labor, insofar as it tended to substitute new reference groups for traditional ones, favored the emergence of broader loyalties among the African population. Together with the economic grievances and psychological insecurities generated by the growth of a money economy, the increase in wage employment prepared the ground for the assertion of a national consciousness. It would be a mistake, however, to exaggerate the causal relationship between the two phenomena. In 1954, for example, as shown by table 7, the Congo ranked far above other African territories in total volume of employment, and only second to Northern Rhodesia in the degree of commercialization of African labor. And yet it remained one of the territories where the evidence of nationalist sentiment was almost totally lacking.

One factor that accounts for the lack of discernible correlation between the growth of wage employment and nationalist activity is the relative absence of associational freedom among Congolese workers. The Congo, although claiming the largest share of wage employment in the African continent, until recently was one of the territories where the number of unionized workers was the lowest. In 1954, for example, the number of Congolese workers affiliated with trade unions was less than 1 per cent of the estimated total labor force; in contrast, Nigeria's trade unions claimed about 47 per cent of the country's labor force.[20]

The weakness of the organized sector of Congolese labor, which appears all the more surprising when compared with the postwar growth of unionization in other African territories, has often been attributed to a fundamental inability on the part of Congolese workers to perceive the advantages of collective bargaining. The truth is that the argument over-looks entirely the crippling limitations imposed on Congolese workers

TABLE 7

COMMERCIALIZATION OF LABOR IN SELECTED AFRICAN TERRITORIES, 1952–1954

| Country | Year | Number in wage employment (in thousands) | Total population (in thousands) | Percentage of population engaged in wage labor |
|---|---|---|---|---|
| Kenya | 1953 | 453 | 5,644 | 8.0 |
| Tanganyika | 1954 | 439 | 8,084 | 5.4 |
| Nigeria | 1952 | 300 | 31,170 | 1.0 |
| Northern Rhodesia | 1954 | 265 | 2,010 | 13.2 |
| Uganda | 1954 | 225 | 5,365 | 4.2 |
| Ghana | 1952 | 216 | 4,478 | 4.8 |
| French West Africa | 1952 | 318 | 15,996 | 2.0 |
| Madagascar | 1952 | 195 | 4,150 | 4.7 |
| French Equatorial Africa | 1952 | 155 | 4,131 | 3.9 |
| Cameroons | 1952 | 112 | 2,854 | 3.8 |
| Algola | 1951 | 156 | 4,037 | 3.9 |
| Ruanda-Urundi | 1954 | 129 | 4,263 | 3.0 |
| Belgian Congo | 1954 | 1,146 | 12,317 | 9.3 |

SOURCE: F. Bézy, *Problèmes Structurels de l'Economie Congolaise* (Louvain: Institut de Recherches Economiques et Sociales, 1957), p. 102.

with regard to the formation and activities of trade unions. In theory, an ordinance of 1946 authorized the organization of *syndicats professionnels d'entreprise,* whose members were employees of the same enterprise, and *syndicats de profession,* whose membership was not limited to the em-ployees of the same enterprise. But they were both subject to important limitations concerning the workers' right to unionize and the unions' right to federate.[21] Moreover, the so-called *curatelle administrative* al-lowed the colonial authorities to keep a close check on the records and activities of unions. Thus, lacking the bare minimum of organizational freedom, the organized sector of the Congolese labor force never at-tracted a very wide following. This situation, unlike that in Ghana and Nigeria where trade-union agitation overflowed into nationalist activities in the late 1940's, and where the unions provided political leaders with an organizational weapon against the colonial administration, was the reason for the relatively minor role of Congolese unions in the struggle for independence.

Legal restrictions were not the only factor militating against the emergence of a vigorous, politicized labor movement. The policy of labor "stabilization" pursued by the Belgian government proved equally conducive to political quiescence. This policy, first initiated by the Union Minière in 1928, was based on the findings of the Commission Gouvernementale de la Main d'Oeuvre, a body of experts appointed in 1924 to report on whatever measures seemed appropriate to "provide European enterprises with the manpower they need without hampering the development of the native population, and at the same time favoring its moral, material, and physical development." [22] In response to the commission's proposals, the large companies adopted a series of measures designed to reduce the incidence of migrant labor. The most significant of these was to encourage long-term employment through a system of financial incentives based on the length of service; by 1952, as a result of this policy, 50.5 per cent of the workers employed by the Union Minière had had at least ten years of continuous service (table 8).[23] A further inducement

TABLE 8

LENGTH OF SERVICE AMONG THE WORKERS OF THE UMHK

| | Number of workers | | Per cent of total labor force | |
|---|---|---|---|---|
| *Length of service* | 1941 | 1952 | 1941 | 1952 |
| Less than 3 years | 6,992 | 6,045 | 46.3 | 31.2 |
| 4–9 years | 6,033 | 3,538 | 39.9 | 18.3 |
| 10–15 years | 1,265 | 6,220 | 8.4 | 32.1 |
| More than 15 years | 823 | 3,566 | 5.4 | 18.4 |
| Total | 15,113 | 19,369 | 100.0 | 100.0 |

SOURCE: F. Bézy, *Problèmes Structurels de l'Economie Congolaise* (Louvain: Institut de Recherches Economiques et Sociales, 1957), p. 135.

to long-term employment was to set wages at a level that would allow workers to support their families. Workers were also protected by an elaborate system of social security, including sickness allowances, old-age pensions, paid vacations, free medical care and hospitalization, and similar fringe benefits.[24] In the workers' camps of the Union Minière, adjacent to the urban areas but separately administered, the Bureau des Palabres was organized to settle whatever litigations might arise among the workers, and in several mining centers—Lubumbashi, Shinkolobwe, Le Marinel, Ruwe, Musoni—native committees (*conseils indigènes d'entreprise*) were set up to "present the workers' desiderata." At best, however, these committees served merely as "instruments of contact and information" for the management.[25] Obviously, the usefulness of this machinery as a safety valve for the settlement of grievances was limited; on the other hand, the policy of stabilization kept such grievances at a minimum. The system sought to insulate the workers from the unsettling influences of their urban environment, and combined the advantages of the welfare state with the virtues of benevolent paternalism to a degree seldom equaled in other parts of Africa.

Undoubtedly, the removal of these disabilities in the status of Congolese workers would have made it easier to organize a broadly based, militant labor movement. But a labor movement alone would not have solved the problem of political integration. The introduction of wage employment also released a host of tensions and divisions among the Congolese societies, which in many instances reflected the uneven spread of modernization.

The distribution of wage employment among the different provinces reveals important area differences in the degree of commercialization of Congolese labor. As table 9 indicates, in 1956 Leopoldville Province

TABLE 9

GEOGRAPHIC DISTRIBUTION OF CONGOLESE WAGE LABOR

| Province | 1947 | 1951 | 1956 |
|---|---|---|---|
| Leopoldville | 26.4 | 28.7 | 27.0 |
| Equateur | 10.1 | 10.6 | 11.4 |
| Orientale | 22.3 | 18.9 | 17.8 |
| Kivu | 16.0 | 17.5 | 18.8 |
| Katanga | 14.6 | 14.8 | 15.8 |
| Kasai | 10.6 | 9.5 | 9.2 |
| Total | 100.0 | 100.0 | 100.0 |

SOURCE: A. Doucy and P. Feldheim, *Travailleurs indigènes et productivité du travail au Congo Belge* (Bruxelles: Institut de Sociologie Solvay, 1958), p. 72.

claimed about 27 per cent of the total labor force of the country, while the joint contribution of Equateur and Kasai provinces was not more than 20.6 per cent. Furthermore, in contrast with Katanga and Leopoldville provinces, where industrial labor was especially abundant, in 1956 Kivu, Orientale, and Equateur provinces had the heaviest concentration of agricultural workers. The number of workers employed in agriculture made up approximately 50 per cent of the wage labor of the Equateur, but only 8.5 per cent of the wage labor of the Katanga (table 10). The fact that Leopoldville claimed the highest proportion of salaried workers and the largest share of clerical employment certainly speeded up the

TABLE 10

CHANGING PATTERNS OF EMPLOYMENT IN THE CONGO PROVINCES BETWEEN 1951 AND 1956

| Province | Year | Agriculture | | Mining | | Industry | | Commerce | | Transportation | | Construction | | Clerical | | Others | | Total | |
|---|---|---|---|---|---|---|---|---|---|---|---|---|---|---|---|---|---|---|---|
| | | Number | Per cent | Number | Per cent | Number | Per cent | Number | Per cent | Number | Per cent | Number | Per cent | Number | Per cent | Number | Per cent | Number | Per cent |
| Leopoldville | 1951 | 41,455 | 14.0 | 1,456 | 0.6 | 51,714 | 17.5 | 21,862 | 7.4 | 29,159 | 9.9 | 31,016 | 10.5 | 7,632 | 2.6 | 111,387 | 37.7 | 295,681 | 100 |
| | 1956 | 36,718 | 11.4 | 685 | 0.2 | 46,095 | 14.3 | 23,785 | 7.4 | 32,181 | 10.0 | 33,092 | 10.3 | 14,421 | 4.5 | 135,398 | 42.0 | 322,375 | 100 |
| Equateur | 1951 | 48,996 | 44.9 | — | — | 14,369 | 13.2 | 10,166 | 9.3 | 4,866 | 4.5 | 10,230 | 9.4 | 2,010 | 1.8 | 18,453 | 16.9 | 109,090 | 100 |
| | 1956 | 67,101 | 49.0 | — | — | 12,410 | 9.1 | 8,151 | 6.0 | 7,605 | 5.6 | 14,005 | 10.2 | 2,813 | 2.1 | 24,774 | 18.1 | 136,859 | 100 |
| Orientale | 1951 | 61,809 | 31.8 | 30,281 | 15.6 | 18,709 | 9.6 | 14,571 | 7.5 | 8,923 | 4.6 | 14,701 | 7.6 | 3,238 | 1.7 | 42,166 | 21.7 | 194,398 | 100 |
| | 1956 | 81,070 | 37.9 | 17,083 | 8.0 | 22,757 | 10.6 | 14,009 | 6.6 | 11,981 | 5.6 | 18,964 | 8.9 | 4,713 | 2.2 | 43,110 | 20.2 | 213,687 | 100 |
| Kivu | 1951 | 60,092 | 33.2 | 42,222 | 23.3 | 18,458 | 10.2 | 7,168 | 6.0 | 6,705 | 3.7 | 15,618 | 8.6 | 2,644 | 1.5 | 27,876 | 15.4 | 180,873 | 100 |
| | 1956 | 85,193 | 37.8 | 35,523 | 15.8 | 16,014 | 7.1 | 9,704 | 4.3 | 9,367 | 4.2 | 21,147 | 9.4 | 5,432 | 2.4 | 42,932 | 19.1 | 225,312 | 100 |
| Katanga | 1951 | 15,613 | 10.2 | 22,273 | 14.6 | 35,535 | 23.2 | 10,170 | 6.7 | 14,213 | 9.3 | 18,064 | 11.8 | 3,504 | 2.3 | 33,504 | 21.9 | 152,876 | 100 |
| | 1956 | 16,091 | 8.5 | 31,253 | 16.3 | 31,948 | 16.9 | 15,811 | 8.3 | 21,025 | 11.1 | 24,510 | 12.9 | 7,650 | 4.0 | 41,484 | 21.9 | 189,772 | 100 |
| Kasai | 1951 | 15,749 | 16.1 | 16,036 | 16.4 | 11,531 | 11.8 | 8,718 | 8.9 | 5,262 | 5.4 | 10,480 | 10.7 | 1,954 | 2.0 | 20,982 | 21.4 | 90,712 | 100 |
| | 1956 | 14,618 | 13.3 | 20,959 | 19.1 | 4,318 | 3.9 | 10,088 | 9.2 | 9,630 | 8.8 | 12,601 | 11.5 | 4,670 | 4.2 | 35,007 | 31.9 | 111,891 | 100 |

SOURCE: A. Doucy and P. Feldheim, *Travailleurs indigènes et productivité du travail au Congo Belge* (Bruxelles: Institut de Sociologie Solvay, 1958), p. 77.

political awakening of the province; on the other hand, the preponderance of agricultural workers in the Equateur partly accounted for the atmosphere of relative quiescence in its political life. These tentative generalizations, however, provide only superficial insight into subsequent political developments. In order to understand the persistence of sectional divisions among the African population, attention must be paid to regional disparities in economic development *within* the provinces.

A glance at the pattern of economic development in the Katanga will illustrate the point. A pivotal feature of the Katanga economy is the overwhelming concentration of industrial activities in the southern part of the province, particularly in the Lualaba and Haut-Katanga districts, where the three major mining centers of Elisabethville, Jadotville, and Kolwezi are located. This unevenness of industrial development, also reflected in regional differences in the distribution of social overhead capital—commercial centers, communications facilities, schools, hospitals, and so on—meant in effect that an important segment of the population of the northern region, the Baluba, had only limited exposure to the influence of Western economic forces.

Second, because of the paucity of Katangese labor resources and the demands of its industrial activities, the Union Minière recruited a substantial part of its labor force from the populations of Kasai Province. In 1956, for example, an estimated 53 per cent of the workers employed by this company at the Lubumbashi mine came from the Kasai.[26] The presence of alien elements whose language, customs, and traditions differed considerably from those of the resident tribes sharpened the consciousness of cultural differences. The Baluba of the Kasai, for example, who constitute the bulk of the workers employed by the Union Minière, although ethnically related to the Baluba of the Katanga, nevertheless form a distinct cultural group. Important cultural, linguistic, and historical factors have also marked them off from the Lunda, the Bayeke, the Tshokwe, and other tribes of the Haut-Katanga. In a real sense, therefore, both factors—the recruitment policy of the Union Minière and the geographical scope of its industrial activities—reinforced latent animosities among the tribes of the Katanga, that is, between northern and southern tribes on the one hand, and southern tribes and Kasaian immigrants on the other.

Another source of tension is the existence of regional differences in the scale of remunerations paid to a given category of workers. In Leopoldville Province, for example, the salaries paid to clerks in 1954 varied from 1,200 to 10,000 francs a month ($24–$200) in the Moyen-Congo District, and from 600 to 5,000 francs in the Bas-Congo District. In Stanleyville, on the other hand, the monthly wages paid to a clerk did not rise above 2,500 francs. Similarly, the daily minimum wages prescribed by the administration—the minimum cash wage together with the ration and housing allowance—fluctuated between 9.20 and 21.90 francs in Leopoldville Province, and between 5.80 and 9.30 in the Kivu.[27] These area differences were further aggravated by the wide gap in the level of wages paid to different categories of workers. In 1954, for example, a clerk in Leopoldville could earn as much as 10,000 francs a month, while an unskilled worker averaged between 680 and 875 francs. When coinciding with tribal divisions, income stratification had the effect of sharpening intergroup tensions. This phenomenon was especially consequential where two or more major ethnic groups were involved in economic competition, as in the Kasai, where the Lulua felt that they were directly threatened by the "acquisitiveness" of the Baluba, or in the Katanga, where the southern tribes took an increasingly dim view of the monopoly exercised by Kasaian immigrants over the clerical jobs available in the province. In these instances affiliation with a tribal party reflected not only the willingness of the individual to assert his cultural identity, but also his desire to retain, or acquire, certain economic privileges.

A third factor that helped to strengthen the attachment of Congolese workers to their respective cultures was the degree of homogeneity of the labor force employed by the large companies. Geographical contingencies and official pressure to limit the recruitment of labor to specific areas often forced expatriate enterprises to draw their workers from a single tribal stock. The Manono plant of the Compagnie Géologique et Minière des Ingénieurs et Industriels Belges (Géomines), located in the northern part of the Katanga, recruited the bulk of its labor from the Baluba populations, within a radius of a hundred kilometers. The workers and their families maintained close contacts with their villages and thus preserved a strong sense of identification with their traditional culture.[28] Similarly, the Baluba employed by the Société Internationale Forestière et Minière du Congo (Forminière) at the Tshikapa plant, in the southern districts of the Kasai, nevertheless continued to take an active part in the village life of their communities. These frequent contacts with the workers' rural homelands helped to minimize the corrosive impact of industrialization. On the other hand, where European enterprises recruited their workers from a tribally mixed population, the disintegrative effect of industrialization was more noticeable. The Leverville plant of the Huileries du Congo Belge (HCB), for example, which employed some 13,000 workers in 1954, recruited most of its labor from a variety of minor tribes of the Kwango area—Bambala, Bapende, Bayaka, Bapindi, Bayanzi, and so forth.[29] In spite of their frequent contacts with their native villages, the HCB workers have been overwhelmingly predisposed to support a panterritorial brand of nationalism.

It has also been suggested that the degree of permeability of certain tribes to the acculturative influences of an industrial environment depends on specific features of their social organization. For example, the degree of "social pressure" exerted on Congolese workers by the clan or the tribe is especially manifest among groups that are organized along matrilineal lines.[30] The attitude of the Bakongo, or of the Baluba Shankadi of the Katanga, both matrilineal, tends to support this view. But it fails to account for the persistence of lineage attachments among such patrilineal societies as the Baluba of the Kasai. Clearly, the mode of social organization of a given society is only one of the many variables that have affected the response of Congolese societies to the impact of commercialization. As has been observed in connection with the Mambwe of Northern Rhodesia, "Whether industrialism will cause a tribal society to cohere or to collapse depends on the interplay of a large number of factors: the internal system of organization and the solution of conflicts that arise within the tribe, the pressure of outside influences on these, the degree of participation in the industrial system, the political activities of the whites, etc." [31]

In evaluating the consequences of industrialization one must take into account not only whatever differences may be discerned in the size and structure of Congolese societies, but also regional discrepancies in the scale and rate of industrialization. Granting that the transition from an agricultural to an industrial society was a prerequisite to the rise of Congolese nationalism, one must also recognize that this process did not affect the attitudes and the interest of the African population in the same fashion throughout the Congo. In many instances "commercialization has either preserved or aggravated old divisions and tensions, or it has created new ones as a result of the unevenness of its incidence, in terms both of areal and class distribution of its material benefits and power potential." [32] Even to this day the conflicts of interests generated by the uneven spread of modernization continue to determine the patterns and the direction of Congolese political developments.

ECONOMIC GRIEVANCES

"African nationalism, like other nationalisms, is in part a revolt against an inferior economic status." Specifically, the fact that "the economic claims and interests of different sections of African societies may be divergent is of subordinate importance, so long as for all sections the colonial regime is regarded as the main obstacle in the way of economic advance." [33] Without attempting to underestimate the extent to which economic grievances have stimulated the growth of nationalist sentiment in the Congo, one must nevertheless recognize that there is no direct relationship between the two. Nor is it entirely correct to assume that the existence of divergent economic interests had only a marginal effect on the development of Congolese political groups.

The abuses perpetrated under the Free State by the intensive exploitation of human labor are sufficiently well known and need not be enlarged upon here. As sympathetic as he was to the cause of the Free State, Viscount Mountmorres admitted in 1906: "No words can convey an adequate impression of the callous and terrible inhumanity which marks the methods of the territorial companies, nor of the abject misery and hopelessness of the native population." [34] After the annexation genuine efforts were made to alleviate the plight of the African population, but the changes did not make themselves felt overnight. In September, 1909, the Conference of Protestant Missionaries, assembled at Stanley Pool, voiced a strong protest against "the continuance of the system of forced labor and taxation which still prevails in various forms throughout large areas of the Congo." [35] Even as late as 1922 an administrative report noted that "thousands of natives are still subject to the *corvées de portage.* . . . The Lulua district alone employs 13,000 carriers a year." [36] Yet these exactions did not lead to the organization of nationalist movements.

Undoubtedly, the ever-present threat of repression partly accounts for the apparent tranquillity of the Congolese population in the period preceding World War II. More important, perhaps, is that the Congolese lacked the psychological inducements and hopes by which nationalist movements are actuated. There is a fundamental truth in the remark that "misery does not automatically generate discontent," and that "people whose lives are barren and insecure seem to show a greater willingness to obey than people who are self-sufficient and self-confident." [37] It is quite true, of course, that the attitude of the Congolese during this period was not always characterized by a "willingness to obey." Despite the insecurity, fear, and suspicion pervading the life of the African, and long before the emergence of a self-sufficient and self-confident class of évolués, economic grievances gave rise to several movements of insurrection. It was not until the postwar years, however, that isolated grievances were translated into specific demands through the medium of voluntary associations, and, at a later stage, inserted into a political program. These demands—for higher wages and salaries for workers; for higher prices for agricultural producers; for more economic opportunities for the Congolese middle classes—all stemmed from the social and economic transformations that took place during and after World War II. This new claimant mood bore testimony to the increasing self-confidence of the évolué population.

The grievances generated by the prosecution of the war effort prepared the seedbed for the development of nationalist sentiment. The demands made upon the African population to increase the production of rubber and minerals, both of strategic importance for the Allies, involved tremendous sacrifices. The production quotas fixed by the governor general were frequently ignored by local officials, many of whom felt that the extortion of a maximum production from the African was the only way to secure victory for the Allies.[38] But for the Congolese worker, what really mattered was the nature and the scale of the exactions, not the motives behind them. Evoking the hardships imposed by "the tremendous war effort," Father Van Wing wrote in 1951: "Wages and prices of native produce were kept so low that only coercion enabled us to reach the end of the war without too much damage." [39] Nevertheless, the compulsory labor demanded for the collection of rubber by the Commission du Caoutchouc led to unrest in urban and rural areas.

It was in the urban areas, however, that the Congolese gave the first sign that they were aware of their collective strength. In 1941 a strike occurred among the workers of the Union Minière in Elisabethville which led to rioting and bloodshed.* Matadi became the scene of similar events in 1945, and in 1944 a mutiny broke out among the soldiers of the force publique in Luluabourg. Shortly after the mutiny, a "supplication" presented by the évolué population of Luluabourg to the governor general urged the administration to consider the following demands: "To be heard periodically by the governor general"; "to obtain decent housing conditions"; "to set aside a day of the week on which they could submit their grievances to a functionary"; to do something about "the effect of public insults." [40] In rural areas the substitution of economic *étatisme* for the "benevolent paternalism" of the prewar period—exemplified by the establishment of the Office des Approvisionnements and the Office de Production Agricole—also brought individual grievances into focus. Speaking before the Conseil de Gouvernement in November, 1943, Governor Ryckmans described the atmosphere of regimentation which prevailed during the war:

La guerre ... affecte la vie quotidienne jusque dans les coins les plus reculés de la brousse. Chaque homme est un mobilisé civil: dans les programmes de travaux et les programmes de production chacun a sa tâche à remplir. ...

---

* According to an official report, the shooting that took place at the Lubumbashi mine in Elisabethville on December 9, 1941, resulted in 45 deaths and 74 casualties. But according to the testimony of an eyewitness, G. Lievens, 95 people were killed and 150 were wounded. The circumstances that led to the shooting are obscure. It would seem, however, that it began when a mob of African strikers approached the provincial governor and his military escort, presumably to discuss their grievances. A Congolese soldier, suddenly panic-stricken, fired a shot into the crowd, whereupon the rest of the detachment started shooting point-blank at the strikers ("Rapport sur la grève des travailleurs de l'Union Minière," Département M.O.I., Union Minière du Haut-Katanga [mimeographed; Elisabethville, n.d.]; cf. G. Lievens, "Note historique sur le massacre de la Lubumbashi" [mimeographed]).

Le solde, c'est une créance sur l'avenir à la quelle la Belgique devra faire honneur.[41]

In the period immediately after the war the elimination of compulsory labor and governmental controls brought relief. On the other hand, the fluctuations in the value of the franc after 1939 led to serious difficulties; while prices of consumer goods steadily rose during the war, salaries and wages remained basically the same. As a result of this reduction in purchasing power, both rural and urban workers were economically worse off in 1946 than in 1939.

Meanwhile the expatriate firms had contributed, albeit unwittingly, to the development of a class of évolués who became increasingly anxious to make good their claims to "equal pay for equal work." Several pressure groups came into being and sought to articulate the demands of elements that shared common grievances. Most notable was the Association du Personnel Indigène de la Colonie (APIC), founded in 1946 by a group of clerks employed in the administration. Its spokesmen made it quite plain in 1957 that their immediate objective was the implementation of the so-called Statut Unique, which meant that Europeans and Congolese with equal qualifications should be granted equal wages and perquisites and equal opportunities for advancement.[42] Similar demands had been voiced a year before by the editorialist of *Conscience Africaine*. Why, he argued, should Congolese workers be subject to the "simpliste" and obsolete *contrat de travail* and the Europeans to the *contrat d'emploi*? Why should Europeans enjoy a paid vacation ten times as long as that allowed to the Congolese? Why should the minimum legal wages be frozen at a level contrary to all norms of social justice? [43] The official answer to these questions was that European expatriate personnel were more qualified and efficient than Congolese personnel, and that consequently they were entitled to higher wages and perquisites. The Congolese would inevitably reply that workers who came from distant provinces could just as legitimately be considered expatriate, and that their productivity was lower than that of European workers only because their salaries were lower.

Furthermore, by 1957 no one could reasonably contend that the system of job reservation applied in the Congo always excluded Europeans from jobs that Africans could do. An increasing number of Congolese medical assistants with a substantial technical background had to compete with European *agents sanitaires* and nurses who had only a few months of preliminary training. Whereas the former earned about 44,750 francs a year, the agents sanitaires and the nurses earned 125,000 and 156,000 francs, respectively.[44] Finally, when in 1957 it became known that the first Congolese to graduate from a metropolitan university earned 30 per cent less than a European employee with similar qualifications, the students of Lovanium issued a memorandum violently criticizing the government's wage policy.[45]

Simultaneously, economic and social unrest developed in the capital and culminated in the riots of January, 1959. Among the factors leading to the crisis, the local repercussions of the economic recession that began in 1957 and the wage policy of the Belgian government seem particularly significant. Partly because of the absence of adequate mechanisms to counteract the fluctuations in world prices, Belgian enterprises were hard hit by the recession. Between 1956 and 1958 profits were no longer reinvested in the Congo, but were transferred to Belgium; this policy drastically reduced the funds available for financing public works. During this period no adequate measures were taken to reduce the spread of unemployment. The situation was further aggravated by the increase in the minimum legal wages. Assuming that salary raises would not necessarily increase the individual output of the Congolese worker, a number of employers decided to cut down their personnel expenses and to increase the mechanization of their enterprises. The result was that in Leopoldville alone the number of unemployed workers rose from 5,321 in December, 1956, to 25,153 in January, 1959.[46]

The economic discontent of the unemployed masses of the capital was certainly an important element in the background of the January riots. The decisive factor, however, was that individual grievances were now couched in political terms by the Congolese leaders, who claimed that political control entailed economic exploitation, and inferentially, that political emancipation would bring economic gains. In other words, the Leopoldville riots signified that the "age of petitions" for the redress of specific grievances was drawing to a close, and that nothing short of independence would assuage the grievance of the nation.

A major source of discontent, which also provided an easy target for the attacks of Congolese nationalists, was the overwhelming concentration of capital in the hands of a few large-scale expatriate enterprises. Since the early days of Belgian rule, five important corporate groups had dominated the economy of the Congo: (1) the Baron Empain banking group, whose main subsidiary was the Compagnie des Chemins de Fer du Congo Supérieur aux Grands Lacs Africains; (2) the Société Commerciale et Minière (Cominière), a holding company founded in 1810 by the Nagelmaekers banking group and counting among its subsidiaries such important societies as the Société Forestière et Agricole du Mayombe (Agrifor), the Chemins de Fer Vicinaux du Congo (Vicicongo), and the Coloniale de l'Electricité (Colectric); (3) the Société de Bruxelles pour la Finance et l'Industrie (Brufina), which controlled through a special holding one of the Congo's two major tin producers (Symétain), one of its major cotton firms (Cotonco), and a colony-wide real estate company

(Crédit Foncier Africain); (4) Huilever, a Belgian subsidiary of the Anglo-Dutch owned Unilever, which controlled the growing, processing, and export of the Congo's vegetable oils; (5) the Société Générale de Belgique (SGB), founded in 1822 by William of Holland, and then known as the Société Générale des Pays-Bas pour Favoriser l'Industrie.[47]

This giant holding company, whose domain extended over industry, mining, and agriculture, illustrates the concentration of economic power in the Congo. Through its participation in a variety of colonial ventures, the SGB controlled approximately 70 per cent of the Congo economy.[48] Its oldest operating subsidiary, the Compagnie du Congo pour le Commerce et l'Industrie (CCCI), has been one of the most effective instruments for government-oligopoly collaboration since 1866. It had a share in almost every exported product through its participation in companies that raised palm oil, coffee, tea, cocoa, rubber, and cattle in five of the Congo's provinces. The SGB also controlled the sole diamond producer of the Congo, the Forminière, and had a substantial, though indirect, interest in Géomines, one of the two major tin producers. It also held important interests in the Compagnie du Chemin de Fer du Bas-Congo au Katanga (BCK), which owns the Port-Francqui–Elisabethville Railroad, as well as in its principal mining subsidiary, the Compagnie Minière du BCK. Last but not least, the SGB controlled through the Comité Spécial du Katanga the Congo's largest operating company, the UMHK. The scale of profits derived by the SGB and the UMHK from the sale of export products is plainly revealed by the data in table 11. In view of the foregoing, it is not surprising that the net profits and royalties of expatriate enterprises equaled the total budgetary expenditures for the colony in 1954.[49]

The Congolese middle classes, represented by the emergent class of entrepreneurs, merchants, middlemen, and artisans, were particularly resentful of the oligopolistic character of the Congolese economy. They felt, with some justification, that the intrusion of European enterprises in certain sectors of the economy denied them the opportunities to which they considered themselves entitled. In 1955, when the public transportation system in Leopoldville was entrusted to a Belgian company, Joseph Ileo denounced the "abuses" perpetrated against "other groups, and the Congolese middle classes in particular," by "Belgian monopolies."[50] Similarly, when a large European retail store decided to extend its business to the cité indigène, an editorialist, speaking on behalf of native interests, openly criticized the intrusion of "alien interests."[51]

The Congolese were equally resentful of the monopoly exercised by Belgian financial groups over banking operations. The issue of bank credit did not, however, arise until 1953, when it became legally possible for Africans to borrow money. Until then, according to the terms of a legislative ordinance of July, 1917, any person lending money to an African was subject to penal sanctions. A legislative amendment passed in August, 1941, authorized loans of 5,000 to 8,000 francs to agricultural coöperatives, extracustomary centers, and *circonscriptions indigènes*, although it

TABLE 11

THE CONGO'S MAJOR EXPORT PRODUCTS, 1958

| Commodity[a] | Tons | Value in millions of dollars | Percentage of world output |
|---|---|---|---|
| Uranium** | b | b | 50 |
| Copper** | 241,345 | 108 | 10 |
| Oil palm products* | 235,762 | 50.5 | 30 |
| Cotton* | 36,781 | 22.9 | 0.6 |
| Tin | 2,580 | 8.3 | 9 |
| Coffee* | 70,603 | 56.3 | 2 |
| Cobalt** | 9,701 | 22.5 | 75 |
| Industrial diamonds* | 15,097,207[c] | 36.6 | 70 |
| Gold | 12,564[d] | 11.6 | 1 |
| Diverse metals* | 441,197 | 35 | — |

[a] Asterisks indicate items produced, processed, or exported through the SGB. Double asterisks identify a major or monopoly role of its principal subsidiary, the UMHK. Diverse metals include manganese, tantalite, cassiterite, tungsten, zinc, etc.

[b] Figures unknown.

[c] Carats.

[d] Kilograms.

SOURCE: Compiled from *La Situation économique du Congo Belge et du Ruanda-Urundi en 1958* (Bruxelles, 1959), p. 197.

prohibited loans to individuals. After the decree of February, 1953, which allowed Africans, whether immatriculés or not, to become landowners in both extracustomary centers and rural areas, it became possible for Africans to obtain loans from European banks. The proceeds these banks received from their European clientele, however, were sufficiently high to prevent them from handling transactions that seemed to involve undue risks.[52] The Société de Crédit au Colonat et à l'Industrie, set up by a decree of July, 1953, did offer credit to Europeans and Congolese alike; but again the same conservatism seemed to prevail when the question of lending money to an African arose. Of 118 demands introduced in 1956, only 17 were taken into consideration. In short, for the vast majority of the Congolese credit facilities were practically nonexistent.[53]

African planters in rural areas were also affected by the squeeze of monopolistic practices. Among the 800,000 Congolese who were engaged in the cultivation of cotton in 1959, many had grown resentful of the monopoly of the Compagnie Cotonnière (Cotonco) over the purchase and marketing of cotton. Their resentment stemmed, to a large extent, from the arbitrary price levels fixed by the Comité de Gérance de la Caisse de Réserve (Cogerco), an institution set up in 1943 to play a role similar to that of marketing boards in British Africa.[54] Administrative reports of 1921 and 1923 revealed that the prices paid to African planters for their crops was the main source of discontent among the rural population,[55] and in 1932 it was estimated that the profits earned by cotton planters were lower than those of the most poorly paid workers in the same area.[56] Again, in 1947, the members of a senatorial commission unanimously declared that the prices paid to native planters were abnormally low.[57] Despite these official warnings, little was done in subsequent years to improve the lot of the rural Congolese; as late as 1959, in a voeu presented to the Conseil de Gouvernement, André Anekonzapa, the delegate from Equateur Province, called attention to the "bad policy" of the Cogerco, and expressed the wish to "have the price paid to the native planters brought up to a higher level." [58]

While these grievances certainly helped to sensitize the rural masses to the appeals of nationalism, they seem relatively innocuous compared with the feelings of intense bitterness arising from the land policy of the Belgian government. In terms of its impact upon the rural societies, perhaps no other feature of Belgian policy has had such far-reaching implications.

## THE LAND PROBLEM

The most deeply resented aspect of Belgian economic policy was the concession of property rights over "native lands" to private companies. This policy, inaugurated by a decree of July, 1885, rested on the assumption that vacant lands did not belong to anyone in particular, and that they could therefore be claimed as property of the state. In the official viewpoint of the Belgian government,

The defence (of the vacant land system) consists in the assertion that the land upon which this produce of commercial value grows (or may be made to grow by cultivation) is not, and has never been owned by the natives; that it is consequently "vacant" land, and as such is the property (together with its products) of the Belgian administration of the Congo, or, indeed, of the Belgian State itself as the Belgian government may think fit. The term "national domain" is thus interpreted not as connoting the patrimony of the aboriginal inhabitants held in trust for them by the Belgian government, but as the "national property" of Belgium.[59]

This legal fiction, which lay at the core of many bitter controversies among Belgian jurists, became in fact the source of the gravest misunderstandings between the administration and the African population. As one évolué queried, "If one denies the natives the right to dispose of their land, on what valid grounds may the state claim title to this property?" [60]

The concession policy pursued by the Belgian government was a carry-over from the system that prevailed under the Free State. The concession of large tracts of land to private enterprises was the method adopted by Leopold II to obtain the capital necessary to finance railway development. The construction of the Matadi–Stanley Pool Railway, for example, was made possible by the concession of an extensive area to the Compagnie du Chemin de Fer Matadi-Leopoldville; similarly, the prospection of the subsoil resources of the Katanga resulted from an agreement between the Congo Free State and the Compagnie du Katanga to grant freehold property to the Comité Spécial du Katanga in a third of the area brought under its jurisdiction.[61] By the time the Free State was annexed by Belgium the total area covered by the grant of freehold property approximated 67 million acres.[62] It is true that after 1908 some of these concessionnaires abandoned their monopoly rights, and that some of the freehold areas granted to them were substantially reduced. But these actions did not bring the concession system to an end; they merely created new conditions for the acquisition of land. Indeed, in the period following World War I and well after World War II, thousands of acres were conceded to missionary societies, private companies, and settlers.

In 1954, in response to a voeu introduced to the Conseil de Gouvernement, the administration carried out a survey of the total area conceded in each province. The survey disclosed that by 1957 only 1.64 per cent of the total area in the Congo had been conceded.[63] Although this percentage is admittedly low, the figure has no meaning so long as the areas conceded are not evaluated in terms of the total area of cultivable land in each province. Moreover, the areas controlled by the Comité Spécial du Katanga (CSK) and the Comité National du Kivu (CNK), two of the Congo's largest concessionnaires, were excluded from the areas surveyed.[64]

The CSK, set up in 1900 after a convention between the Free State and the Compagnie du Katanga, was given jurisdiction over some 112 million acres and freehold rights over some 35 million acres. In the words of one official publication, "le CSK a les droits les plus absolus de disposition des terres mises en indivision." [65] The only restriction to this broad sweep of power was embodied in Article 15 of the Colonial Charter which required that concessions of more than 10,000 hectares be submitted to the Belgian Chambers for approval. Despite this provision, by 1957 the CSK had alienated 3,289,690 acres of land in Kasai and Katanga provinces. The freehold rights of the CNK, created in 1928 to administer and exploit the vacant lands appropriated by the Compagnie des Chemins de Fer des Grands Lacs, covered 800,000 hectares in the Kivu area. But the exceptionally high population density of the area made the expropriation of African lands all the more difficult, and in 1933 the total area subject to the administration of the CNK was reduced to 400,000 hectares. Of these, about 150,000 had been conceded to settlers and private companies by 1957. Once carried to its logical conclusion, this system could have resulted in the establishment of native reserves, as in the Union of South Africa.[66]

The African reaction to the predatory concession system is exemplified by the following statement made in 1959 before the Conseil de Legislation by the Congolese delegate from the Kivu:

In our country, everyone knows that the land always belongs to the clan or to the tribe. If, at an earlier date, our chiefs have conceded our lands to [European] societies, it is only because of ignorance, and also because they did not understand the terms of the contracts. . . . It should not be surprising, therefore, that the local populations should have come to regard the annexations by the Comité National du Kivu and the Comité Spécial du Katanga as unbearable and revolting.[67]

Such criticisms, which explain the inclination of the population of the Kivu toward an agrarian socialist ideal, are corroborated by the report of the Commission for the Study of Land Problems: "Local enquiries allow us to affirm that the feelings of hatred which the natives harbor against the Comité National du Kivu are surpassed only by those they have against the Institut des Parcs Nationaux, and especially the Parc National Albert." [68] Undoubtedly, the alienation of some 2,022,000 acres to the Parc National Albert seriously aggravated the problems caused by the scarcity of cultivable land. In 1957 the Jomba area, in the vicinity of Lake Albert, was officially described as being "oversaturated"; each family head had only 1.90 hectares of land to raise his crops and cattle, a situation described as "catastrophic" and likely to produce "all the ferments of grave social and political troubles." [69] There is little question that the concession policy was nowhere more deeply resented than in the Kivu, but other provinces were not exempt from similar difficulties.

The land hunger created by the sale of African lands intensified the hostility of the rural population toward the administration. It also gave rise to tensions among the Africans themselves. In many instances the migration of rural inhabitants toward other areas led to the usurpation of property rights, thereby creating a host of latent animosities. The Congolese delegate to the Conseil de Législation declared in 1959 that the "acquisition of 'vacant' lands . . . lies at the root of all the debates, quarrels, and ancestral enmities among neighboring tribes." [70]

The conflicts between the Lulua and Baluba populations of the Kasai provide a tragic illustration of the tensions created by the expropriation of native lands. The origins of the feud lay in the continued allocation of land to Baluba immigrants in the vicinity of Luluabourg, in an area over which the Lulua held customary proprietary rights. At the beginning this policy caused little dissension, but the steady influx of Baluba into the Lulua district made land hunger more acute. Moreover, because vast areas had been conceded to European enterprises, the shortage of land was all the more unbearable; it was estimated in 1957 that the Elkasai and the Société d'Elevage et de Culture au Congo Belge (SEC), two subsidiaries of the Forminière, together owned 226,670 acres of land in the Lulua district, and that the Catholic mission of Kamidji owned some 52,000 acres.[71] The territorial expansion of the Baluba naturally aroused anti-Baluba feeling among the resident tribes. The Lulua became increasingly reluctant to abandon their prescriptive rights of occupation to the Baluba, who not only deprived them of their lands but refused to acknowledge the authority of their chiefs.[72] As the administration automatically ruled out the possibility of reinstating land that had already been alienated to European enterprises, the intrusion of Baluba peasants inevitably led to conflict and resistance. By 1959 the whole district was rife with animosities; under the circumstances very little was needed to ignite the smoldering tinder of tribal antagonisms.

The main conclusion to be drawn from this discussion is that the social and economic changes introduced by the development of a money economy, while providing the conditions necessary to the rise of nationalist sentiment, also created situations that led to fundamental divisions among, and within, the Congolese societies. Certain factors of disunity in some places tended to reinforce one another. In the Kasai, for example, the overflow of Baluba elements into the urban areas of the province, where they monopolized most of the clerical positions, significantly heightened intergroup tensions produced by the shortage of land; similarly, the enormous concentration of wealth within the boundaries of the Katanga, coupled with the discriminatory recruitment policy of the Union Minière, fostered conflict between the resident tribes and the Kasaian immigrants. In each instance the cumulative effects of economic forces raised serious obstacles to natural unification.

In the last analysis, what needs to be emphasized is that the social mobilization* fostered by the introduction of a money economy, the spread of urbanization, the growth of a salaried class, and the diversification of labor did not proceed at the same rate throughout the Congo.

---

* "Social mobilization" is the expression used by Karl W. Deutsch to describe the societal changes that lead to the birth of a nation. Among the basic uniformities involved in this process of national integration, Deutsch mentions "the shift from subsistence agriculture to exchange economies," "the growth of towns and the growth of social mobility within them," "the growth of basic communication grids," "the differential accumulation and concentration of capital skills . . . and the lift-pump effect on other areas and populations" (Karl W. Deutsch, "The Growth of Nations: Some Recurrent Patterns of Political and Social Integration," *World Politics*, no. 2 [Jan., 1953], 168–195).

When a set of conditions favorable to the emergence of an integrated community was created, only particular groups were affected. To put it another way, the social updraft resulting from new patterns of social and economic intercourse was restricted to specific nationality groups, with the result that the rate of social mobilization varied not only from region to region, but from one group to another. Certainly, the discontinuities arising from this situation have made it all the more difficult for the forces of nationalism to transcend ethnic and regional boundaries. It is well to bear in mind, however, that the circumstances conducive to the growth of an integrated community are not found exclusively in the economic realm. Just as important are the cultural transformations brought about by Western education and Christianity, the two major vehicles of social change in Africa.

# VI. THE INFLUENCE OF CHRISTIAN
# MISSIONS AND EDUCATION

The impact of missionary activities and the spread of Western education are among the factors that have most profoundly affected the traditional order in the Congo. Catholic missions were at the forefront of European intrusion in the Lower Congo, both chronologically and instrumentally. Similarly, in the nineteenth century Christian missionaries not only assisted professional explorers, but were themselves responsible for exploring extensive areas. The missionary endeavor, however, exerted its strongest influence on the growth of a national consciousness in the field of education: "The one aim of education which has had a continuous history from primitive times to the present has been to induct the young into the membership of the group, community, or nation." [1] In this respect the role of the missions was of critical importance.

Until 1954, when the Belgian government decided to support the organization of lay schools, education for the Congolese was entirely in the hands of missionaries: "Even on a continent where the association of education with religious mission is a commonplace, the reliance of the Congo on this type of educational organization is striking." [2] This relationship, officially justified on the assumption that the African is naturally inclined toward the supernatural, and therefore that the "teachings of the missionaries correspond to the mentality of the blacks," has profoundly influenced the form and content of Belgian education in the Congo.[3] A preliminary discussion of the role of Christian missions is indispensable to an understanding of the social and political consequences of the Belgian Congo educational system as it operated until 1954.

## The Social and Political Consequences of Evangelization

Unlike the first wave of evangelization, which was a pre-Reformation movement, the nineteenth-century missionary movement carried into the African continent the sectarian divisions engendered by the Reformation. Yet, despite the fact that the Berlin Act gave equal protection to all Christian orders, historical factors and Belgian national interest greatly favored the expansion of Catholic orders.

Leopold's concern over the danger of Protestant attacks on the Free State was the principal motive behind his efforts to attract Catholic mis-

122

sionaries to the Congo. As early as 1903 he sought to enlist the support of the Vatican against "les sectes non-conformistes qui essayent de mettre leur insuccès évangéliques sur le compte des crimes imaginaires du gouvernement et de ses agents." [4] After various attempts to gain the support of Catholic opinion in England and the United States, Leopold reached an agreement with the Vatican in 1906 which decisively strengthened the influence of the Belgian Catholic missions. According to the terms of this concordat, national missions were given perpetual grants of land and subsidies to help them carry on their educational, scientific, and religious activities.[5] But as "national" missions were those having their administrative headquarters in Belgium, the agreement automatically favored Catholic orders. Between 1891 and 1931 the total number of Catholic missionaries increased from 11 to 1,870, whereas the number of Protestant missionaries increased only from 79 to 740.[6] By 1954 there were 6,335 missionaries in the Congo, of whom 4,978 were Catholic. In the same year Catholic missions claimed 28.05 per cent of the total Congolese population among their baptized followers, while Protestant missions claimed only 5.72 per cent.[7]

Both Catholics and Protestants were determined to eradicate the "evil influence of heathen customs," and both were equally eager to win converts. Their zeal was abundantly, and sometimes persuasively, criticized by various pamphleteers at the turn of the century, and above all by E. D. Morel, the founder and chief spokesman of the Congo Reform Association: "It is from them [the missionaries] in the main," wrote Morel in 1909, "that has grown up the conviction . . . that nothing in the structure of African social life is worth preserving; that everything . . . is bad and corrupt, and must be pulled down—tribal systems, communal tenure, and marriage laws." [8] Although they share the responsibility for eliminating rituals and customs that formed the fabric of the traditional society, Catholic missionaries have been far more disruptive than Protestant missionaries in terms of the scope and depth of their activities.

Unlike the Protestants, who used a small number of African evangelists as intermediaries between the tribal society and the Church, the Catholics concentrated their efforts on the community as a whole.[9] The function assigned to the Protestant evangelists was to serve as the "nervous system through which we transmit our impulses to the great hosts in the villages, and through whom come to us the reactions of chiefs, officials, and people to the work, through whom come to us the reactions of Truth opposed to heathen custom and thought." [10] The Catholic approach, on the other hand, was to remove a group of prospective converts from their customary areas, and organize separate communities under the supervision of the mission. This system, initiated about 1895 by the Jesuit Father Van Hencxthoven in the Kwango vicariate, became identified with the *ferme-chapelle,* an institution that combined evangelistic, educational, and religious activities.[11] "The aim of the fermes-chapelles," said one Catholic missionary, "is to spread around us easily and rapidly the practical knowledge of our holy religion. They are established with the authorization of the native chiefs, in the vicinity of one or several villages. Each has one main shack [*chimbeck*] for the purpose of religious activities, near which we construct a dwelling for our young Christians. Thatched huts provide a shelter for the livestock we give them: chickens, hogs, goats, sheep, etc."[12] The evidence suggests, however, that the consent of the chiefs was frequently the result of bribery, and that all sorts of pressures, including physical violence, were used by the Catholic missions to expand their influence.[13] In December, 1911, the issue of the fermes-chapelles brought the government under violent attack from the leader of the opposition, Emile Vandervelde; among the several charges brought by the Socialist leader against the Jesuit fathers of the Kwango, the chief one was that "the majority of the children living on the fermes-chapelles [had] been stolen by the catechists of the missionaries, and were illegally detained."[14] As a result of the campaign led by the Belgian Socialists, the Catholic missionaries were instructed to abandon the ferme-chapelle system for a method more in keeping with the aims of Belgian policy. But the new system merely transferred Christian acculturative influences into the villages; it did not significantly attenuate their effect.

Second, Catholic missions were involved in a comparatively broader range of activities than Protestant ones: "While the Catholic missions have organized and pursued a variety of undertakings," wrote Father Vermeersch in 1909, "the Protestant missionaries are almost exclusively concerned with the schools. . . . They are not interested in crop cultivation, nor in the education of orphans."[15] "Manual work," he added, "and above all agricultural work, . . . [is] the most apt to fix the African population on the land."[16] Another reason for encouraging the development of agricultural work, and manual skills in general, was that the financial resources of the missions were not always sufficient to meet the operating costs of the stations; the agricultural produce raised by their dependents could provide an additional source of revenue. Reporting the impressions of a European observer, Emile Vandervelde gave the following assessment of the work done by the Jesuit missionaries: "Their aim is excellent, but their means are open to criticism. They keep at Kisantu, and also in the other stations, more children than they can feed with their own resources. They obtain their food by forcing the population of the neighboring villages to work for them. . . . On the whole, because of their zeal in hunting for children and collecting taxes in kind, . . . they end up being viewed unfavorably by the natives." [17]

Finally, the close working relationship established by the Church with the administration conferred upon Catholic missionaries a semi-official role that allowed them to extend their action far beyond the limits of evangelization.* They not only participated in the elaboration of colonial policy through their membership in the advisory organs of the colony, but in its execution as well. For example, they did not hesitate on some occasions to use their influence to remove Catholic converts from the authority of Protestant chiefs, either by dividing the chefferies into separate units, or simply by substituting the authority of a catechist for that of the chief. But the way in which these catechists used their prerogatives created numerous difficulties between the missions and the local officials, and in 1922 Governor Lippens severely criticized the missions for "imposing on the native chiefs the authority of catechists who, without any legal power, exert pressure upon them . . . [to] abduct children and adults against the protests of the chiefs and the parents in order to bring them to the mission, or [to] displace them, according to their own fancy or interest, without bothering about kinship ties or local customs." [18] Again in 1924 a Belgian publicist, Paul Coppens, reported that "their office is [for the catechists] nothing but a pretext for indulging in exactions, thefts, abuses, and excesses of all kinds," and that the territorial administrators were inevitably charged with anticlericalism whenever they denounced their actions to the mission.[19] More important than the immediate administrative implications were the social consequences, in particular the fact that the prestige and authority of the traditional chiefs were considerably diminished.

The impact of Christianity, however, should not be evaluated exclusively in terms of its negative aspects, though these undoubtedly form an important element in the psychological makeup of Congolese nationalists. Indeed, Christianity not only shattered the traditional society, but also endeavored to create a new one, and a better one. In so doing it provided the Congolese with a means of rehabilitation and reintegration through corporate membership in the Church.

One of the most important contributions toward this social and religious transformation was the creation of an African clergy. In 1917 there was only one African ordained priest, but by 1954 the number had grown to 349, and by 1959 to more than 600.[20] About the same time

---

* In the Katanga, where Monsignor de Hemptinne once enjoyed a position of virtual omnipotence, this relationship caused a European functionary to quip: "Il y a quatre puissances au Katanga—le gouvernement, le Comité Spécial, l'Union Minière et Monseigneur de Hemptinne—et les trois premières ne sauraient réussir sans la quatrième."

the Protestant missions claimed more than 500 African pastors. This policy, which stemmed from the belief that "native Christian leaders must be encouraged to assume responsibility . . . and must progressively be expected to make decisions and to direct policy," [21] gave the Congolese an opportunity to share a common ideal, and hence a broader set of loyalties.

This process of reintegration occurred within the framework and under the guidance of different religious communities, each having its own set of principles and values, and "each passing on to the African a strange caricature of the other's faith and practice." [22] True, religious differences did not lead to such fundamental political cleavages as some observers once believed, though they may have aggravated existing tensions. But they certainly caused serious friction between Catholic and Protestant missionaries, and this friction had important repercussions on the attitude of the Congolese toward Christianity in general.

A standard argument leveled against the Protestants by the Catholic missionaries was that they "denationalized" the African and brought divisions into the country. "In his simplicity," one Catholic missionary states, ". . . [the African] believes that religious differences can be reduced to a dispute among the whites and that Catholicism is the religion of the 'little Belgians,' while Protestantism is that of powerful nations like England and the United States." [23] There was also a strong suspicion that the Protestant missions were directly responsible for the emergence of nativistic sects.[24] According to Monsignor de Hemptinne, apostolic vicar of the Katanga, the Protestant societies were consciously attempting to hasten the political emancipation of the Congolese, through outside intervention if necessary. At the General Conference of Protestant Missionaries, held in 1929 in Leopoldville, he expressed the conviction, in what is probably the most virulent diatribe ever written by a Catholic clergyman against the Protestant Church, that the program adopted by the conference constituted an implicit recognition of the "Wilsonian principle of self-determination," and hence would surely prepare the ground for the intervention of the League of Nations in the affairs of the Congo.[25] The Protestants, on the other hand, denounced the collusion of the Catholic Church with the administration, a collusion that resulted in discriminatory efforts against their work: "Bribery and intimidation have been used, as well as lies and calumnies. Priests have lavished gifts upon the chiefs and notables whose favor they wished to procure, and on the children whom they wish to enroll in their schools. . . . Sometimes threats and blows are employed to prevent Africans from attending Protestant services and schools." [26] To the African, the conflict between Protestant and Catholic missions seemed singularly inconsistent with the "unity of all men in Christ," which they were told was one of

Christianity's fundamental ethical principles. It therefore led to religious indifference and disaffection among a great many Congolese communicants and seminarists who, once estranged from the Church, became more vulnerable to the appeals of nationalism. Whether viewed in a tribal or a territorial perspective, nationalism as an ideal seemed less remote and, in their eyes at least, more worthwhile than Christianity.

Evangelization was not only conducted along different religious lines but through the medium of different vernaculars, thereby accentuating cultural differences among the Congolese. In fact, the most significant contribution of the Christian missionaries to the growth of ethnic nationalisms was their maintenance of the vernacular languages through the development of a system of orthography, the publication of dictionaries, and the translation of biblical texts. The growing body of religious and secular literature produced by the Christian missions provided the means through which the African retained or recaptured the cultural identity of his tribe, and which enabled him at a later stage to give it a political meaning.

The pioneering work accomplished by the missionaries in the field of linguistics is illustrated by the following survey. In 1887 the Baptist missionary W. H. Bentley published his *Dictionary and Grammar of the Kongo Language, as Spoken at San Salvador*; it was supplemented in 1910 by A. Seydel and E. Struyf's Kikongo phrase book, *La Langue congolaise*. Father Cambier's *Essai sur la langue congolaise* (Bruxelles, 1891) offered the first systematic study of the Iboko dialect, and in 1920, long before the publication of Father Hulstaert's monumental *Dictionnaire Lomongo-Français* (2 vols.; Tervueren, 1957), E. A. and L. Ruskin compiled the *Dictionary of the Lomongo Language*. In 1903 W. H. Stapleton of the Baptist Missionary Society wrote his *Suggestions for a Grammar of Bangala, the Lingua Franca of the Upper Congo* with a view to standardizing the various language groups of Equateur Province. Similarly, J. and L. F. Whitehead's *Manuel de Kingwana* (1928) provided one of the earliest standardized versions of the Swahili spoken in the eastern region. The Kasai dialects were investigated by Father Vandermeiren in *Grammaire de la langue Bena Lulua* (Bruxelles, 1877); by Father Gabriel in *Vocabulaire Kanioka Français* (Vanves, 1901) and *Grammaire de la langue Kiluba-Hemba* (Bruxelles, 1912); and, at a later date, by A. de Clercq in *Langue Lebeo: Grammaire et vocabulaire* (Bruxelles, 1924). To this brief list must be added a voluminous body of religious literature—catechisms, prayer books, Bibles—which also aided the diffusion of the vernacular.

It is quite true, of course, that these efforts sometimes helped to develop a lingua franca which then became the vehicular language of a particular area. For example, the books and periodicals published in

Lingala under the auspices of the missions, and the efforts made by the Bible Society to unify this language, facilitated communication among the tribes of the Equateur.[27] Elsewhere the missions introduced the use of a single vernacular among different tribes, thereby giving it the standing of a lingua franca, as in the Kasai where Tshiluba is now spoken by many other tribes besides the Baluba.

On the other hand, the highly empirical manner in which the missionaries approached the study of African dialects, and the absence of concerted efforts among the various congregations, sometimes contributed to the accentuation of certain variations within the same linguistic group. In his article, "Kikongo Language Situation," the Reverend George W. Carpenter stated:

Each [missionary] learned the local dialect and wrote it down as he heard it. This work was fundamental, but it had limitations. It reproduced very colloquial forms of language, full of localisms and aberrations. The tremendous amount of local variation between village and village could hardly be appreciated by the earliest workers, each of whom assumed what he had learned to be more or less a norm of the language as a whole. Moreover, each heard in his own way, according to the vocalics of his own mother tongue, and so even a single original word might presently blossom out in two or more different orthographies. . . . Each important mission station thus became a kind of bridgehead from which the exploration of the language phenomena could be carried out and its literary development begun.[28]

Describing the linguistic diversification of the Lower Congo, the same author reported that

There are at least four written forms of Kikongo that are vigorously propagating themselves with more or less official standing, and still a larger number of variant forms in which more or less literature has been and is being produced. Two of the major varieties are those sponsored by the Roman Catholic Missions, as illustrated by the publications of Tumba and Kisantu respectively. The other two are those based on the work of Dr. Bentley of the BMS, and Dr. Karl Laman, of the SMF.[29]

According to Father Hulstaert, a somewhat similar situation prevailed in Equateur Province, where the dialects spoken in the Coquilhatville area differed markedly, both in phonetics and in vocabulary, from those spoken in the Basankusu or Lulonga areas, in spite of the fact that these dialects were the vehicle of thought of the same ethnic group, the Mongo. Evoking the possibility of a linguistic unification, Father Hulstaert noted that a major obstacle was the "individualism of the different missions," and their tendency to ignore the identity of the tribes located outside their jurisdiction: "Each mission clings to its own ideas, without taking into account the particular [tribal] interests at stake." [30]

Broadly speaking, it may be said that the perpetuation of linguistic differences through the literary work of the missionaries tended to encourage cultural divisions. But where these differences, whether natural or artificial, cut across otherwise tribally homogeneous communities, it has at times stimulated an opposite reaction among the members of the groups in question. The efforts of the Bakongo to seek unity through the unification of the Kikongo language is a case in point.

In this connection, it is interesting to note that in 1935 an *ad hoc* commission had been set up on the initiative of Father Van Wing, after consultation with the apostolic vicars of Boma, Matadi, Kisantu, and Leopoldville, for the purpose of unifying the Kikongo language. This commission, the only one of its kind ever established in the Congo, set out to adopt a common system of orthography for each of the three dialects then in existence, and to standardize the vocabulary used in each of the vicariates.[31] Because of technical difficulties, however, the commission never completed its work. But it provided the initial stimulus which some fourteen years later led to the organization of the Association of the Bakongo for the Unification, Preservation, and Expansion of the Kikongo Language, better known as the Abako.*

The parochial outlook of the religious congregations, and the way in which they set about the task of recording African dialects, were not the only factors that operated to preserve the vernacular, or what seemed to be the vernacular. Equally important was the tendency of certain members of the Flemish clergy to project their own experiences, as members of a linguistic and cultural minority, against those of the tribes with which they came into contact. They naturally identified the significance of the vernacular with the cultural values they attached to the use of Flemish in their homeland, and thus displayed a special sympathy for what they called the "cultural language" (*cultuurtaal*). "The cultural language," stated Father Van Bulck, "must be a means of cultural development for the natives. . . . A cultural language cannot be based on an artificial language, or on a mixed language, but on a common language based on the mother tongue. . . . A good vehicular language will never serve the purpose of a cultural language." "The Negro," he added, "is not a *tabula rasa;* he has his own culture which must be preserved." [32]

---

* In the course of an interview Father Van Wing told me that the founder of the Abako, Edmond Nzeza-Nlandu, arrived at the *petit séminaire* of Lemfu, near Kisantu, the year that the commission was set up. Although Nzeza-Nlandu was initially partial to the French language (Father Van Wing described him as a "Fransquillon") he subsequently developed a genuine interest in the Kikongo language, partly as a result of his contacts with the Bakongo seminarists who participated in the work of the commission, in particular the late Abbé Jean Loya, Pierre Mpase, and Henri Matota. All three were ardent supporters of the Abako, and Matota's work, *Ntuka Kongo* (Leopoldville, 1960), was clearly written to widen the appeal of the Abako among the Bakongo population.

This somewhat ethnocentric attitude regarding the utility of a "cultural language" explains why some Flemish missionaries have developed an active interest, not only in the language of certain tribes, but in their traditions, customs, and history, as shown by the writings of Father Van Wing on the Bakongo, Fathers Boelaert and Hulstaert on the Mongo, and Fathers Vandermeiren and Verhulpen on the Baluba.[33] As much as other publications in the vernacular, these works decisively aided the cultural and political awakening of the groups concerned. The literary contributions of Father Van Wing, as he once admitted, were intended to give the Bakongo "a certain sense of national unity, a pride in their culture." [34]

The foregoing observations suggest that the impact of Christianity has tended to preserve tribal loyalties among the Congolese. But one must also bear in mind that the several functions performed by the missionaries conditioned nationalist developments in different, and sometimes contradictory, ways. Equally significant are the variables pertaining to the social and political systems of the Congolese populations, insofar as they facilitated or hampered adaptability to the impact of Christianity. Likewise, the extent to which missionary activities stimulated grievances on the part of Congolese nationalists raises further questions concerning the cultural predispositions of the groups concerned, the methods of evangelization adopted by the congregations, and the official position of the Church at any given time.

Among the more Islamized segments of the Congolese population, for example, Christianity has become the object of a deep and lasting resentment, illustrated by the universal hostility that to this day characterizes the attitude of the Bakusu toward the White Fathers. The missionaries helped to destroy a religion that was officially regarded as a subversive movement—even to the point of identifying the Koran as a source of "communist propaganda" [35]—and regarded Islam as a scourge on the face of Africa. And because it inspired "a more elevated and efficient fear than human justice," only Catholicism, according to Monsignor Roelens, could eradicate "the hateful practices authorized by the Islamic religion." [36] Yet it is doubtful that the zeal of the Catholic missionaries could have evoked such hostility unless Islam had already won the spiritual allegiance of the Africans, either because it provided moral or psychological compensation for the attenuation of tribal sanctions, or simply because its dogmatic content was judged by the Africans to be more satisfying than that of Catholicism. In any event, the uncompromising attitude of the missionaries regarding Islamic practices and beliefs, and the fact that they could count on the backing of the administration, were reasons for the appeal and success of nationalism in such predominantly Islamized areas as the Maniema district in the Kivu and the territoires of Stanleyville, Ponthierville, and Bunia in Orientale Province.[37]

The evidence available is far too scanty to permit a final judgment on the methods of evangelization adopted by certain congregations, and the way in which they influenced the attitude of Congolese nationalists. Only in the instance of the Jesuit fathers of the Kwango vicariate, whose practices are on record, is it possible to suggest a relationship between the ferme-chapelle system and the distinctively anticlerical orientation of the tribes of the Kwango-Kwilu area. Even then one would have to take into account a host of other factors which cannot be fully explored here.

One of these is the official position of the Church at any given time. A turning point in the policy of the Church was the bishops' declaration of June, 1956, recognizing the right of the Congolese to control their political destinies. "All the inhabitants of a country," the declaration stated, "have the duty to collaborate actively for the common good. They have therefore the right to take part in the conduct of public affairs." [38] This sudden change of attitude, though possibly motivated by opportunism, indicated a positive commitment to the cause of Congolese nationalism and was of crucial significance. For the first time in the history of Belgian colonization, the Catholic Church did not hesitate publicly to dissociate itself from the official policy of the Belgian government.

But this measure was not enough to assuage the grievances of Congolese nationalists, and even after 1956 there was a lingering suspicion that the Church continued to lend its support to the administration in order to perpetuate the status quo. In the eyes of some nationalists the real aim of the Church was not to "civilize" but to "colonize," not to spread the gospel for the sake of Christianity but to "evangelize [the Congolese] down to the marrow of their bones so as to ensure their docility." [39] There is some evidence, however, that the missionaries on certain occasions took up the defense of African interests against the policy of the administration. Because such intervention, carried on behind the scenes, was probably unknown to the Congolese masses, their attitude seemed to be one of tacit approval of all governmental policies.

Among the specific charges directed against the Church, one of the most prominent concerned its failure to fulfill its educational tasks. By many thoughtful Congolese the Catholic clergy was held responsible for withholding opportunities for higher education from the Congolese, in a deliberate effort to obstruct their political advance.[40] Another was that its professed dedication to Christian virtues seemed hardly compatible with its actual behavior. As one nationalist newspaper editorialized, "Les Jésuites prêchent la pureté; la chasteté est un voeu pour eux, mais la réalité déçoit. ... Les Jésuites prêchent la justice, mais la Compagnie de Jésus est remplie de gens au coeur de pierre, de jaloux, de calomnieux et de méchants." [41] For the harshness and the sweeping character of these charges there is in fact little justification. But there is enough evidence to show that the attitude adopted by certain members of the Catholic clergy was not always in harmony with the acknowledged principles of the Church. For example, the statement made by Monsignor de Hemptinne before the Comité Régional du Katanga in 1926 conveys sentiments that are quite remote from the spirit of Christian charity expected of a clergyman. Commenting on the advisability of corporal punishment for Africans, the prelate stated: "Je me rallie entièrement à la suggestion faite par Monsieur le Président que seule la punition du fouet était d'une efficacité certaine pour réprimer les infractions commises par les noirs, par exemple en matière d'indiscipline ou d'irrégularité au travail. Cette mesure est nécessaire pour le bien même du noir."

The Congolese also entertained a suspicion that the attitude of the Church was not exempt from racial prejudice, insofar as it claimed that moral improvement, and indeed salvation, necessarily required the abolition of "pagan customs," the "extirpation of prejudices and superstitions." [42] This assumption found expression in a condescending and holier-than-thou attitude toward the Congolese, "these poor savages just emerging from barbarism, and clinched to error and vice, so to speak, by a secular atavism." [43] Racial discrimination was also apparent in the organization of the missions, which tended to give the African priests an inferior position in the daily activities of the *chrétientés*.[44] These evidences of a feeling of superiority stung the pride of the African and stimulated protest against the "cultural imperialism" of the Church.[45] The Congolese wanted to replace a European importation by a church of their own, a desire that led to the organization of messianic and nativistic movements like Kimbanguism, Kitawala, and many others.

The positive achievements of the Church were just as important as its shortcomings in stimulating the political consciousness of the Congolese. The most consequential of these was the early and massive Africanization of the clergy, as it encouraged demands for similar measures in governmental and administrative spheres. One nationalist, for example, after paying a vibrant homage to the Church for playing a vanguard role in the "Africanisation des cadres," and for "understanding that this country belongs to the Congolese and must be directed by the Congolese," contrasted this policy with that of the administration: "Bravo Eglise! Tu as formé des prêtres au même titre que tous les prêtres du monde ... mais où sont nos Administrateurs Territoriaux, nos Gouverneurs de Province, nos ingénieurs, nos médecins?" [46]

The formation of an indigenous church offered a means of access to positions of responsibility which served to alleviate individual frustrations. And because it helped to deflect the hopes and aspirations of the

Congolese from the path of nationalist activity to the path of Christianity, it could be argued that the Church, in a sense, encouraged the maintenance of the status quo. But only up to a point, for once nationalism had reached the "take-off" stage, many Congolese priests gave their support to the movement for political emancipation. Until then, however, it was from the former seminarists, from the renegades and backsliders, that Congolese nationalism received its main impetus. ". . . lacking Christianity as a focus for their interests and loyalty," as Professor Coleman points out, "[they] were adrift and ripe for an integrating ideology." [47] Another predispositional factor lies in the character of the educational system introduced by Belgium.

THE CHARACTER AND CONSEQUENCES OF THE EDUCATIONAL SYSTEM

As a means for communicating ideas and feelings across the language barriers inherent in the traditional society, and as a tool that could be used to challenge the legitimacy of colonial rule, education played its part in the development of Congolese nationalism, but to a much more limited extent than it did in other parts of Africa. Unlike their counterparts in French and British Tropical Africa, the Congolese leaders who displayed the strongest commitment to nationalist ideas had relatively little formal education. Except for Justin Bomboko, not a single one had had the opportunity to acquire a university education, and only a few had completed secondary school. Yet on the eve of independence the Congo claimed a higher rate of literacy than any other territory on the African continent.

This rather unique situation must be attributed to the assumption underlying Belgian educational policy that vocational training, limited to a few technical skills, would best serve the ends of paternalism. As Lord Hailey pertinently observed, "Belgian policy may be said to assign a different cultural future from that which is envisaged by the French, for it looks less to his association with European civilization than to his fuller development within the range of his own economic and social environment." [48] In the minds of Belgian officials this philosophy was fully consonant with the broad objectives of Belgian policy. The late Governor Ryckmans conceded that

No doubt such a policy would not be justified in an independent country like Libya, or in one that has been promised independence within a very brief lapse of time, like Italian Somaliland. In such countries one must somehow train the cadres of the native society. If we have no black doctors, veterinarians, engineers, it is because we can send white doctors, veterinarians, and engineers.[49]

This policy was largely responsible for the relative quiescence that characterized the Congolese political scene until 1956. But, while tending to lessen the pressure of nationalist sentiment, it did not prevent its emergence. At this stage, however, the lack of opportunities for higher education imposed serious limitations on the goals and aspirations of the new elite.

The broad principles governing the Belgian educational system in the Congo were formulated for the first time in 1924, on the recommendations of a special commission appointed by Minister Franck in 1922, which included representatives from the government and the missions.[50] In its final report, based on the findings of a "mission d'études" sponsored by the Phelps-Stokes Fund,[51] the commission urged, among other measures, (1) the adaptation of education to "the natives' environment," (2) the development of a "new moral discipline . . . to prepare the natives to furnish the continued effort that is essential to the progress of civilization," (3) the use of "the native language" as the only medium of instruction, and (4) "the collaboration of the religious missions." [52]

In brief, the consensus was that education for the Congolese should be patterned along the lines advocated by the American Negro leader, Booker T. Washington, who favored a strong emphasis on agricultural and vocational training, and its extension to the masses. The same opinion was held by the Permanent Committee of the National Colonial Congress, which cautioned the government against the danger of a "bookish" education, and insisted on the advantage of "sustained and efficient work." [53] This principle, "on which were founded the great American schools for the blacks, thanks to the patient and clear-sighted efforts of such great philanthropists as Armstrong and Booker T. Washington," [54] formed the keystone of the program adopted by the Belgian government in 1924.

The system introduced in 1924 included a two-year primary course (*écoles primaires du premier degré*), followed by a three-year higher primary course with strong emphasis on vocational training. After completion of this second cycle, the most promising students—about 1 per cent of the primary school population—were directed to the so-called *écoles spéciales pour la formation de l'élite*. These schools were classified as (1) normal schools, also known as *écoles de moniteurs*, where future schoolteachers were inculcated with "a love of work, the habit of continuous effort, . . . and respect for the authorities"; (2) commercial schools for the training of clerks, accountants, typists, and so forth; and (3) vocational schools for the training of carpenters, metalworkers, printers, and the like.[55] These schools, though frequently referred to as secondary schools, were largely vocational. In fact, the only institutions dispensing more than the mere rudiments of a literary education were the *petits* and *grands séminaires* established by the Catholic Church for the training of the African clergy, and the school for medical assistants at Leopoldville. By 1938 the grands séminaires of Beaudoinville, Lulua-bourg, Mayidi, and Kabwe, where "the highest degree of intellectual culture . . . [could] be attained by a native," were attended by 135 Congolese priests.[56]

Aside from a few minor alterations introduced in 1929 in the curriculum of the higher primary cycle,[57] the system remained virtually unchanged until 1948, when the government decided to organize a program of secondary education for qualified students. Its aims were (1) to ensure a "good general training which will permit the students to gain desired employment," and (2) to prepare selected students for university training, an objective which was itself said to be subordinate to "the presence of an elite from which it will be possible to choose those who are not only intellectually but morally fit to receive and benefit by superior training." [58] In line with these stated objectives, secondary education was divided into "general secondary schools," to prepare the students for higher education, and "special secondary schools," with a strong vocational bias. The former, like the Belgian schools, were patterned along two different lines: "secondaire latine," with emphasis on liberal arts, and "secondaire moderne scientifique," with emphasis on mathematics and sciences. Yet, as the record indicates, very few students made their way to secondary schools. In 1958–59, for example, only one primary school student out of eighty-three attended a secondary school, one of the lowest ratios in Africa, after Kenya and Tanganyika.[59] Accordingly only a small number of students were admitted to institutions of higher learning when they were finally established.

In 1947, as a first step toward the organization of higher education, the Catholic University of Louvain created at Kisantu, near Leopoldville, the Centre Universitaire Congolais Lovanium, an institution that coördinated the medical and agronomical training offered by the Fondation Médicale de l'Université de Louvain au Congo (Fomulac) and the Centre Agronomique de l'Université de Louvain au Congo (Cadulac), founded respectively in 1923 and 1925, with a four-year course in "commercial and administrative sciences." At the time, however, the idea of university education for the Congolese was still "out of the question"; what was envisaged was "a progressive elevation of vocational schooling to the university level," and only after "a series of carefully studied stages." [60] The penultimate stage began in January, 1954, when the Centre Universitaire Congolais Lovanium, now established at Kimuenza, organized a two-year preuniversity course for students who had successfully completed their secondary schooling, provided that they could show a "certificate of good behavior delivered by the apostolic vicar, the director of the secondary school, or the civil authorities." [61] According to the review *Lovania*, published under the auspices of the University of Louvain, of thirty-one students enrolled for preuniversity courses in 1954, seventeen "became discouraged" and five flunked their examination, which meant that less than one-third of the student body "made the grade." [62]

The two-year preuniversity course was eventually reduced to one year, and in October, 1954, Lovanium University inaugurated its first academic session. Courses of study were offered in four fields of specialization—medicine, agriculture, pedagogy, and "social and administrative sciences." Although Governor General Pétillon had consistently opposed the introduction of a liberal arts program on the grounds that it would "turn the heads of the Congolese," a faculty of "philosophy and letters" was created in the fall of 1956 in order to set up preparatory courses in law.[63] But it was not until the fall of 1958 that a faculty of law was formally organized. Of the eleven Congolese who graduated from Lovanium in 1958, not a single one had had the opportunity to acquire a legal training.

In response to the initiative taken by the University of Louvain, and under the pressure of metropolitan circles identified with the nonconfessional Université Libre de Bruxelles, an official university was established at Elisabethville in 1956. The curriculum, like that of Lovanium, included courses in philosophy and letters, natural and medical sciences, and pedagogy. But in contrast with Lovanium, the majority of the students enrolled at the University of Elisabethville were European (table 12).

TABLE 12

NUMBER OF STUDENTS ENROLLED IN CONGOLESE UNIVERSITIES, 1954–1959

| | *University of Lovanium* | | *University of Elisabethville* | |
|---|---|---|---|---|
| *Year* | Africans | Europeans | Africans | Europeans |
| 1954 | 30 | 3 | 0 | 0 |
| 1955 | 77 | 10 | 0 | 0 |
| 1956 | 122 | 47 | 8 | 86 |
| 1957 | 177 | 72 | 17 | 107 |
| 1958 | 248 | 117 | 44 | 155 |
| 1959 | 344 | 136 | 77 | 199 |

SOURCE: Albert Pevée, *Place aux Noirs* (Bruxelles, 1960), p. 32.

In 1958, for example, fewer than one-fourth of the students enrolled at the University of Elisabethville were African.

The absence of a substantial number of university-trained elite, with the intellectual concerns that are usually associated with advanced education, decisively helped to stunt the growth of nationalist sentiment in the Congo. The reason for this, as E. Shils has pointed out, lies in part in "the special affinity which exists between the modern intellectual orientation, and the practice of revolutionary politics, of politics which are uncivil in their nature." [64] At a certain stage, however, this type of affinity did exist, to some extent, among the évolués—clerks, medical assistants, former seminarists, and so on—and in the absence of university-trained leaders they came to exercise political leadership. But they lacked the manipulative skills that place intellectuals in a position to create and impart a sense of nationality to their countrymen. Moreover, lacking the prestige and status of an intelligentsia, most of them tended to derive their appeal from sources other than those identified with a modern intellectual culture, that is, from their professed attachment to certain aspects of the traditional culture.

The content of the Belgian educational system is equally relevant to an understanding of the political orientation of the Congolese elites. All efforts were made to encourage the development of vocational training in primary and secondary schools: "Le carcatère éducatif de l'enseignement au second degré ordinaire se traduira par une attention marquée à l'égard du travail manuel et des branches telles que l'hygiène, l'éducation physique, la déontologie élémentaire, l'histoire locale et le folklore." [65] Beginning in 1948 with the introduction of "general secondary schools," Belgian policy underwent a shift of emphasis from an almost exclusively vocational education to "the formation of Bantu humanists, rather than copies of European humanists." [66] In this policy the Belgian government received the full support of missionary societies: "Assimilation pure and simple is not the ideal," explained Father Mosmans. "What we need is an intelligent adaptation of a superior civilization to an inferior civilization." [67] The teaching of geography was to be essentially "practical and intuitive"; the aim of history was "to fortify the loyalty of the natives toward Belgium." [68]

This policy accounts in part for the shortcomings of the Belgian educational system in the Congo. Commenting on the "slant" given to the teaching of history, L. Ballegeer observed in 1949: "How many erroneous ideas, how many untruths have gained currency; the *pax belgica* supposedly brought to an end slavery, despotism, and barbarism, and inaugurated an era of civilization!" [69] In 1954 a commission of inquiry appointed by the Minister of Colonies called attention to the inadequacy of the curriculum in the fields of history and geography:

C'est en matière de géographie et d'histoire que nous avons trouvé les plus grandes faiblesses; des élèves de dernière année du secondaire qui ignoraient comment on pouvait se rendre du Congo en Italie, par exemple. ... Pour l'histoire, la situation dans l'enseignement indigène est pire encore. Pour les mêmes raisons: faute de documents et d'éléments concrets, on se contente trop souvent d'ânonner péniblement des bribes d'histoire à la mode d'Epinal, où il y a surtout des rois installés sur des trônes, avec pourpre et couronne, et qui font des guerres, marient leurs filles (nous avons été frappés par la précision des informations en ce domaine) et tiennent tellement de place qu'on en oublie qu'il y a encore des sujets autour d'eux.[70]

To the Congolese who wished to emancipate themselves from the shackles of traditional society, this kind of educational system had very little to offer in the way of a modern intellectual training. It provided only for a limited exposure to a liberal arts education, and then persistently endeavored to adapt the curriculum to the tribal context. In other words, Western acculturative influences were always kept under control so as to prevent the emergence of a modern intellectual elite.

Another factor that contributed to the preservation of tradition concerns the use of languages in schools. In contrast with the policy adopted by the French, which, as Thomas Hodgkin reminds us, was based on the assumption that "the vernacular was a prison-house, holding back the African's intellectual development," [71] the Belgians repeatedly emphasized the utility of the "native language." As Minister Louis Franck stated to the Conference on the Christian Missions held at Le Zoute, Belgium, in 1926, "We want Central Africa to remain a black man's country. If we want that, we must instruct the natives in their own language first. To think that if you teach these natives pidgin English, pidgin French or pidgin anything else, you will give them a higher mental evolution or development is quite wrong." [72] In 1929 Minister Franck cautioned his audience against the "social peril" presented by the tendency of European-educated Africans to live outside their "own racial community," and their general propensity to look upon their "frères de race" with contempt.[73]

Official preference for the "native language" as a medium of instruction was intimately connected with the policy of indirect rule advocated by the Belgian government. In the eyes of Belgian officials and missionaries the use of the vernacular was indispensable to the development of the African "along his own lines." Father R. Van Caeneghem emphasized the point as follows:

With regard to the cultural development of the community as a whole, let us bear in mind that the language is not only a means of communication among individuals, but an integral part of the community; it is intimately linked to each aspect and manifestation of its life. . . . To civilize with a foreign language is a hybrid endeavor, contrary to the nature of things.[74]

Similarly, according to the Dominican Father V. Vekens, the abandonment of the vernacular would lead to "a radical and immediate destruction of the native customs," which would be "de la folie révolutionnaire et bolshevisante." [75]

These motives, reinforced by the personal convictions of the Flemish clergy, were important factors militating against the use of the vehicular language as an alternative to French. But they were not the only ones. Because of the intrinsic limitations attached to the use of vehicular languages as instruments of communication and education, the missionaries found the vernacular more useful to the intellectual development of the African. To cite Father Hulstaert: "C'est précisément parcequ'elles sont des langues passe-partout, parce qu'elles sont abâtardies et apauvries que les linguae francae jouissent d'une grande faveur dans toutes les colonies. ... Tant pour le développement intellectuel que pour la création d'une littérature, pareil parler reste toujours inférieur à une véritable langue indigène, car il manque de richesse et de souplesse." [76] Apparently this statement was especially true of the Lingala, described by the Reverend Mr. Whitehead as a "hotch-potch of ignoramuses": "As a means of conveying thought," the author added, "it is of less value than the lowest savage dialect." [77] Swahili proved to be a more adequate medium, but the Catholic missionaries objected to it as the "vehicle of Islam," and felt that its use was therefore incompatible with their apostolate.[78]

Thus, despite the efforts of Belgian officials to standardize the use of a single vehicular language, the tendency was to resort to the vernacular as a medium of instruction. In areas where linguistic diversity did not permit the application of this principle, however, standard practice was to extend the use of the most important dialect to other tribes located in the area. The Kikongo language, for example, is widely spoken among the tribes of the Kwango-Kwilu area. And in Kasai Province, where "the Catholic and Protestant missionaries have united in using the Baluba-Lulua [*sic*] dialect," Tshiluba is now the lingua franca.[79] In Equateur Province, on the other hand, a number of different dialects are spoken in schools—Lomongo, Lonkundu, Lingombe, Ngbaka, or Ngbandi, depending on the area. In Orientale and Katanga provinces, except for a few local deviations, Kingwana was used by Catholic and Protestant missionaries alike as an alternative to the coast Swahili. In practice, therefore, the instructions of the Belgian government concerning the use of any one of the "four official languages"—Kikongo, Lingala, Tshiluba, and Swahili—were not always heeded.[80]

Regardless of the medium employed in any given area, French was taught only as a foreign language, and not before the third year of primary school. At the secondary level French was to be "the exclusive vehicle of instruction," but the curriculum reserved an important place for the "careful study of a native language." [81] In addition, Flemish was taught as a second language at the beginning of the fourth year, along with Latin, which meant that completion of a secondary schooling required a working knowledge of at least three different languages besides the lingua franca. Aside from the fact that the curriculum left little room for other subjects, the emphasis given to the vernacular decisively encouraged the attachment of the Congolese to their traditional culture, not only because it made cross-national communication all the more difficult, but also because of the emotional connotations attributed to the use of the "cultural language."

A final aspect of the Belgian educational system concerns the lack of opportunities offered to graduates of postprimary schools to study abroad. Addressing the Institut Royal Colonial Belge, a Belgian functionary, J. Vanhove, declared in 1951: "It seems clearly inadvisable, for moral and political reasons, to send colored students to our universities." [82] Pointing to the difficulties encountered by Holland, France, and Great Britain, he cautioned his audience against a policy that would inevitably lead to "unfortunate experiences."

At least until 1952, this warning was carefully heeded. In 1953 one African student was admitted for the first time to the University of Louvain. The precedent established by this bold initiative was followed on a very limited scale: five Congolese students were officially enrolled at Louvain for the academic year 1954–55; two more were admitted in the following year; and by 1958 a total of ten had registered for courses at Louvain. It was not until 1955 that a Congolese student was admitted to the University of Brussels, the second institution of higher learning in Belgium, next to Louvain. By 1958 only three Congolese students were attending the University of Brussels. The University of Liège, the third major university of Belgium, did not count a single African student before 1958.[83]

Like their counterparts in British and French Africa, these students became ardent supporters, and in some instances the founders, of nationalist movements. But they constituted only a tiny fraction of the évolué population, and by the time they became available for political action, the less well educated had already seized the initiative. For this reason the few Congolese who studied in metropolitan universities played a minor role in the development of nationalist activity.

Clearly, the Belgian educational system, with its emphasis on "controlled" acculturation, was in large measure responsible for the long-delayed political awakening of the Congolese elite. The possibility of vocational achievement provided a counterattraction to the appeal of nationalist activity, and hence operated to divert the aspirations of the Africans from the sphere of revolutionary politics. Gradually, however, the évolués became aware of the qualitative and quantitative deficiencies of the Belgian educational system, and in time their grievances found a natural outlet in agitational politics.

By 1958 there was widespread dissatisfaction over the government's neglect of education at all levels. This stand is clearly indicated by the content of petitions addressed to the groupe de travail that visited the Congo in 1958; the "immediate improvement of education in quantity and in quality" was a recurrent theme in the list of grievances submitted by the évolués.[84] Even among rural Africans, however, the lack of secondary schools was bitterly resented.[85]

Most of the criticism centered on the lack of opportunities for higher education. In 1953, when the Belgian government stubbornly insisted on a go-slow policy, one évolué pointed out that the University of Louvain had been established in the fifteenth century, when "the lettered could be counted on one's fingertips," and that, in view of this historical precedent, there was no reason to defer the creation of a Congolese university to a later date.[86] Despite the efforts of the Belgian government to provide some educational opportunities, there existed a strong suspicion that the European teachers and the missionaries were deliberately attempting to obstruct the advancement of otherwise qualified students. As one nationalist stated, "Certains professeurs colonialistes voyaient d'un très mauvais oeil le progrès de quelques uns de leurs élèves autochtones. Donc, au lieu de les encourager à faire davantage, ils mettaient en oeuvre tous les moyens possibles pour les rebuter." [87] For many educated Congolese, "the right to excel," as one of them put it, "was a right . . . exclusively reserved to the colonialists and their progeny." [88]

Many Congolese, of course, were painfully aware of the literary inadequacy of the curriculum. Commenting on the "miserable situation of the vocational school of Luluabourg," one student declared: "Dans notre école, en dehors de la technologie, on ne voit rien d'autre. Français: Programme des écoles primaires modifié; mathématiques: Il n'y a pas de programme précis." [89] Sometimes these shortcomings were attributed to the presence of Flemish teachers and their alleged tendency "to treat [the students] in the old manner [*à la manière de l'ancien Congo*]." [90] There was some feeling, too, that the use of the dialects in schools hampered the intellectual development of the students. Because they felt that "the knowledge of French [was] the only means to gain full access to Western civilization," the évolués frequently criticized the policy of the Belgian government for its "backward" and "reactionary" implications.[91]

But while the majority of the évolués looked upon the vernacular as a "prison-house," the more culturally conscious of the Congolese regarded the vernacular as a valuable element of their traditional culture which, they felt, "should be jealously preserved by all children worthy of their ancestors." [92] Indeed, one member of the Bakongo clergy, Father Matota, felt so strongly about the issue of languages that he once suggested that higher education be given in the vernacular.[93] To the more nationally minded of the évolués, whose efforts and ambitions tended toward the goal of "national emancipation," such views were anathema. Not only did they contest the utility of the vernacular as a medium of instruction, but they were acutely aware of the political difficulties that would result from a perpetuation of linguistic differences. "Without a common national language," one of them asked, "how can we hope to form a nation when we eventually become independent?" [94]

After what has been said about the content of the curriculum introduced by Belgium, it is not surprising that most of the grievances concerning educational matters were identified with specific ethnic or regional groups, rather than with the nation as a whole. Another reason for this orientation, however, lies in the uneven distribution of educational facilities, a fact that also tended to restrict vocational opportunities to the inhabitants of particular regions. In those areas where education was lagging, either because of the delayed penetration of missionary enterprise, or because they happened to be located outside the mainstream of economic activities, the local population gained the impression that they were the victims of discrimination, that they were deliberately left in a state of stagnation while every effort was made to promote the educational advancement of other tribes. Writing in 1953, one African described the situation prevailing in the Lac Leopold region in these terms:

Au Lac Leopold nous ne bénéficions d'aucune école secondaire, telle une école moyenne ou normale, comme d'autres régions. Après l'école primaire, soit cinq années, si un élève ne va pas frapper à la porte du séminaire, son sort est définitivement arrêté. Il doit revenir dans son milieu coutumier pour reprendre sa place de simple autochtone. ... Il est grand temps que les autorités responsables examinent la question et essayent d'y remédier, sinon le retard prolongé apportera au pays un préjudice irréparable.[95]

In 1957, a Congolese journalist observed that the école normale of Inongo, and the petit séminaire of Bokoro, both located in the Lac Leopold II district, served only the Ekonda, the Ntombe, and the Nkundu, but excluded such tribes as the Basakata, the Baboma, and the Wadia.[96] About the same time a Muluba journalist from Elisabethville lamented that the Haut-Lomami district (Katanga) had virtually no secondary schools, the latter being exclusively found in the "big towns," in Elisabethville, Jadotville, and Albertville.[97] As a result of this situation, he added, the Baluba school-age population was automatically excluded from the "grandes écoles." In other words, regional discrepancies in the distribution of educational opportunities often perpetuated or reinforced ethnic antagonisms by creating a sense of grievance among those groups that otherwise could have expected better jobs and higher salaries. In particular, the Baluba of the Katanga always felt treated like "second-class citizens" in relation to other tribes.

Reflecting on the shortcomings of Belgian educational policy, J. S. Harris wrote in 1946: "Only if it is intended that the Congolese people remain permanently under European tutelage, can a disjointed system of education, which denies them effective training beyond the rudimentary and limited vocational levels, be justified." [98] Regardless of whether or not educational means were entirely justified by the ends of Belgian colonial policy, the general character and content of Belgian education go far to explain the quiescence of the Congolese political scene, at least until 1956. Indeed, it is perhaps not coincidental that the first overt manifestations of Congolese nationalism should have followed so closely on the heels of the establishment of the first institution of higher learning. Until then, however, the calculated adaptation of the curriculum to the social and economic needs of the colony, and the complete absence of opportunities for higher education, were hardly compatible with the ascendency of revolutionary sentiments.

Whatever achievement may be credited to Belgian educational policy, its overall effect has been to divide rather than unite. The quasimystical properties attributed to the use of the vernacular, the emphasis placed on a "Congolese pedagogy inspired by real Congolese requirements," [99] and the uneven distribution of secondary schools fostered basic contradictions and incompatibilities within the Congolese society. More specifically, the situation discouraged the emergence of crosscultural, supraethnic patterns of social communication. If there is any truth in Professor Deutsch's thesis that such patterns are among the most effective "building blocks of nationality" [100]—and the evidence shows that there is—the conclusion which suggests itself, then, is that the chances of success of a unified, territorial nationalist movement were seriously compromised by the absence of cultural bridges to initiate and carry on the process of national unification. In terms of its long-range consequences, therefore, the failure of Belgian educational policy to ease and accelerate the cultural assimilation of the Congolese seems far more significant than its obvious lack of success in stemming the tide of nationalist assertions.

# VII. EXTERNAL INFLUENCES

Ruth Slade has recently observed that "if the isolation of the Congo from the rest of the world could have continued indefinitely . . . [Belgian policies] might have met with an outstanding success." [1] This view cannot be accepted without certain reservations, for even when contacts with the outside world were minimal or nonexistent, a number of sporadic revolts occurred which in one way or another expressed a reaction against Belgian domination. But it rightly emphasizes the extent to which outside influences have stimulated the growth of political activities in the Congo.

External factors and influences have operated in different ways and with varying degrees of intensity over time; not only did they produce a psychological climate favorable to the development of nationalist sentiment, but they also shaped, directly or indirectly, the political outlook and objectives of African leaders. Particularly significant in this respect was the part played by metropolitan interest groups and personalities during the terminal phase of Belgian colonialism. Because the colonial situation implied a large measure of dependence on metropolitan institutions, a number of Congolese leaders tended to look to Belgian politicians for guidance and inspiration. But this state of affairs could not come about while the Congo remained hermetically sealed against the penetration of political currents and ideas from Belgium.

The first sign of an incipient transformation appeared in 1954 as a result of the projection of metropolitan issues into the colonial arena, and the consequent disruption of the traditional alliance among Catholic missions, the administration, and business interests. As the process of disintegration gathered momentum, transforming the Congo into an ideological battleground, a number of politically conscious Africans felt that they could better attain their ultimate objectives if they could identify their aspirations with those of Belgian interest groups. If nothing else, they would thus acquire a stronger bargaining position for the achievement of limited goals. More important perhaps, from a psychological standpoint, is that for the first time in the history of Belgian colonization a substantial number of Congolese became aware of the profit that could be drawn from the existence of divisive forces within the European oligarchy.

To the ferment of ideas that came from Belgium must be added the leavening influence of political developments in neighboring African territories. Despite the rigorous censorship exercised by the administration, the advance of constitutional reforms in British and French Tropical Africa did not go unnoticed among the évolués, and undoubtedly helped to awaken their political consciousness. At a later stage it led to the organization of nationalist movements explicitly aimed at the "political emancipation" of the Congo. While these different stimuli, some originating from Belgium and others from African territories, tended to operate in concomitance, it will be convenient, for the sake of analysis, to treat them separately.

THE INTRUSION OF METROPOLITAN ISSUES

Until the accession to power of the Socialist-Liberal * cabinet of Prime Minister Gaston Eyskens in April, 1954, and the appointment of the Liberal Minister of Colonies Auguste Buisseret, Belgian colonial policy had never been a major issue among Belgian political groups. Differences of opinion which arose among the metropolitan parties on colonial matters were generally kept within bounds, for they never involved the substance of the government's policy in Africa. A leading personality of the Social Christian Party (PSC), Raymond Scheyven, could declare in 1956:

Before M. Buisseret I have known two ministers of colonies, both Social Christian, Messrs. Wigny and Dequae. I do not recall that in the course of the discussion of the colonial budget . . . M. Housiaux in the name of the Socialist Party, or M. Demuyter in the name of the Liberal Party, ever expressed a formal disagreement on behalf of their respective parties with regard to the substance of our colonial policy. I inferred therefrom that each of our ministers conducted, as they should, a grand national policy [*une grande politique nationale*].[2]

By then, however, the colonial policy of the government had become the focal point of partisan struggles between the clerical Right, represented by the Social Christian Party, and the secular Left, represented by the Liberal and Socialist parties (PLB, PSB). What were the factors responsible for this sudden transformation, and how did it affect political developments in the Congo?

*The "Question Scolaire"*

A central element was the reversal of the government's long-standing position on educational policy in the Congo, or what became known in Belgium as "la question scolaire." Partly because of his personal com-

---

* In Belgium, as elsewhere in Europe, the Liberal position is characterized in economics by a commitment to the laissez-faire policy, in politics by opposition to government intervention and regulation, and in religion by a strong anticlerical bias.

mitment to the anticlerical tradition of European liberalism, and also because this tradition happened to meet the expectations of many Congolese,[3] the new minister resolved to use his power to break the monopoly of the Catholic missions in the field of education. A timid step in this direction had already been taken in 1946 by the Liberal Minister of Colonies Godding, when he decided to set up a number of secondary lay schools (*athénées royaux*) for European children. Now the Minister announced his intention to set up lay schools for African children as well, and to make substantial cuts in the subsidies granted to mission schools.

In order to appreciate the importance of the issue, certain facts of Belgian political life must be borne in mind. For one thing, the lines of political cleavage among Belgian parties are largely determined by their stand on the religious issue. For this reason the question of state subsidies for Belgian denominational schools has occasionally led to bitter controversies between the Liberal and Socialist parties on the one hand, and the Social Christian Party on the other. Moreover, because the stronghold of conservative Catholicism is the Flemish-speaking provinces, the question of state subsidies inevitably arouses cultural as well as religious antagonisms. Viewed against the background of domestic politics, the measures announced by M. Buisseret carried strong emotional overtones.

In the context of the colony these measures had revolutionary implications. In effect, by questioning the monopoly of the missions in the field of education, the Minister questioned the very foundation of Belgian colonial policy. This point was made by Senator Pholien on June 26, 1956, when he reminded the "Honorable Ministre" of his obligations toward the missions:

You have the positive duty of helping and supporting the missions because Belgium has found in the missions the best possible collaborator. . . . It is to the missions that the great founder of our colony, King Leopold II, addressed himself, and it is they who for seventy years have been dispensing education. . . . You must protect the missions because their teachings correspond to the mentality of the blacks who, let me repeat it, respect the supernatural.[4]

Although few Liberals clearly foresaw the ultimate consequences of laicization on the political evolution of the Congo, most of them were prepared to admit that they had more in mind than just altering the educational system.

After setting up the Advisory Council for Education (Conseil Supérieur de l'Enseignement), one of the first measures taken by the Minister toward the realization of his plans was to send a commission of inquiry to the Congo. The final report of the commission (known as the Coulon Report), published in December, 1954, systematically criticized every aspect of Belgian educational policy.[5] Its main significance is that it was "unquestionably the most outspoken and explosive official document dealing with any aspect of Belgian policy in the Congo that [had] appeared in recent years." [6] Primary education was criticized for the inadequacy of the curriculum, the inefficiency of teaching methods, the lack of equipment and facilities. Commenting on the "value and atmosphere of the bush schools" (*écoles de brousse*), the authors of the report noted that 50 per cent of the schools they visited were empty during school hours: "Sometimes the pupils were at work in the fields, and not always the school's fields, according to unfriendly testimonies, for Monsieur le Maître had planted coffee and groundnuts—even more than he could cultivate himself." [7] The commissioners were equally critical of the state of secondary education, described as inadequate from the standpoint of the "qualifications of the teachers, the spirit, and the methods." [8]

The commission recommended that the development of lay schools would attract teachers of higher ability and hence raise the general level of education. Anticipating the objection that a lay teacher would cost the state 450,000 francs a year ($8,000), while a missionary would cost only 75,000 francs ($1,500), the commissioners contended that a cheap education would always produce cheap results: "The trouble here is that the state is getting only its money's worth." [9] Perhaps the most explosive of the arguments advanced in the report was that only a modern, secular education would provide the intellectual and philosophical freedom that the Congolese so ardently desired. In other words, the position of the Church in Africa was stigmatized as being hopelessly anachronistic, both politically and intellectually: "The Congo is reasonably regarded by some as the last surviving theocratic state since the disappearance of the old Paraguay. . . . [The Congo is a state] where, in the political and intellectual spheres at least, the missionary world stands in relation to the people as a suzerain to his vassal, respected by some, feared by others, but always obeyed." [10]

The controversy unleashed in Belgium by the publication of the Coulon Report found expression in a violent parliamentary battle between the Right and the Left. The essence of the accusations launched against the Minister by the opposition was that his policy was entirely motivated by his anticlerical bias. As Pholien acidly stated before the Senate in 1956, "L'Honorable Ministre est un satrape velléitaire, entouré de maires du palais, avec une seule constante, son anticléricalisme!" [11] The consensus of the Social Christian deputies was that the shortcomings of missionary education had been deliberately overplayed, and that the general picture of education in the Congo was not nearly so grim as the report suggested. And besides, even if there were sufficient grounds for some of the criticisms contained in the report, argued Pholien, its findings would probably be invoked in the United Nations to weaken Belgium's position in Africa. "I find it truly disappointing," he said, "that the mandatories of the Minister should make such invidious comments, even if they are confronted with imperfect results; without attempting to predict the future, I am convinced that this report will be invoked in the United Nations to criticize Belgian colonial administration." [12] Despite continued attacks on his policy, Buisseret decided to take appropriate measures to carry it into effect.

According to the so-called Buisseret-Moermans-Thompson agreement, concluded in March, 1956, by representatives of Catholic and Protestant missions and the Minister, 45 per cent of the subsidies granted for the construction of new schools were to be allocated to Catholic missions and 10 per cent to Protestant missions; the remaining 45 per cent would be spent for the construction of lay schools.[13] In addition, the missions were required to resort to the procedure of *adjudication publique* for the construction of their schools; instead of relying upon the services of their personnel they would from now on hire the services of a contractor. The arrangement decisively favored the growth of lay schools between 1956 and 1958, and while it did not cause a drastic reduction in confessional schools, it nevertheless placed the missions in a difficult financial position.

But the Church had a deeper reason for discouragement in taking stock of the situation. The attitude of the Minister was regarded not only as an affront but as a potential threat to the spiritual mission of the Church in Africa. In order to counter this threat the Catholic hierarchy showed an increasing disposition to repudiate its long-standing collaboration with the administration. For example, Father Mosmans openly declared that a major "imperative" of missionary action was to avoid the stigma of "collaboration." [14] Two months later the Catholic bishops of the Congo issued a formal declaration publicly expressing their intention to withdraw from collaboration with the government:

All the inhabitants of a country have the duty to collaborate actively for the common good. They have therefore the right to take part in the conduct of public affairs. The trustee nation is obliged to respect this right, and to favor its exercise by progressive political education. . . . It is not for the Church to pronounce on the precise form in which a people's emancipation may come. She considers this to be legitimate as long as it is accomplished in charity and the respect of mutual rights.[15]

The real significance of the bishops' declaration is that it gave the imprimatur of the Church to the principle of self-government as the major alternative to the maintenance of the status quo. Although it did not specify when or how self-government was to be attained, it nevertheless recognized the right of the Congolese to "take part in the conduct of public affairs." Some Africans were therefore encouraged to raise the questions that the Church declined to answer. The évolués had perceived the possibility of this alternative, however, long before the issuance of the bishops' declaration. Many of them realized at the outset that the debate over educational policy involved a fundamental revision of the principles underlying the old doctrine of paternalism, and that the government, by challenging the authority of the Church in the field of education, also challenged a fundamental principle of colonial control. For this reason they looked upon the Minister as their "great defender," as the "friend of the blacks," and regarded his policy as a major step toward political emancipation. Evaluating the implications of the controversy, Lumumba tersely stated: "Anyone who is against the state secular schools is also against the emancipation of the Africans."[16]

Moreover, in seeking a justification for his policy in the "irresistible pressure" of the évolués' opinion, the Minister gave them the impression that their views could become a significant factor in the formulation of metropolitan policy. This impression was further strengthened by the development of friendly societies (*amicales*), discussion groups, and similar pressure organizations, for the most part identified with metropolitan parties, and operating as "transmission belts" between the Congo and Belgium. In fact, the initial success encountered by these associations did not lie so much in the receptivity of the Africans to metropolitan ideologies as in the fact that they came to be viewed as valuable instruments for enlisting the support of the metropolitan government against the local administration, and for playing one off against the other. A Congolese writing in 1955 referred to the "action of Belgian parties" as the best guarantee available to the Africans against the "unscrupulousness" of the colonial oligarchy: "Refuser l'action des partis politiques belges au Congo serait nous asservir et nous livrer, nous Congolais bien protégés et défendus par les instances metropolitaines, aux ravisseurs peu scrupuleux ... et laisser le peuple congolais à la convoitise d'une minorité de personnes avides."[17] In brief, the mere presence in the Congo of metropolitan political groups, or their affiliate organizations, indicated that there was such a thing as a legitimate alternative to the status quo.

Perhaps the most promising sign in the entire picture, from the standpoint of Congolese nationalists, was the effect of the crisis on the stability and prestige of the colonial administration. The internal rifts engendered by the *question scolaire* virtually destroyed the monolithic unity of the sacred alliance among the Church, the administration, and big business, and therefore considerably weakened the capacity of the government to resist the pressure of nationalist assertions. Into this situation there was injected another element which gave the Africans further evidence of disunity among their "civilizers."

*The "Question Linguistique"*

Next to the question scolaire, the most divisive issue that appeared on the colonial scene during the years preceding independence concerned the use of languages in schools and court proceedings. Anticipating the difficulties that would inevitably result from the "exaggerated pretensions of a few exalted minds," Alexandre Delcommune wrote in 1919: "One must hope that the knowledge of the Flemish language will not be imposed upon the natives. . . . The question of languages must not be raised in the Congo, because it does not exist, and because no claims could possibly justify this pretension." [18] This warning was carefully heeded during most of the colonial period, and, in spite of the constitutional guarantees offered by the Colonial Charter, the Flemish community of the Congo made no effort to claim equality of treatment for its language. By 1954, however, it became increasingly clear that the Congo could not long remain insulated from the linguistic conflict that has opposed, and continues to oppose, the Flemish and Walloon communities of Belgium.*

In a sense, the controversy over the use of languages was a by-product of the question scolaire. When, in December, 1954, the Minister announced before the Chambers that French would be the only medium of instruction used in the official schools, he immediately aroused the suspicion of the Flemish communities both in Belgium and in the Congo.[19] With the appointment of school officials who were mostly of Walloon extraction, he became increasingly suspect of "cultural chauvinism." In December, 1955, two important metropolitan pressure groups, the Vlaams Economisch Verbond and the Economische Raad Voor Vlaanderen, both dedicated to "the promotion of Flemish economic and social interests," issued a joint memorandum urging the Minister of Colonies to "propose the appointment of candidates having a perfect knowledge of the Flemish culture as well as a sufficient national spirit." [20] In the Congo, the spokesmen of the Vlaamse Vriendenkring, a Flemish cultural association with representatives in each of the provinces, became equally apprehensive of a policy which, in their opinion, smacked of "fransquillonisme."

Actually, even before Buisseret was appointed to office, intense feel-

---

* Although the Belgian Constitution of 1830 stipulated that "the use of languages is free," French was the only language used in the administration, the army, and the universities until 1850. The "equality law" of 1898 provided for equal treatment for both French and Flemish, but in practice French continued to be given precedence over Flemish. The "linguistic frontier" established in 1932 divided the country into unilingual Flemish and Walloon regions, but failed to satisfy the demands of the Flemings for bilingualism in Brussels and for teaching languages in schools located in the border areas. In recent times the linguistic claims made by the Flemish movement have found expression in a vigorous campaign for a federalized Belgium.

ings had been aroused over the issue of languages in Congolese courts. The issue arose early in 1954 in connection with "l'affaire Grootaert," in which the Court of Appeals of Elisabethville annulled the decision delivered by a district judge of the Katanga, Grootaert, on the sole grounds that it had been worded in Flemish.[21] In response to the vehement protestations voiced by Grootaert, the incumbent minister, M. Dequae, threatened him with disciplinary sanctions.[22] The incident aroused passionate discussions both in the Congo and in Belgium, and in June, 1956, a Belgian deputy bitterly attacked the government for its failure to implement the provisions of the Colonial Charter concerning the use of languages in the Congo.[23] Following the quashing of the decision of the Court of Appeals of Elisabethville by an *arrêt* of the Cour de Cassation of Brussels, in June, 1957, the Flemish community was stimulated to press its claims for equal treatment of its language not only in the courts, but in the field of education as well.

Meanwhile, in the face of the continued discrimination evidenced by the Minister, the Flemish minority of the Congo sought to bring pressure to bear on the Governor General. In July, 1955, the Vlaamse Vriendenkring of Elisabethville presented the Conseil de Gouvernement with a petition which pointed out that Article 3 of the Colonial Charter should have been implemented by way of decree "within five years following the promulgation of this law," and that the failure of the government to promulgate such decrees was tantamount to a violation of the rights of the Flemish population.[24] The petition went on to urge the Governor to take appropriate action to remedy this "flagrant violation of the fundamental law," which might otherwise provoke "an extreme reaction from the Flemish population." These demands, ardently supported by the Flemish press—represented in the Congo by the weekly newspaper *De Week*, and the monthly review *Band*—were given partial satisfaction by a decree of January 5, 1957, on the use of languages in court. At best, however, this accomplishment was regarded by most Flemings as a halfway house to the full recognition of their constitutional rights.

In May, 1957, the Socialist Senator de Block, speaking on behalf of the Flemish community of the Congo, suggested before the Senate that the University of Elisabethville be transformed into a bilingual institution, offering the same courses in both languages, and that all Belgian students be required to learn the second national language.[25] The Vlaamse Vriendenkring of Elisabethville carried the argument a step further, insisting that Flemish be maintained as a compulsory second language for all students, regardless of race. In an effort to rationalize its position, the association pointed out that a good command of the Flemish language would enable the Africans to communicate with their "frères de race" in South Africa; that it was a necessary qualification to gain access to administrative posts; and that it was the only means of safeguarding the Belgian cultural heritage, while providing the benefit thereof to the Africans.[26] Similar demands were voiced by the Flemish members of the Colonial Council, and by Father Van Wing in particular, who put his views on record when he declared before the council in April, 1958, that "the learning of Flemish as a second language should be compulsory for all, without distinction of race."[27] About the same time, Professor L. O. J. de Wilde, a longtime member of the Colonial Council, felt that it was possible to adopt no other attitude toward the "staunch cultural colonialists [*les colonialistes indécrottables*] than to coerce them with all the means available in the fatherland." Speaking before the Alumni Association of the University of Ghent, he urged the Flemish leaders of the three major metropolitan parties "to collaborate with a perfect solidarity, as they did to push through the decree on judicial matters."[28]

What were the effects of the controversy on the attitude of the Africans? Some Congolese reacted by pointing out that there was no reason that they, too, should not be entitled to claim equal treatment for their own languages. Once carried to its logical conclusion, noted Désiré Mobutu, this reasoning would lead to the adoption of 127 national languages, "two for Belgium, and 125 for the Congo." Commenting on the possible implications of the language controversy, he added:

Do not say tomorrow that the blacks are . . . nationalists because they demand the recognition of 125 dialects, on equal terms with French and Flemish. This fantasy will not come from the blacks, but from those who originated it. . . . The unanimous opinion of our compatriots is that the language of Voltaire, and it alone, must become our national language.[29]

If this last sentence truly expressed the "unanimous opinion" of the Africans, one may wonder why the author should anticipate the eventuality of 127 national dialects. Actually, what appears at first sight as a contradiction merely reflects the concern of some Congolese nationalists over the divisive implications of the language issue. Although they were frequently suspected by the Flemish press of yielding to the pressure of the *fransquillons,* their aversion to Flemish as a second national language was but one symptom of their growing national consciousness.

The natural rights arguments used by the Flemish population in defense of its constitutional prerogatives were also implicit in the arguments proffered by certain Congolese leaders to justify the right to "self-determination" of their own people. They argued, with common-sense deduction, that if the will of the Belgians was not a single will, even after living for some 160 years under the same institutions, one should not a fortiori expect the will of the Congolese, however numerous, to be identified with the will of the whole. As claimants of minority rights, therefore, the more culturally conscious of the Flemish community somehow gave a sanction of legitimacy to the separatist claims of ethnic minorities, thereby causing deep anxieties among those Africans who, like Mobutu, strove for the attainment of "national" independence.

At the same time, the language issue accentuated existing differences among the European population. Indeed, just as the question scolaire brought the Congolese to realize the existence of an open tug-of-war between clericals and anticlericals, the *question linguistique* made them fully aware of the historic rift between Flemings and Walloons. This combination of internal strains and rivalries, and the fact that many Africans could sense its corrosive impact, created an environment favorable to the development of nationalist activity.

The Van Bilsen Proposal

What finally prompted a group of educated Congolese to seize upon the latent opportunities of this situation was the publication of Professor A. A. J. Van Bilsen's *Thirty-Year Plan for the Political Emancipation of Belgian Africa*, in December, 1955. The timing of the proposal, rather than its substance or novelty, assured its author an immediate popularity among the Africans.

Van Bilsen, who was at the time professor of colonial legislation at the University Institute for Overseas Territories at Antwerp, first went to the Congo in 1946 as a consultant to the official news agency, Agence Belga. From then on he developed a growing interest in Africa. His travels took him to Rhodesia and South Africa in 1947, and to the Ivory Coast, Nigeria, and the Cameroons in 1954 and 1955. Between 1950 and 1954, while serving as chef de cabinet of Minister of Education Harmel, he had the opportunity to gain firsthand knowledge of educational problems in Belgian Africa. As a result of his professional background and personal intuition, he became keenly appreciative of the danger inherent in the continuation of an essentially static colonial policy. On October 4, 1954, in his inaugural address to the Institut de Formation Sociale Coloniale, in Brussels, he launched the idea of a thirty-year plan of political emancipation, emphasizing the need to prepare the Congolese for the responsibility of self-government. In November of the same year he persuasively argued in favor of "une nouvelle politique coloniale de mouvement," based on a thirty-year timetable.[30]

The 1955 version of the Van Bilsen plan, initially published in the Flemish Catholic review, *Gids op Maatschappelijk Gebied*,[31] refined and developed the argument presented by the author a year earlier. By setting a timetable, argued Van Bilsen, the government would avoid the "two classic faults" of colonial authorities, their tendency (1) to "make concessions only when they can no longer do otherwise," and (2) to "give too little attention not only to the formation of a competent indigenous elite, but above all to the awakening among them of a sense of responsibility." In other words, the plan would allow the government to retain control over the pace and direction of the process of emancipation, and would at the same time lessen the danger of "being caught unawares by the march of events." In a letter to F. Grévisse, dated April 11, 1956, Van Bilsen reiterated his conviction that "a bold policy of emancipation," along the lines suggested in his plan, was the sole alternative to the "terrible impasse" that would otherwise confront the government:

Mon souci est plus exactement de suggérer que l'on entame, sans perdre un jour de plus, la mise en place des cadres et des dispositifs indispensables pour que le jour venu, l'émancipation ineluctable puisse se faire sans trop de dommage pour le Congo et le Ruanda-Urundi. Je suis persuadé que l'actuelle politique, si nous ne renversons pas la vapeur, nous mène d'ici dix ans à une terrible impasse, tandis qu'une politique hardie d'émancipation nous permettrait de continuer à guider nos pays Africains pendant plusieurs décades, soit pendant tout le temps voulu.[32]

Why, then, suggest a thirty-year limit for independence? The avowed reason was that it would presumably take thirty years to prepare the Congolese for the tasks of self-government. The truth, however, is that the author felt an obligation to take a conservative stand on the issue of a target date, so as to allay possible charges of demagoguery from his countrymen. As he later admitted in a letter to Wilfrid Benson, director of the Division of Information on Non-Self-Governing Territories of the United Nations:

Le fait d'avoir proposé un plan de trente ans me fait passer dans mon pays pour un dangereux agitateur. ... En essayant de faire pénétrer des idées progressistes en matière de politique coloniale, je dois tenir compte des préjugés qui règnent dans mon pays, et c'est dès lors avec prudence que j'avance. J'ai voulu éviter que ceux qui me feraient le reproche de "ruiner" l'action gouvernementale ne puissent m'accuser de faire de la démagogie.[33]

Despite the absence of intermediate target dates for specific political reforms, the plan recognized the possibility of a progressive transfer of autonomy to territories or regions "whose maturity was judged sufficient." Only a federal structure, argued Van Bilsen, could offer the flexibility required by this formula. A federal government would not only allow a decentralization of authority from Brussels to Leopoldville, and from Leopoldville to "the autonomous Congolese countries," but would also act as "an arbiter, preventing or cushioning the impact of whatever crisis might arise." Two other reasons favoring a federal system were the very size of the Congo, which made "all attempts at political centralization illusory," and the economic weakness of Ruanda-Urundi: "No more than Buganda could Ruanda and Urundi hope to become independent states, for these countries would not be viable. Even united they would still form a precarious political entity because they are too weak economically." In sum, the formula proposed by Van Bilsen entailed a gradual transfer of powers within the framework of a federal governmental structure.

Although Van Bilsen's plan was primarily intended to offer a concrete basis for the revision of Belgian colonial policy, the metropolitan government turned a deaf ear to the proposal. The official position of the Belgian government on the issue of a timetable for emancipation had remained basically unchanged since January, 1952, when Governor General Pierre Ryckmans declared before the General Assembly of the United Nations: "It should be recognized that premature emancipation would not be of advantage to the people concerned, while fixing an overdistant date might, on the other hand, tend to retard rather than promote development." [34] Once the influence of Van Bilsen's ideas on the Congolese came to be realized, however, the Minister of the Congo did not hesitate to heap scorn on the "irresponsible strategists who fix dates; such an attitude shows either that they know nothing or that they understand nothing of Africa." [35]

Van Bilsen's plan provoked an enthusiastic response from the few Africans who heard about it. Several students at Lovanium sent him wheedling letters asking for copies of the plan. Justin Bomboko, at the time attending the Université Libre de Bruxelles, congratulated Van Bilsen for elucidating the basis of the Belgo-Congolese community in a way that "fully meets the aspirations of the Congolese":

Le problème que vous soulevez dans votre étude est très important; il est regrettable que l'on n'y ait pas songé depuis longtemps. Il est très beau de parler de Communauté Belgo-Congolaise, mais faut-il encore définir exactement la base sur laquelle on fonde son édification. C'est cette base que vous venez de préciser et qui, sans aucun doute, répond pleinement aux aspirations des Congolais.[36]

But at the same time Bomboko asked: "Will the autonomous Congolese states coincide with the present administrative boundaries, or will they reflect ethnic and cultural affinities?"

Eventually, these hopes and ideas found expression in a lengthy editorial statement which appeared in the July-August, 1956, issue of the Leopoldville newspaper *Conscience Africaine*. In this epoch-making document, better known as the manifesto of *Conscience Africaine*, for the first time in the history of Belgian colonization a group of Congolese explicitly stated their desire to see the Congo "become a great nation in the center of the African continent." In retrospect, however, this document looks like a relatively mild statement of nationalist objectives. To be sure, "total political emancipation" was specifically mentioned as the only alternative to colonial rule, but the emancipation was to be "progressive," extended over a period of thirty years. Referring to the Van Bilsen plan, the authors of the manifesto openly stated: "We believe that such a plan has become a necessity. . . . This plan should express the sincere will of Belgium to lead the Congo to complete political emancipation in a period of thirty years." In the meantime, specific measures should be introduced to bring about a progressive democratization of existing institutions:

On the one hand, existing institutions must become more and more representative, by replacing progressively the present system of nominations with a system in which the population itself will designate its representatives. On the other hand, the councils which are now purely consultative must receive a true power of decision and control in increasingly extended matters in order to arrive finally at a responsible government at the head of our nation.

Emancipation was to be attained not only gradually, but peacefully and lawfully. Rejecting all forms of violence on the grounds that "those who use violence show that they are not ripe for democracy," the authors of the manifesto went on: "We have only one aim: the good of the Congolese nation. We will make this aim triumphant in lawfulness and by peaceful means."

Finally, although they firmly rejected the idea of a Belgo-Congolese community, as defined by Belgium, for fear that it might "put a brake on the total emancipation of the Congolese people," they made a strong plea in favor of the "union of Africans and Europeans living in the Congo." Their conception of the "Congolese nation of tomorrow," they said, was that of "a human fraternity based on the fundamental equality of all men without racial distinction." This gradualist, pacific approach clearly shows the ties between the manifesto and Van Bilsen's ideas. But it also indicates a tacit acceptance of the views of the Catholic Church regarding the problem of emancipation, a fact that seemed all the more natural in view of the associational nexus between the authors of the manifesto and the Catholic hierarchy.

It must be noted, in this connection, that the editorial committee of *Conscience Africaine* was identified with a small cultural group organized by the Abbé Joseph Malula in 1953 to serve as a forum for the discussion of social, economic, and cultural problems. In time the substance of these discussions was reproduced in a modest newspaper, edited by Joseph Ileo, under the title of *Conscience Africaine*. Until the publication of the manifesto, however, the newspaper had never displayed the overtones of a nationalist press. Indeed, the rather innocuous criticisms occasionally voiced by the editor against the colonial regime confirmed the impression that he and his collaborators were under the influence of the Church.

In the light of this relationship, some observers were tempted to conclude that the manifesto was nothing more than the mouthpiece of the Church. One Leopoldville newspaper, for example, described it as "une auto-défense de l'Eglise contre les partis belges," thereby suggesting that it was the result of a clerical conspiracy directed against the implantation of partisan ideologies.[37] At first sight, this view seems to be corroborated by an impressive body of circumstantial evidence. For one thing, the manifesto immediately followed the bishops' declaration, as if to give added emphasis to the principles enunciated by the Church; also, it appeared shortly before the annual meeting of the PSB, quite possibly to cut the ground from under the feet of the Socialists; finally, the "technical assistance" extended to the editor of *Conscience Africaine* by two European professors at Lovanium University provided further evidence in support of this contention. Nevertheless, although the evidence available clearly indicates that the authors of the manifesto enjoyed the blessings of the Church, they were not necessarily the agents of a clerical conspiracy. Rather, they decided to seize the opportunity offered by the publication of Van Bilsen's plan to further their own political aspirations, and they did so in circumstances that were consciously intended to maximize their influence.

The publication of the manifesto caused a considerable stir among Africans. It was widely circulated among the évolués of the provincial capitals, and even reached into the rural areas. Although many educated Africans were favorably impressed by the revolutionary character of the initiative, others felt that its goals fell short of their expectations. On August 24, 1956, the Abako responded to the manifesto in a devastating critique of the ideas advanced by the editor of *Conscience Africaine*. Far more impatient in tone, and radical in its objectives, the so-called countermanifesto categorically stated: "Rather than postponing emancipation for another thirty years, we should be granted self-government today." [38] The Abako said that it did not "wish to participate in the elaboration of this plan, but purely and simply to annul it because its application would serve only to retard the independence of the Congo. Our patience is already exhausted. Since the hour has come, emancipation should be granted us this very day." Arguing that "political maturity precedes, in many cases, administrative capacity," it went on to urge the Belgian government to grant full political rights and unrestricted civil liberties to the Congolese: "Our position is clear and we demand: (1) political rights; (2) all the liberties of the individual, of thought, of opinion, and of the press; liberty of assembly, of association of conscience, and of religion."

The only area of agreement between the two manifestos concerned the conditions under which a Belgo-Congolese community might come into being: "Before thinking of the foundation of such a community," stated the Abako, "the Belgians ought to realize that it must be neither solicited nor imposed, but freely chosen and accepted." Even then, the Abako was much more outspoken in its criticisms of the Belgian conception of the community:

A caricature of the community copied from the famous French Union is not at all plausible for us; it is only a modified form of domination. Is it possible to conceive how this Congo, eighty times larger than Belgium, could become its tenth province? Would Belgium be able to tolerate having the inhabitants of her "tenth province" form the majority of the representatives in the Chamber?

Turning to the problem of "the Congolization of the staffs in the administration," the Abako lamented the absence of "true offices where the Negro assumes real responsibilities." Citing Van Bilsen, it pointed out that it was the fault of the Belgians, not of the Africans, if no Africans were doctors, engineers, civil servants, or officers. Again, quoting Van Bilsen, its spokesmen concluded:

The time is ended when colonization could be justified by the right of the first occupant or the conqueror or the treaties settled with illiterate and uninformed native princes who were incapable of opposing the colonial penetration. Only one claim justifies colonization and that is consent, the attachment of the native population to those who are their educators, to those who bring them the key to a new and better world, a world of well-being and liberty.

Despite obvious differences in the language and objectives of the two manifestos, the source from which they drew their inspiration was the same. More selective than its earlier counterpart, the manifesto of the Abako categorically rejected the idea of a thirty-year timetable, but then sought to justify its position by the very same arguments advanced by Van Bilsen in support of his plan. In other words, the main significance of Van Bilsen's plan is that it created the issue around which nationalist sentiment crystallized. It not only brought to light different brands of nationalist sentiment, but gave impetus to different types of nationalist activity, based on divergent conceptions of nationhood.

THE INFLUENCE OF POLITICAL DEVELOPMENTS IN AFRICAN TERRITORIES

In the meantime the political developments that occurred in other African territories had further stimulated the political awakening of the Congolese. It made them all the more aware of the *immobilisme* that seemed to govern Belgian colonial policy, and hence intensified their desire to change the status quo. Indeed, it is perhaps not entirely coincidental that the first nationalist-inspired manifesto appeared at a time when the demands for self-government were more pressing than ever before in the African continent.

Long before they decided to voice their aspirations, some Congolese understood the significance of the administrative reforms introduced in certain other parts of Africa. One of them, for example, writing in *Congo Pratique* in March, 1953, drew attention to the measures adopted by the British government to Africanize the civil service of the Gold Coast, and sourly commented: "A quand le tour des Congolais? Quand les poules auront des dents? Alors, nous attendons avec patience." Another, taking note of the antidiscriminatory legislation passed by the Legislative Council of Uganda, suggested a similar initiative from the Belgian government. The Congolese, however, were more sensitive to the developments that took place in the neighboring territories of former French Equatorial Africa (AEF), partly because they shared with them a common vehicular language, and also because of the proximity of Brazzaville, separated from Leopoldville only by the width of Stanley Pool.

There are several ways in which the influence of former French Equatorial Africa made itself felt. For one thing, in contrast with the situation existing in Leopoldville, relations between Africans and Europeans in Brazzaville were relatively free of racial discrimination. Comparing the social atmosphere of Brazzaville with that of Leopoldville, a Belgian observer, Pierre Mernier, noted in 1948:

The example of neighboring territories has produced a strong impression on our blacks. The Belgians have evidently gone far beyond the French in the way of social benefits for the Africans. But the French are more humane. In Brazzaville the whites and the blacks commingle in the same cafés. In the stores the whites stand in line behind the blacks. There are no racial priorities.[39]

While many Congolese were favorably impressed by the relative absence of social distance between the African and European communities of Brazzaville, some of them were even more sensitive to the intellectual ferment of French Africa. Commenting on the literary achievements of French-educated Africans, the editor Antoine-Roger Bolamba noted in 1953 that "in French overseas territories French poetry centers upon a special theme, one that seeks to link poetry to politics: Aimé Cesaire, Léopold Senghor, and all the more talented African poets have taken it as a rule." [40] Actually, it was not so much the literary talent of these personalities as their conscious attempt to promote an African cultural renaissance which impressed them. Above all, the kind of political consciousness displayed by French-educated Africans reminded the Congolese of the greater intellectual and political freedom prevailing in the French territories.

That the Congolese were keenly aware of the measure of political freedom enjoyed by the Africans of Brazzaville is clearly evidenced by the general tenor of the letter addressed by the Abako to the Abbé Fulbert Youlou after he was elected mayor of Brazzaville in late 1956: "Ce n'est pas sans enthousiasme que les Bakongo rassemblés dans l'Abako ont suivi le déroulement des dernières élections qui devaient aboutir à la libre expression de la volonté du peuple Congolais. Ce franc succès augure un avenir de paix et de justice dont les Africains ont soif, et pour l'établissement duquel ils se solidarisent de plus en plus." [41] About the same time the constitutional changes introduced by the Loi-Cadre of June 23, 1956, further intensified the desire of the Congolese to acquire effective political rights. With the substitution of universal suffrage on a common roll for the previous system of separate electorates, the Africans of Brazzaville were extended the dignity of citizenship as well as a meaningful share of political participation in the government of their territory. The Africans of Leopoldville, on the other hand, continued to be treated as subjects. Under the circumstances one can better understand the feelings of impatience and frustration of Congolese Africans in the face of the persistent immobilisme of Belgian policy. As one Congolese bitterly remarked, in 1957: "Alors que chez nous on hésite à confier aux Noirs des postes de confiance, nous assistons à une réele émancipation politique, économique, et sociale des colonies françaises, dont les indigènes ne sont pas plus évolués que nous. ... Des personalités de renom telles que Jacques Opangault et l'Abbé Fulbert Youlou ont été élues par le peuple pour servir les intérêts supérieurs du pays." [42]

Just as significant, from a psychological standpoint, was the introduction of popular elections in the trust territory of Ruanda-Urundi. When in August, 1956, the resident general of Ruanda-Urundi, Jean-Paul Harroy, announced that popular elections to the *collèges de sous-chefferies* would soon replace the old system of designation, many thoughtful Congolese felt that they should be extended the same political rights. They could not understand why Ruanda-Urundi, which had been under Belgian administration for thirty-three years, should take "giant strides toward autonomy" while the Congo was being kept in a state of political stagnation. As Lumumba put it,

The fact that Ruanda-Urundi, a territory which has been under Belgian mandate since August 31, 1923, is more favorably situated than the Congo from the administrative point of view is not without influence on the Congolese. Whereas Ruanda-Urundi, which had the good fortune to be placed under international trusteeship in 1923, is taking giant strides towards autonomy, we Congolese, who have been under the same Belgian administration for more than three quarters of a century—much longer than Ruanda-Urundi —are far behind our neighbour. [43]

Meanwhile, the accession of Ghana to independence, and the emergence of nationalist movements in some of the territories adjacent to the Congo, were bound to encourage demands for autonomy on the part of the évolués. It was not until 1958, however, that the relationship between such outside influences and nationalist developments appeared in full light.

One event that had a determinative influence on the growth of Congolese nationalism was the visit of General de Gaulle to Brazzaville in the summer of 1958. In his speech there on August 24, de Gaulle reiterated his intention to give French overseas territories the choice between immediate independence and participation in the French Community: "Whoever desires independence," said de Gaulle, "can immediately obtain it." As one observer correctly noted, "The visit of the chief of government at Brazzaville was noted at Leopoldville . . . with as much intensity as in the capital of French Equatorial Africa. The words of the General touched the Congolese of Leopoldville with equal vigor." Two days later, a group of évolués of Leopoldville presented M. Pétillon, then minister of the Congo, with a petition denouncing the "anachronistic political regime" of the Congo and demanding the fixing of a date for "complete independence." [44] It should be noted that this petition was signed by a number of individuals who later became associated with the Mouvement National Congolais (MNC), including Lumumba, Ileo, and Adoula. In fact, it was only a matter of weeks before they decided to follow up their demands by organizing the MNC, thereby indicating that Congolese nationalism had gone beyond the "age of petition" and had entered the militant phase.

Another significant event was the All-African People's Conference, a nongovernmental conference of political parties held in Accra in December, 1958. Among the delegates to the conference were Lumumba, Gaston Diomi, bourgmestre of the commune of Ngiri-Ngiri of Leopoldville, and Joseph Ngalula, editor of the weekly *Présence Congolaise*, all three representing the MNC. Upon their return to Leopoldville on December 28 they held a public meeting in the commune of Kalamu, before an audience of some 7,000, in which they developed the major themes discussed at Accra. The general tenor of Lumumba's exhortations reflected the vigorous support of the conference for independence movements in Africa. "Independence is not a gift," said Lumumba, "but a fundamental right of the Congolese." After noting that the Accra conference "marked a decisive step toward the self-realization [*la pleine affirmation*] of the African personality, and toward the total unity of all the peoples of the African continent," the MNC leader went on to "record with satisfaction that the resolutions adopted at the conference coincide with the views held by our movement." [45]

Although it is almost impossible to establish a precise relationship between Lumumba's speech and the riots of January, 1959, there is no denying that his performance of December 28, 1958, added an important element to the social and political unrest that led to the rioting. If nothing else, his presentation of the work of the conference conveyed a sense of urgency which helped to accelerate the trend toward independence. More important, perhaps, was the effect of the All-African People's Conference on Lumumba's thinking, as it certainly strengthened his personal inclination toward the ideal of Pan-Africanism and stimulated his efforts toward the attainment of this goal.

Meanwhile, on the occasion of the Brussels Exhibition, which took place during the summer and fall of 1958, a substantial number of Congolese had come in contact with the environment of the metropolis. Although this stimulus had a different impact from those we previously examined, its formative influence on the development of nationalist activity cannot be overlooked.

### The Brussels Exhibition of 1958

Until 1958 only a handful of Congolese had been given the opportunity to go abroad; in 1955 sixteen notables from various provinces had visited Belgium at the invitation of the Minister of Colonies, five Bakuba weavers had attended the Brussels Textile Exhibition, and one trade-union official had taken part in the International Labor Conference in Geneva. But except for these limited contacts "there was no precedent for the influx of several hundred Africans from all parts of the Congo and and Ruanda-Urundi which occurred during the period of the Brussels Exhibition." [46]

The cosmopolitan environment of the Belgian capital was highly congenial to the development of nationalist sentiment. Here, as Thomas Kanza pointed out, the Congolese delegates discovered for themselves that "human qualities as well as virtues and faults are not the monopoly of any people or race." [47] They could mix with people of different origins, observe different patterns of behavior, and compare them with those of Belgian colonials. As a result of their exposure to these new and unsettling influences they became increasingly receptive to liberal ideas.

But they also began to search for common political grounds. At the Centre d'Accueil du Personnel Africain (CAPA) of Tervueren, where lodgings had been provided for the delegates, a number of Congolese from different provinces could exchange impressions about the political future of the Congo, and seek tentative agreement on how best to achieve their goals:

In the splendor of the park at Tervueren . . . life went on until late at night. The people there were already divided into two groups: those who would return immediately to their native country and those who had decided to know Europe better before returning. . . . Among the first group were a number of actual political leaders of the Congo.[48]

One of the results of this cross-fertilization of ideas between the Congo and the metropolis was the organization of the Mouvement pour le Progrès National Congolais (MPNC), a short-lived political movement whose membership was exclusively made up of Congolese who attended the exhibition. Its program stressed the need to preserve the "national unity of the Congo," but was extremely noncommittal on the issue of independence, merely indicating that "the attainment of a minimum of material and intellectual development is a precondition to the acquisition of independence." [49] In addition, the political fortunes of the party were seriously compromised by the circumstances in which it came into being. Aside from the fact that it was the outgrowth of an alien environment, it had been organized at the instigation of a Belgian functionary, M. C. C. de Backer, presumably to counteract the influence of the Abako.[50] In any event, a number of Congolese who initially belonged to the MPNC —Jean Bolikango, Jacques Massa, Albert Kalondji, and Jason Sendwe, among others—became the leaders of their own political formations once they returned to the Congo. But if the experiment attempted by the founders of the MPNC failed to achieve more than a fleeting success, it was nonetheless indicative of a growing political consciousness.

In conclusion, external influences affected the growth of nationalism in the Congo in two ways. First, they brought into the Congo a social and political ferment which predisposed the Congolese elites to engage in nationalist activities. We have seen how the intrusion of metropolitan issues, together with the occurrence of political reforms in neighboring African territories, helped to foster new hopes and expectations among the évolués, and how they sought to exploit to their advantage the opportunities created by this situation. Similarly, the incidence of political reforms in neighboring territories served to intensify their hopes and expectations. In addition, external influences in some instances precipitated the organization of political groups, or the politicization of nonpolitical groups. Unquestionably the most significant of such influences was the Van Bilsen proposal. Because it created the issue that provided the initial stimulus to the rise of nationalist assertions, it may well be regarded as the starting point of political developments in the Congo.

# PART THREE

*The Development of Political Groups*

# VIII. THE GENESIS
## OF CONGOLESE PARTIES

Like most parties in Africa, Congolese parties came into being through the initiative of Westernized elements whose immediate objective was the political emancipation of the group they claimed to represent, for the purpose of creating an independent nation-state possessing all the trappings of sovereignty. As a form of colonial protest, however, they must be distinguished at the outset from such earlier traditionalist or syncretistic manifestations as the initial movements of resistance organized by Arabized chiefs against the Free State, or the messianic movements initiated by African "prophets" to assert their independence from European churches. These protonationalist manifestations have one common denominator with modern political movements: their opposition to alien control. But otherwise they lack most of the structural and functional characteristics of political parties.

Second, as a formal type of organization, political parties must also be distinguished from such nonpolitical organizations as tribal and kinship associations, cultural organizations, and economic interest groups. Admittedly, these groups share many important characteristics with political parties. Most of them have specialized functions of some kind, some form of organizational structure, and a leadership drawn from Western-educated elements. Unlike political parties, however, they do not seek to overthrow the colonial status quo, or to gain control over the government through periodic elections. Rather, they tend to operate like pressure groups on behalf of their members, seeking to exert some influence upon the government within the framework of the colonial situation.[1]

Yet, once these broad distinctions are made, it must be recognized that Congolese parties are very closely related to the nonpolitical organizations that preceded them. Most of them came into being through a process of politicization of preëxisting associations, or as a result of a split in, or a regrouping of, preëxisting associations. This process of adaptation has inevitably affected the structure, leadership, and goals of political parties, especially if the parent organization had an ethnic or regional basis. Moreover, in view of the extraordinary proliferation of nonpolitical associations in postwar years, one can easily understand why this process led to a multiplicity of political groups. The relationships

between political parties and messianic movements are perhaps not so
easily discernible, partly because of the aura of secrecy surrounding the
latter. Nonetheless, although their instigators usually disclaimed all motives of a political nature, the evidence shows that they played an important part in the development of political activities. In brief, to understand the origins of Congolese parties it is necessary to look at the social
and historical context in which they arose.

### Early Nativistic and Messianic Movements

The Congo became at an early date the scene of sporadic protest
movements which found expression in a variety of messianic and nativistic
sects.* In 1904 a magico-religious movement, "une sorte d'organisation
magique et en partie secrète de la société indigène totale," [2] appeared in
the region of Bena Dibele, in the Sankuru district of the Kasai. Under
the leadership of a certain Epikilipikili, the movement rapidly spread
among the Bakuba, the Bangende, and the Bashilele in neighboring
areas. The magical virtues attributed to the fetish of the sect (Tonga-
Tonga) precipitated a series of revolts among the populations of the
Sankuru which led to a bloody repression.[3] Again in 1919 and 1920 serious
uprisings occurred among the Basonge-Meno, in the same region and
under very similar circumstances. This time the movement spread from
the Sankuru to Equateur Province, all the way to the Lac Leopold II
district, and to the Kwango.[4] The revolt was not quelled until the early
part of 1921, after an impressive show of force: "Un déploiement con-
sidérable de forces produisit l'effet qu'on attendait; dès le mois d'avril
nous avions obtenu la soumission de toutes les populations insurgées
contre notre autorité." [5] In 1931, however, some ten years later, further
unrest developed among the Bapende of the Kwango under the influence
of a nativistic movement instigated by a group of appointed chiefs. Here
again the movement led to a series of spontaneous uprisings which resulted in a military expedition that caused the loss of approximately 500
lives among the Bapende.[6] This manifestation of protest was undoubtedly one of the most serious ever faced by the colonial authorities, but it
was by no means the last.

Meanwhile the Lower Congo saw the emergence of a number of
messianic movements, roughly similar to those previously mentioned

---

* In this context the term "nativism" refers to "any conscious, organized attempt
on the part of a society's members to revive or perpetuate selected aspects of its
culture" (see Ralph Linton, "Nativistic Movements," *American Anthropologist*, XLV
[April–June, 1943], 230–240). "Such movements," adds the author, "are comparable
in many respects to the messianic movements which have arisen in many societies
in times of stress. They usually originate with some individual who assumes the role
of a prophet, and is accepted by the people because they wish to believe. They
always lean on the supernatural and usually embody apocalyptic and millennial
aspects" (p. 232).

except for the fact that they contained an element of rationality that was almost totally lacking in nativism. In such movements "moribund elements of culture are not revived for their own sake or in anticipation of practical advantages from the elements themselves. Their revival is part of a magical formula designed to modify the society's environment in ways which will be favorable to it." [7]

One of the first indigenous messianic movements was the so-called sect of the Antonians, founded in 1704 by a young Congolese "saint," Dona Beatrice, in the vicinity of San Salvador at a time when the old Kongo Kingdom had already fallen prey to bitter dynastic rivalries between the chiefs of Soyo and those of San Salvador. According to the testimony of Father Bernardo da Gallo, a Capuchin missionary who lived in the Congo between 1701 and 1709, the king of San Salvador, Pedro IV, had fled from his capital and established his court near Mount Chibango, presumably because he found this location more easily defendable against the incursions of his rivals. For some thirty years before the emergence of the sect the kingdom had been in the throes of a bloody civil war, accompanied by innumerable successoral fights among the various pretenders to the throne. These circumstances help to explain the curious political complexion acquired by the sect. Although the movement started as a typical syncretistic manifestation, directed in part against the control of the Church, it soon developed political objectives of its own. While Dona Beatrice went about the countryside telling her listeners that Christ was born in San Salvador, she also urged the King to return to San Salvador and restore the political unity of his realm. In time, with the assistance of a certain Chibenga, she managed to organize a strong opposition movement against King Pedro, whose authority was so heavily dependent upon the support of the Catholic clergy that he had no choice but to dissociate himself from the Antonians. Condemned by the Church as a heretic, Dona Beatrice died at the stake on July 1, 1706, but the sect continued to exert a profound influence on the political life of the kingdom. Until the defeat of Chibenga in 1709, the Antonians were in fact the chief source of opposition to both the clergy and the king. The main significance of this early prophet movement is that it possessed striking similarities to the syncretistic cults that have proliferated in the Lower Congo in more recent times. In the sect of the Antonians "can be seen a movement that is the precursor of modern politico-religious agitations, like Kimbanguism and its derivatives." [8]

Kimbanguism,* the best known of the messianic movements, was founded in 1921 by the "prophet" Simon Kimbangu, a former catechist

---

* Kimbanguism was also known as Kintwadi, Ngunzism, the Disciples of Simon Kimbangu, and, most recently, as the Church of Jesus Christ on Earth by Simon Kimbangu.

of Bakongo origins who was educated at the Protestant mission of Ngombe-Lutete.[9] This magico-religious movement had as its manifest objective the constitution of an independent African church incorporating into its dogmas some of the elements found in the Bible. But in its latent forms, at least, it represented a spontaneous movement of resistance directed against European domination. Indeed, in the minds of many converts, Kimbangu was the "elect" who would expel the whites and then become the "ruler of Africa." And for some he was the heir apparent to the throne of the old Kongo Kingdom. This peculiar combination of traditionalist, nationalistic, and antiwhite elements is clearly reflected in some of the "Heavenly Songs" written by Kimbangu's disciples, and in their tendency to accept from the Bible whatever messages of freedom could be read into it.[10]

Kimbanguism spread like wildfire through the Lower Congo, gaining an increasing number of devotees in both rural and urban areas. The movement rapidly assumed "such unwieldy proportions that Kimbangu could no longer attend to the details of the organization himself. He was obliged to seek for assistants, and there was no lack of volunteers." [11] In September, 1921, however, Kimbangu was arrested, along with 248 of his disciples, and sentenced to life imprisonment. But the appeals of his doctrine did not end with his martyrdom, for "Kimbangu's disciples remain profoundly faithful to his doctrine. They confidently believe in the coming of a Messiah, a black Christ who will liberate the country of their ancestors and establish a kingdom of love and justice." [12]

The deportation of Kimbangu to Elisabethville did not diminish the strength of their convictions; indeed, it added new fervor to the zeal of his disciples. Despite numerous attempts at suppression on the part of the administration, the movement (subsequently known as Ngunzism) continued to show a remarkable vitality. In December, 1923, in Thysville, several thousand Ngunzists participated in a public demonstration, presumably to obtain the release of Kimbangu, and in subsequent years similar incidents occurred at Tumba, Kilange, Nkamba (Kimbangu's birthplace), and elsewhere in the Lower Congo.[13] At the same time the movement's xenophobic and nationalistic tendencies became increasingly manifest. The fact that it had been driven underground at the time of Kimbangu's imprisonment, and the growing influence of André Matswa's Amicale Balali—a protonationalist organization founded in Brazzaville in 1926 [14]—decisively contributed to the radicalization of the movement:

From a movement in which spiritual revival was the central feature, even if elements of nationalism were by no means lacking, it has developed into a movement almost entirely hostile to foreigners and with obviously national and revolutionary aims. . . . The aims of the movement are more political than religious. There is more talk of Ntotila's coming and of the establishment of the national kingdom than of Christ as a Savior for the sins of the individual and the people.[15]

This trend became even more accentuated during the postwar years. In 1956, for example, a group of Kimbanguists from Leopoldville sent a memorandum to the United Nations denouncing "the colonialist governments of Belgium and Portugal . . . who introduced themselves illegally into the ancient Kongo Kingdom," and suggested that they be replaced by a Kimbanguist government.[16] As on earlier occasions, the colonial authorities responded to this political resurgence by deportations and other punitive measures. In 1956 forty-six leaders of "subversive sects" were arrested in Leopoldville, and fifty-seven Ngunzists were reportedly arrested in Matadi, while in other parts of the Congo similar movements reached an alarming scale.[17]

Only a few years after the emergence of Kimbanguism another messianic movement of major importance, the Watch Tower Movement, better known as Kitawala, appeared in the eastern part of the Congo.[18] Founded in America in 1874 by Charles Taze Russell, and propagated in the United States and abroad by the Jewish judge, J. E. Rutherford, it became affiliated with the American Methodist Episcopal Church in 1894. The movement seems to have been introduced into South Africa about the turn of the century at the instigation of H. M. Turner, bishop of the Negro branch of the American Methodist Episcopal Church. From then on it rapidly gained ground in Rhodesia, Nyasaland, Angola, and the Belgian Congo.

From a doctrinal standpoint Kitawala resembles Kimbanguism in its millennial character and its heavy reliance on biblical texts, its vehement opposition to "imported religions," and above all in its insistence on the slogan "Africa for the Africans." Unlike the Kimbanguists, however, the members of the sect make no conscious attempt at cultural revival. Actually, Kitawala is "scarcely a religion in the usual sense of the term, but rather a sort of philosophy of history, a rational account of the divine plan for the world that Russell thinks he had found." [19]

The influence of Kitawala manifested itself in the Congo for the first time in 1923, when a group of propagandists from Nyasaland and Northern Rhodesia attempted to set up local branches in the southern part of the Katanga.[20] Similar attempts were made in 1925 in the territoire of Sakania and in 1927 in Elisabethville. From the beginning of the 1930's the movement underwent a rapid expansion, recruiting an increasing number of adherents in Elisabethville, Kipushi, Manono, Shinkolobwe, Jadotville, and Albertville, as well as in many rural areas of the Katanga where it seemed to enjoy "the complicity of the customary authorities." In Elisabethville alone it claimed about a thousand members in 1932. By 1936 the workers' camps of the Union Minière in Jadotville were reported to be "infected" by Kitawalist cells: "Leurs propagandistes prêchent l'égalité des races, l'égalité des salaires et l'Afrique aux noirs. Ils prêchent la lutte contre l'Eglise Catholique appelée par l'Etat pour tromper les noirs." The petulance of the sentiments animating the adepts of the sect is perhaps best illustrated by the words of one Emile Ilunga, who was arrested in Elisabethville in 1937 along with several other ringleaders:

We blacks are here in our country and what we want is to be considered as Europeans, for the Bible makes no distinctions between whites and blacks. Our Watch Tower Movement seeks to put an end to all this, for it is only here in the Congo that the government considers the natives as slaves. We are fed up with this, and the new God of the Kitawalist doctrine is here to help us. . . . Look at this man on the brochure of the Watch Tower: "Toward Deliverance"; this man laden with chains represents all the natives.

During these years, in an effort to forestall the expansion of the sect, the Katanga authorities deported thousands of adepts to other regions of the Congo. But instead of thwarting the movement it merely exported its influence to the other provinces. Thus, thanks to the camp for deported persons at Lubutu, the sect made rapid headway in Orientale Province, gaining important strongholds in Ponthierville and Stanleyville. Similarly, it was the "relégués" of Yakoma who introduced the movement to Equateur Province. By 1946 the Tshuapa district was reported to be undergoing "a recrudescence of Kitawalist activity," and, in 1947, 300 members of the sect were arrested in the territoire of Bokungu. The same pattern repeated itself in the Kivu, where the local populations proved notably receptive to the appeals of the Watch Tower. In 1942 a number of cells appeared among the workers' camps of the Comité National du Kivu in Muhulu, territoire of Masisi, where the movement caused some serious disturbances in March of the same year. Under the leadership of the famous Bushiri, also known under the pseudonym of Mulumozi wa Yesu (the representative of Jesus), a group of Kitawalists conceived the idea of capturing the European personnel of the mining camps of Nyamasa and Muhulu, and then attacking Costermansville (now Bukavu). After a bloody uprising at Jembe where 58 rebels were killed, some 379 suspects were arrested, of whom 74 were sentenced to death and the rest to penal servitude. Despite this brutal repression the movement continued to attract a substantial number of adherents, especially among the Bakumu, the Wanianga, the Bakano-Bakondji, and the Bakusu; by 1955 the territoire of Walikale claimed an estimated 7,000 sect members. But it also continued to show many signs of vitality in Orientale, Equateur, and Kasai provinces, where the movement coexisted with numerous fetish societies.

The vulnerability of the Congo societies to the influence of nativistic and messianic movements depends to some extent on the social and political structure of these societies, as well as on the transformations they have undergone since they came into contact with Western influences.[21] In general, however, their origins are to be found in the emotional strains and stresses of the colonial situation. In the absence of meaningful, regular channels of political expression, they provided alternative outlets for the discharge of grievances and tensions.

How did these movements affect subsequent political developments? First, by creating a climate of social and political unrest which in turn invited stringent repressions, they provoked intense nationalist feelings among the local populations. And at a later stage these feelings were capitalized upon by political leaders to mobilize support. The extraordinarily rapid expansion of nationalist activities through Orientale Province, the Kivu, and the eastern part of the Equateur, especially in the Tshuapa district, is largely attributable to the heritage of protest created by movements of a nativistic or chiliastic character. Similarly, against the background of unrest caused by the emergence of prophet movements, one can better understand why the Lower Congo was the area where organized nationalist activities first came into existence.

Furthermore, such movements afforded subsequent generations of nationalists ways and means of furthering their immediate political goals. In some instances, by a curious process of identification, the magico-religious qualities of a prophet were attributed to a political leader, hence adding an element of mysticism to his personal prestige. For example, after the riots of January, 1959, Kasa-Vubu seems to have been regarded by some Bakongo as the reincarnation of Simon Kimbangu, and pictures that were circulated among the African population of Leopoldville showed Kasa-Vubu receiving his powers from Jesus Christ at the request of Kimbangu.[22] This kind of imagery is not only indicative of the immense prestige enjoyed by Kasa-Vubu, but it also helps to explain the rapid rise to prominence of a party like the Abako. More often, a conscious effort was made by Congolese leaders to force the grievances of certain sects into political channels. Although this practice was not restricted to any single political group, no other party resorted to it so frequently and successfully as the Abako; without in any way identifying its political objectives with the contents of the Kimbanguist doctrine, the Abako never missed an opportunity to pay homage to Simon Kimbangu and to those of his followers who suffered martyrdom at the hands of the administration. And when the remains of Kimbangu were transferred from Elisabethville to Matadi-Mayo, in April, 1960, several Abako leaders, including Kasa-Vubu, expressed their grief by attending the funeral ceremony.

Third, these movements sometimes contributed to the cultural revival that attended the emergence of some political groups. The continued diffusion of the Kimbanguist faith, with its emphasis on the traditional aspects of the Bakongo culture, probably stimulated the rise of cultural nationalism among the Bakongo. In a sense the syncretism of Kimbanguism found a counterpart in the combination of modernist and traditionalist strands discernible in the Bakongo nationalist movement. But this factor is only one of those that encouraged cultural revivalism among the Bakongo; equally important was the part played by tribal unions in perpetuating certain aspects of the traditional culture.

Finally, certain manifestations of messianic or nativistic character were instigated by Africans to further their immediate political goals. In the Kasai, for example, one Sébastien Kapongo was reported in 1954 to have launched a Mau-Mau sect in order to widen the appeal of the Association Lulua-Frères among the population of the Demba territory. Kapongo was described in a Sûreté report as the "promoter, initiator, and high priest of a sect that he calls Mau-Mau." [23] According to the same report, the "number of devotees, recruited exclusively among the members of the Lulua-Frères, . . . [was] extremely high, and the movement [had] gained a strong foothold in the Demba territory." The organization of the sect was apparently built around a paramount chief (*grand chef*), who would delegate his authority to a group of subalterns referred to as *conducteurs* or *conducteurs en chef,* depending on their position within the hierarchy of the movement. Except for the facts that these officials "wore long black robes and a fez" and "prayed on a sheepskin," the information disclosed by the Sûreté concerning their role and identity is very scanty. All we know is that the "paramount chief organized meetings at night in the villages" and distributed fetishes made of soap, which presumably would "make the Lulua people courageous, invisible to the armies of the enemy, and superior to anyone." Despite the absence of recognizable similarities between the ritualistic aspects of Kapongo's sect and the Mau-Mau movement in Kenya, the movements were alike in serving as instruments for the political mobilization of the rural masses. In fact, the extremely rapid development of the Lulua-Frères must be largely attributed to its nativistic underpinnings. By 1955, for example, the association had organized nineteen branches in the Kasai, twelve in the Katanga, two in Leopoldville, one in Stanleyville, and another in Usumbura (Burundi); in the Kasai alone the total membership of the association was estimated at 8,679.[24]

THE GROWTH OF VOLUNTARY ASSOCIATIONS

Just as nativistic and messianic movements represent a distinctive form of adjustment, or maladjustment, to the challenge of European domination, voluntary associations represent a specific response to the disintegrating influences of modernity and the opportunities for reintegration arising therefrom. They made it possible "for Africans to recover . . . the sense of common purpose which in traditional African society was normally enjoyed through tribal organization." [25] At the same time they provided the organizational framework through which Congolese nationalists mobilized and channeled the energies of the African masses into an effective political apparatus.

In its most generic sense, the term "voluntary association" covers many different types of institutionalized groupings: tribal and regional associations, alumni societies, coöperatives, trade unions. For the sake of analysis, however, it will be useful to distinguish between "functionally diffuse" organizations in which membership criteria were chiefly determined by ethnic, linguistic, or communal ties, and "functionally specific" organizations in which membership was determined by criteria other than those previously mentioned.*

*Functionally Diffuse Associations*

In postwar years a multitude of tribal associations suddenly sprang up in the major urban centers of the Congo. They involved the coöperation of individuals drawn from one or several ethnically related groups, and their leadership usually consisted of Westernized elements who sought to preserve or strengthen the identification of the members with their traditional milieu, as well as to "improve" the social, economic, and cultural level of their ethnic community.[26] The activities carried on by these associations illustrate the "diffuseness" of their goals:

Dans toutes les circonstances, fastes ou néfastes les membres se réunissent autour de celui d'entre eux qui souffre ou se réjouit. Ils s'organisent et se cotisent pour gâter les hospitalisés, les femmes accouchées. Ils se mettent en peine pour accueillir héberger et diriger les nouveaux arrivés, pour apaiser les conflits entre époux, pour intervenir en cas de maladie prolongée et de chômage involontaire, lors des naissances, mariages ou décès, pour participer aux frais de voyage de ceux qui vont en congé dans le milieu natal pour soutenir et rapatrier les veuves et les orphelins.[27]

Some of these associations can be traced back to an early date. For example, the Association des Lunda, subsequently known as the Groupe-

---

* "A functionally specific relationship is defined as one in which the activities, or considerations, or rights and obligations covered by the relationship are precisely defined and delimited. A functionally diffuse relationship is defined as one in which the activities, rights, etc., are vaguely defined and delimited" (Marion J. Levy, "Some Sources of Vulnerability of the Structures of Relatively Non-industrialized Societies," in *The Progress of Underdeveloped Areas,* ed. Bert Hoselitz [Chicago: University of Chicago Press, 1952], p. 117). In the context in which they are used these terms designate certain patterns of relationship in an "ideal" way, for a number of these associations combined functional specificity and functional diffuseness.

ment des Associations Mutuelles de l'Empire Lunda, was recognized by the district commissioner of Elisabethville on April 24, 1932.[28] Most of them, however, appeared in the early 1950's as a result of the postwar influx of rural inhabitants into urban centers. By 1956 as many as eighty-five tribal associations were officially registered in the Leopoldville area.[29]

Undoubtedly the most powerful of all the tribal associations of Leopoldville was the Abako, officially recognized by the district commissioner of the Moyen-Congo on July 7, 1953.[30] Under the leadership of its founder, Edmond Nzeza-Nlandu, the association rapidly grew in strength and influence. As the name indicates—Association pour le Maintien, l'Unité et l'Expansion de la Langue Kikongo—its immediate objective was "to unify, preserve, and spread the Kikongo language." This objective was accomplished mainly through the publication of a weekly newspaper, the *Kongo Dia Ngunga,* which, according to the statutes of the organization, "sera l'expression de tout Mukongo et de toutes les associations Bakongo-Kwangolaises de Léopoldville." [31] From its inception, therefore, the association showed considerable interest in the cultural improvement of its members, who were recruited among the Bakongo population exclusively.

Next to the Abako, the most important of these associations in Leopoldville was the Liboke Lya Bangala, founded on December 4, 1954, by a former seminarist and newspaper editor, Jean Motingia, and primarily intended for the so-called Bangala and the tribes that had been officially recognized by the association as related to the Bangala, namely, Lokele, Basoko, Bapoto, Ngombe, Motembo, Bangbandi, Mbanza, Ngbaka, and others.[32] Like the Abako, the Liboke Lya Bangala was formed to give its members some sense of identification with their traditional milieu. But, unlike the Abako, whose major focus of activity was the preservation and expansion of the use of the vernacular of the particular group, its interests were not directed toward any specific objective. Because of the diversity of its tribal components it never acquired the degree of social and cultural cohesion displayed by the Abako. In fact, it may well be regarded as a regional rather than a strictly tribal association.

The main types of regional associations found in Leopoldville were the *associations de ressortissants,* the most notable of which were the Fédération Kwango-Kwiloise, founded by Gaston Midu in July, 1953, and the Fédération Kasaïenne, founded by Eugène Kabamba in May, 1955. Membership in each of these "federations" was determined by regional criteria; for example, the Fédération Kwango-Kwiloise drew its members from one or the other of the several tribes located in the Kwango-Kwilu area (Bambala, Bapende, Batshokwe, Bayaka, Bayanzi, etc.), just as the Fédération Kasaïenne included in its membership expatriate elements who belonged to one or another of the Kasaian tribes. Within the federation, however, association by tribal affiliation was the rule rather than the exception. In 1955 the Fédération Kasaïenne comprised some thirty different *associations primaires*, based on tribal and kinship ties: Jeunesse Bena Mukuna, Association Familiale Bakwa-Ntembe, Association Bena Koshi, Association Mutuelle Bakuba de Lusambo, Association Bakwa-Dishi, Association des Basonge de Lubefu, and others. These associations were represented by an equal number of *comités de groupments* which were in turn responsible to the central committee of the federation. But there was in fact little or no coördination between the central organs and the associations primaires.[33] On the whole, these federations were not so much the expression of residential affiliations as the projection of aggregated tribal loyalties.

The proliferation of associations also hit several other urban centers besides Leopoldville. In Luluabourg some members of the Baluba tribes organized a number of kinship and tribal associations—Association Bena Mpuka, Association Bakwa-Dishi, Association Bena Tshiamba, Association Mutua Mukuna, and so forth. By far the most active, however, was the Association Lulua-Frères, founded in 1951 by a Lulua chief, Sylvain Mangole Kalamba, for the purpose of "improving the situation of the Lulua people, culturally, morally, and socially." [34] Beginning in 1953, the association undertook to set up branch unions in the other provinces as well as in territories outside the Congo. In 1954 the Luluabourg section reportedly sent recruiting agents to Kitwe, Northern Rhodesia, with membership cards for Rhodesian members,[35] and by 1955 it had set up branches in each of the major mining centers of the Katanga, including Elisabethville, where the association counted more than 1,000 active members.[36]

A host of other associations sprang up in Elisabethville, among them Association des Baluba du Katanga, Fédération des Tribus du Haut-Katanga, Groupement des Associations Mutuelles de l'Empire Lunda, Association des Ressortissants Bahemba de Kongolo, and Association des Basonge du Katanga. Likewise, Bukavu became the scene of intensive organizational activity. There were, for example, the Union d'Entraide Batembo du Kivu, the Association Batetela, the Association Bakwa-Luntu, and the Caisse d'Entraide de l'Elite Bashi. Similar developments occurred in Stanleyville, Coquilhatville, and other urban centers.

Many of these associations proved to be ephemeral. Some merely collapsed because they were too parochial to survive, or because they did not serve the purpose for which they were initially set up; others merged into broader units or split up into separate factions. In several instances, however, they served as "the real focus of the migrants' political interests and activities," [37] and hence became the direct precursors of organized political groups.

By agitating in favor of social, economic, and political reforms, sponsoring motions to the provincial councils, "advising" the administration on the choice of customary or invested chiefs, and nominating candidates for election to the communal councils, they performed increasingly significant pressure-group functions. Eventually, they came to be regarded by the administration as legitimate interest groups whose views should be taken into consideration whenever circumstances so required. Some évolués even contended that the "multiplication of clan associations" was owing essentially to the abusive complacency of the administration: "The administration lends a special attention to the development of clan associations. Their presidents form a special council which is consulted on every occasion. This initiative has consequently produced a multiplication of clan associations." [38] In any event, the associations were important training grounds for future political leaders. Long before they had had a chance to engage in political activities, the leaders of these associations learned how to organize and manipulate a mass apparatus, articulate grievances, and disseminate information and propaganda, thereby massing much valuable experience.

At the same time, however, they tended to perpetuate certain aspects of the traditional culture, either by stimulating interest in the language, customs, and history of the tribe, or by facilitating contacts between customary and extracustomary centers. But this does not mean that they were inevitably conservative in outlook. Their primary concern was to control and synchronize processes of acculturation, with a view to bringing some measure of harmony between the évolué population and the rural masses, and unifying all clan and kinship groups within the same nationality group. This point was made by one Bonaventure Makonga, a Baluba of the Katanga, in the July 11, 1957, issue of the Elisabethville newspaper *L'Etoile-Nyota:*

Elles [les associations tribales] sont une réalité exigeante, émanant du peuple tout entier. Elles unissent les déracinés à ceux qui sont restés dans les milieux d'origine, les évolués à la masse. Elles unissent à l'échelle non plus clanique mais tribale, grâce à l'effort du blanc promoteur de vastes agglomérations facilitant la rencontre des membres des mêmes tribus longtemps séparés par le temps et les distances. *Elles écartent les notions de coutumier et d'extra-coutumier pour plus former qu'un seul groupe de gens attelés à une même tâche: l'évolution systématique de tous les habitants d'un même pays* [italics added].

The extent to which the leaders of these associations actually endeavored to promote the "systematic evolution of all the inhabitants of the same land" varied substantially depending on the groups concerned. This tendency was perhaps most clearly evidenced among such large-scale entities as the Bakongo, the Baluba, and the Lulua. In any event,

1. The late Patrice Lumumba, first prime minister of the Congo and national president of the Mouvement National Congolais (MNC). By permission of Photo Africapress.

2. Joseph Kasa-Vubu, president of the Republic of the Congo and former president of the Alliance des Bakongo (Abako). By permission of Photo Africapress.

3. *Albert Kalondji, mulopwe (king) of the short-lived mining state of South Kasai and at one time national president of the dissident wing of the Mouvement National Congolais (MNC). By permission of Photo Africapress.*

4. *Cléophas Kamitatu, provincial president of the Parti Solidaire Africain (PSA). By permission of Photo Africapress.*

5. *Antoine Gizenga, national president of the Parti Solidaire Africain (PSA). By permission of Photo Africapress.*

6. Paul Bolya, president of
the Parti National du Progrès
(PNP), in full regalia. By permission of Courrier d'Afrique.

7. Albert Kalondji, carried in triumph by his supporters. By permission of
Photo Africapress.

8. *A political meeting of the Union Kwangolaise pour l'Indépendance et la Liberté (Luka). By permission of Photo Africapress.*

9. *A group of Bangala warriors on their way to a meeting of the Parti de l'Unité Nationale (Puna). By permission of Photo Africapress.*

10. A militant of the Alliance des Bakongo (Abako) with Kasa-Vubu's effigy on his garment. By permission of Photo Africapress.

11. A Leopoldville voter ponders the ballot. By permission of Photo Africapress.

12. A Tshokwe dancer entertains a group of kinsmen in the Ruashi commune of Elisabethville. Photo by the author.

13. *A group of Baluba of Leopoldville demand the division of the Kasai Province and the constitution of a Baluba state. By permission of Photo Africapress.*

14. *A Muyaka of Leopoldville is clubbed to death. By permission of Photo Africapress.*

15. *A patrol of Congolese soldiers attempts to maintain "peace and order" in the cité indigène of Leopoldville during the electoral campaign. By permission of Photo Africapress.*

16. *Albert Ndele, at one time chef de cabinet of the Minister of Finance in Lumumba's government, has just escaped an attempt against his life. A United Nations soldier watches the scene. By permission of Photo Africapress.*

17. *Moise Tshombe, president of the Conakat and later president of the Independent State of the Katanga. By permission of Pix Inc.*

18. *Anicet Kashamura, president of the Cerea and later Minister of Information and Cultural Affairs in Lumumba's government. By permission of Pix Inc.*

by placing a strong emphasis on ethnic solidarity, they played a decisive role in strengthening the group consciousness of their people; they also set important limits on the range of political goals and activities which they assigned to these associations, thus preparing the way for the emergence of political parties based on cultural, historical, or ethnic ties, or a combination of these.

In a sense this is also true of the associations de ressortissants, since so few could resist the centrifugal pressure of their ethnic components once independence came within the foreseeable future. The result was that they usually broke up into splinter groups, each drawing its support from separate tribal entities. In many instances, however, their influence was restricted to expatriate elements of particular urban localities, hence favoring the growth of "dwarf" parties.[39]

A third type of voluntary grouping was the so-called *cercles d'évolués,* whose membership was restricted to Westernized elements which are sometimes loosely referred to as "detribalized." * The nature of their objectives is illustrated by the statutes of the Association des Evolués de Stanleyville, whose purposes were to "group all the évolués of Stanleyville, to create an atmosphere of understanding and solidarity among its members, to organize their leisure according to their level of education, and to improve their intellectual, social, moral and physical formation." [40] In other words, one finds here the same diffuseness of objectives which characterized tribal and regional associations, with the difference, however, that the principal motive for joining a cercle d'évolués was to transcend the pale of tribal and ethnic loyalties, and seek reintegration through a broader ordering of human relationships.

By 1947, 113 cercles d'évolués, with a total membership of 5,609, had been organized in the several towns of the Congo. Between 1952 and 1956, however, their number increased from 131 to 317, and their membership from 7,661 to 15,345.[41] The rapid growth of the évolué population, together with the prospect of immatriculation, accounts in part for the success encountered by these clubs. But the main reason for their popularity is that they came to be regarded as instruments for "the gradual initiation [of the Congolese] to the administration of our own affairs." According to Antoine Marie Mobe, former president of the Association des Evolués de Stanleyville, there were in 1956

two kinds of organs through which the natives are gradually becoming initiated to the stewardship of the affairs of the country: (*a*) the official ones

---

* Like the term "évolué," the term "detribalized" has different connotations and meanings, for it has never been defined with any precision. In this context "detribalized" is used to refer to a category of individuals who have "taken over new primary loyalties and values, along with new ways of living and new occupations" (see M. Herskovits, *The Human Factor in Changing Africa* [New York: Knopf, 1962], p. 288).

. . . such as the *conseils d'entreprise,* the *commissions régionales et provinciales du TEPSI,* the *conseils de province,* and the *conseil de gouvernement;* and (*b*) the unofficial ones . . . born out of the initiative of the natives, directly or indirectly. As long as local contingencies will not permit a better mode of representation in the official assemblies we do not see why these associations should not be allowed . . . to discuss some of these problems in order to allow us to obtain a gradual initiation to the administration of our own affairs.[42]

Like the tribal and regional associations, these cercles became natural outlets for the expression of grievances; they provided their members with a forum for the discussion of social, economic, and political problems; and they served as informal training grounds for the rise of their more dynamic elements to positions of leadership. But they made no effort whatsoever to cultivate the tribal loyalties of their members. As Robert Rotberg noted in connection with similar associations in East and Central Africa, "these voluntary, atribal groupings would not have existed had it not been for the de-emphasis on tribal ties that was apparent fairly early among the more educated, and more urbanized, Africans." [43] One result of the deëmphasis on tribal ties is that it favored the rise of broadly based parties led by modernist, Westernized elites. Among the more prominent leaders of such groups were Patrice Lumumba, at one time president of the Association des Evolués de Stanleyville, Cléophas Kamitatu, a leading personality of the Cercle des Evolués de Kikwit, Chrysostome Weregemere, president of the Cercle des Evolués de Costermansville, and many others.

A fourth type of association that had a formative influence on Congolese parties is represented by the several alumni associations that came into being during the interwar period. As their names indicate (Association des Anciens Elèves des Pères de Scheut, Association des Anciens Elèves des Ecoles Chrétiennes, Union des Anciens Elèves des Frères Maristes, etc.), they were sponsored by religious congregations for the purpose of promoting a Christian esprit de corps among their members. One of them, the Association des Anciens Elèves des Pères de Scheut, better known as Adapès, underwent a rapid development after the war, eventually claiming a membership of some 15,000.[44] In 1945 some of its members decided to expand the scope of their activities by organizing in Leopoldville the Union des Intérêts Sociaux Congolais (Unisco), a study group aiming at "the total suppression of all internal and external signs of racial discrimination, the improvement of the social conditions of the natives in general, and the defense of the rights of the évolués in particular." [45] Under the leadership of its first president, Eugène Kabamba, who subsequently became the organizer of the Fédération Kasaïenne, the Unisco displayed an increasing vitality, organizing re-

unions, sponsoring lectures, setting up libraries, and even sending petitions to the colonial authorities for the redress of social and economic
grievances. At the time, however, the association was entirely composed
of clerks or *moniteurs* who had had only a rudimentary education, a de-
fect that was regarded by some as a serious handicap. They felt that in the
absence of a strong representative personality who could act as an "inter-
locuteur valable" on behalf of the association, they would never be in a
position to apply effective pressure on the administration. It was to
remedy this situation that the president of the Unisco, Jean Bolikango,
called upon Joseph Kasa-Vubu to act as spokesman for the association.
As a former seminarist, Kasa-Vubu was eminently qualified for this
position, which he held until 1956. From the very beginning, however,
Kasa-Vubu showed himself much more eager to assert the claims of the
Bakongo against the Bangala than to press the demands of the association
against the colonial administration. In 1946, in a lecture to the Unisco
entitled "The Right of the First Occupant," he argued that since the
Bakongo were the first occupants of the territory surrounding the capital
they were its sole legitimate owners, a thesis which "provoked the consternation of the assembly." [46] The incident has more than a historical
significance; it also illustrates the kind of tensions that have so frequently arisen within the alumni associations. But while many of them
failed to resist the pressure of tribal particularisms, they nevertheless
contributed to the political awakening of their members. In this respect
their role was similar to that played by other types of associations.
Partly because of their early exposure to Christian influences, the elites
who emanated from their ranks tended to be of a moderate kind. Jean
Bolikango, at one time president of both the Adapès and the Unisco, and
Jean-Pierre Dericoyard, once president of the Union des Anciens Elèves
des Frères Maristes, are examples.

### Functionally Specific Associations

Other associations were organized to perform specialized functions
for their members. Most often the tendency to satisfy social and economic
needs through associational specialization occurred within the tribe or
kinship group, as evidenced by the growth of mutual-aid societies and
coöperatives organized along ethnic lines. But it also led to the growth of
voluntary groupings that cut across ethnic ties. In the Congo this latter
form of associational interest is best exemplified by the development of
trade-union activities.

Until 1946 labor activities were exclusively carried out by the Confédération Générale des Syndicats (CGS), a left-wing organization restricted to European workers, which came into being in 1944 after several
professional organizations decided to merge into a single union. Viewed

as a Communist-inspired organization by the administration, the CGS subsequently lost most of its following to the Christian trade unions affiliated with the metropolitan Confédération des Syndicats Chrétiens (CSC). As the socialist labor leaders of the metropolis at one point refused to compete with the Christian trade unions on the grounds that they were "under the tutelage of Belgian functionaries," [47] the CSC virtually monopolized the field of labor organizational activity. By 1953, for example, of sixty registered trade unions, fifty were affiliated with the CSC. [48]

Because of legal restrictions imposed upon them, the trade unions never succeeded in attracting more than a small fraction of the wage and salary earners of the Congo. In 1956 they claimed a total membership of 8,829, which at the time represented less than 1 per cent of the estimated total wage labor force. [49] More than half of the registered unions were located in Leopoldville, and at least until 1957 there were none in Kasai and Equateur provinces. Some measure of liberalization was introduced by the decree of February, 1957, which recognized the right of the agents and auxiliary agents of the administration "to join occupational associations devoted to the study, defense, and furtherance of their economic, occupational, and social interests," and by the legislative ordinance of September, 1957, which recognized the right of trade unions to have recourse to a strike or walkout in the event of "a final failure of the conciliation and arbitration procedure" prescribed by the ordinance. [50] But the reform had apparently very little impact on the attitude of the African masses. [51] However, as Father Bruyns pointed out, "one immediate consequence of this enactment is that the socialist and liberal unions made a bid for African membership whereas in the past ten years only the Christian unions took action to organize manual and nonmanual unions." [52]

Rather than the unions per se, it was their satellite organizations, represented by a host of amicales, cercles, study groups, and the like, which provided the main stimulus to the growth of political activity. On the side of the CSC were found a variety of sociocultural groups, such as the Jeunesses Ouvrières Chrétiennes (JOC), the Centre d'Etudes et de Recherches Sociales (CERS), the Ligue des Employés Chrétiens, all of which served as agencies for the diffusion of Christian democratic ideas. Whereas the Amicales Libérales served a similar purpose for the adepts of the Liberal doctrine, in Leopoldville the Amicale Socialiste, affiliated with the metropolitan-sponsored Fédération Générale des Travailleurs Belges du Congo (FGTBC), became the main carrier of Socialist ideas. Under the leadership of Alphonse Nguvulu, at one time president of the Leopoldville provincial committee of the FGTBC, the Amicale Socialiste developed into a small militant organization whose members did not hesitate, on occasion, to attack the administration. In early 1958, for example, the association took a firm stand in favor of a genuine democratization of the colonial institutions, advocating "une reille autonomie communale et la disparition d'une contrainte administrative intolérable en régime démocratique." [53] Although its leader once expressed his admiration for the "noble ideology (of the FGTBC), which is at the forefront of the economic, social, and political emancipation of the Belgian workers," [54] the association owed its initial success to the belief of some Congolese that the aid and support of the metropolitan parent organization would enable them to gain a strong bargaining position vis-à-vis the administration. However, once they realized that most of the European socialists acted like members of the "exploiting class," many Congolese deserted the ranks of the Amicale Socialiste.[55] On the whole, the main contribution of these associations to the development of Congolese parties was not ideological but educational. They were the agencies through which a number of future Congolese leaders, including Cyrille Adoula, Joseph Ileo, and Patrice Lumumba, received their initial political education, and learned the techniques of propaganda and agitation.

With the exception of the Amicale Socialiste de Leopoldville, which transformed itself into a minor political group (the Parti du Peuple) whose ideology smacked of socialism, these organizations were unable to bring about a lasting ideological commitment on the part of their members. Under the pressure of events a number of trade-union militants formerly associated with metropolitan-sponsored organizations joined the ranks of the nationalist movement. And yet, though Congolese workers rapidly disengaged themselves from the hold of metropolitan trade unions, their previous exposure to different ideologies and methods of political action carried within itself serious portents of dissension.

It would be wrong to conclude that the metropolitan model was the only one to find acceptance among the African workers. The Association du Personnel Indigène de la Colonie (APIC), founded in 1946, remained unaffected by metropolitan influences, even when the pressure of partisan ideologies reached its highest point. Explaining the motives that prompted the APIC to take an independent route to social and economic advance, its president, Arthur Pinzi, stated in 1957 that "the Congolese elites would betray the future aspirations of their children if they admitted that the only independent trade union, created and managed for and by the Congolese, could possibly disappear." [56] For this reason the APIC proved to be more successful than its rival organizations in securing "equal pay for equal work" for Congolese workers, despite the vehement opposition of European functionaries affiliated with the Association des Fonctionnaires et Agents de la Colonie (AFAC). The APIC stood as a "united front," unhampered by the internal divisions that affected the Socialist and Christian trade unions and often frustrated the efforts of their members in the field of collective bargaining.[57] The fact remains, however, that the APIC never played an active political role, mainly because the legal restrictions imposed by the administrations made it impossible for its leaders to coördinate and politicize trade-union activities. By the time some of these restrictions were lifted the Abako had already seized the initiative.

The limited amount of organizational freedom enjoyed by the Congolese workers, coupled with the equally limited educational opportunities dispensed by the Belgian colonial regime, helped to channel political activities along ethnic or tribal lines. Contrary to what happened in some territories of French West Africa, where trade unions provided the nuclei for broadly based nationalist movements, the part played by Congolese trade unions in the organizational development of nationalist activity seems negligible. In fact, most political groups turned out to be the lineal descendants of associations functionally diffuse in purpose and orientation, such as tribal and regional associations. Indeed, the first manifestations of militant nationalism originated in a party that emerged from a preëxisting tribal association.

THE ABAKO ENTERS THE POLITICAL ARENA

Long before the Abako transformed itself into a militant nationalist organization, its founder gave a clear hint of the ultimate objectives of the association. In an open letter to his "dear Bakongo compatriots," dated June 15, 1953, Nzeza-Nlandu urged all the Bakongo "to work for the common good of their race," and concluded, "Thus united in their heart and spirit, the Bakongo will become some day a great and prosperous nation in Central Africa." [58] These early efforts of the Abako leaders to spread the idea of a Bakongo nationality among their followers were largely overshadowed in public attention by their renewed interest in the history and culture of the tribe. The reassertion of the values of the Bakongo culture and the early manifestations of Bakongo nationalism cannot, however, be entirely separated. Not only did this cultural revival give a legitimate basis to the "myth" of the Kongo Kingdom on which modern nationalist claims are based, but it also built up the confidence of the Bakongo in their ability to challenge Belgian colonial rule.

Although the Abako was officially recognized by the administration in 1953, it had been active since 1951. Its founder attended at one time the grand séminaire of Mayidi (Kasai) where he became acquainted with Father Van Wing.[59] Only a few months before his ordination, however, he abandoned the priesthood, moved to Leopoldville where he found employment as a clerk in the local branch office of the Huileries du Congo Belge (HCB), and almost immediately set about the task of organizing the Abako. This initiative was partly motivated by a sincere attachment to the culture of the Bakongo, for which he had gained a deeper appreciation and a better knowledge in the course of his frequent contacts with Father Van Wing. But it was also prompted by considerations of a more practical nature. Anticipating the constitutional reform of the Statut des Villes, Nzeza-Nlandu was already aware of the potential advantages that could result from a strong organizational apparatus.

True, a number of Bakongo, mostly students of the Jesuit fathers of Kisantu, had already organized themselves into an association, the Renaissance Bakongo (Renaibako); yet, according to Nzeza-Nlandu, its activities had lapsed into quiescence. His arrival in Leopoldville reactivated the Kisantu-centered Renaibako, infused a new dynamism in the organization, and broadened its organizational bases. By late 1951 the Abako had extended its action to Isangila, and by 1953 to Thysville and its vicinity. Once it had won official recognition, the organization became increasingly active in two ways. It sought, first, to spread its activities from Leopoldville, Thysville, and Matadi to the rural areas, and, second, to establish organizational linkages with special interest groups identified with the kinship system, such as coöperatives, youth groups, and students' organizations.

Meanwhile, positive efforts were made to stimulate the interest of educated elements in the history and culture of the Bakongo, largely through the organ of the association, *Kongo Dia Ngunga*. The circular announcing the foundation of this newspaper stressed the fact that "all the Bakongo are issued from the same stock: *Kongo Dia Ntotila* [the Kongo of the King of San Salvador]." [60] The cultural unity which at one time prevailed among the Bakongo was evoked as the explicit goal toward which all efforts should be directed: "Since the fall of our beloved kingdom brought about by constant warfare against our neighbors, the Yaga, and the slaving activities conducted during the past three centuries, we are no longer united." Nothing short of the collaboration of "all the Bakongo intellectuals," continued the circular, could restore the unity of the Bakongo:

Tous les intellectuels Bakongo de toutes catégories en commençant par nos prêtres, nos députés ou conseillers au gouvernement, nos divers commis, nos chefs de secteur, nos étudiants en théologie et en philosophie, nos étudiants de Lovanium, nos collègiens et nos séminaristes, nos pasteurs, nos instituteurs, nos commerçants, nos chefs de village et tous nos autres chefs doivent se faire les premiers abonnés et les premiers correspondants de notre journal, les propagandistes et les interprètes de ce que nous venons d'exposer.[61]

About the same time, in late 1953, in response to the charge that the composition of the directing organ of the association had been unduly weighted in favor of the Bantandu subgroup, Nzeza-Nlandu called upon a Mayumbe, Joseph Kasa-Vubu, to join the Central Committee of the Abako. Since his lecture to the Unisco in 1946, Kasa-Vubu's personal identification with the interests of the Bakongo had become a matter of common knowledge among the évolués of Leopoldville. In 1953 he reiterated his attachment to the traditional culture of his group in an article entitled "La Coutume Bantoue ne disparaîtra pas mais elle fera des progrès," [62] in which he criticized "certains Africains progressistes" for ignoring the capacity of adaptation of Bantu customs. Citing the example of the Belgians, who "after centuries of Greco-Latin civilization . . . have preserved their own qualities and talents . . . but never converted themselves into Greeks and Romans," Kasa-Vubu argued for a progressive evolution of Bantu civilization:

La coutume Bantoue n'a eu dans son passé qu'un défaut. Ce défaut est celui de n'avoir jamais progressé. ... Or la coutume Bantoue ne disparaîtra pas mais elle fera des progrès. La civilisation qui est elle-même une coutume n'a pas le pouvoir de faire disparaître celles qu'elle rencontre sur la voie du progrès, ni de s'y substituer, mais de les complèter tout en se complètant elle-même et en s'assimilant les nouvelles qualités qu'elle découvre chez les autres peuples. [63]

This particular aspect of Kasa-Vubu's personality, his acceptance of certain Western innovations combined with a manifest attraction to the Bakongo traditional culture, assured him an extraordinary popularity among both the rural masses and the more Westernized elements.

The rapid growth of the Abako was mainly owing to Kasa-Vubu's own dynamic personality. As chairman of the Association des Bourses d'Etudes du Mayombe, an association designed to give "moral and material support to gifted students attending secondary schools and universities," Kasa-Vubu rallied a number of educated elements to the cause of the Abako, and thus gave added impetus to the organization. His promotion to the rank of president of the association early in 1954 added a militant twist to its activities. In some quarters the association came to be viewed with such deep suspicion that in March of the same year its leaders felt the need to issue a public statement to refute the charges made by a local newspaper identifying the Abako with Matswanism, Kimbanguism, and communism. [64]

It was not, however, until August, 1956, with the publication of its countermanifesto, that the Abako actually transformed itself into an overtly political organization. The leaders of the Abako responded to the manifesto of *Conscience Africaine* by a decidedly more outspoken statement, in which they brushed aside all solutions short of immediate self-government. The political awakening of the Bakongo was prompted not only by their opposition to the gradualist character of the timetable suggested by the manifesto, but also by their obvious distaste for the kind of political organization it envisaged to lead the Congolese to self-government.

Taking strong exception to the views advanced by Joseph Ileo concerning the advisability of a "single united front," the leaders of the Abako denounced at the very outset any attempt "to rally all the Congolese to the same opinion" as "sheer utopia." In presenting their argument for what amounted to a multiparty system, they sought to rationalize their position by pointing out that political parties do not reflect "historical circumstances," but "opinions," and hence constitute the indispensable elements of a truly democratic system. "The struggle of parties," they said, "although dangerous, is very necessary in a democracy. It stimulates competition; each party wants to prove to its voters that it knows better than the other what to do to improve the well-being of the people." [65] Yet, although the language of the Abako revealed a certain attachment to democratic principles, it concealed an even deeper commitment to historical, ethnic, and linguistic loyalties. In essence, affiliation to a political party was viewed as secondary to, and derivative from, affiliation with the tribe.

The position of the leaders of the Abako was understandable, considering the potential advantage they could reasonably expect from their numerical strength and previous years of organizational activities. But it also reflects some deeper aspirations. Since their main concern was to preserve the Bakongo cultural heritage, the Abako leaders were naturally apprehensive of being absorbed into an all-embracing political organization, which evoked the threat of domination by alien tribes as well as the abandonment of their own cultural distinctiveness. In other words, it meant abandonment of the very values and objectives for which they stood.

What made them especially aware of this threat was that the authors of the manifesto of *Conscience Africaine* were for the most part of Bangala origins. They not only felt that the Bangala were about to steal their thunder, and possibly claim the role of a vanguard in the struggle for emancipation, but were consciously attempting to assert their hegemony over the Bakongo. Although this was probably not true, such feelings were not unnatural in view of the latent animosities which had previously envenomed the relations of the Bakongo with their neighbors from the north.

But the immediate circumstances that brought about the transformation of the Abako into a political party should not obscure the fact that this transformation was essentially the product of a nationalist reaction against the continuation of Belgian colonial rule. In fact, no sooner had the Abako issued its countermanifesto than it rapidly asserted itself at the vanguard of the "anticolonial struggle," continually assailing the administration for its persistent refusal to introduce free political institutions. With the publication of the decree on the Statut des Villes, in March, 1957, the Abako quickly seized the opportunity to call attention to the more restrictive features of the reform. In a communiqué issued on April 7, 1957, the Abako dismissed the entire project as a "model of racial discrimination," pointing out that "everything in these reforms [was] arranged for the blacks [but] without the blacks, and away from the blacks." [66] But this did not prevent the Bakongo from contesting the elections, which enabled them to score a spectacular victory against their opponents; they won 62 per cent of the vote, and eight posts of bourgmestre out of ten.

From then on, emboldened by this electoral success, and, above all, by the election of Kasa-Vubu to the post of bourgmestre of the Dendale commune, the Abako displayed an increasingly militant mood. On the occasion of his installation, in April, 1958, Kasa-Vubu urged the Belgian government to hold democratic elections and grant the Congo its internal autonomy without further ado. In the same speech, the Abako leader vehemently protested against the "systematic surveillance" exercised by the government over the nascent African press: "We strongly protest against this inhuman attitude and demand immediate freedom of the press and association. . . . We demand general elections and internal autonomy." [67] Despite the threat of disciplinary sanction issued by the colonial authorities, Kasa-Vubu continued to agitate in favor of "immediate and total independence," ever anxious to reaffirm the determination of the Abako to "liberate the Congolese people from the shackles of colonialism."

By the end of 1958 the Abako had organized an impressive network of local sections, and, while still feebly developed in the countryside, its influence was felt in many of the villages outside Leopoldville, Thysville, and Boma; it could now count on the support of a solid phalanx of *militants* in each of the communes of Leopoldville. In December, 1958, official contacts had been established with the Abbé Fulbert Youlou, who had just been elected premier of the (formerly French) Republic of Congo. [68] These organizational moves were suddenly cut short by the administrative sanctions that followed the Leopoldville riots; the Abako was dissolved and its leaders were arrested. But the party continued to function underground. While the party militants turned to clandestine activities, the rump of its leadership—the so-called Comité de la Défense Abako, headed by Antoine Kingotolo—found in Brazzaville the "active sanctuary" that enabled them to carry on the fight for independence.

Since the Abako clearly stood at the forefront of the resistance movements that led the Congo to independence, one question must be raised at this point: Why was the nationalist drive spearheaded by the Bakongo people, rather than the Bangala, or any other group? Part of the answer lies in the cultural gestation that preceded the political awakening of the Bakongo. We have seen how the Abako sought from the very beginning to inculcate a sense of cultural unity in its members by offering a net-work of communications through which traditional symbols, beliefs, and customs were kept alive. Over a period of years these people developed a considerable pride in being members of the Bakongo race; looking back on their historical and cultural heritage, they discovered that they "belonged to an old non-Western civilization, one which the West could not question [*récuser*] in any of its forms." [69] This consuming urge to reassert and rehabilitate their past led the Bakongo to challenge the legitimacy of Belgian colonial rule.

Added to the feeling of cultural unity, from which the Bakongo nationalist movement derived its initial impetus, was an element of messianic fervor, originating from the prophet movements inaugurated by Simon Kimbangu. The popular unrest instigated by Kimbangu made the Bakongo especially susceptible to the appeal of nationalism. Even more significant, however, from a psychological standpoint were the extraordinary vitality of the Kimbanguist movement, and, in particular, its ability to evade the repressions of the colonial authorities. The staying power of Kimbanguism inspired a tremendous self-confidence among the Bakongo; it made them feel that the Abako, like Kimbanguism, would never be wiped out, no matter how stringent the repressions. As one Bakongo tract put it, "Think of the history of Kimbanguism. It began in 1920 and continues to spread to this very day. There have been arrests and relegations, but they did not discourage its adepts." [70] In other words, the Bakongo found in Kimbanguism a powerful psychological induce-ment to move ahead toward the realization of their objectives.

Third, the proximity of Leopoldville to the traditional Mukongo habitat facilitated horizontal mobility between urban and rural areas, and hence made it relatively easy for urbanized elements to spread the political ideas of the Abako in their rural homelands. This situation ren-dered the Bakongo more vulnerable to the appeal of nationalism than groups not so closely situated to their traditional milieu. In the final analysis, the driving force behind the political awakening of the Ba-kongo may well be the product of a unique combination of cultural, historical, and ecological factors, resulting from the accidents of coloniza-tion.

The prominent part played by the Bakongo in spurring the forces of nationalism had profound repercussions on subsequent developments. Not only did they give an ethnic and cultural content to the brand of nationalism for which they stood, but this kind of nationalism came to be regarded as a model by many potential nationalists. In their efforts to achieve "immediate and total independence," the Bakongo persuasively demonstrated that the restoration of a people's cultural individuality was fully compatible with its claims for self-government. In their search for an acceptable base of their own, many of the more politically conscious elites felt attracted toward the ideal of pantribalism advocated by the Bakongo.

# IX. THE DISPERSION
## OF POLITICAL FORCES

The sudden proliferation of Congolese political groups provides the example of a developmental pattern which finds virtually no counterpart in other African territories. Whereas in November, 1956, the Abako was the only significant party in existence on the Congolese scene, by November, 1959, as many as fifty-three different political groups were officially registered. In the few months preceding independence the number had grown to 120.[1] This plethoric growth of parties reflects the extent to which they tended to rely on the support of tribal groupings as a means of entry into the political arena.

We have already mentioned some of the factors that helped to maintain or reinforce the attachment of certain Congolese tribes to their traditional culture: the uneven penetration of Western influences, the presence of tribally homogeneous minorities in certain urban areas, differences in the scale and structure of traditional societies, and so on. This situation was further aggravated by the incidence of other discontinuities. One of these was the lack of coincidence between ethnic and administrative boundaries, a fact that frequently led to the emergence of political cleavages within the same ethnic community. Another type of discontinuity is exemplified by the existence of social and political differences between rural and urban elements. Although there were notable exceptions to the rule, urban elements, on the whole, were not nearly so tradition-bound and inward-looking as the people living in the bush. This generalization applied particularly to expatriate elements that were separated from their traditional habitat by geographical barriers, as were the Baluba and Mongo minorities of Leopoldville. Then, in some instances, divisions were accentuated by specific administrative measures designed to tear asunder the organizational web of tribal federations.[2] These conditions created a host of internal fissures which at one time or another found expression in the emergence of parties with local affiliations.

The elements of disunity were not restricted to the Congo, and there is no reason to believe that they constituted from the outset an insurmountable obstacle to the establishment of a viable party system. What made the obstacles so difficult to overcome was that, unlike most newly independent states of Africa, the Congo experienced an exceedingly short

191

period of transition from colonial rule to self-government. In the absence of previous political experience, the abrupt withdrawal of Belgian rule deprived the centrally minded nationalists of the opportunity to gather sufficient strength to resist the divisive pulls of sectional interests. The history of Congolese political groups in the period preceding independence is largely the story of ethnic and sectional rivalries, with the centrally minded nationalists seeking survival in the interstices of the ethnic struggle.

## THE EMERGENCE OF ETHNIC NATIONALISMS

Ethnic competition was endemic in the Congolese situation long before the introduction of electoral processes. For example, according to Joseph Ngalula, the origins of the rivalry between Bakongo and Bangala may be traced back to 1955, when the office of chef de cité of Leopoldville became vacant. In attempting to have the vacancy filled by their own candidates, the Abako and the Liboke Lya Bangala found themselves engaged in pressure-group activities which led to a bitter competition between their respective leaders.[3] The "main precipitants of tension," however, as Professor Coleman reminds us, were the formal steps taken by the Belgian government to grant the franchise to the inhabitants of the Congolese communes. Beginning early in 1957 with the announcement that communal elections were soon to be held in Leopoldville, Elisabethville, and Jadotville, the recrudescence of ethnic group activity was accompanied by a renewed intensification of communal antagonisms.

This phenomenon is best illustrated by the feud between the Abako and the Liboke Lya Bangala in the months preceding the elections. On January 6, 1957, Kasa-Vubu delivered a speech before the General Assembly of the Abako in which he described at great length the ancestral virtues of the Bakongo people, illustrating their generosity, trustworthiness, and peace-loving character by reminding his audience of all the help and assistance that Stanley had received from the Bakongo.[4] A few days later, in response to what they considered "a provocation directed against the tribes of the Upper Congo," the leaders of the Liboke Lya Bangala wrote an open letter to the Governor General to protest against the "dangerous regionalism" of the Bakongo:

Conscious of our responsibilities, and in view of the Bakongo's increasing tendency to vilify the other tribes, we have decided to raise the most vehement protests against the attitude of their leaders. . . . Their ideal aims at fostering the belief that we, the Bangala, are intruders in Leopoldville, which, according to the Directing Committee of the Abako, is the land of the Bakongo. . . . By spreading such groundless rumors, we fear that the Abako will end up deceiving the public and influencing the administration.[5]

This declaration did not go unheeded by the leaders of the Abako. On February 3 they issued a counterdeclaration in which they categorically asserted that "Leopoldville, Brazzaville, the Lac Leopold area, Angola, and Pointe Noire were an integral part of the ancient Kongo Kingdom, a state that was divided in 1885, at the Berlin Conference, among France, Belgium, and Portugal." [6] Shortly therafter, on February 21, the Agence Dia—a Catholic press agency in Leopoldville—published an article which further aggravated the tensions between Bakongo and Bangala. In brief, the article purported to show that the claims of the Bakongo were based on historical aberrations. According to the article, the Leopoldville area, initially the property of the Bateke, was gradually occupied by the Bangala, the Mongo, and the Libinza, for the Bakongo allegedly "avoided all contacts with the whites." Furthermore, added the article, "the Bakongo, until recently, suffered from an inferiority complex toward the Bangala," as still did "the great mass of the Bakongo population." The upshot of the argument was that the "fanaticism" and the "revolutionary outlook" of the Abako were essentially directed against the Bangala.[7]

These charges provoked a violent reaction on the part of the leaders of the Abako. On April 7 they issued a retaliatory statement reasserting their claims, adducing for this purpose the testimonies of Jérôme de Montesarchio, Monseigneur Cuvelier, and Professor Georges Balandier.[8] In the same breath they explained away the position of the Church by its commitment to a policy of "divide and rule": "La réalité est que vous souhaitez cette division pour appliquer vos principes 'divide et impera.'" One may of course wonder to what extent the efforts of the Abako did not precisely tend toward this goal. In any event, as a result of this violent press war, tribal animosities were at a new high in the Lower Congo.

The resulting tensions were dramatically brought to light during the communal elections. Since the voting behavior of the Africans was largely determined by tribal or ethnic affiliations, the outcome of the electoral contest tended to confirm the numerical or organizational strength of specific tribes. In Leopoldville, for example, the Bakongo inflicted a resounding defeat upon the Bangala, sweeping 130 out of 170 councilors' seats, and 8 posts of bourgmestre out of 10. In Elisabethville, 3 posts of bourgmestre out of 4 fell into the hands of Baluba from the Kasai.[9] Frustrated by their opponents' victory, and determined to avoid similar setbacks in the future, the defeated tribes sought better to organize themselves so as to add cohesiveness to their ranks.

In April, 1958, shortly before his departure for Brussels where he represented the Catholic missions at the International Exposition, Bolikango founded the Fédération des Bangala, a party based exclusively on the presumed solidarity of the so-called Bangala tribes.[10] As he realized that this foundation was rather shaky, Bolikango subsequently decided to enlarge his bases of support by setting up the Interfédérale. Founded in late 1958, the Interfédérale was an assemblage of disparate elements, a potpourri of the different tribal and regional associations of Leopoldville. In addition to the Fédération des Bangala the new party included in its membership the Fédération des Basonge, the Fédération Kwango-Kwiloise, the Fédération Kasaïenne, the Fédération des Bateke, the Fédération du Kivu-Maniema, the Fédération des Batetela, and several other smaller federations.[11] As subsequent events were to demonstrate, this roof organization, which might be described as an aggregate of "federated federations," constituted a very fragile edifice.

In the Katanga the Union Congolaise, founded in late 1957 at the instigation of a Belgian lawyer, had presented the voters with a program in which, according to its progenitor's own terms, "Congolese nationalism and Christian-Social doctrines were intermingled with Socialist ideas." [12] But this program, despite or because of its novelty, held little attraction for the native tribes of the Katanga; their efforts were primarily aimed at checking the control of Kasaian immigrants over the municipal institutions of Elisabethville. In order to resist the inroads of these alien tribes, the leaders of several associations of tribes indigenous to the Katanga decided in November, 1958, to form a coalition behind the Confédération des Associations Tribales du Katanga, better known as the Conakat. In September of the same year the Baluba of the Kasai, who previously had been affiliated with the Fédération des Baluba Centraux du Katanga (Fedebaceka), founded, under the leadership of Isaac Kalondji, the Fédération Kasaïenne (Fedeka). Like the Interfédérale, the Conakat included in its membership a number of minor tribal groupings previously affiliated with separate associations. Unlike the Interfédérale, however, the Conakat managed to create among its constituent units a strong sense of corporate solidarity.

Tribal solidarity also played an important part in determining the outcome of the communal elections of December, 1958. In Luluabourg the same factors that enabled the Abako to carry the elections of December, 1957, allowed the Lulua to score a decisive victory against the Baluba. Thanks to their high degree of tribal cohesion, they managed to gain control of the majority of the seats available.[13] As elsewhere in the Congo, this tribal challenge was met with a tribal response. In the early part of 1959 the leaders of several clan associations of Luluabourg (Association Bena Mpuka, Association Bena Tshiamba, Association Bena Kalondji, etc.) founded the Mouvement Solidaire Muluba (MSM), to which belonged the overwhelming majority of the Baluba of Luluabourg.[14] The tensions between Lulua and Baluba reached a climax in the summer of 1959, when a wave of hatred and violence suddenly swept over the entire province, causing hundreds of casualties in both camps.

The same pattern of challenge and response repeated itself in Equateur Province. Shortly before the elections of December, 1959, a group of Ngombe elements of Coquilhatville founded the Fédération du Nord de l'Equateur (Feduneq), a party that became identified with the Ngombe tribes of the Equateur. According to an African journalist of Mongo extraction, "cette association ... donna l'éveil politique à l'esprit encore endormi de nos amis Ngombe. Leur président cherchait toutes les possibilités de passer au pouvoir et se servait de l'association pour assouvir son appétit [sic]." [15] Confronted with what they deemed to be an "openly racist" attitude on the part of the Ngombe, the Mongo, who until then had hoped for an atmosphere of "peaceful coexistence," felt obliged to organize their own party, the Union Mongo (Unimo). While the tension between these two groups never reached a degree of intensity comparable to that which continues to oppose the Lulua to the Baluba, it nevertheless led to sporadic violence in those areas where the Ngombe elements predominate, as in the territories of Lisala and Gemena.[16]

In the meantime, the Belgian government's declaration of January 13, 1959, gave a new stimulus to the growth of ethnic nationalisms. With the prospect of independence finally in sight, the Congolese leaders became increasingly anxious to seek the support of their own tribal groupings. As a result, a number of "supratribal" associations suddenly collapsed under the centrifugal pressure of their ethnic components. In March, 1958, the Association des Batetela and the Association des Basonge bolted the Interfédérale to form, respectively, the Fédération des Batetela (Fedebate) and the Parti de l'Unité Basonge.[17] Then, in April, 1959, the leaders of the Fédération Kwango-Kwiloise issued a formal statement in which they publicly "disapproved of the procedure through which they had become affiliated with the Interfédérale," and stated their intention to withdraw from the party.[18] Ultimately, the Fédération Kwango-Kwiloise split up into three contending groups, each drawing its support from different tribal groupings: (1) the Parti Solidaire Africain (PSA), founded in April, 1959, by Sylvain Kama, former vice-president of the Cercles des Evolués de Kikwit, and drawing its support from a variety of small tribal entities of the Kwilu area (Bambala, Bapende, Babunda, Lampuku, Badjinga, etc.); (2) the Union du Kwango pour l'Indépendance et la Liberté (Luka), founded by André Peti-Peti, which rallied the support of the Bayaka of the Kwango; and the Alliance des Bayanzi (Abazi), founded by Gaston Midu, which drew its membership from the Bayanzi. While some of these defections might have been encouraged by Bolikango's moderate leanings, they were also motivated by a nearly universal desire to gain participation in the emergent political order.

By November, 1959, the proliferation of parties had reached an unprecedented scale. The prevailing situation was aptly summarized by a Belgian deputy, H. Lahaye, when he declared before the Chamber of Representatives: "Not a week goes by without the announcement that a few clerks decided to meet in order to found a new party. Or else the initiative comes from some tribal chief [*chef de brousse*]. On the other hand, the earlier parties break up into different factions." [19] This already frantic competition was to reach a new climax after the Brussels Round Table.

Once it became known that the Congo would accede to independence on June 30, a new flurry of minor parties came into being. In Leopoldville, for example, the collapse of the Interfédérale led Bolikango to seek the support of the Bangala, through the Front d'Unité Bangala, founded in January, 1960. As his "grande ethnie Bangala" was actually much smaller than he was willing to admit, Bolikango again sought to enlarge his bases of support by inviting several minor parties of the Equateur to join the Parti de l'Unité Nationale (Puna). Founded at the Lisala Congress, in March, 1960, the Puna was supposedly interethnic, but in fact drew most of its membership from the Ngombe populations of the Equateur. About the same time Jacques Massa founded the Rassemblement Démocratique du Lac, Kwango et Kwilu (RDLK); Gabriel Fataki, the Alliance des Bateke; and Victor Gafani, the Fédération des Bahumbu.[20]

In those provinces where two or several major tribal groups seemed to enjoy equal support, local politicians sought to capitalize on marginal tribal entities in the hope of gaining control over the balance of forces. In Luluabourg, for example, Grégoire Kamanga founded the Coalition Kasaïenne (Coaka) in order to bring the pressure of several minor tribes of the Kasai (Babindji, Basala, Bena Mputu, etc.) to bear against either one of the two major contestants, the Lulua and the Baluba.[21] Among dispersed tribal groupings the tendency was to set up provincial parties operating independently from one another, even though their bases of support were ethnically the same. The division of the Basonge of Leopoldville, Luluabourg, and Elisabethville into three separate political groups, albeit all committed to the ideal of "Basonge unity," is an example. These few examples illustrate the extent to which the distribution of certain ethnic groups among the several provinces has contributed to the fragmentation of the Congolese political scene.

In early 1957 an évolué of Luluabourg asked:

One has already spoken of a Congolese nationalism; but does it exist in the full sense of the term? Do the Basala Mpasu of Luisa and the Azande of the Uele have anything in common? Is there a community of ideas between the Bakongo of the Mayumbe and the Babemba of the Katanga? [22]

Subsequent events indicated that the answer was largely negative. Yet it would be incorrect to conclude that all Congolese were inveterate tribalists, incapable of transcending their tribal perspectives, let alone of organizing national parties, for this view fails to do justice to the efforts of those nationalists who strove toward the ideal of a truly panterritorial nationalist movement. This countertrend is best illustrated by the uphill struggle fought by the leaders of the Mouvement National Congolais (MNC) to transform their country into a viable nation-state.

FORMATION AND TRANSFORMATION OF THE MNC

Technically, the MNC was the outgrowth of the manifesto of *Conscience Africaine*. It came into being in August, 1956, through the initiative of Ileo and Ngalula, to concretize their commitment to a program of national union, "to give a more precise form to the advancement of the ideas [they wished] to promote." [23] The goals of the newly created movement were officially described in the November, 1956, issue of *Conscience Africaine*: "To lead the Congolese toward the consciousness of their national unity and responsibilities. To pursue the emancipation of their country. To make the Congolese nation a living reality based on the equality of races, mutual respect and social justice." According to the authors of the manifesto, this meant that "the organization will be able to form sections, affiliate members, and hold meetings, in order to realize the considerable work of education which is indispensable in the service of the elite and the masses of our people." [24] For all their efforts to stir up the national consciousness of the Congolese masses, however, the creation of the MNC had no immediate impact on the attitude of the Africans. In Leopoldville, where the rivalry between Bakongo and Bangala had already come into focus, the movement held little attraction for either group. And where such polarities did not exist, its fame was largely eclipsed by that of the Abako, justly considered after 1956 as the only militant nationalist organization. Yet from such unauspicious beginnings the MNC was destined to grow into the most extensive nationalist organization to appear on the Congolese scene.

What retrieved the MNC from the state of limbo in which it seemed to stagnate was the visit of the groupe de travail appointed by Minister Pétillon for the purpose of "conducting an inquiry into the aspirations of the inhabitants of the Congo." In August, 1958, anticipating the arrival of the groupe de travail, several évolués of Bukavu founded the

Centre de Regroupement Africain (Cerea), a party that was to assume a dominant position in Kivu Province. Shortly thereafter, in October, 1958, a group of Congolese of Leopoldville formally announced the formation of the Mouvement National Congolais, dedicated to the goal of national liberation. In a motion presented to the groupe de travail, the leaders of the MNC stated their objectives as follows:

Le MNC a pour but: ... d'obtenir la démocratisation des institutions consultatives existantes; de lutter en faveur du peuple congolais pour l'acquisition immédiate des libertés fondamentales garanties par la Charte des Nations Unies; de combattre avec force toutes formes de séparatisme régional; de mettre tout en oeuvre enfin pour libérer le Congo de l'emprise du colonialisme impérialiste en vue d'obtenir dans un délai raisonnable et par voie de négociation pacifique l'indépendance du pays.[25]

The MNC of October, 1958, differed in several respects from the MNC of August, 1956. The maintenance of national unity was still the paramount objective of the party, but the terms on which independence was to be granted had become characteristically less compromising. Instead of timidly advocating a thirty-year timetable, the MNC now pressed for "a rapid democratization of advisory organs," "the immediate acquisition of fundamental liberties," and the "liberation of the Congo from the shackles of colonialism." Its membership was no longer confined to a mere handful of literati; it now included, in addition to its progenitors, Ileo and Ngalula, a number of dedicated nationalists, most of them drawn from trade-union organizations. Among them were Cyrille Adoula, secretary general of the FGTBC; Antoine Ngwenza, secretary general of the Groupement des Employés Chrétiens; Maximilien Liongo, vice-president of the Leopoldville section of the APIC; Pierre Tona and Albert Nkuli, respectively permanent secretary and undersecretary of the CSCC; Gaston Diomi, president of the Mutualités Chrétiennes. Finally, its leadership had changed hands; with the arrival in Leopoldville of Patrice Lumumba the MNC entered its militant phase.

Early in his career Lumumba displayed an organizational bent which remained unmatched among other Congolese leaders. Unlike other politicians who tended to use their respective tribal associations as a means of access to the political arena, Lumumba entered politics through broadly based associations. As early as 1951 he had become a member of one of the most active and numerically important of all the clubs d'évolués of Orientale Province, the Association des Evolués de Stanleyville. In the same year he was appointed secretary general of the Association des Postiers de la Province Orientale (APIPO), a professional organization of which he became a member while working as a postal clerk in Stanleyville. A couple of years later he was holding the post of vice-chairman of the Association des Anciens Elèves des Pères de Scheut (Adapès). In 1955 he became chairman of both the Association des Evolués and the Association du Personnel Indigène de la Colonie (APIC), and founded the Amitiés Belgo-Congolaises, a cultural organization grouping Africans and Europeans. Following the visit of the minister of colonies, August Buisseret, to Stanleyville, Lumumba founded the Amicale Libérale de Stanleyville in the hope that it would give him leverage against the colonial authorities.

A member of the Batetela tribe,* Lumumba was born on July 2, 1925, in Onalua, in the territoire of Katako-Kombe in Kasai Province.[26] In 1943, after completing his primary education at the Catholic mission school of Tshumbe Sainte Marie, he went to Kindu, in the Maniema district of Kivu Province, where he found employment as a clerk at the local branch office of the Symétain company. He then moved to Leopoldville to attend a vocational school, but was subsequently sent to Stanleyville to work as a clerk at the Office des Chèques Postaux. The fact that he had received only a primary education did not prevent him, while employed in a Stanleyville post office, from becoming the editor of *L'Echo Postal*, the quarterly review of the Amicale des Postiers. He also made frequent contributions to local newspapers, such as *Le Stanleyvillois*, and to more widely read publications, such as *La Voix du Congolais* and *L'Afrique et le Monde*. But while the vast majority of Congolese writers of the period emphasized the cultural heritage of their own tribes, Lumumba's material emphasized—within the limits tolerated by Belgian officialdom—problems of racial, social, and economic discrimination.[27] At the same time Lumumba devoted much of his energies to the activities of the Association des Evolués de Stanleyville; thanks to his personal efforts the association, which claimed only 162 members in 1951, counted more than 1,000 regular members in 1956.

In 1952, while employed as a part-time research assistant by the French sociologist Pierre Clément, Lumumba already showed a remarkable intellectual curiosity. According to Clément, "Patrice was insatiable, and was interested in everything and as curious as an ethnographer. We had hardly returned (from our trip to the Kasai) when he wrote a long article on the causes for the exodus towards the cities. He had gathered the material by interrogating the chiefs and notables of his country." [28] Yet, eager as he was to receive a formal education, Lumumba was denied access to Lovanium University on the ground that only bachelors could be admitted. Clément vividly described Lumumba's disappointment,

---

* The term "Batetela" is used by the Baluba of the Kasai to designate the Ankutshu Membele, a relatively small tribe located in the territories of Katako-Kombe and Kole (Kasai). While the members of the tribe claim to descend from a common ancestor (Okutshu Membele), they also acknowledge their cultural relatedness to the Bahamba, Basongomeno, Bakusu, Bangengele, and Mongo peoples.

"after having nourished the ardent desire of being able to study at the interracial Lovanium University, at having to renounce this project because its doors were not open to married people." In any event, his career as a postal clerk was suddenly interrupted on July 1, 1956, when he was arrested on the charge of embezzling 126,000 BF ($2,520) from post office funds. He was condemned to serve two years in prison. On June 13, 1957, the sentence was commuted on appeal to eighteen and finally twelve months, after the évolués of Stanleyville had reimbursed the sum in question. Lumumba subsequently moved to Leopoldville where he found employment as the sales director of the Bracongo brewery.

In the meantime, while serving his term in the prison of Stanleyville, Lumumba wrote *Congo My Country,** a document of great historical significance which provides many revealing insights into the author's personality. The book offers a convincing refutation of the charge that he was nothing more than a "school-grader" and derived most of his grievances from the fact that he realized it.[29] But it also sheds light on some of the real grievances from which he derived a sense of frustration and revolt—his burning desire to gain recognition as a human being, to be treated on equal terms with the whites, and to share in the political life of the Congo. Finally, while some of the statements contained in the book were obviously intended for "official" consumption, one nevertheless gets the impression that even in 1956 Lumumba was firmly committed to the cause of Congolese nationalism. He saw a distinction between what he termed "true" and "false" nationalism:

A man without any nationalist tendencies is a man without a soul. . . . What we have to avoid in our country is false nationalism, the cramped nationalism that conceals forms of racialism and hatred for those of another race. . . . This struggle against racialist nationalism can be effective only if we are able to abolish its causes.[30]

His dedication to the cause of Congolese nationalism stemmed from different sources. His coming from a tribal society whose traditional value system had been profoundly altered by Arab influences, his early career as a clerk in the Maniema, and his protracted sojourn in Stanleyville all helped to erode his tribal loyalty.[31] One must also remember that he came of age in the postwar period, when nationalist ideas had already captured the imagination of Africans. Furthermore, his visit to Belgium in 1956 brought him into contact with a new and unsettling environment, and this contact apparently had a profound psychological effect on his attitude. On his return from Belgium Lumumba commented: "I am most

---

* Lumumba's work was posthumously published in Brussels in 1961 under the title *Le Congo terre d'avenir est-il menacé?* The obvious resemblance between the title of Alexandre Delcommun's famous work, *L'Avenir du Congo Belge menacé* (Bruxelles, 1919), and that of Lumumba's book is the only parallel between the two.

anxious that a large number of Congolese elite be allowed to explore the mother country, people who can profit by the experience of getting to know the Belgians and can return to pass on this experience to their own people." [32] Finally, the fact that he suffered imprisonment at the hands of the Belgian administration predisposed him to a radical orientation. His meteoric rise within the hierarchy of his own party must be explained in part by the title deed to eminence conferred on politicians who served sentences for engaging in "subversive activities." But his personality also played an important part. Thanks to his own charisma, Lumumba rejuvenated the MNC and gave a fresh élan to its cause. Yet, as he cast himself in the role of a "national" leader, he created a public image of himself which provoked the suspicion of other Congolese leaders, both within and outside the MNC.

Lumumba's sojourn in Leopoldville represents a crucial phase in his political career. Like many other uprooted Africans, Lumumba sought to adjust himself to his new urban environment by joining a tribal association. But his motives for joining the Fédération des Batetela were quite remote from the feeling of parochialism which usually accompanies such moves. His main preoccupation was to break down the barriers of particularism and ethnicity which then seemed to circumscribe the outlook and behavior of the Batetela of Leopoldville. In a speech to the federation on April 13, 1958, Lumumba urged his audience to "liquidate ethnic antagonisms" and to strive instead for a "rapproachement of all, regardless of origin":

Les citadins émigrés d'unités coutumières souvent étrangères, sinon hostiles les unes aux autres, ne sont pas encore parvenus à se fondre en une société nouvelle organisée, "intégrée" comme on dit en langage sociologique. Les particularismes, qui restent encore tenaces, entravent le développement de la coopération et de la mise en commun des efforts en vue de réalisations profitables à tous. La solidarité a persisté ou est réapparue, parfois même plus forte que naguère, au niveau des groupes familiaux, claniques, villageois, reconstitués en miniature dans les villes sous forme d'association; mais elle les dépasse rarement. Notre Fédération ferait oeuvre utile en s'assignant, entre autres tâches, la liquidation des antagonismes ethniques, et le rapprochement de tous sans considération d'origine, de classe, ou de fortune. ... Les élites Batetela doivent rejeter tout nationalisme réactionnaire et destructif, mais opter plutôt pour un nationalisme intelligent, ce nationalisme qui n'est autre chose que l'amour de son pays et le désir de voir régner l'ordre.

In 1958, while serving as vice-president of the Amicale Libérale de Leopoldville and as president of the Fédération des Batetela, Lumumba joined the Centre d'Etudes et de Recherches Sociales (CERS), a study group that had been formed in 1955 by Jacques Meert. Among the prominent members of the CERS were Ileo and Ngalula. As they were both anxious to broaden the ideological bases of their movement in order to avoid the stigma of parochialism, they made overtures to Socialist and Liberal *sympathisants* to join their ranks. Thus it was that Cyrille Adoula joined the MNC. A few other militant trade-unionists then associated with the FGTBC initially entered the movement, but subsequently decided to form an independent Socialist party. Thus, late in 1956, shortly before the December elections, Alphonse Nguvulu founded the Action Socialiste, which changed its name to Parti du Peuple in April, 1959. In the meantime Ileo and Ngalula called on Lumumba—who was then regarded as the most eminent spokesman of Liberal ideas—to join the MNC. From then on he rapidly asserted himself as the dominant figure of the party.

In December, 1958, shortly after proclaiming himself president of the MNC's Central Committee, Lumumba left for Accra to attend the All-African People's Conference. On his return from Accra he proceeded to consolidate his support at home and abroad by agitating for a rapid emancipation of the Congolese from Belgian tutelage. He responded to the Belgian government's declaration of January 13, 1959, by stating that "the document must be considered as the beginning of talks and negotiations" with the metropolitan authorities.[33] The first congress of Congolese parties, held in Luluabourg April 7–12 under the auspices of the MNC and the Union Congolaise, provided him with the opportunity to set the stage for "talks and negotiations." In a motion that he apparently urged upon the delegates Lumumba declared: "It will be the responsibility of the government which the Congolese demand be installed in January, 1961, to determine on what date the Congo will accede to its total independence." [34] Shortly before the congress adjourned, Lumumba left for Belgium via Conakry, where he attended a meeting of the Directing Committee of the All-African People's Conference.

While in Brussels Lumumba delivered several speeches under the auspices of Les Amis de Présence Africaine, a Belgian organization dedicated to the promotion of African culture.* On this occasion he credited the Belgians with certain advantages that had accrued to the Congolese through economic and social developments, but he also deplored the "bastardization and destruction of Negro-African art" and the "depersonalization of Africa," and reaffirmed his party's determination to elect an independent Congolese government in 1961. His visit was prompted not only by his desire to air his grievances and thus exploit whatever differences existed among Belgian politicians. His primary concern was to establish contacts with other leaders—Kasa-Vubu and Bolikango in

---

* The Amis de Présence Africaine (APA), founded in May, 1958, is organically linked to the Society for African Culture (SAC), led by Alioune Diop (Senegal) and based in Paris, but it should not be confused with the official publication of the SAC, *Présence Africaine*.

particular—in order to explore what kind of alliances, if any, could be worked out.[35] But he was equally eager to secure the moral support and financial assistance of Belgian politicians. His efforts brought him into contact with virtually all shades of the Belgian political spectrum—left-wing Catholics, Liberals, Socialists, Christian Syndicalists, Communists, and Freemasons. As one of his rare Belgian friends put it, Lumumba "was concerned only with one thing, which he used to express in the following manner: 'Whatever your opinions, I shall accept your help if you earnestly desire the independence of my people.'"[36] Just how much "help" Lumumba actually received from Belgian politicians is difficult to say; but it undoubtedly contributed to the sense of self-confidence—and self-importance—which was one of Lumumba's most marked qualities at this stage of his career.

Ideological differences among Belgian politicians, and the growing influence of anticolonial sentiment in the metropolis, had insured the MNC leader a wide hearing. His domestic hearing, however, was mostly confined to Leopoldville. It became increasingly urgent, at this particular juncture, to expand the territorial spread of the MNC—to set up provincial headquarters and local cells, to establish parallel women's and youth organizations, to hold political meetings: in short, to transform the Leopoldville-centered MNC into a mass movement.

As early as February 15 Cléophas Mukeba, a Muluba from the Kasai, had organized a provincial section of the MNC in Elisabethville, and a few days later another one in Kolwezi.[37] But this was a small beginning in view of the task that lay ahead. On May 27, returning from Brussels, Lumumba stopped in Coquilhatville, where he held a meeting before the Cercle des Amis du Progrès, and thanks to his oratory rapidly converted the majority of its members to his cause.[38] In Stanleyville, where he was accorded an enthusiastic reception, Lumumba made further organizational moves. He was immediately recognized as a "favorite son" by the members of the Association des Evolués, and it was among them that he recruited most of the shock troops of the MNC, as well as its provincial leadership: Joseph Kasongo and the late Jean-Pierre Finant, who became respectively president and vice-president of the Provincial Committee of the MNC; Antoine Kiwewa, who was appointed secretary general; Bernard Salamu, to whom was entrusted the task of organizing the Jeunesse MNC of Stanleyville; the late Alphonse Songolo; and many others. They rapidly transformed Orientale Province into a major stronghold of the MNC. By October, 1959, the Stanleyville organization had extended its ramifications to Bengasina, Opala, Buta, Aketi, Bondo, Wamba, Paulis, and Faradje.[39] In the Kivu, MNC sections were set up in Bukavu, Panju, Samba, and Kimbombo, and in the Kasai, where Lumumba conducted a *tournée de propagande* in August, 1959, the organizational network of the MNC gradually expanded through the Sankuru District.

Meanwhile, as the competition among parties reached an unprecedented scale, Lumumba became more intransigent in his demands concerning the timing of a political transfer—and more vociferous in stating these demands. On July 1, 1959, he called a general assembly of the MNC and on this occasion delivered a violent attack against "Belgium's policy of intimidation" and the "saboteurs of national independence." [40] A few days later, on July 13, he intensified his attacks against the allegedly "neocolonialist" maneuvers of the Belgian government:

The Belgian government, in promising independence to the Congolese, wishes to achieve it not through the aspirations and wishes of the Congolese people but according to its own aims. And what are these aims? To put in power white colonialists and black colonialists; to set up a puppet government in the framework of which the old colonial administration will continue to pull the strings, thanks to the marionettes which it will have placed in power. The regime will thus not be changed, only the actors.[41]

Partly because he felt that his position was being undermined by the efforts of the administration to regain a measure of control over the situation, Lumumba became increasingly inclined to arrogate to himself unfettered authority over the affairs of his party.

As a result, a major schism occurred in the leadership of the MNC in July, 1959, when Ileo, Adoula, and Ngalula decided to set up their own moderate wing. On July 16 a communiqué was issued which announced a drastic alteration of the directing organ of the MNC and the promotion of Joseph Ileo to the rank of secretary general. Lumumba's riposte came the next day, in the form of a brief statement which categorically denied the announcement and confirmed Antoine Ngwenza in his functions of secretary general. Ileo responded by castigating Lumumba's "personal rule" and by emphasizing the "democratic character of the measures taken by the Central Committee of the MNC." [42] A series of charges and countercharges followed which further divided the contending factions.

Although the dissident wing of the MNC became known as the MNC-Kalondji, it is worth noting that Albert Kalondji—a Muluba of the Kasai who acted as one of the delegates of the provincial branch of the MNC at the Luluabourg Congress—was not personally involved in the organizational reshuffle of July, 1959. His subsequent endorsement of a federal formula, which Lumumba persistently rejected, must be viewed, therefore, as a symptom of more fundamental differences. In contrast to Lumumba's preference for a highly centralized organization, Ileo, Adoula, and Ngalula insisted on revamping the Central Committee of the MNC along collegial lines, with equal weight assigned to each of the various functional committees. In short, the essential difference between the two groups lay in their divergent conceptions of decision-making processes within the party rather than in their respective stand on the issue of federalism versus centralism.

In any event, the effect of this rift on subsequent political developments can hardly be overestimated. Not only did the defections of Ileo, Ngalula, and Adoula deprive the leadership of the MNC of some of its ablest elements, but it considerably narrowed its potential territorial spread. In the Katanga, for example, where a provincial branch of the MNC had already been established, the conflict split the party into hardly reconcilable factions. The president of the Provincial Committee, Jean Yumba, eventually joined the Balubakat; the first vice-president, Ambroise Muhunga, founded the Association des Tshokwe du Congo, de l'Angola et de la Rhodésie (Atcar); the second vice-president, Pierre Mishakabo, became provincial president of the Kalondji wing of the MNC, followed by Cléophas Mukeba, who became its first vice-president; and Dominique Tshiteya, who previously held the post of director of the Political Bureau, rallied the Leopoldville branch of the Lumumba wing. In the Equateur the MNC underwent similar convulsions. Victor Likinda, who had been appointed president of the Provincial Committee of the MNC during Lumumba's visit to Coquilhatville, resigned his position, to be replaced by Louis Elonga. Léon Engulu, who formerly held the rank of deputy secretary general in the MNC, joined the Unimo, while Laurent Eketebi, who also held an important position in the provincial leadership of the party, joined Bolikango's Parti de l'Unité Nationale (Puna).[43] In the Kasai, Lumumba's party was deprived of its most important center of influence when the Baluba elements of the MNC almost unanimously joined the ranks of the Kalondji wing. While it may be that some of these defections were prompted by opportunistic motives, they also tended to reflect the ties of ethnic solidarity that linked the Leopoldville organization of the MNC with its provincial branches.

In fact, the single most important consequence of the split is that it gave a renewed intensity to the competitive struggle among certain ethnic groups. Thus, Kalondji's commitment to the "moderate" views of Ileo and Ngalula did not prevent him from seeking the support of his own group, the Baluba, in a move that was all the more understandable since he had already become a symbolic figure among the Baluba as a result of his previous involvement in the Lulua-Baluba conflict. As will be shown presently, while the Kalondji wing of the MNC came to identify itself with the cause of the Baluba, the Lumumba wing responded by throwing its weight behind the Lulua, thereby aggravating a conflict which even to this day seems to defy solution.

THE LULUA-BALUBA CONFLICT

Before we examine the circumstances that led to the Lulua-Baluba conflict, certain basic historical facts must be borne in mind. According to all the available evidence, until the European penetration there were virtually no cultural or linguistic differences between the Baluba and the so-called Lulua (sometimes called Bena Lulua, meaning "the people of the Lulua River"). Both were regarded as belonging to the Baluba group. "Until 1870," writes Van Zandijke, "there was no generic term to designate those people who are conventionally called Bena Lulua. When they wished to designate themselves by a common appellation they called themselves Baluba immigrants, from the south." [44] The name Lulua was apparently adopted by the German explorer Von Wissmann around 1885, to designate a group of Baluba located on the western bank of the Lulua River who were called Bashilange by the neighboring Tshokwe. They retained the name after 1885 to distinguish themselves from those Baluba elements who followed the European colonizer in the northern part of the Kasai, and assisted him in the foundation of the first stations—Malange (today Luluabourg), Luebo, Kabinda, and so forth. In brief, as Professor Vansina points out, "what we have here is a new 'tribe' which was born after 1885 in the same way most tribes are born; they came to be regarded as culturally different among themselves and by other tribes, and they expressed their differences by a tribal name." [45] Thus, even though both groups actually share the same cultural features, their *consciousness* of belonging to different tribes is what lies at the root of their mutual antagonisms.

But the mere existence of different types of tribal consciousness would probably not have led to such bitter animosities had not these been further stimulated by socioeconomic differences. We have already noted how the territorial expansion of the Baluba beyond their customary areas tended to arouse the hostility of the resident tribes. As they took over the lands of the Lulua, they came to be regarded as usurpers of immemorial prescriptive rights, and were treated as such. Already in 1957 an administrative report blandly referred to the Lulua's "tendency to expel peacefully the Baluba peasants" from the overcrowded areas of the Lulua District.[46] In the meantime, however, in response to the pressures generated by the shortage of cultivable land, Baluba elements moved in increasing numbers to the urban quarters of Luluabourg where they managed to acquire a virtual monopoly of the clerical jobs available. As social stratification tended to coincide with tribal cleavages, the Lulua became increasingly sensitive to the threat of Baluba domination. In fact, it was this very fear of domination, and their desire to "catch up" with the Baluba, that led a group of Lulua to organize the Association Lulua-

Frères in 1952.[47] However, their efforts did not bring significant changes and in subsequent years the Baluba retained their dominant position in Luluabourg. Describing the psychological climate engendered by this situation, the administrator of Luluabourg wrote in 1958: "Confidence has disappeared from the relations between the two races; each side multiplies minor vexations; a climate of insecurity reigns." [48]

The relations between Lulua and Baluba reached a crisis point in July, 1959, when an official report, stating the position of the local administration, fell into the hands of the Baluba. In this report, prepared by the assistant district commissioner of Luluabourg, Dequenne, in response to the demands of Chief Sylvain Kalamba Mangole that he be recognized as King of the Lulua, the administration openly acknowledged the "immense prestige" of Kalamba, and further suggested that his request be referred to the Lulua customary chiefs.[49] More important, however, was the emphasis placed on the Lulua's "imprescriptible customary rights over the land which became gradually occupied by the Baluba." Proceeding on the assumption that the claims of the Baluba were in conflict with customary rights, but ruling out the possibility of their evacuation from the rural lands of the Lulua, the report went on to suggest that they be granted a mere right of occupancy, of a usufructuary rather than proprietary character.

This proposal, intended to meet the demands of both parties, satisfied neither one. The Baluba argued that they were the sole legitimate owners of the land since their titles had been formally guaranteed by the Belgian authorities. The Lulua, on the other hand, carrying the argument of the administration one step further, adamantly insisted that the concessions made by the provincial authorities clearly violated customary law and could therefore be declared null and void at any time.[50] Even less acceptable to the Baluba was Dequenne's suggestion to subordinate the right to vote in the urban constituencies of Luluabourg to the length of residence of the inhabitants, for the proposed period of "at least ten years of effective and continued residence" as a voting qualification would have automatically disfranchised the overwhelming majority of the Baluba living in Luluabourg.[51]

Regardless of the intrinsic worth of such proposals, the mere fact that they became known and publicized immediately sharpened the tension between the two groups. True, the Provincial Governor publicly repudiated the views expressed in the report, stressing the fact that they should not be identified with the official position of the provincial administration. To the Baluba, however, Dequenne's views appeared as a sign of an irrevocable commitment of the administration to the cause of the Lulua. They gained the impression that the Belgian authorities were deliberately playing favorites so as to exacerbate tensions between themselves and the Lulua. On July 9, the president of the Mouvement Solidaire Muluba, Evariste Kalondji, wrote an open letter to the presidents of the Belgian Chambers in which he bitterly criticized the Belgian administration for its "scandalous attitude" which was "the cause of all the social and political troubles." [52] With the support of Albert Kalondji, who was at the time a member of the Legislative Council and president of the provincial section of the MNC, the MSM also protested by staging public manifestations. On August 9, the provincial governor, de Jaeger, anticipating a worsening of the situation, proclaimed a state of emergency and arrested Albert Kalondji along with several other leaders of the MSM.

To the Baluba, the repression was the acid test of Belgium's intentions. It reinforced their conviction that the administration was playing off the Baluba against the Lulua, and intensified their fear that the latter would seek to exploit the situation to their advantage. The developments that took place between July and December, 1959, confirmed their expectations, thereby dashing all hopes for a viable and lasting solution.

For one thing, the Lulua, now engaged in a bitter fight for supremacy and determined to recoup themselves at the expense of the Baluba, grew increasingly provocative in their attitude and ruthless in their actions. All the more so, in fact, since the administration had given them plenty of evidence that it supported their claims. As Antoine Rubbens noted: "It seemed that they were trying to put the programme of the report in practice through terror and violence; huts were burned down, cultivators chased from their land, families were molested and men were killed." [53] The Association Lulua-Frères, suddenly transformed into a natavistic-cum-terroristic organization, provided an outlet for the fanaticism of both rural and urban elements. The armed raids conducted by the association became more frequent, and the resulting casualties more numerous. On October 11, some thirty Baluba were reported massacred in the *zone annexe* of Luluabourg. If this clash was not the first sign of a festering hatred between the two tribes, it certainly was the most alarming symptom of its depth. In the Kasai, it marked the beginning of a long-drawn-out exodus of the Baluba populations from their rural homelands to the towns, accompanied by a recurrence of violence and bloodshed. But occasional rioting also flared up wherever Lulua and Baluba elements happened to be in contact with each other, for example in Jadotville, Elisabethville, Tshikapa, Bakwanga, and Leopoldville.

While the administration had long been aware of the gravity of the situation, it was not until December 12 that the Governor General decided to send a commission of conciliation to the spot. The commission, headed by Mr. Rae, honorary president of the Court of Appeals of Leopoldville, reported after investigation that the only way out of the dilemma was the displacement of some 100,000 Baluba from Luluabourg and its vicinity to the southern part of the province. Although the suggestion was based on a preliminary agreement treached between the customary chiefs of the two tribes at the Lake Munkamba conference, held on January 11, 1960, under the auspices of the commission, it was categorically rejected by the Baluba leaders. In fact, the substance of the agreement reached at Lake Munkamba did not reflect a common consensus, but merely the special interests of customary authorities.[54] In the case of the Lulua, the difference was not so apparent since Kalamba's views on the question were in complete harmony with those of the modernist leaders of the Association Lulua-Frères. The position of the Baluba chiefs, on the other hand, was clearly at odds with that of the MSM leadership. Although they subsequently sought to exculpate themselves by arguing that they had negotiated the agreement under duress,[55] a more plausible explanation lies in their hope that the agreement, once implemented, would allow them to reassert their authority over some 100,000 D.P.'s.[56] In any event, the Governor General refused to ratify the agreement; instead, he called a state of emergency and entrusted the vice-governor general, M. Lafontaine, with the task of maintaining order. In the meantime, some 35,000 refugees had already left their villages to seek shelter in the southern part of the province.

Not only did the aggravation of political tension, together with the massive influx of Baluba elements into the southern territories of the Kasai, prepare the ground for the secession of South Kasai; it also helps to explain the nature of subsequent political alignments within the province. Mainly because of Albert Kalondji's ethnic origins, a close rapprochement was established between his party and Evariste Kalondji's MSM in the latter part of 1959. Shortly thereafter, the Lumumba wing of the MNC, which had until then done its best to steer a neutral course between the two contending factions, countered the move of its rival by entering into an alliance with the Lulua.

Meanwhile, the tactics employed by certain segments of the European population to offset the influence of militant nationalism added another element of division among Congolese parties.

## COUNTERNATIONALIST TRENDS

While the promises contained in the declaration of January 13, 1959, had aroused great hopes among Congolese nationalists, among the European population they were generally interpreted as a sign of naïve idealism which, for all intents and purposes, was tantamount to a capitulation. As one évolué put it, "the government's declaration [was] viewed by many Europeans as a gift offered by metropolitan cowards to a handful of demagogic agitators." [57] To be sure, there were important differences in the degree of recalcitrance displayed by European elements to the reforms announced by the metropolitan government, and in the way they ultimately sought to accommodate themselves to the new circumstances. Their initial reaction, however, was very much the same throughout the Congo; in each province attempts were made to organize "moderate" groups, either on a uniracial or multiracial basis, with a view to resisting the onslaught of the more militant parties.

As noted earlier, an important move in this direction had already been made in the Katanga in May, 1958, when the president of the Ucol-Katanga, Achille Gavage, took the initiative in organizing the Union Katangaise, a multiracial party which, as the name suggests, was aimed at the construction of a "genuine Katangese community." According to the main points of its program, there was to be "a massive immigration" of European elements, with first priority accorded to Belgian applicants; an extension of compulsory military service to both Africans and Europeans, and stationing of metropolitan troops in "all the major urban centers of the Katanga"; a regime of tax exemption applicable to all "new activities" and "reinvested benefits," and an obligation for all "organs of public interest" to reinvest their capital funds in the regions in which they were raised. Furthermore, the Congo was to be divided into "large territories enjoying internal autonomy," federated with Belgium "on the basis of equal partnership," with the seat of the federation in Brussels.[58] This program, formulated in April, 1958, was in perfect harmony with the views expressed by the Central Committee of the Ucol-Katanga a year or so earlier.[59]

Similarly, beginning in early 1959, Kivu Province saw the emergence of several multiracial parties of a "moderate" tendency. Some, like the Union Belge des Populations Congolaises, founded in June, 1959, by a chef de secteur of Kindu (Maniema), were organized by appointed chiefs; others, like the Rassemblement Congolais, came into being through the initiative of European settlers. The latter, founded by a Belgian lawyer associated with the Capricorn Society,* M. Raoul Piron, stated that its primary objective was to "create, with the assistance of our friends from Kenya and Rhodesia, a permanent Pan-African organization destined to defend the ideal of increased coöperation between Europeans and Africans against the demagogues of Cairo and Accra."[60]

---

* The Capricorn African Society, founded in Salisbury (Southern Rhodesia) in 1949, is a multiracial society dedicated to the attainment of "an interracial, integrated society in which the different races cooperate without regard to color for the common material and spiritual enrichment of all." This version of "partnership" is based on the conviction that the doctrines of white domination and African nationalism are both morally objectionable, and practically impossible to realize (J. H. Oldham, *New Hope in Africa* [London: Longmans, Green, 1955], pp. 17 ff.).

The Rassemblement Congolais was replaced in July, 1959, by the Alliance Rurale Progressiste, a party which, despite its label, was anything but progressive. Its specific objectives were to promote rural interests and safeguard clan civilization: "L'Alliance Rurale Progressiste cherchera à promouvoir les intérêts ruraux, sauvegarde de la civilisation clanique et de la structure clanique dans ce qu'elle a de bon; et l'évolution clanique dans le domaine social et culturel sous la direction des chefs coutumiers progressistes et éclairés." [61] As the foregoing statement suggests, the Alliance Rurale Progressiste, though placed under the presumptive control of Africans, was, like the Union Katangaise, the brainchild of settler interests; but it differed from its Katangese counterpart in one major respect—it took a firm stand in favor of a unitary system of government for the Congo.

Further steps in the development of counternationalist activities were taken in the other provinces. In Leopoldville, for example, a Congolese journalist, Camus Mwissa, had already taken the lead in October, 1958, by organizing the Union Progressiste Congolaise for the purpose of "maintaining friendly relations with Belgium." [62] Between January and July, 1959, this initiative prompted similar moves on the part of moderate elements, which resulted in a new and bewildering array of more or less ephemeral groupings such as Sébastien Kini's Parti Démocrate Congolais, Jean-Pierre Dericoyard's Parti Travailliste, Justin Disasi's Mouvement Libéral Congolais, Jean Yoka's Mouvement National de la Protection du Droit Coutumier, and many others.[63] In Stanleyville, a European settler, Charles Bonté, founded in June, 1959, the Parti Economique et Agraire, while in the Ituri a native planter of Bunia, Albert Djulu, founded the Parti pour l'Avancement de la Démocracie en Ituri. About the same time, a group of European settlers of Coquilhatville organized the Parti de l'Indépendance Congolaise, followed by the Mouvement Traditionaliste Congolais, founded in August, 1959. Finally, in Luluabourg, moderate tendencies were represented by the Union des Populations Rurales et Extra-Rurales, and the Union des Intérêts Locaux, both organized by European settlers in coöperation with customary authorities.

Whether organized at the instigation of European settlers, or on the initiative of Africans who had some vested interest in the maintenance of the status quo, a universal characteristic of these political formations was structural weakness. Like most "patron" parties, they were "weakly articulated, comparatively undisciplined, with little if any membership participation," [64] and tended to rely for their influence on the prestige of local personalities whose status in the colonial society depended on their acquiescence with the "powers that be." Under the circumstances, with the approach of the elections of December, 1959, a number of moderate politicians* felt the need to consolidate their bases of support through a broad coalition front.

Their efforts toward a regroupment of moderate political forces led to the creation of the Parti National du Progrès (PNP) at the so-called "Congrès des Honnêtes Gens," held in Coquilhatville, November 11–16, 1959. The new party emerged out of a fusion of some twenty-seven different parties, representing the allegedly "honest" elements of each province.[65] Equating honesty with conservatism, Jean-François Iyeki, secretary general of the Interfédérale, declared in his opening address to the delegates: "Nous sommes des hommes tranquilles, des pères de famille, nous sommes conscients de nos responsabilités. ... *Nous ne sommes pas des révolutionnaires.*" [66] Here conservatism meant in essence the endorsement of the government's declaration of January 13, 1959, as interpreted by Minister de Schrijver, and its corollary objective—a united Congo. In view of the emphasis placed by the PNP leaders on the desirability of a "strong, united Congo," the absence of the Union Katangaise at the Coquilhatville Conference does not seem too surprising. As will be shown in a subsequent chapter, its leaders had already opted for a different strategy, entirely dictated by considerations of expediency.

Though handicapped politically by its pro-Belgian leanings, the PNP, under the leadership of Paul Bolya, managed to extend its ramifications to each of the six provinces. After December, 1959, however, once the Union Congolaise had withdrawn from the PNP after a dispute that broke out over party finances, its influence in the Katanga became nil.[67] And where the political scene had already been preëmpted by one or two major parties, as in the Kasai or in Orientale Province, its chances of success were minimal. Actually, its main centers of influence were in Leopoldville Province, where its alliance with the Luka insured the support of the Bayaka tribes of the Kwango, and Equateur Province, where its alliance with the Ngwaka Mina Ngende—an ethnic association founded in Gemena before the 1959 elections—and the Mouvement d'Evolution Rurale du Congo (Mederco)† enabled its leaders to earn

---

* The term "moderate" in this context refers to Congolese leaders who, regardless of their ultimate political objectives, favored close coöperation with Belgium during the transition from colonial rule to independence, which, in practice, also meant adherence to the timetable established by the government.

† The Mederco, founded in July, 1959, in Gemena by André Anekonzapa—at one time president of the Cercle des Evolués Van Gèle—was intended to aggregate the support of all people of Sudanese extraction, including the Ngwaka. Its initial appellation was "Association des Ressortissants des Peuples Soudanais." The defection of the Ngwaka, according to Anenkonzapa, was owing to the efforts of European settlers to pit the Ngwandi against the Ngwaka. Nevertheless, it must also be recognized that their efforts could hardly have succeeded unless there were important linguistic and cultural differences between the two groups. These differences are indicated in H. Burssens, *Les Peuplades de l'Entre Congo-Ubangui* (Tervueren: Annales du Musée Royal du Congo Belge, Monographies Ethnographiques, 1958).

the support of such groups as the Ngwaka (or Mbwaka), Ngwandi (or Ngbandi), Mbubu, Mbandja, and Bagiro, all located in the Mongala and Ubangui districts. In brief, despite its label, the PNP could hardly claim "national" support.

The obvious conclusion to be drawn from this rapid survey is that the patterning of Congolese political groups at this particular stage of their development is extremely complex and mutable—more so in fact than in any other African territory at a similar point of its evolution. This bewildering picture reflects in part the complete absence of previous political training, and the passionate desire of the Congolese elites to seize the opportunities which they had so long been denied. Indeed, one of the striking aspects of this situation was the tendency of Congolese politicians to seek power through whatever means were deemed expedient. An extreme example is found in the announcement made in the issue of September, 1959, of *La Voix du Congolais* that a new party, labeled the Parti d'Opposition, had recently been founded for the purpose of "exercising a close check on the future government." "Son but," said the announcement, "n'est pas de faire concurrence aux autres partis mais de surveiller de très près les travaux du futur gouvernement." A more typical attitude of Congolese politicians was to use their own tribal bases as stepping-stones to positions of leadership, a fact that has led some observers to conclude that Congolese parties were nothing more than a manifestation of the personal ambitions of self-seeking individuals.[68] If, in some instances, there may be a basis for this view, the fact is that most Congolese leaders had as their primary objective the emancipation of the "people" whom they claimed to represent. This latter point brings us back to what must be regarded as a major source of political fluctuation, namely, the inability of Congolese leaders to conceptualize the promise of independence otherwise than in terms of ethnic reference. As they projected the position of their own group of origin into the context of an independent nation-state, they became deeply aware of the threat of "tribal domination," and thus tended to cast about for whatever alliances seemed most likely to offset this threat. It was in the midst of this extraordinary proliferation of parties and alliances, unparalleled even among the more seasoned examples of multiparty systems, that the Congo approached its first national elections.

# X. THE GENERAL ELECTIONS

The general elections of May, 1960, represent the final phase of a process of political transfer which formally began in January of the same year at the Brussels Round Table Conference. Although the Round Table had once and for all settled the issue of a target date for independence, there was still considerable uncertainty as to which group would acquire a dominant position in the new political order—if only because the contestants were so numerous and their bases of support so unstable.

The tensions arising from this atmosphere of uncertainty were further heightened by the suspense created by the expectation of independence. Since the struggle for power was also a struggle for the leadership of an independent state, one can easily understand why the elections caused such deep anxieties among the electorate. One must remember finally that, unlike what happened in other African territories which are now independent, the vast majority of the Congolese had no previous experience with electoral processes, and consequently few Africans outside the main towns really understood the purpose and meaning of an election, and even fewer grasped the mechanics of the electoral procedure. Consequently the elections seemed to resemble a highly improvised operation, conducted in the midst of great and disorderly popular excitement, and with little or no understanding of the issues involved. Before we turn to a discussion of the electoral campaign and its outcome, a preliminary survey of the constitutional machinery devised at the Brussels Round Table will provide the necessary background to an understanding of subsequent developments.

CONSTITUTIONAL BACKGROUND

It was decided at Brussels that the constitutional provisions laid down in the resolutions adopted at the Round Table would serve as a basis for the drafting of the *loi fondamentale,* the basic law which was to provide the emergent nation with a workable institutional framework until the elaboration of a constitution by the Congolese Chambers.[1] However, regardless of whether or not a common consensus could have possibly emerged in the period following independence, the patent incompatibility of the loi fondamentale with the context of Congolese politics portended political instability. Not only was the absence of parliamentary traditions in itself a serious obstacle to the transfer of Western institutions, but the very fidelity with which the "framers" sought to apply certain features of the Belgian constitution cast doubt on the merits of their work.

Summing up the broad similarities of the loi fondamentale with the Belgian constitution, Raymond Scheyven, then minister in charge of economic affairs for the Congo, observed on June 8, 1960: "We have presented the Congolese with a political system similar to ours. . . . It features communes, provincial assemblies, a bicameral system, and a political system where the head of state is irresponsible." [2] The division of executive leadership between the head of state and the head of government, with the former presumably acting as a symbol of authority, was the most conspicuous—and potentially dangerous—of the features borrowed from the Belgian constitution. In line with the tradition of parliamentary government, executive powers were to be exercised by a prime minister and a cabinet responsible to parliament. Accordingly, the introduction of a motion of censure could lead to the overthrow of the government in case it no longer enjoyed the confidence of the Chambers; but the passage of such a motion required a two-thirds majority of either one of the Chambers, or a simply majority of both Chambers, and it could occur only after a cooling-off period of at least forty-eight hours following the introduction of the motion. In contrast, the head of state was inviolable and irresponsible. His powers were limited to the ratification of treaties, the promulgation of laws, and the nomination of high-ranking officials, including the prime minister and the members of his cabinet. But whereas in Belgium these powers have been largely emasculated by the predominant role assigned to the prime minister by parliamentary tradition, in the absence of such a tradition conflicting claims to "legality" were bound to arise.

The loi fondamentale provided for a chamber of representatives of 137 members "elected by universal and direct suffrage according to the procedure fixed by the electoral law," on the basis of one deputy for every 100,000 inhabitants, and for a senate essentially composed of members designated by the provincial assemblies on the basis of 14 senators for each province, including at least 3 "customary chiefs" or "notables." However, as many as 12 additional members could be added to the Upper Chamber by "co-optation" of the elected senators.

A unicameral system was adopted at the provincial level. The size of the elected membership of the provincial assemblies varied from 60 in those provinces with a population of less than two million inhabitants, to 90 in those provinces with three million or more. Additional members, representing from 10 to 15 per cent of the elected membership of the assemblies, were to be elected subsequently from a list of "customary chiefs" or "notables." A provincial executive would then be elected by an absolute majority of at least two-thirds of the membership of the provincial assemblies. Finally, a state commissioner, appointed by the head of state with the approval of the Senate, would represent the central government in each province; according to Article 184 of the loi fondamentale, his main function was to "administer state services" and "assure the coördination of provincial and central institutions."

The distribution of powers between the central government and the six provinces is defined in Article 219 and 220 of the loi fondamentale. The provincial authorities were given competence in such fields as "the organization of the political structures of the province within the framework of the general principles contained in the loi fondamentale," provincial police, judicial police officials attached to the provincial parquets, provincial finance, education other than higher education, agricultural and mining concessions, provincial and local railways, roads and public works. Except for such concurrent powers as social legislation and national minimum wages, all other powers were vested with the central government.

On the whole, with its 259 articles, 7 titles, and 6 chapters, the loi fondamentale was certainly one of the most complicated and cumbersome instruments the Congolese could possibly have anticipated. As many of the issues of public law involved the loi fondamentale were not susceptible to definitive interpretation, they became the source of considerable misunderstandings among officeholders, at both the national and provincial levels.

Equally complicated was the voting system prescribed by the electoral law of March 23, 1960.[3] This provided for a method of election patterned on the system of proportional representation known in Belgium as the *scrutin de liste à un tour*. Under this procedure, the number of votes cast for each slate of candidates is divided by 1, 2, 3, and so on depending on the number of seats available in each constituency. The resulting figures, known as the "electoral quotient," are then rated in order of importance to determine the number of seats to be allotted to each party. Furthermore, by casting his ballot for a candidate of his choice instead of for a list as a whole, the voter could, in effect, alter the order of priority reflected by the respective positions of the candidates on the list.

Voting was compulsory for all "male citizens of Congolese status"; but in order to be qualified for registration, the voters had to be at least twenty-one years of age, and domiciled in the constituencies concerned for at least six months. Aspirants to both federal and provincial office had to be at least twenty-five years of age, domiciled in the Congo for at least five years, and born of Congolese parents, or of a Congolese mother.

Prescriptions regarding eligibility to the Senate were the same, except that the minimum age was thirty instead of twenty-five.

Although it is quite improbable that any other system could have produced a very different result, given the localization of most parties, one could argue that the application of the Belgian model has unduly enhanced the position of marginal groupings in the assemblies. More important, perhaps, were the rather anomalous results produced by the proportional representation system, which fostered the impression, among Africans, that the administration had "rigged" the elections so as to favor certain parties at the expense of others. In any event, the technicalities of the electoral procedure were certainly a key element in the state of confusion which prevailed during the electoral campaign.

## THE ELECTORAL CAMPAIGN

The electoral campaign, officially scheduled to start on May 11, was accompanied by serious disturbances in many constituencies. Several casualties were reported from Luluabourg, where the feud between Lulua and Baluba reached a new climax shortly before the polling date. Similar unrest was reported to have occurred in the Maniema and North-Kivu districts (Kivu), in the Haut-Congo and Ituri districts (Orientale), in the Kabinda and Sankuru districts (Kasai), and in the Haut-Lomami District (Katanga). In each of these constituencies, the methods of intimidation employed by the contestants ranged from acts of sabotage directed against party headquarters and cold-blooded murders to slanderous accusations and threatening statements.

In general, intimidation and violence were the result of the activities of the young and militant cadres of the more extremist parties. "Abuses and violence," wrote Walter J. Ganshoff van der Meersch, "were most noticeable in those areas where the influence of Cerea-Kashamura, Abako, PSA, MNC-Lumumba, and MNC-Kalonji was the strongest." [4] Such practices were owing not only to ideological differences between themselves and their immediate opponents, but to an understandable suspicion that the administration would automatically favor moderate candidates. In a message to the Collège Exécutif Général, Lumumba said that the prevailing unrest was "precisely the result of interference on the part of certain functionaries who deviously [sournoisement] sabotage the nationalist parties." [5] In the same message, Lumumba stated that "the overwhelming majority of the presidents and assessors of the polling stations [in the Orientale Province] were members of the PNP." "The responsibility of this situation," he added, "must be attributed to the Governor General, who rejected the political dosage [between the MNC and the PNP] suggested by the Governor of Stanleyville." Despite the absence of conclusive evidence to substantiate these charges, the fact is that there was a widespread suspicion of administrative interference, and this was enough to exacerbate feelings.

Another possible source of suspicion stemmed from the general unfamiliarity of voters and candidates with the electoral machinery. Professor Alan P. Merriam's description of the situation which he observed in a Kasaian village is applicable to other rural areas: ". . . [The inhabitants] were not instructed in any way in what voting meant, for whom they were voting, why some candidates were on the ballot and others were not, how the democratic processes can include voting against rather than voting for, and how, though defeated in one election, a person can be elected in the next." [6] Thus in some places electoral lists were incomplete, or candidates forgot to file for candidacy; or, when they did file, it was only to discover that they could not meet the conditions for eligibility. Inevitably, this situation led to serious misunderstandings, and these in turn led to violent reactions on the part of the African population.

Finally, as the campaign got under way, the acerbity of political propaganda added another element of tension to the electoral struggle. The electoral campaign was carried out with the aid of two principal media: the parties' press and oral propaganda. The former was abundantly used by those parties, such as the MNC-Lumumba, MNC-Kalondji, Abako, Conakat, and Balubakat, which had already secured a solid foothold in urban areas. On the other hand, the abnormal concentration of the nationalist press in Leopoldville was a serious handicap to those parties, such as the Cerea, which directed their appeal to the more distant areas of the country. In such cases, the parties' primary reliance was on the *tournée électorale*, generally conducted by the *présidents sectionnaires*.

Aside from the Conakat, the Puna, and the PNP, which carefully refrained from flogging the moribund horse of colonialism, most of the parties focused their attacks on Belgian policies and practices. But criticisms were generally attuned to local circumstances. Where economic grievances were most acute, campaign speeches and tracts would emphasize the material benefits which independence would presumably bring to the local population. In specific areas, the popular discontent caused by arbitrary land concessions to the Comité National du Kivu and the Comité Spécial du Katanga, and by the monopolistic practices of the Union Minière and other large-scale companies, received first priority. And where repressive measures against separatist churches and Islam had been especially stringent, the right to religious freedom formed an important ingredient of the parties' propaganda. Thus, the monopoly of the Catholic Church in the field of education came under frequent attack in the columns of *Solidarité Africaine* (PSA) and *La Verité* (Cerea); but most of the blame put on Catholic missionaries lay in the suspicion that their role had been one of active collaboration with the administration. Educational demands were generally related to the opportunities offered in each province, and hence most noticeable in the Equateur, Kivu, and Orientale provinces.

Perhaps the most striking aspect of the propaganda themes developed during the campaign was their failure to emphasize the positive meaning of independence, except in the vaguest terms. Indeed, the dominant impression that one gets from the general content of political tracts and campaign speeches is that, for most Congolese, independence meant little more than the absence of constraints and equality with the whites. Thus, according to an MNC-Lumumba tract, issued by the Kazombo branch,

Independence means total equality between blacks and whites. . . . if you must travel by foot to go somewhere, and happen to meet a European who drives a car, he must stop and pick you up if you think there is room for you. Otherwise do not hesitate to take down the license plate number and report it to the national president. . . . [The European] will be brought to trial in Leopoldville and will be forced to go back to Europe, for he is an enemy of the Congolese. . . . After independence every Congolese who so wishes and who can afford it may buy a double-barreled gun.[7]

In a somewhat similar vein, Theodore Nguba, president of the Kipaka (Kivu) section of the Cerea, explained to an African audience:

Independence means that the Maringa can live among the Bakwanga, that the Bakongo can go to Bukavu, that all black-skinned people can circulate freely through the whole of the Congo. . . . Independence is like a house that is given the name of those who decided to build it. . . . If you always stay in the back seat you'll never know how to drive. You must move up to the front seat and grab the wheel. That is what independence means.

These random examples suffice to indicate the flavor of some of the campaign speeches; what needs to be noted here, however, is the absence of public debate on national issues other than those pertaining to the unitary vs. federal question, and even this never commanded more than passing attention.

Among the several techniques utilized by competing groups to increase their electoral chances, at least three deserve mention. One, illustrated by the Abako, consisted in appealing to the cultural values associated with particular groups. The historical origins of the Bakongo, for example, provided one of the major themes of the Abako propaganda. It found expression in such slogans as "Congo—with C—refers to colonized Africa; Kongo—with K—refers to the African empire founded by Ne-Kongo, or King Kongo, of which the Kongolese are the descendants."[8] The restoration of ancestral traditions and beliefs was constantly emphasized by party propagandists as an objective which only independence could achieve. And the propitiating virtues of certain dates, anniversaries, and numbers were skillfully exploited in the party press as so many favorable omens of victory at the polls.

Another technique, exemplified by virtually all parties, consisted in alienating an opponent from his following by pointing to his connections with the administration, his tribalist or separatist leanings, and the like. The PNP leaders, for example, failing to qualify as "authentic Kongolese," became the object of many caustic diatribes in *Notre Kongo* (Abako), while Lumumba came under attack for identifying the destinies of the Bakongo with the rest of the Congolese population—a fact which, in the eyes of the Abako, betrayed an amazing lack of "historical sense." [9] Lumumba's alleged sympathies toward the Soviet Union were denounced by the Conakat through the use of such dubious quips as "MNC-Moscou nous conseille," or "MNC-Mouvement National Communiste." [10] In response to these accusations, the MNC invariably taunted the "stooges of Belgian imperialism" and those "tribalists" who sought to undermine the strength and unity of the Congo by using "Belgium's favorite weapon: *divide et impera*."

Finally, nationalist parties also attempted to meet the expectations of those elements that had a vested interest in the maintenance of the status quo. Thus, in order to extend their influence to the rural areas, they frequently dwelt upon the fact that independence would not bear prejudice to the authority of the chiefs as long as they refrained from obstructing the tide of nationalism, and from acting as accomplices to the Belgian authorities. And in the urban areas, where the economic advantages derived from the Belgian presence were most apparent, the grudging promises made by nationalist spokesmen sounded unusually reassuring to European-employed Africans.

Since the MNC's rise to national prominence must be essentially credited to Lumumba's skill at maneuvering for the best leadership position, one must take a closer look at the campaign strategy laid out by the MNC leader.

In spite of his repeated efforts to affirm the national vocation of his party, Lumumba clearly saw the tactical advantage which could be gained from a proper manipulation of a tribal environment. Not only did he manage to earn the support of a large segment of those tribes that were ethnically related to his own, such as the Bakusu and "Batetela Mongo," but he adroitly exploited the occurrence of tribal conflicts to play one group off against the other. As already mentioned, he won the sympathies of the Lulua by posing as their staunchest ally against the incursions of the Baluba, but this did not prevent him from retaining the support of a considerable segment of Kalondji's following, in Leopoldville, by denouncing his "tribalist" attitude as a threat to the unity of the Congo. Elsewhere, as in the Maniema and South-Kivu districts, a substantial number of small tribal entities rallied to his cause as a result of a careful selection of party officials and propagandists according to ethnic criteria. Furthermore, party workers concentrated their energies on those areas which seemed most likely to respond to the appeal of a territorial party, areas where tribal loyalties were the most disparate, and hence the most tenuous.

As the election date approached, Lumumba sought to transform the MNC into an integrating structure within which sectional and ethnic interests would be represented. To a considerable extent this goal had already been realized through a number of tactical alliances with minor parties: in the Kasai, for example, the Union Congolaise, the Mouvement Politique Kanioka, the Alliance des Basonge, the Coalition Kasaïenne, and several others, had clearly committed themselves in favor of the MNC. In order to enhance further the position of his party, Lumumba felt the need to adopt a more flexible position on certain issues. This shift in doctrinal orientation was dramatized at the Luluabourg Congress, held April 3–4, 1960, a major landmark in the history of the MNC.[11]

From the substance of the resolutions adopted by the congress it seemed that the intransigent opposition of the MNC leader to all forms of "regionalism" had undergone considerable dilution. While the need to transcend particularistic loyalties was still recognized, allowance was made for "a certain degree of autonomy for each of the six provinces, insofar as matters of provincial interest are concerned." The congress also recognized that "the participation of customary authorities in the political institutions of the country [was] necessary in order to ensure the social equilibrium and stability of the nascent Congolese state," though it also cautioned the chiefs against the "corruption" and "delusion" to which they would expose themselves if they became the victims of colonialist propaganda. Finally, the participants admitted that "the presence of Europeans, once deprived of its oppressive aspects, will constitute a valuable factor of economic, social, and scientific progress within the context of a free and independent Congo," a move which was obviously intended to reconcile the objectives of the party with the economic demands of those Congolese who derived special advantages from the maintenance of Belgian enterprises. In any event, as a result of this maneuver, a number of "uncommitted" tribes—the Ba-Dekese, the Basala Mpasu, the Babindji, the Ba-Luntu, and so forth—joined the Front Commun Kasaïen, an electoral coalition organized under the auspices of the MNC.

The same themes were developed at the Coquilhatville Congress, held April 10–11, and the Inongo Congress, held May 1–2. On each of these occasions Lumumba paid lip service to the chiefs, reaffirmed the determination of his party to maintain the unity of the Congo and Africanize the administration. At the Stanleyville Congress, however, held on May 22, Lumumba displayed his favorite stock in trade: he bitterly attacked the Belgian administration for its "discreditable and manifest efforts to sabotage the elections," and violently protested against the arrival of metropolitan troops at the bases of Kamina and Kitona. Furthermore, anticipating an eventual defeat at the polls, Lumumba introduced a resolution in which he demanded "the organization of new elections by a provisional government, as was the case for Belgium in 1830," and "the election of the head of state by direct and universal suffrage." [12] Undoubtedly, this sudden hardening of attitude was essentially motivated by the decision of the Belgian government to send reinforcements to the Congo, in anticipation of a further deterioration of the situation. But it also reflects Lumumba's tendency to gauge his appeal to his audience, and to change his tactics according to the requirements of the situation.

The several congresses held by the MNC in the months of April and May, 1960, were intended not only to provide its leader with a forum for the ventilation of his grievances; they were also intended to bring the masses into contact with Lumumba's personality, which alone constituted the MNC's most valuable asset during the campaign. His ability to sense and articulate the demands of his public, coupled with his talent for meeting a wide range of expectations, was a key element in the popular appeal of the MNC. Above all, Lumumba possessed a special knack for setting people in motion, for arousing an emotional response from his audience, for whipping up enthusiasm for his ideals. His own excitement, as well as his ideas, was infectious. In other words, as much as the effectiveness of his tactical maneuverings, it was Lumumba's own dynamic behavior and charismatic appeal which helped the MNC to score a victory at the polls.

A final aspect of the electoral campaign which needs to be stressed has to do with its repercussions on the most publicized, and least understood, of postindependence developments—the mutiny of the force publique. There is obviously no room in this study for a detailed analysis of the factors that led to the revolt. Here one needs only to underline the climate of chronic unrest in which the electoral campaign was conducted, and which made it necessary for the Belgian authorities to keep the force publique on constant duty to restore order in the more troubled parts of the Congo, and to ensure observance of the curfew. This, and the fact that relatively little attention was paid by Congolese politicians to the demands voiced by the military, were among the major factors which predisposed the Congolese soldiers to go on rampage after independence, and to destroy at the same time what little hope there was of forming a stable central government. Another contributory element, which will be discussed in the last section, has to do with the outcome of the negotiations which preceded the investiture of Lumumba's government.

## THE RESULTS

The extreme competitiveness of the electoral struggle is best illustrated by the high proportion of candidates who ran on individual lists. Approximately 46 per cent of the lists competing for seats in the lower house, and 60 per cent of those competing for seats in the provincial assemblies, were introduced by individual candidates, which meant that among the 250 lists competing for election to the Chamber of Representatives, only 142 could be identified with one party or the other.

Consequently, where the number of lists presented exceeded the number of seats available, the proportion of lists which failed to meet the electoral quotient, and hence failed to elect a candidate, was relatively high. As was to be expected, the proportion of lost votes was the highest in those constituencies where individual lists were the most numerous, as in the Kivu, for example, where approximately 40 per cent of the votes cast went to individual lists that failed to elect a candidate. This proportion reached 35 per cent in the Equateur, 30 per cent in the Katanga, and 15 per cent in the Leopoldville Province.[13] Conversely, where strongly organized parties competed with individual lists, chances were that the dispersion of the vote would turn to the former's advantage. For example, in the Equateur, the Puna obtained 39 per cent of the seats available in the provincial assembly with only 25 per cent of the vote; in the Katanga, the Conakat polled 32 per cent of the vote, and the Balubakat 24 per cent, and they respectively won 50 per cent and 37 per cent of the seats in the assembly; and in the Kivu, the Cerea swept 43 per cent of the seats with less than 23 per cent of the vote.

With one important exception, territorial parties were less successful than ethnic or regional parties in terms of seats won. As shown by the figures in table 13, the MNC-Kalondji and the PNP suffered a crushing defeat, with only 7 and 8 seats, respectively, whereas Lumumba's MNC emerged as the strongest party in the Chamber, with 33 seats out of 137. Subsequently three minor parties of the Kasai—the Coaka and the Union Nationale Congolaise, which controlled 3 seats each, and the Mouvement d'Union Basonge—entered into an alliance with Lumumba's party, which brought his total up to 41. The PSA and the Abako, holding respectively 13 and 12 seats, stood as the second and third largest parties. Next came the Cerea, with a total of 10 seats, the Conakat with 8, and the Balubakat and the Puna with 7 each. The remaining 25 seats were distributed in varying proportion among a flurry of minor parties of purely local interest.

TABLE 13

PARTY STRENGTH IN NATIONAL ASSEMBLY, BY PROVINCE, MAY, 1960

| Party | Leopold-ville | Equa-teur | Orientale | Kivu | Katanga | Kasai | Total |
|---|---|---|---|---|---|---|---|
| MNC-Lumumba | 1 | 2 | 21 | 5 | — | 4 | 33 |
| PSA | 13 | — | — | — | — | — | 13 |
| Abako | 12 | — | — | — | — | — | 12 |
| Cerea | — | — | — | 10 | — | — | 10 |
| PNP | — | 2 | 3 | — | — | 3 | 8 |
| Puna | — | 7 | — | — | — | — | 7 |
| Conakat | — | — | — | — | 7 | — | 7 |
| MNC-Kalondji | — | — | — | — | — | 8 | 8 |
| Balubakat | — | — | — | — | 6 | — | 6 |
| Independents | 1 | — | 1 | 1 | 1 | 1 | 5 |
| Reco | — | — | — | 4 | — | — | 4 |
| UNC | — | — | — | — | — | 3 | 3 |
| Luka | 3 | — | — | — | — | — | 3 |
| Local interests | — | 2 | — | — | — | — | 2 |
| Association Ngwaka | — | 2 | — | — | — | — | 2 |
| Mederco | — | 2 | — | — | — | — | 2 |
| Customary chiefs | — | — | — | 1 | 1 | — | 2 |
| Coaka | — | — | — | — | — | 2 | 2 |
| Front Commun | 1 | — | — | — | — | — | 1 |
| Abazi | 1 | — | — | — | — | — | 1 |
| RDLK | 1 | — | — | — | — | — | 1 |
| Unimo | — | 1 | — | — | — | — | 1 |
| Cartel MNC-Lumumba–Unebafi | — | — | — | 1 | — | — | 1 |
| Cartel ARP-PRC | — | — | — | 1 | — | — | 1 |
| Atcar | — | — | — | — | 1 | — | 1 |
| Cartel MNC-Lumumba–Coaka | — | — | — | — | — | 1 | 1 |
| Total | 33 | 18 | 25 | 23 | 16 | 22 | 137 |

SOURCE: *Congo 60* (Infor-Congo, June, 1960), no. 6, p. 5.

The landslide victory scored by Lumumba's party in the Orientale Province where it polled 340,511 votes, or 271,000 more than its nearest opponent, the PNP, accounts for its strong position in the Chamber: of the 25 deputies allotted to the province, 21 were elected on an MNC ticket. In the other provinces, however, owing in part to the ethnic character of the contest, the fortunes of the MNC were far less impressive. In the Kivu, where it polled 17.44 per cent (73,326) of the provincial vote, 6 seats fell to the MNC-Lumumba, four of which came from the Maniema constituency. In the Kasai and Equateur provinces, the MNC candidates polled 15.95 per cent (80,895) and 8.45 per cent (30,626) of the vote. In the Leopoldville Province, where the MNC's share of the provincial vote fell to 2.36 per cent (15,353), its defeat must be attributed to the strong positions held by the Abako and the PSA, which respectively won 32 and 42.94 per cent of the vote.

The relative strength of the parties competing at the provincial level is accurately mirrored by the balance of forces in each of the provincial assemblies (table 14):

TABLE 14

PARTY STRENGTH IN THE PROVINCIAL ASSEMBLIES, MAY, 1960

| Party | Leopold-ville | Equa-teur | Orientale | Kivu | Katanga | Kasai | Total |
|---|---|---|---|---|---|---|---|
| MNC-Lumumba and affiliates | 2 | 10 | 58 | 17 | 1 | 25[a] | 113 |
| PNP and affiliates | 11[b] | 10[c] | 6 | 5 | — | 4 | 36 |
| Reco | — | — | — | 6 | — | — | 6 |
| PSA | 35 | — | — | — | — | — | 35 |
| Abako | 33 | — | — | — | — | — | 33 |
| Cerea | — | — | — | 30 | — | — | 30 |
| Conakat | — | — | — | — | 25 | — | 25 |
| MNC-Kalondji | 1 | — | — | — | 1 | 21 | 23 |
| Cartel Katangais | — | — | — | — | 23[d] | — | 23 |
| Puna | — | 11 | — | — | — | — | 11 |
| Unimo | — | 8 | — | — | — | — | 8 |
| Abazi | 2 | — | — | — | — | — | 2 |
| RDLK | 2 | — | — | — | — | — | 2 |
| Front Commun | 2 | — | — | — | — | — | 2 |
| Union Congolaise | — | — | — | — | 1 | — | 1 |
| Union Nationale Congolaise | — | — | — | — | — | 10 | 10 |
| Coaka | — | — | — | — | — | 5 | 5 |
| Mouvement Populaire Congolais | — | — | — | — | — | 1 | 1 |
| Parti de l'Indépendance Lulua | — | — | — | — | — | 2 | 2 |
| Parti du Peuple | — | — | — | — | — | 1 | 1 |
| Local interests | 2 | 8 | 2 | 7 | 4 | 1 | 24 |
| Independents | — | 13 | 4 | 5 | 5 | — | 27 |
| Total | 90 | 60 | 70 | 70 | 60 | 70 | 420 |

[a] Includes six seats controlled by the Parti de l'Unité Basonge and two controlled by the Cartel MNC-Lumumba–Coaka.

[b] Includes nine seats controlled by the Luka, one by the Cartel Arek-Unilac-PNP, and one by the Union Economique Bolobo.

[c] Includes five seats controlled by the Mederco and five controlled by the Association Mbakwa.

[d] Includes eighteen seats controlled by the Balubakat, two by the Atcar, and three by the Cartel Balubakat–MNC-Lumumba.

SOURCE: *Congo 1960* (Bruxelles: CRISP, 1961), pp. 156, 166, 172, 183, 215, 263.

1. In the Orientale Province, with a total of 58 seats, the MNC-Lumumba controlled the overwhelming majority of the seats in the provincial assembly, and was therefore in a position to manage provincial affairs there free of all meaningful opposition.
2. In the Kasai Province, the MNC-Lumumba captured 17 seats out of a total of 70, whereas its immediate opponent, the MNC-Kalondji, gained 21. But thanks to the support of its associate formations—the Mouvement d'Unité Basonge, the Coaka, and the Union Nationale Congolaise, which obtained, respectively, six, two, and ten seats in the assembly—the "cartel" controlled by Lumumba's party then commanded a total of at least 35 seats.
3. In the Equateur Province, 28 seats out of a total of 60 fell into the hands of candidates who ran on independent lists. The MNC-Lumumba, which encountered its greatest success in the Tshuapa District, contiguous to the Orientale Province, managed to obtain 10 seats, while Bolikango's Puna, thanks to its alliance with the Association des Ressortissants de Banzyville (Assorbanzy), and Bomboko's Unimo respectively obtained 11 and 8 seats. The PNP, divided into two wings—the PNP-Mederco, which scored a relative success in the Ubangui District, and the Association Mbwaka—could presumably count on 10 seats in the provincial assembly.
4. In the Leopoldville Province, the assembly was almost evenly split between the PSA and the Abako, holding respectively 35 and 33 seats. The remaining 22 seats were shared among the Luka (9 seats), the Abazi (2 seats), the RDLK (2 seats), and representatives of local interests.
5. In the Kivu Province, the Cerea, though dangerously weakened by internal divisions, won 30 seats out of a total of 70. The MNC-Lumumba, partly because of its alliance with the Union des Bazembo de Fizi (Unebafi), which got 3 seats, emerged with a total of 17 seats in the assembly, the remaining ones almost evenly distributed among the Reco, the Unerga, and representatives of local interests.
6. In the Katanga, the assembly was split between the Conakat and the Balubakat, which held respectively 25 and 18 seats. Thanks to its alliance with the Atcar, Fedeka, and MNC-Lumumba, the Balubakat could count on at least 23 seats. The balance of forces was eventually upset to the advantage of the Conakat when several candidates who had been elected on individual lists threw their weight behind Tshombe's party. On June 1, the Conakat controlled 32 seats, and the Balubakat 22.

At this point, a brief examination of the social background and characteristics of the Congolese deputies may provide some useful insights into the character and behavior of the new political elite.

Probably the most remarkable feature of the new Congolese elite was its youthfulness. As shown by the data in table 15, the median age of candidates elected to the Chamber of Representatives varied between thirty and thirty-nine. While twenty-four were in their middle or low twenties, only five were in their fifties, and none were over sixty. Because of proscriptions regarding eligibility to the upper house, the average

age of senators was slightly higher than that of deputies, their median age varying between the high thirties and low forties. Only seven were over fifty, and only one was over sixty.

In terms of party affiliations, the deputies elected on an MNC-Lumumba ticket were by far the youngest, their median age fluctuating

TABLE 15

AGE OF CONGOLESE LEGISLATORS, 1960

| Age | Chamber of Representatives | Senate |
|---|---|---|
| 25–29 | 24 | 0 |
| 30–39 | 68 | 50 |
| 40–49 | 36 | 22 |
| 50–59 | 5 | 7 |
| 60 and above | 0 | 1 |
| Unknown | 4 | 0 |

between thirty and thirty-nine.[14] Equally significant is the youthfulness of the deputies elected on a Cerea or PSA ticket. Conversely, the candidates who were supported by the more conservative parties were generally older. An examination of the age of senators by party affiliation reveals the same relationship between the degree of conservatism or radicalism of any particular group and the age of its affiliate members, the only exception to this rule being represented by the Abako, whose members averaged between forty and fifty years of age. The reason for this deviation would seem to lie in part in the history of the Abako, and also in the prestige-giving qualities attached to old age in the Bakongo traditional society.

Table 16 reveals that close to 50 per cent of Congolese deputies, and more than one-third of the senators, were members of the civil service. Among the legislators falling in this category, thirty-one were employed in the lower echelons of the administration in the capacity of *commis chefs, commis principaux, rédacteurs,* or *agents de la quatrième catégorie.* The last one excepted, most of these administrative grades were determined by seniority and none involved positions of responsibility beyond those assigned to junior clerks and secretaries. Among those deputies who belonged to the "fourth" category (agents de la quatrième catégorie, only one—Justin Bomboko—had had the opportunity to receive a university education. The private sector was mostly represented by clerks, accountants, and commerçants; with the exception of Senator Promontorio, the only Congolese lawyer at the time, few of the legislators included in this category had studied beyond the primary level. Most of the customary chiefs, represented by three deputies and fourteen senators, were illiterate.

As might be expected in view of its doctrinal orientation, the MNC-Lumumba supported candidates who belonged to a variety of social cate-

TABLE 16

OCCUPATIONS OF CONGOLESE LEGISLATORS, 1960

| Occupation | Chamber of Representatives | Senate |
|---|---|---|
| *Public sector* | | |
| Civil servants[a] | 20 | 11 |
| Professional civil servants[b] | 17 | 6 |
| Clerks | 19 | 9 |
| Teachers | 10 | 5 |
| Total | 66 | 31 |
| *Private sector* | | |
| Lawyers | 0 | 1 |
| Commerçants | 14 | 3 |
| Accountants | 4 | 6 |
| Farmers | 5 | 0 |
| Clerks | 7 | 2 |
| Others | 4 | 4 |
| Total | 34 | 16 |
| *Native authorities and local government* | | |
| Customary chiefs | 3 | 14 |
| Chefs de secteur | 12 | 13 |
| Bourgmestres | 5 | 0 |
| Total | 20 | 27 |
| *Unknown* | 17 | 6 |

[a] Includes *commis principaux, commis chefs, rédacteurs,* and *agents de la quatrième catégorie.*

[b] Includes medical assistants, *infirmiers,* and agronomists.

SOURCE: P. Artigue, *Qui sont les leaders Congolais?* (Bruxelles: Editions Europe-Afrique, 1960), and mimeographed documents from the *bureaux* of the assemblies.

gories. The fact that it supported three bourgmestres for election to the lower house, and not a single customary chief, is of course illustrative of its modernist outlook. Conversely, the large number of chefs de secteur and customary chiefs among PNP members emphasizes the extent to which this party sought the support of conservative elements. In proportion to its strength in the Chamber of Representatives, the PSA ranked highest in terms of members drawn from the public sector, but the

Abako, Cerea, and MNC-Lumumba also included a large number of civil servants—a fact which exemplifies the extent to which radicals sought to exploit the grievances caused by the exclusion of Africans from higher administrative posts.

Compared with the membership of legislative assemblies in other African territories, the new Congolese elite shows a strikingly low educational level. In contrast with the situation in Ghana or Nigeria, for example, the membership of the Congolese Chambers includes only a tiny proportion of teachers, and virtually no professional people, which after all is not surprising considering the nature of the Belgian educational system. As in some of the territories of former French West Africa, one finds a heavy proportion of fonctionnaires, but here again their educational background was not exactly of the caliber that one could expect from a graduate of the Ecole Normale–William Ponty at Dakar. In fact, it is not an exaggeration to say that the new elite is represented for the most part by individuals whose formal education did not reach beyond the grade-school level. Aside from the difficulties arising from the political fragmentation of the assemblies, this state of affairs was to make the formation of a parliamentary majority an even more arduous task.

## THE INVESTITURE OF LUMUMBA'S GOVERNMENT

The details of the protracted negotiations which preceded the investiture of Lumumba's government, on June 23, have been recounted elsewhere by an eminently qualified observer.[15] Here we need only to discuss the general development and final outcome of the negotiations.

In line with Belgian parliamentary procedure, Walter Ganshoff van der Meersch, minister in charge of Belgian affairs, called on Lumumba on June 13, shortly after the election results were in, to explore what combinations, if any, could be worked out among the leaders of the different groups. In the Minister's mind, the only acceptable formula was one of a broad coalition in which as many tendencies as possible were to be represented. This indeed was a *sine qua non* if, as he insisted, the future government was to obtain a comfortable majority in the Chambers. But Lumumba realized that an extension of his bases of support in parliament could only be achieved at the expense of governmental cohesion. His preference at the outset was for a "cartel des gauches" which would have included a majority of PSA, MNC, and Cerea members, and only a marginal representation of moderates. For this purpose an agreement was concluded between Lumumba and the PSA, Cerea, and Balubakat leaders which said: "In order to assure our final victory over Belgian colonialism, the MNC, PSA, Cerea, and Balubakat have decided to pool their strengths in view of the formation of a central government." [16]

But in order to minimize the chances of conflict between potential secessionists and the central government, both the Abako and the Conakat had to be given an adequate share of ministerial posts. For this reason, and also because of the Minister's insistence on a "gouvernement de large union nationale," Lumumba recognized the need to enlarge his "cartel." To the Conakat leader, who categorically demanded the Ministries of Economic Affairs and National Defense, Lumumba was willing to concede the Ministry of Economic Affairs and the vice-presidency of the Chamber of Representatives. To the Abako leader, he offered the post of prime minister, reserving for himself the presidency. Finally, after a period of uneasy maneuverings, marked by considerable reticence on the part of the Abako and the sudden defection of the Conakat, Ganshoff issued a brief communiqué on June 17, indicating that the "*informateur* [had] failed in the mission that [had] been entrusted to him." [17] He then called on Kasa-Vubu to form a government.

In view of the existing situation, the least that can be said of Ganshoff's second choice is that it was anything but judicious. For one thing, it fortified the nationalist leaders in their belief that Belgium was engaged in a last-ditch rearguard action intended to frustrate the nationalist parties in their victory. For another, since Lumumba, in response to Ganshoff's decision, now declared his intention to form a separate government, the range of prospective *ministrables* was automatically reduced. Finally, Kasa-Vubu's personality conjured up threats of separatism among both radical and moderate unitarians.

Yet, on June 19, Kasa-Vubu presented the Minister with a draft proposal of a cabinet composed of nineteen ministers and twelve secretaries of state, none of whom belonged to Lumumba's party. As he realized the urgency of effecting a reconciliation, Ganshoff attempted to mediate an agreement between the Abako and the MNC leaders. But in spite of his personal efforts to elicit a constructive solution, the negotiations ended in a deadlock.

The impasse was now reaching a critical state. On June 20, the Cerea, Balubakat, PSA, and UNC leaders addressed a memorandum to the Minister announcing that they would support Kasa-Vubu's candidacy to the presidency if Lumumba was given a free hand in the formation of his cabinet. The next day, in what proved to be the real test of Lumumba's strength, the MNC candidate was elected to the presidency of the Chamber by 74 voices against 58. Lumumba seized the occasion to reaffirm his intention to seek the investiture of his government by the Chambers.

Faced with this new development, Ganshoff decided to call again on Lumumba, and on June 23, barely a week before the date of independence, the Chamber of Representatives, by 74 voices, and the Senate, by 60, gave their reluctant support to what appeared to be one of the most disparate coalitions that could possibly be anticipated. The uneven distribution of some 23 ministerial chairs among twelve different parties was in itself a symptom of the fragility of the coalition. Prime Minister Lumumba's MNC effectively controlled 8 ministries, the PSA 3, and the Cerea 2, and the remaining 9 offices were shared equally by the lesser members of the cabinet: PNP, Unimo, Conakat, Puna, Abako, Assoreco, UNC, and independents.

The position occupied by each of the afore-mentioned participants in the central government throws a revealing light on the degree of cohesion that prevailed among them. Four key ministries were held by the MNC-Lumumba: National Defense, controlled, significantly enough, by Lumumba himself; Interior (Christian Gbenye); Economic Co-ordination (Alois Kabangi); and Agriculture (Joseph Lutula). The PSA leader, Antoine Gizenga, held the post of deputy prime minister, while Jacques Massena and Pierre Mulele, also of the PSA, were respectively in charge of two important ministries, Commerce and "Information and Cultural Affairs." Albert Delvaux, national secretary of the PNP, was given the symbolic mission of representing the Congo in Belgium as *ministre résident en Belgique*—an ironic homage to the political affinities of one of the PNP leaders.

The Abako, which emerged as the third-largest party in the Chamber, secured only one ministerial post—Finance. It was also represented in government by one secretary of state and one minister of state, both chosen from the rank and file of the party. On June 24, however, Kasa-Vubu was formally elected head of state by a strong majority in a joint session of both houses. Although Kasa-Vubu's bid for the presidency constituted a formal guarantee of his willingness to collaborate with the central government, and therefore seemed to eliminate the possibility of a secessionist move, his election had important repercussions on subsequent events.

What needs to be remembered is that Kasa-Vubu won the election against Bolikango, who had agreed to support Lumumba's bid for the premiership after a previous understanding that his candidacy to the post of president of the Republic would then be supported by the MNC. In fact, during the period of indeterminate maneuverings which preceded his investiture, Lumumba had publicly stated that he gave his "personal support" to Bolikango, and "hoped that others will do likewise." [18] Despite this enticing promise, however, Bolikango was denied his share of the spoils, to the anger and consternation of his Bangala followers. Bolikango's defeat affected the attitude not only of his supporters within and without parliament, but also of the Bangala elements of the force publique. For if the electoral campaign provided the predisposing conditions for a violent uprising of the military, the setback suffered by Bolikango was certainly a key factor behind the anti-Lumumba demonstrations staged by the Bangala mutineers.

In the state of political confusion created by postelection maneuverings, the immediate result of the mutiny was to intensify the separatist urges of certain ethnic minorities, and make their containment, or suppression, well-nigh impossible. As early as June 4 the Unimo had warned the Collège Exécutif Général that it would form a separate state of its own in the southern part of the Equateur unless it received an adequate share of ministerial posts in the provincial government.[19] On June 9, the Abako issued a memorandum in which it formally announced its intention to set up a separate and autonomous government, so as to give the Bakongo "all the rights which are recognized in the free world." The Abazi followed suit a few days later, and on June 23 several deputies of the Kivu declared their intention to form "an autonomous and sovereign province" in the Maniema. To be sure, these various attempts at secession, motivated by an ever-increasing "fear of domination" on the part of ethnic minorities, are not unusual in territories moving toward self-government. However, nowhere else on the African continent have these efforts been so numerous and so persistent. That this should be so is as much a reflection on the past policies and practices of the Belgian authorities as an indication of the helplessness of the newly invested government in the face of the situation created by the mutiny of the force publique.

# XI. THE SECESSION OF THE KATANGA

Unlike most of the separatist moves that have accompanied the liquidation of Belgian rule in the Congo, the secession of the Katanga was not so much the result of the fear of domination of one ethnic group by another, as the end product of a combination of historical, economic, and social forces converging toward the same end. As already mentioned, the separate administrative status enjoyed by the province during the early phase of Belgian rule, coupled with the receptivity of its non-African population to the ideas and influences emanating from the Rhodesias and South Africa, had already generated strong separatist feelings among the settler community of the Katanga. However, such dispositions could not have led to the secession of the province unless they were shared and abetted by a substantial segment of the African population. In order to understand how this identity of interests came about, special attention must be paid to at least two important factors of disunity between the Katanga and the rest of the Congo: (1) area differences in the numerical importance and the economic status of the settler population, and (2) regional differences in the scale of economic development. These differences have been the major determinants of the recurrent conflicts between the Katanga provincial authorities and the central government on the one hand, and among the provincial leaders on the other. A preliminary examination of the patterns of economic and social development found in the Katanga will provide the necessary background to an understanding of the sequence of events that led to the secession.

PATTERNS OF ECONOMIC AND SOCIAL DEVELOPMENT

With a population of 1,709,659—approximately 13 per cent of the total population of the country—the Katanga was in 1960 one of the most sparsely populated of all the Congo provinces, but one where European settlers were the most numerous. The Katanga claimed in 1956 a non-African population of 34,047—about 31 per cent of the total European population of the Congo—and a ratio of Europeans to Africans approximating 20.8 per thousand, as against 10.3 for the Leopoldville Province.[1]

The influx of European elements into the Katanga is a relatively recent phenomenon. The province counted only 4,824 Europeans in 1924 and 11,341 in 1947.[2] By 1958 some 31,847 Europeans lived in the Katanga, but only 2,310 of these could be regarded as bona fide settlers, the

233

rest consisting of temporarily employed or assigned civil servants, industrialists, technicians, and missionaries. Moreover, only 52 per cent of Katangese settlers could claim Belgian nationality. Finally, the occupational distribution of the settler population, though indicating a heavy proportion of merchants and industrialists as well as a generous sprinkling of professional people, remained highly diversified.

The absence of a numerous, homogeneous, and permanently settled non-African population, which was in a large measure the result of a conscious attempt on the part of the Belgian government to retain unfettered control over the affairs of its former colony, admittedly weakened the prospects of European dominance in the Katanga. Similarly, the recency of European settlement as well as the lack of a strong cultural cohesion among the colons has probably limited the latter's capacity to identify their future with that of the province. Yet, despite these potential handicaps, the European population of the Katanga has been at the vanguard of prosettler activities.

Because of the diversity and sheer abundance of its subsoil resources, the province underwent a rapid and spectacular development in postwar years. Between 1950 and 1957 the total value of its mineral output increased by 57 per cent, jumping from 5,569.3 to 8,764.5 million Belgian francs; the latter amount was estimated to be about 80 per cent of the total value of the minerals extracted in the Congo in 1957. The province's main source of revenue was its copper deposits, so vast and so easy of access that they have been called a "geological scandal." Moreover, some 60 per cent of the world's cobalt and an appreciable, though undisclosed, percentage of its uranium came from the Katanga. It also held a virtual monopoly on the Congo's production of tin, silver, platinum, lead, palladium, and zinc.[3]

This wealth is sometimes identified with one of the Congo's largest operating companies, the Union Minière du Haut-Katanga (UMHK), founded in 1906 to prospect the mineral resources of an area some 20,000 square kilometers in extent.[4] The UMHK was one of the free world's largest producers of cobalt and uranium, and the world's third-largest producer of copper; this is a rough indicator of its part in developing the economic potential of the province. In 1955 the company had gross profits of $125 million, of which $54 million were distributed in dividends after taxes and other prior charges. Furthermore, it produced for its own consumption or for sale a variety of industrial by-products, and held a substantial share of the Compagnie du Chemin de Fer du Bas-Congo au Katanga (Beceka). Ultimate control over the UMHK, however, was exercised by the Société Générale de Belgique, unquestionably the most powerful of the five corporate groups which, until recently, dominated the Congo economy.

This overwhelming concentration of economic resources within the boundaries of the Katanga, and of capital in the hands of a single expatriate enterprise, has obvious political implications. For one thing, the dependence of the Katanga on Belgian technicians and investments suggests that the success of a secession largely depended on the support of Belgian interests. But this limitation did not make secession less desirable in the minds of European colons. In fact, as already noted, the position of the Katanga in relation to the other provinces has always been the source of profound economic grievances on the part of its resident population. Like the Ivory Coast in relation to the other states of French West Africa, the Katanga was viewed in some quarters as "the cow that the other territories never tired of milking." [5]

The same feeling permeated the attitude of the resident African population toward Kasaian immigrants, whom they tended to regard as the main beneficiaries of the economic opportunities offered in the province.* And just as the settlers repeatedly heaped scorn on the Leopoldville authorities for depriving the Katanga of its wealth, at one point the Africans openly criticized the Governor General for allowing Kasaian elements to reside in the province. For example, on February 13, 1959, Godefroid Munongo wrote a strongly worded letter to the Belgian authorities which stated, among other things:

Les Katangais d'origine se demandent avec raison si les autorités ne font pas exprès en accordant le séjour définitif aux gens du Kasai dans nos centres pour que les ressortissants de cette province puissent, grâce à leur nombre toujours croissant, écraser ceux du pays. Ce fait pourrait faire déclencher dans un avenir plus ou moins proche des bagarres entre les habitants des deux provinces. [6]

According to some observers this animosity, though intensified by the prospect of independence, was already noticeable in the early forties— if not before. [7] At any rate, the crucial point here is that while the European and African communities derived their sense of economic grievance from different sources, their respective roles cannot be fully understood independently of each other, for it was the presence of "alien" tribes which provided the *raison d'être* of the alliance of European vested interests with those "natives" of the Katanga who claimed to be "genuine" Katangese.

However, one must add that this feeling was not uniformly shared by the resident African population. Nor was it sufficiently strong to super-

---

* It was estimated in 1956 that about 35 per cent of the population of the centre extra-coutumier of Elisabethville originally came from the Kasai. For the most part of Baluba origins, these immigrants held the most lucrative jobs and virtually controlled the local advisory councils. For example, of twelve members seated on the conseil de centre of Elisabethville, nine were from the Kasai; of these, seven were of Baluba extraction.

sede all tensions among ethnic groups. In some cases, the uneven spread of industrial activities has tended to reinforce ethnic particularisms among the resident tribes. The heavy concentration of economic resources in the southern districts of the province—Lualaba and Haut-Katanga—has meant in effect that the Baluba populations of the province have remained largely insulated from the unsettling influences generated by urbanization. Qualifications must therefore be attached to the proposition that the Katanga represents, in terms of its economic development, a distinct geographical entity. In point of fact, the impact of urbanization has been confined to specific areas, and insofar as it has affected specific tribes to the exclusion of others, it has produced not only striking contrasts in the ecology of the province but profound social and political tensions among its indigenous populations.

POLITICAL PRESSURES AND CLEAVAGES

The catalytic agent behind the emergence of political parties in the Katanga, as elsewhere in the Congo, was the constitutional reform introduced in 1957 by the Statut des Villes. In Elisabethville the communal elections of December, 1957, which gave three bourgmestre posts out of four to Baluba elements from the Kasai, reinforced whatever ties of solidarity previously existed among the indigenous tribes of the Katanga. As noted earlier, it was their common antipathy toward the Kasaians, whom they regarded as "aliens," which led a group of self-styled "genuine" Katangese to organize the Confédération des Associations Tribales du Katanga (Conakat) in November, 1958. What came to be officially described as "une fraternité purement Katangaise" [8] was actually a federation of preëxisting tribal associations representing the several ethnic groups of the Katanga—the Groupement des Associations Mutuelles de l'Empire Lunda, the Association des Baluba du Katanga, the Fédération des Tribus du Haut-Katanga, the Association des Basonge, the Association des Bena Marunga, and so forth. For a time, the most important of these numerically was the Association des Baluba du Katanga (Balubakat), founded in 1957 by Jason Sendwe for the purpose of "promoting the unity of the Baluba." [9]

The Conakat incorporated in its leadership several prominent personalities who could bring themselves into active relationship to their ethnic surroundings. One of these was Bonaventure Makonga, a Muluba who claimed to be the son of paramount Chief Kinda Ilunga of Kamina (Katanga). A member of the conseil de centre extra-coutumier of Elisabethville from 1947 to 1954, and editor in chief of the weekly *Etoile-Nyota*, published in Elisabethville, Makonga became actively involved in the activities of the Balubakat, at least until April, 1958, when he decided to resign from his post of secretary general of the cultural section of the association to assist in the foundation of the Conakat. He was joined in his efforts by Moise Tshombe, at one time president of the Association Mutuelle de l'Empire Lunda, member of the conseil de territoire of Sandoa, and member of the Conseil de Gouvernement. In spite of his official functions and his personal connections with the paramount chief of the Lunda, the Mwata Yamvo, Tshombe did not harbor much sympathy for the European colonizers. Quite to the contrary, his personal experience with the Europeans of Elisabethville, when his firm (Société Kapenda Tshombe) went bankrupt, tends to suggest that he had no reason whatsoever to pose as a friend of the whites.[10] But the strongest and most interesting of the personalities associated with the Conakat was Godefroid Munongo, grandson of the Bayeke Chief Msiri, who held the functions of judge at the *tribunal de territoire* of Elisabethville before he was appointed *agent territorial* in 1959. His inborn dislike of the Europeans was further strengthened after November, 1959, when he was dismissed as president of the Conakat by the provincial authorities on the grounds that these functions were incompatible with his administrative duties. Yet, as we shall see, he promptly realized, along with the other members of the triumvirate, that he needed the Europeans more than they needed him.

From the outset, the anti-European orientation of the Conakat leaders found a specific target in the provincial administration, which they accused of favoritism toward the Kasaians.* Thus, in January, 1959, shortly after Mr. Schoeller took over the post of provincial governor, the Conakat leaders did not hesitate publicly to express their concern over "the somewhat preferential policy of the administration," calling attention to the "flagrant injustices" committed during the term of office of Schoeller's predecessor, Governor Paelinck:

Jusqu'ici, il nous est pénible de le dire, l'Administration a pratiqué quelque peu une politique préférentielle. Nos régions ont été délaissées; nos milieux coutumiers ne connaissent pas le developpement de l'enseignment. L'Administration, ou mieux, certains de ses fonctionnaires, prenaient notre silence, notre bonne humeur devant certaines injustices flagrantes, pour une lâcheté de notre part. Ils en profitaient pour saper notre âme [*sic*], notre présence. Jusqu'à

---

* These charges were not unfounded. During Governor Paelinck's term of office, from about 1954 to 1958, these immigrants received special favors from the provincial administration, partly because Paelinck had spent his preceding term of office in the Kasai, where he had developed a deep and lasting sympathy for the local Baluba tribes. Thus the provincial governor was frequently reminded by his "Kasaian friends" of his own words, spoken in Tshiluba on the occasion of his investiture: "You Kasaians, who live in the Katanga, do not forsake me; I, for my part, will not forsake you. . . . Ask me for what you need and you will get it" (from a petition submitted by the Fédération des Baluba Centraux to Governor Paelinck, Jan. 10, 1958 [unpublished document]). In a real sense, therefore, the Kasaians became the protégés of the provincial administration, or at least were so viewed by other tribes.

naguère certains proclamaient que seuls des gens remuants, agissants, avaient droit à tous les égards, tous les titres. Eux seuls pouvaient nous représenter dans toutes les assises. ... Des injustices délibérément commises devront au plus tôt être redressées. Des notifications nettes et claires devront être faites à ceux qui ont sali la réputation de la Belgique et son administration coloniale.[11]

At the same time, in an effort to dispel "false rumors without foundation," they vehemently denied that they had any separatist leanings, and insisted that their only goal was to bring to an end the role of "second-class citizens" hitherto played by the Katangese. However, this claim was seriously open to question after May, 1959, when the Conakat responded to the overtures made by the European settlers by entering into an alliance with the Union Katangaise.

A number of circumstantial factors confirmed the impression that the alliance was little more than a marriage of reason. Indeed, after the government's declaration of January 13, 1959, few Europeans could reasonably expect the Katanga to become a bastion of white supremacy, at least in the form that was initially contemplated. Furthermore, the resolutions adopted at the first congress of Congolese parties, held at Luluabourg in April, 1959, made it quite plain that the Katanga would in all likelihood enjoy even less autonomy under a centralist Congolese government than it ever did before independence. For the so-called "genuine Katangese," on the other hand, the dominant position assumed by the MNC during the congress carried ominous implications. It conjured up the threat not only of "alien domination," but of Baluba domination, because at the time the top leadership of the MNC consisted essentially of Baluba elements. In brief, the alliance could not fail to benefit both sides, even though some Katangese Africans viewed it as nothing short of an act of treason on the part of the Conakat leaders.

This move, though bitterly denounced by some nationalists, was presented by the Conakat leaders as perfectly natural, given the similarity of interests existing between the settlers and themselves.[12] But the colons were now in a position where they could exercise some control over the affairs of the Conakat. While their influence gradually dwindled within the party, initially at least they seemed to have had a considerable say in the decisions of the Conakat. For example, in a memorandum submitted to the Minister on June 25, 1959, the Conakat leaders paid homage to a statement by Monsignor de Hemptinne which a few months later would have been sheer anathema to all "genuine" Katangese: "La race noire n'a rien derrière elle. Peuple sans écriture, peuple sans histoire, sans philosophie, sans consistance aucune. ... Le sionisme nègre est une trouvaille à nous d'origine communiste [*sic*] idéologique ou politique, peu importante; ce mouvement est factice." [13] From the very beginning, this collusion of interests caused many ill feelings between the African leadership of the Conakat and some of its constituents.[14] For the time being, however, any attempt to curtail the influence of the settlers would have been impolitic.

The support of the colonat added to the ambitions and gave increased confidence to the aspirations of the Conakat leaders. In May, 1959, they publicly announced the need to transform the Katanga into "an autonomous and federated state" with political control vested in the hands of "authentic Katangese." [15] Shortly thereafter, Moise Tshombe expressed his commitment to a "federal system uniting the Congolese provinces and Belgium in the framework of a Belgo-Congolese community, with each of the constituent units preserving its internal autonomy," a proposal that seemed directly lifted from the program of the Union Katangaise.[16] Finally, the party propagandists began to place increased emphasis on the claims made by the Katangese against the Kasaian immigrants. Thus, on the inauguration of a Conakat section in Kolwezi, an eminent personality of the party, after paying lip service to the "legitimate rights of the inhabitants of this province," went on to declare that all non-Katangese would be automatically excluded from the political and administrative posts of the province.[17] In fact, the parochial outlook of the Conakat developed into an increasingly xenophobic attitude; according to an impartial observer of the Katangese scene,

Immigrants and their descendants would be thrown out of the Katanga; jobs made scarce by the recession would be left to the natives of the province; in any event, the foreign labor that the industries might need would not be part of the community and would not participate in polls—these would be reserved exclusively to genuine Katangese and their civilizers.[18]

By October, 1959, the relations between the Kasaian elements and the Katangese had deteriorated almost beyond repair. They were so bad that on October 10, 1959, the Kasaian bourgmestre of the Ruashi commune in Elisabethville, Laurent Musengeshi,* took the initiative in organizing a reunion of the provincial leaders to explore the possibility of a rapprochement. The Katangese were represented, among others, by Moise Tshombe and Jean Kibwe, respectively president and vice-president of the Conakat, and the Kasaians by Isaac Kalondji and Hilaire Katoto, respectively president and vice-president of the Fédération Kasaïenne (Fedeka), a political group identified with the Baluba of the Kasai. Although the initiative did not succeed, some of the declarations made by the participants are worth quoting, for they cast a revealing light on the existing situation:

---

* Because he was born in Kabinda, which until 1933 was included within the boundaries of the Katanga, Musengeshi was regarded by the Conakat leaders as a "Katangese," and was therefore not suspected of partiality.

*Musengeshi:* Le bruit court avec véhémence que l'on va tuer et même ravager tous les ressortissants de la province du Kasai, il parait que le mot d'ordre serait donné par les dirigeants de la Conakat, surtout dans l'intérieur. Ce langage malveillant me fait peur. ...

*Tshombe (Conakat):* Je vous trouve un garcon très courageux d'affronter ce grave problème, mais le moment est très malheureux; il vous a fallu faire cela entre les mois de mars et avril 1958, c'est trop tard pour le moment. ... Quelques éléments ambitieux se trouvant parmi les Kasaiens ont rendu un mauvais service dans la province du Katanga. Lorsque ces messieurs disent qu'ils sont nos civilisateurs, nous ne sommes pas contents. Soyons sincères. ... Nous avons pris notre position, elle est irrévocable. Nous défendrons le FEDERALISME, c'est notre droit politique, comme le votre est UNITE DU CONGO. Cela ne changera pas notre optique SOCIALE. Pour votre information, nous venons d'envoyer Monsieur Nyembo dans l'intérieur pour faire des tournées de propagande sur le FEDERALISME.

*Kalondji (Fedeka):* C'est bien, mais la masse Katangaise ne comprend pas la différence entre POLITIQUE et SOCIAL. On peut avoir des idéologies politiques; c'est un droit, mais socialement nous devons tous rester frères, je crois.

*Tshombe:* Nos amis Kasaiens ont méfiance à notre égard. Par exemple, les quatre bourgmestres ont commis des abus. Vous devez aller vous-même à la commune Kenya: Sur 28 unités, vous n'en trouverez que deux Katangais. Lors de l'invitation BCB à son cinquantenaire, des anciens amis ne voulaient pas me dire bonjour ni s'approcher de là ou je me trouvais. Vous ne voyez pas que c'est un danger SOCIAL?

*Tukula (Fedeka):* Pourquoi Monsieur Tshombe vous êtes si sceptique en disant que le mal est fait et est palpable? Beaucoup de mes amis katangais se basent sur une chose—que les Kasaiens sont et se prétendent des civilisateurs. C'est faux. N'ecoutez pas les paroles de personnes qui sont irresponsables. Ils s'amusent. Ne souffrez pas du complexe d'inferiorité. ...

*Kibwe (Conakat):* Tous les Kasaiens sont complexés parce qu'ils croient qu'ils ont appris beaucoup. C'est vrai. Ce sont les blancs qui ont fait cela a notre détriment. C'est les blancs qui ont tort.

*Tshibanda (Fedeka):* Croyez-vous que la masse katangaise a un complexe d'infériorité?

*Kibwe:* C'est un pur hasard. La chance a voulu que ce soit ainsi. Vous avez pu remarquer cela lors des élections de décembre 1957. On n'avait pas designé les Katangais, mais bien les Kasaiens. C'est alors par après que la masse s'est rendue compte de son erreur. Une réaction était tout à fait indiquée. Elle est née. Maintenent nous assistons à une prise de conscience de la masse katangaise. Cela avec la nomination de quatre bourgmestres qui ont mené une politique TRIBALE. Ce geste nous a provoqué la reaction que nous vivons ce jour. ...

*Kalondji:* Nous connaissons qu'il existe des abus de part et d'autre, mais nous ne pouvons pas nos permettre de nous arrêter là. Cherchons tout ce qui nous unit, et évitons tout ce qui nous sépare.[19]

Despite their conciliatory attitude, and their earnest desire to insulate local politics from the sphere of social relations, the Kasaian leaders failed in their effort to ease the tension between the two groups. As a result of this situation, rendered even more explosive by the inflammatory statements made by the propagandists of the Conakat against the Kasaian tribes, the party underwent a major crisis when, a few weeks later, its most important constituent unit, the Balubakat, decided to withdraw. Indeed, if substantial cultural differences exist between the Baluba of the Kasai and those of the Katanga, they are at any rate not so fundamental as to leave each indifferent to the other's fate.[20]

But Sendwe's move was also symptomatic of personal rivalries in the leadership of the Conakat. In fact, it was only after many hesitations that he had agreed to join the Conakat on February 5, 1959, and then on the condition that it would still retain a large measure of autonomy.[21] This reticence was due in large measure to Sendwe's personal dislike of certain leaders of the Conakat, of Evariste Kimba and Bonaventure Makonga in particular, who once belonged to the Balubakat but subsequently withdrew from the association after being denied the leadership positions to which they aspired.[22] Under the circumstances, Sendwe felt understandably lukewarm at the prospect of an alliance with his former rivals.

In addition, like many other Katangese, Sendwe took a very dim view of the merger of the Conakat with the Union Katangaise. His reaction was not unnatural considering that the leadership of the Union Katangaise was made up of individuals whose reputation as "white supremacists" was already well established. To cite the words of Jean Brabon, who was for a time adviser to the Balubakat:

Les buts [de la Conakat] pouvaient être louables; Malheureusement, l'Union Katangaise avait à sa tête un triumvirat dont la personalité inspira d'office une grande méfiance aux Bantous: Ce sont Messieurs Gavage, Calonne et Onckelynckx. Les deux premiers surtour étaient irrémediablement compromis. Mr. Gavage avait en effet il y a quelques années publié dans la presse Katangaise une série d'articles où il préconisait déjà la séparation du Katanga et son rattachement éventuel à la Rhodésie. ... Quant à Mr. Calonne, son attitude quotidienne envers les Congolais constituait à elle seule un motif suffisant. Si l'on connait la mentalité Bantoue, toujours tentée de donner beaucoup plus d'importance aux individus qu'aux causes qu'ils défendent, on comprend aisément la réticence des Baluba devant cette union—Conakat–Union Katangaise.[23]

In any event, the secession carried several important consequences. For one thing, since the Balubakat attracted the overwhelming support of the Baluba of the Katanga, who represent by far the largest ethnic group of the province, it considerably weakened the bases of support of the Conakat. Moreover, the formation of the Cartel Katangais, on November 1, 1959—which included, besides the Balubakat and the Fedeka, the Association des Tshokwe du Congo, de l'Angola et de la Rhodésie (Atcar) of Ambroise Muhunga—radically altered the previous lines of cleavage. No longer were divisions drawn between "genuine" Katangese and "immigrants," but between Baluba and Tshokwe on the one hand, and the remaining tribes on the other. Finally, the schism provoked the emergence of new identifications between metropolitan or colonial interest groups and parties.

In assessing the nature of the relationships between European interests and political groups, one should stress at the outset that Europeans did not stand as a monolithic or undifferentiated bloc. While close organic ties existed between the Conakat and the white settlers through the Union Katangaise, the connections between the Balubakat and Belgian Liberals—often associated with the Belgian Socialist Party—were initially due to the presence of isolated personalities upon whom the party had devolved advisory functions. Some were drawn from the provincial cadres of the administration, others from the administrative personnel of the Université Officielle of Elisabethville, and still others from the research staff of the Institut de Sociologie Solvay of Brussels which as early as 1955 had organized a number of *foyers sociaux* in the Katanga and Kivu provinces.[24] Most of these personalities, however, had been appointed to official positions under the Liberal ministry of Auguste Buisseret, who held office from 1954 to 1958.

Second, the means of pressure available to the Conakat were far more effective than those at the disposal of its rivals. They could count on the active support of several local pressure groups, such as the Ucol-Katanga, the daily newspaper *L'Essor du Congo,* and the Zionist Association of Elisabethville, as well as on the financial backing of powerful corporate interests, including the UMHK.[25] As one might expect in view of the magnitude of the stake held by the Société Générale in the mineral resources of the Katanga, it was to the utmost advantage of Belgian banking interests that the Conakat should score a decisive victory at the polls. This point, however, needs qualification.

In the first place, the Board of Directors of the Société Générale held different opinions concerning the degree to which they should intervene in local politics, and the manner in which any intervention should be carried out. Even sharper differences of opinion divided the colonial personnel of the Société Générale from its metropolitan executives, the former being far more outspoken in their preference for a separate political status for the Katanga. Secondly, at least until the convening of the Brussels Round Table, the contributions of campaign funds made by the Société Générale were mainly channeled through semi-independent agents, a fact which helped in no small way to increase the fragmentation of the Congolese political scene.[26] Finally, when it appeared that the balance of power was almost evenly shared between the Conakat and the Balubakat, the Société Générale, out of sheer opportunism, decided to dispense its financial aid to both the contenders, thus canceling the potential advantage it might have derived from a more discriminating disposition of its resources.

The net involvement of European metropolitan interests in the politics of the Katanga is admittedly difficult to ascertain. But most informed observers would agree that the competition among parties served as an outlet for the expression of personal and ideological antagonisms between conservatives and liberals, or clericals and anticlericals. As a result, Katangese leaders have been led to adopt far more intransigent stands on concrete issues than they might otherwise have adopted. One may also wonder if the secessionist efforts of the Katanga leaders could have succeeded if they had not been sustained, morally and financially, by Belgian interests.

### THE POLITICS OF SECESSION

The chain of events which led to the secession comprised two distinct major phases. One, which immediately followed the general elections, ended with the neutralization of the forces opposed to the ambitions of Tshombe and the Conakat. The other, triggered by the mutiny of the force publique in the early days of July, 1960, relates more specifically to the circumstances which brought about the erection of an independent state in the Katanga.

The electoral campaign that began in April, 1960, accelerated competition among groups and led to bloodshed on numerous occasions, in Kamina in particular, where the Balubakat-pro-Conakat—a dissident wing of the cartel organized by Bonaventure Makonga only a few weeks before the polling date[27]—clashed with members of the opposing group. But the battle for ballots was especially tight between the Conakat and the Balubakat, the two principal dramatis personae: of the 160 lists which competed for seats in either the provincial or the central assemblies, 24 had been introduced by the Conakat and 16 by the Balubakat. In the end, however, neither of the two contestants could claim a decisive victory over its opponent. As shown by the figures in table 17, the provincial assembly was almost evenly split between the Conakat and the Balubakat, with the former controlling 25 of the total of 60 seats. Thanks to its alliance with the MNC-Lumumba and the Atcar, the Balubakat could presumably count on 23 seats in the assembly.

This precarious equilibrium was eventually upset to the advantage of the Conakat by two unforeseen developments. On May 27, the dissident wing of the MNC, led by Albert Kalondji, drew away the support of two Baluba elected on a cartel ticket.[28] Almost simultaneously several deputies who had been elected on lists of "local interests" joined the Conakat. Thus, on June 1, when the assembly held its inaugural session, the Conakat controlled 32 seats and the cartel, 22.

TABLE 17

PARTY STRENGTH IN THE KATANGA PROVINCIAL ASSEMBLY

| District | Conakat | Balubakat | Cartel Balubakat–NMC-Lumumba | Atcar | MNC-Lumumba | MNC-Kalondji | Union Congolaise | Local interests | Total |
|---|---|---|---|---|---|---|---|---|---|
| Elisabethville | 3 | 2 | | | | | 1 | | 6 |
| Jadotville | 1 | | 2 | | | | | | 3 |
| Tanganyika | 3 | 6 | 1 | | 1 | | 1 | 4 | 16 |
| Lualaba | 6 | 1 | | 2 | | | | 3 | 12 |
| Haut-Lomami | 3 | 9 | | | | | | 1 | 13 |
| Haut-Katanga | 9 | | | | | | | 1 | 10 |
| Total | 25 | 18 | 3 | 2 | 1 | 1 | 1 | 9 | 60 |

SOURCE: *Congo 1960* (Bruxelles: CRISP, 1961), I, 243.

The electoral procedure also had important consequences on the outcome of the party struggle. As stipulated by the *loi électorale*, the elections to the provincial and federal assemblies were held concurrently; but the candidates were selected from different lists and in different constituencies. Consequently, those parties which favored a unitary formula, such as the Balubakat and its coalition partners, tended to reserve their "safest" candidates for federal offices, while separatist parties, on the contrary, tended to develop their strategy along opposite lines. This policy considerably enhanced the position of the Conakat in the provincial assembly.

Second, the odd results produced by the scrutin de liste à un tour, directly borrowed from the Belgian electoral system, led the members of the opposition to believe that the elections had been systematically "rigged" by the administration.[29] Whether or not the evidence upheld this belief is difficult to say. The crucial point here, however, is that the members of the opposition were unanimously convinced that they were the victims of electoral fraud. Although twenty-one complaints seeking the quashing of the elections had been introduced by the cartel in the period following the publication of the electoral returns, none were acknowledged. Thus on June 1, as a sign of protest against "the way in which electoral processes had been conducted," the members of the cartel walked out of the provincial assembly.

Realizing that a prolonged boycott of the assembly would prevent the formation of a provincial government unless the two-thirds quorum prescribed by the loi fondamentale was reduced to a simple majority, the provincial governor, Mr. Schoeller, appealed to the Minister of the Congo in Brussels and urged him to promulgate an amendment to that effect. At the same time Schoeller informed the leaders of the Balubakat that the amendment to the loi fondamentale would still allow them to get an "equitable share" of the ministerial posts. Indifferent to the Governor's placatory statements, the leaders of the Balubakat immediately cabled the Governor General and the King and prophetically warned them against the "promulgation of a law [that] would inevitably lead to civil war after June 30." [30] On June 15, the Belgian Chamber of Representatives, by a vote of 98 to 5, with 66 abstentions, and the Senate by 66 votes with 33 abstentions, enacted the amendment. Even at this late date the cartel could have secured at least four ministerial seats if it had chosen to attend the session, owing to the procedure stipulated by the loi fondamentale.[31] But at the insistence of its European adviser, Madame Perrin, the cartel decided otherwise, and the following day the provincial assembly elected a government in which all ministerial chairs but one were occupied by members of the Conakat.[32]

In yielding to the joint pressures of the colonat and "genuine" Katangese, the Belgian government had not only relieved the Conakat from the compromises on offices that would have been necessary if the two-thirds requirement had been retained; it had in effect deliberately played into the hands of the "separatists." If indeed ruthless repression was the only means available to the Conakat leaders to come to terms with the demands of the cartel once the latter had walked out of the parliamentary arena, secession became the only solution to escape the control of the central government.

On June 23, barely a week before independence, the Congolese Chambers had finally given their reluctant approval to Lumumba's cabinet. As could be expected, Tshombe received the news with a mixture of astonishment and indignation. In a statement to the Belga news agency, the President of the provincial government of the Katanga gave the following hint of his ultimate intentions:

It is with astonishment that I have heard on the radio the final composition of the central government. I note that the Ministry of National Defense has been attributed to Mr. Lumumba and the Interior to a member of the MNC, although it had been decided that National Defense, in order . . . to avoid the control of a single party, would be administered by a college of all the ministers, with the secretaryship of National Defense going to a member of the Conakat. It had also been agreed that another key ministry, Interior, would be assigned to the Abako which shares the federalist ideas of the Katangese. The post of head of state had been formally promised to Mr. Kasa-Vubu, and the vice-presidency to Mr. Bolikango. It is only on these conditions that the Conakat agreed to lend its support to the government formed by Mr. Lumumba.[33]

That Tshombe intended to proclaim the independence of the Katanga on June 26, or shortly thereafter, is now a well-established fact.[34] But the Belgian government was too much aware of its responsibilities toward the central government, and of the consequences that would have resulted from its failure to meet them, to allow the secession to occur at this particular juncture. Belgian financial interests, moreover, were not unreservedly committed to Tshombe's views. Indeed, a Belgian deputy who cannot be suspected of sympathies toward Belgian capitalist enterprises, Ernest Glinne, recognized that the UMHK favored other methods than secession. This possibility, according to him, was viewed rather as a means of "blackmail" or "an alternative linked to an eventual catastrophe." [35]

The catastrophe occurred on July 5 with the mutiny of the Congolese National Army. Difficult though it may be, even at this time, to separate fact from rumor in recording the developments and implications of the mutiny, it is nevertheless beyond question that the revolt which exploded at Camp Massart on July 9 threatened the entire province with violence and confusion. Order was finally restored after the intervention of the Belgian paratroopers stationed in Kamina, and on July 11 the President of the provincial government officially proclaimed the independence of the Katanga. Shortly thereafter, the Belgian government, now regarding itself as freed of its obligation toward the central government of the Republic of the Congo, delegated d'Aspremont Lynden to the Katanga as "chief of the Belgian Technical Mission." While the Belgian government refused to extend official recognition to the newly born republic, it nevertheless "acknowledged" the independence of the province, and the King paid a public homage to the "tribes which have conserved their amity with Belgium and ask her to remain independent." [36]

As the foregoing discussion tends to suggest, the secession of the Katanga was not made inevitable, although it may have been precipitated, by any single set of factors. The fact that Belgium shares a heavy responsibility in the secession does not make her alone responsible for it. Indeed, one could possibly argue that the reason that it did not take place before June 30, 1960, was precisely because the Belgian government was willing to recognize and honor its legal obligations toward the central government. On the other hand, it could also be argued that the amendment to the loi fondamentale, which made it legally possible for the leaders of the Conakat to set up a government unhampered by the forces of the opposition, and their conviction that Belgian interests would then support their claims, did encourage the Katanga authorities to proclaim the independence of the province after June 30. But neither of these factors is sufficient to explain the existence of strong separatist sentiments in the Katanga. Nor do they provide a basis for predicting the occurrence of similar situations in a colonial context.

Among the several factors which predisposed the Katangese leaders to claim self-determination, at least three deserve emphasis. One is the sense of economic grievance which shaped the attitude of the Katangese toward the inhabitants of the other provinces. As already noted, regional differences in the distribution of economic resources operated to aggravate latent tensions among ethnic groups, so that economic stratification tended to coincide with tribal divisions. In a sense, therefore, sectional and tribal antagonisms must be viewed as symptoms of economic grievances. The fact that the Conakat succeeded in rallying the support of otherwise unrelated entities (Lunda, Bayeke, Batabwa, etc.) suggests indeed that these grievances were an important source of solidarity among its members. A second determinative factor was the part played by the white settlers in making the idea of secession both economically attractive and politically meaningful. The alliance between settler interests and "genuine" Katangese, prompted by the decision of the Belgian government to grant the Congo its independence, did not imply a fundamental change in their objectives. On the contrary, the tactics employed by the colonat consisted in communicating its political conceptions to the Conakat without in any way attempting to exercise exclusive control over the affairs of the party. By a process like osmosis, the Conakat identified itself with the ideas and attitudes which gave the settler community of the Katanga its distinctive outlook. A third explanatory factor lies in the outside support accorded by Belgian metropolitan interests to the advocates of the secession. This support by itself did not provoke the emergence of separatist claims, but it provided the external stimulus that made the prospects of a secession increasingly attractive. And it was the external stimulus that made the secession feasible.

# PART FOUR

*Organization and Functioning of Congolese Parties*

# XII. PARTY ORGANIZATION

In the course of previous chapters we have attempted to relate those factors and circumstances that have conditioned the growth of nationalist sentiment and activity to the pattern of political fragmentation that has taken form in the years preceding independence. We must now turn to an examination of the internal organization and functioning of Congolese political groups, and, on the basis of the evidence available, consider the way in which political fragmentation has affected the distribution of power within individual parties. Conversely, we must ask ourselves whether certain forms of organization, or certain elements of the parties' structure, have not contributed to the internal dislocation of some parties.

MASS PARTIES AND ELITE PARTIES

It is now clear that generalizations about the structure of Congolese parties can be only tentative. Most of the parties never advanced beyond an embryonic stage of development; many of them disappeared without even having had a chance to contest elections; and, at least until 1959, very few attempted to extend their ramifications to the rural areas. Under the circumstances, it would be presumptuous to ascribe to such inexperienced political groupings quite the same structural qualities as one finds among political parties in other parts of Africa. Some of them, however, do not seem so amorphous or transitory that they do not lend themselves to analysis. If Congolese parties are unique from the standpoint of their fluidity and variety, and hence cannot be identified with any other party system, this does not mean that they do not share certain common characteristics with political parties elsewhere in Africa.

Thus the classic distinction made by Thomas Hodgkin between "mass" and "elite," or "patron," parties suggests a set of basic characteristics concerning the organization, membership, and ideology of African parties which has considerable applicability to at least *some* Congolese parties, even though these characteristics may be found only in embryonic form.[1] "The essential characteristics of mass parties," writes Hodgkin,

is that they seek to enroll the mass of the population as members, or at least supporters, of the party. Elite parties, on the other hand, consist essentially of a nucleus of persons enjoying status and authority within the existing social

251

order—an elite of chiefs, religious leaders, or wealthy bourgeois—and depend largely upon established ties of obligation and loyalty between the "elite" and the "people." [2]

Admittedly, this rather broad classification tends to blur the contours of the various species included within the spectrum of Congolese parties. As a scalar model, however, the dichotomy between mass and elite parties does not exclude a more detailed characterization of individual groups.

In this context, elite parties are those personal and factional cliques that came into being on the eve of independence through the combined efforts of white settlers or customary authorities, or as a result of factional divisions within a given party. The term "mass party," on the other hand, designates those relatively disciplined and cohesive organizations that sought, regardless of their ultimate political objectives, to mobilize the support of a broad popular following. Unlike the former, which tended to operate more like electoral machines, their main concern was to bring about a radical transformation of the existing political order, preferably through revolutionary action rather than electoral or constitutional means.

Thus, however different in their goals and orientation, parties like the MNC, PSA, Centre de Regroupement Africain (Cerea), and Abako all tended to take on the characteristics of popular movements approximating the structural properties of mass parties. On the other hand, the Reco and the Alliance Rurale Progressiste (ARP) in the Kivu Province, the Parti Travailliste in the Leopoldville Province, the Parti Traditionaliste and the Mederco in the Equateur Province, were little more than conclaves of local notabilities, and consequently never acquired much of a "grass-roots" appeal among the African masses. Even in the case of a party like the Parti National du Progrès (PNP), which at one time established branch organizations in several provinces, the evidence shows that it was neither "national" in scope nor "progressive" in character, but consisted rather of dispersed clusters of factional interests based on ethnic and sectional ties.

At the same time, the extent to which Congolese parties can be said to fit into either one of these categories varied markedly from one party to another, and "nationwide" parties differed widely from one province to the next. For example, no other party reached a degree of structural cohesion and internal discipline comparable to the Abako; and while the organization of the MNC-Lumumba in the Orientale Province would seem to approximate that of a mass party more closely than the Cerea or the PSA, in the Leopoldville Province it could hardly be described as a mass organization. Furthermore, some parties combined the characteristics of mass and elite parties depending on their field of operation. In some urban areas of the Katanga, for example, the Conakat functioned as a mass party, whereas in the countryside, where its influence was largely dependent on the support of customary chiefs, it acquired the characteristics of an elite party. The same holds true, to some extent, of the MNC-Kalondji and Lulua-Frères in the Kasai. Nevertheless, however arbitrary, this distinction provides us with a clue to an understanding of the organization and behavior of Congolese parties.

First of all, in the Congo as elsewhere in Africa, the opposition between mass and elite parties reflects fundamental differences in the ways in which party leaders sought to legitimize their claims to authority. By and large, the authority of mass party leaders tended to be of a charismatic type, that is, dependent upon their extraordinary personal qualities, whether actual or imagined. But this does not mean that *all* mass party leaders enjoyed the same type of charisma. Some, like Kasa-Vubu, enjoyed charisma only among a particular group (the Bakongo), while others claimed a nationwide charismatic appeal. The latter type is best exemplified by Lumumba, a leader not only endowed with a special knack for projecting the image which he sought to create of himself, but one who was remarkably successful in attracting the solid loyalties of a tribally heterogeneous body of militants. Moreover, while some leaders accepted certain procedural restraints upon their charisma, others, like Lumumba, made comparatively short shrift of such limitations and used their personal appeal to the fullest extent.

In the case of elite parties, on the other hand, claims to authority stemmed from the acceptance of traditional norms, that is, from "piety for what actually allegedly or presumably has always existed." [3] The PNP leaders, for example, repeatedly emphasized their devotion to ancestral patterns of authority and bitterly criticized any departure from these time-honored customs. As Jean-François Iyeki pointed out in his address before the delegates to the Coquilhatville Congress, in November, 1959: "Naguère au village quand il fallait prendre und décision lourde de conséquence, on écoutait le chef et les notables, et puis les villageois venaient lui donner raison ou évoquer d'autres arguments. Aujourd'hui nous constatons que certains de nos frères ont oublié la leçon de leur jeunesse." [4] According to this view, authority is legitimized by the fact that it has always been so, and will continue to remain so in the future social order.

True, in some instances the authority of a leader stemmed from a combination of charismatic and traditional elements. A leader like Kasa-Vubu, for example, derived his authority partly from his personal charisma, partly from the fact that he came to be regarded by the Bakongo as the embodiment of their traditional values. Indeed, it was his alleged commitment to some of the traditional values of the Bakongo society which gave sanction to, and hence limited, Kasa-Vubu's authority. That this implied a real check on his power and influence was admitted by Kasa-Vubu himself when he declared to the correspondent of *La Libre Belgique,* shortly before the opening of the Brussels Round Table:

J'estime que ma mission est de réaliser la volonté de mon peuple. Mais je suis aussi son guide: S'il s'égare je lui dirai qu'il fait fausse route. Jusqu'ici j'ai usé de mon influence morale pour le garder des explosions passionnelles; j'ai ordonné la non-violence et j'ai été ecouté. Mais l'influence morale ne suffit pas. Il n'est pas toujours possible de contenir les foules par la seule persuasion.[5]

Similarly, when they saw that their charisma tended to become somewhat watered down among a particular segment of their following, some leaders sought to legitimize their authority on purely traditional grounds. Thus, as he realized that he was losing the support of the Baluba intellectuals of Leopoldville, shortly after independence, Albert Kalondji did not hesitate to cast himself in the role of the paramount chief (*mulopwe*) of the Baluba.

Another significant difference between mass parties and elite parties concerns the social origins of their respective leaders. As might be expected of individuals who placed so high a premium on tradition, the leaders of elite parties were usually recruited among customary or appointed chiefs—chefs de secteurs, chefs de territoire, and so forth—or from the membership of advisory organs. It is interesting to note, in this connection, that out of twenty-four Congolese who served on the Conseil de Gouvernement from 1957 to 1959, nine became identified with elite parties. Among them, Antoine Lopez, Sylvestre Mundigayi, and André Edindali became vice-presidents of the PNP; André Anekonzapa became the founder and self-appointed leader of the Mouvement d'Evolution Rurale du Congo (Mederco); and Abraham Lwanwa founded a pro-settler party in the Kivu, the Reco, which became affiliated with the PNP after the Bagira Congress, held in this locality in March, 1960.[6]

In contrast, the leadership of mass parties was generally recruited from discontented elements who felt that they had something to gain and nothing to lose from a termination of colonial rule. One important social category from which they were drawn is represented by those clerks who were employed by private enterprises. Among the more prominent leaders who originated from this clerical class were Patrice Lumumba; Albert Kalondji; Isaac Kalondji, founder of the Fedeka; Sylvain Kama, founder of the PSA; and Anicet Kashamura, secretary general of the Cerea. Unencumbered by the handicaps suffered by government-employed clerks, they became involved in nationalist activities at a relatively early date, much earlier at least than those elements employed by the colonial administration. Africans who belonged to the latter category —commis, commis chefs, rédacteurs, and so forth—were generally reluctant to join the nationalist crusade lest they lose their jobs.[7] By April, 1959, however, twenty-one agents de la quatrième catégorie* applied for a *mise en disponibilité* and consequently resigned from their posts. Among them were Justin Bomboko, founder of the Unimo, and several other personalities who reached prominent positions in the MNC-Lumumba.[8] A third group from which mass parties recruited some of their cadres is represented by the medical assistants. By virtue of their training, they were expected to play a variety of roles which predisposed them to positions of leadership, and because of the system of wages and perquisites enforced by the administration, they felt more acutely than any other group the effects of racial discrimination. This, and the fact that they had been exposed to a broad liberal arts education, made them notably receptive to the appeals of nationalism. It is not surprising therefore that two of the most able members of the provisional committee of the MNC set up in 1958, Gaston Diomi and Martin Ngwete, should have been employed at one time as medical assistants. A final category is made up of former seminarists who, for some reason or another, abandoned the priesthood to join the nationalist crusade. For example, seven of the ten members of the Central Committee of the PSA attended at one time a *grand* or *petit séminaire*. Similarly, the founder of the Abako, Nzeza-Nlandu, is a product of the grand séminaire of Mayidi, and its chairman, Kasa-Vubu, spent three years at the grand séminaire of Kabwe. Despite their different social backgrounds, these leaders all shared a common urge to bring about a radical transformation in the status quo, and this alone suffices to mark them off from other leaders.

A third major difference between mass and elite parties refers to the degree of commitment of the rank and file to party directives. Unlike elite parties, which tended to be loosely organized and comparatively undisciplined, mass parties were comparatively more disciplined, and on occasion did not hesitate to root out "deviationist" elements. Just how effective some of them actually were in maintaining discipline within the party is indicated by the percentage of electoral participation during the communal elections of December, 1959. Thus, in the predominantly Bakongo areas the overwhelming majority of the African population abstained from voting, in conformity with the directives issued by the Abako. In Matadi, for instance, 98.27 per cent of qualified voters abstained from voting, and in some territories—Luozi, Songololo, and Madimba— this proportion reached 100 per cent.[9] The same rigorous discipline was shown by the MNC-Lumumba in the Orientale Province, where the last-minute decision to participate in the elections was carefully heeded by

* In official Belgian terminology, agents de la quatrième catégorie were clerks (commis principaux and rédacteurs) employed in the colonial bureaucracy. Until enactment of the Statut Unique in January, 1959, this category included the highest administrative positions to which a Congolese could aspire.

the rank and file of the party. In the Kasai, however, the electoral boycott advocated by the Kalondji wing of the MNC was not uniformly observed. In Luluabourg, for example, where the MNC-Kalondji polled twice as many votes as its nearest opponent, the Union Congolaise, the electoral participation of the Baluba was just as high as that of the Lulua. Like the Balubakat in the Katanga, and the Lulua-Frères in the Kasai, the MNC-Kalondji never managed to infuse its members with a strong sense of party discipline—not so much because of a deficient organization or an inadequate communications system but mainly because their leadership was unable to cope with the pressure generated by ethnic tensions. In the case of the PNP, Puna, ARP, RDLK, Abazi, and similar elite-type parties, organizational laxity originated in weak articulation and loose structure.

In brief, the foregoing survey suggests that the general contours of Congolese parties are best delineated by reference to the sources of authority and social origins of their leadership as well as by the degree of commitment of their members to the central directives. At one end of the scale are found parties like the Abako, MNC, Cerea, and PSA, which tended to gravitate in the direction of tightly knit mass organizations. At the opposite extreme, parties like the ARP, Reco, and PNP tended to take on the characteristics of electoral machines functioning at the beck and call of local personalities whose position of prestige and influence depended on their acquiescence to the established order. A middle category, represented by the Conakat, the MNC-Kalondji, and the Lulua-Frères, tended to operate like mass parties in urban areas and elite parties in the countryside. As we shall see, these differences suggest corresponding variations in the distributions of power within the party hierarchy.

INTERNAL PARTY ORGANIZATION

At one time or another, most parties underwent some sort of structural transformation, either because of internal dissension, or simply because their leaders felt the need to build a more effective organization. Moreover, except for the Abako, which by then had set up local branches in the countryside, none had the occasion to sink their roots into the rural areas before the elections of December, 1959. In other words, the organizational framework of Congolese parties did not begin to take shape until the early part of 1960, and even then coördination between the basic units and the headquarters remained extremely inadequate.

In general, the usual form of organization at the local level was the cellular type, with sections and subsections reaching down from the various urban communes to the chefferies and the villages. Most often these units were organized on the basis of existing administrative subdivisions. In the Lower Congo, for example, the Abako set up local sections—

known as *cellules mères* after December, 1959—in each secteur, and by November, 1959, regional sections—designated alternatively as *sections régionales, sections territoriales,* or *fédérations*—were added in each territoire for purposes of coördination.[10] In the towns, the *sections communales* functioned as the primary units. Furthermore, in the case of "national" parties, or parties which aspired to build a "national" organization, intermediary links were established in the provincial capitals in the form of provincial branches directed by a *comité provincial.*

At the central level, despite wide variations in their formal organization, Congolese parties tended to fall into two distinctive categories. One, characteristic of mass parties, featured a central committee or a political bureau composed of a small nucleus of party officials to whom all other functional bodies and field units were subordinated. And the central position in this body was occupied by the president who, in theory at least, enjoyed unfettered control over the affairs of the party. The other, typical of elite parties, made allowance for greater flexibility in decision-making processes, usually through the use of a collegial device of some kind or another.

Thus, following the split of the MNC, in July, 1959, and as a safeguard against the recurrence of similar crises, the presidency of the MNC-Kalondji was assumed by a collegial body composed of the heads of the various functional committees attached to the party. In default of collegial devices, some parties have attempted to satisfy the aspirations of different ethnic groups through a system of rotation, as in the case of the Interfédérale where the presidency was to be assumed alternatively for a one-year term by each of the presidents of the various tribal associations incorporated into the party. Another formula consisted in creating as many positions as could be reasonably filled by prospective candidates. For example, the Central Committee of the PNP included, in addition to a national president, three national vice-presidents, and as many as eighteen councilors appointed on the basis of three from each province. In short, while the procedures differed from one party to the other, a common characteristic of elite parties was the loose structuring of their central organization.

In contrast, the hallmark of mass party organizations was the centralized character of their directing organs. For example, a striking feature of the organization of the Abako was the broad sweep of authority devolved upon the Central Committee, and, within it, upon the president. According to Article 14 of the *règlement intérieur,* the Central Committee —later known as the Political Bureau—"is responsible for the activities of the party and its formations, and application of the *règlement intérieur,* and the execution of the decisions adopted by the National Congress." [11] It had full control over each of the various functional commit-

tees (*sécrétariats*) attached to the party, and enjoyed exclusive authority
to call a meeting of the National Congress, to determine the number of
fédérations and their jurisdiction, and to suspend or dissolve a *comité
fédéral.* Its membership included one president and ten members who
became qualified for office by "militating" for at least three years on
behalf of the party. The key position, however, was held by the president, who "controls the activity of the party and its subordinate organs.
He orients his policy in accordance with the motions adopted by the
party congress. He decides on all matters that have been submitted to
the attention of the Political Bureau. He watches over the life of the
party." [12] As a meeting of a party congress was a procedural rarity,
Kasa-Vubu, as president of the Central Committee, clearly enjoyed a
predominant position in the party hierarchy.

The structure of the leadership of the MNC-Lumumba is equally
symptomatic of the centralizing tendencies of mass parties. Its highest
executive organ was the National Central Committee, composed of one
national president, one national vice-president, and six provincial presidents. According to Article 12 of the party statutes, "the National Central Committee is the principal organ of the movement: It ensures its
proper functioning and decides on all questions of general interest related
to the activities of the party." Even more significant, however, were the
powers vested in the National Bureau—a four-man directorate consisting
of a national president, a secretary general, a deputy secretary general,
and a treasurer. Besides acting as the "official representative" of the party,
the National Bureau was given exclusive responsibility to determine the
"party line" at the national level; as stipulated by the party statutes, "a
local or provincial committee may not decide on matters of national concern without consulting the National Bureau." Moreover, compliance
with the central directives was ensured by the obligation, imposed on all
party members and organizations, "to observe the party discipline and
carry out the decisions taken by the directing organs of the MNC." In
sum, the National Bureau functioned as a "party within the party";
operating under the direct patronage of Lumumba, this inner grouping
of party faithful was the core agency from which all important directives
emanated.

Viewed from the angle of their formal organization, then, mass
parties looked like strongly centralized "machines," enforcing a rigorous
discipline from the top of the hierarchy down to their basic units. This
picture, however, bears only a distant relation to the facts of party life.
Whether they tended to be of a mass or elite type, the outstanding characteristic of Congolese parties is the decentralized nature of their organization. In general, local and provincial officials retained a considerable
power of initiative, especially where constituency organizations were

spread over two or more provinces. But even in a party like the Abako "regional presidents" in practice enjoyed wide autonomy.[13] This concentration of power in the hands of these officials has frequently led to friction, and on some occasions the heads of the local sections did not hesitate to go over the heads of the comités régionaux to present their case to the Central Committee in Leopoldville.

The jurisdictional controversies that broke out among local officials are best illustrated by the dispute that took place shortly before independence, in Tshela, between Emmanuel Kini and Samuel Tati, both well known among the local Abakiste community. Kini was a member of the local section of the Abako who simultaneously held the posts of territorial assistant, member of the *conseil de territoire*, and president of the *tribunal de territoire* of Tshela. He bitterly criticized the Abako leadership for its decision to substitute political tribunals composed of "reliable" elements for those instituted by the administration. In Tshela the decision was carried out by Tati, regional president of the Abako, apparently without consulting the members of the local Abako committee. Because he resented Tati's "dictatorial" methods and regarded this gesture as a challenge to his authority, Kini ventilated his grievances before the Central Committee of the Abako. When the quarrel worsened, Kasa-Vubu appointed a commission of inquiry to investigate the situation. By then, however, relations among the various echelons of the party hierarchy had deteriorated beyond repair. In Tati's words, "Déjà dans notre milieu Abako nous sommes menacés d'échec par la mésentente qui existe entre les présidents des sections et des sous-sections, et entre comités des sections voisines. A cause de ce danger que nous voudrions créer nous mêmes [*sic*], je me declare personellement contre ces tribunaux." [14] This state of affairs, Kini added, was largely owing to Tati's dictatorial attitude and to his repeated efforts to pit Catholics against Protestants, and the évolués against the uneducated masses; he then told the commission that the regional president had endeavored to organize a party of his own "où il n'y aurait comme membres que des gens qui n'ont pas fait des hautes études, tels que les maneuvres, les commerçants." According to the report of the commission, after a bitter exchange of charges and countercharges the dispute was eventually settled, "thanks to the firm and skillful diplomacy displayed by the delegation." But that it should have occurred at all bears testimony to the internal conflicts that erupted from time to time within party hierarchies.

At the central level ultimate control over party affairs was frequently exercised by a dominant personality. This personalization of power is perhaps best illustrated by the role played by Lumumba in managing the affairs of the MNC. He controlled virtually all aspects and phases of policy making, and, moreover, in doing so paid relatively little attention to formal procedures. Decisions involving day-to-day questions of policy, such as the appointment of party officials, the selection of candidates for elections, and other matters of lesser importance, depended in last resort on the will of the MNC leader. Similarly, Kasa-Vubu's personality overshadowed all other offices in the hierarchy of the Abako. But whereas Lumumba consciously sought to impose his will on his following, Kasa-Vubu conceived his role somewhat differently: like de Gaulle, Kasa-Vubu looked upon himself as a "guide," but he also insisted on the fact that his real "mission" was to consummate the will of his people. To cite Kasa-Vubu's own words: "J'estime que ma mission est de réaliser la volonté de mon peuple." [15] On some occasions, however, the Abako leader did not hesitate to make unilateral decisions, as when he suddenly decided to leave the Brussels Round Table in protest against the refusal of the delegates to consider the issue of a provisional government.[16]

In the case of the PSA, this concentration of authority was perhaps less apparent; yet, important decisions were ordinarily subject to the approval of a duumvirate composed of Antoine Gizenga and Cléophas Kamitatu, respectively national and provincial presidents of the PSA, and both equally popular among certain segments of the Kwilu population— the former among the Bapende, and the latter among the Bambala. On the surface, while the leadership of the PSA retained some measure of unity, differences of character and personality between the two leaders, and the different ways in which they interpreted their functions, have produced occasional tensions at the top level of the party hierarchy. In time Gizenga became identified with the more radical, militant wing of the party, and Kamitatu with the more moderate; but neither faction achieved a position of dominance in the party, at least not until independence.

The conflicts of leadership which have affected the relations between the provincial committee of the PSA, based in Kikwit, and the national committee, based in Leopoldville, were owing to a large extent to disagreements over the distribution of authority between the provincial and national organizations of the party. The national committee would frequently criticize the provincial leaders for their lack of trust in their superiors, and for their tendency to make decisions on their own. The provincial committee, on the other hand, did not hesitate to blame the national leaders, and Gizenga in particular, for being "inert" and "incompetent" to handle the affairs of the party. For the young local elites of the PSA, who felt that they had done the most to give the party a solid armature in the countryside, the interference of the national committee was a source of considerable animosity. Bickerings over the proper allocation of party funds between the national and provincial committees pointed to another source of friction. At one point, for instance, the national committee criticized the provincial leaders for their failure to transfer a sufficient share of membership dues to Leopoldville, a gesture that naturally antagonized the provincial cadres. Basically, the tug of war between Kikwit and Leopoldville tended to reflect the conflicting claims to leadership made by Gizenga and Kamitatu; and the reason for its continuing so long without breaking into the open was that each contestant realized the potential popular support enjoyed by the other. But it also illustrates the kind of leadership problems faced by nationwide parties when they attempted to coördinate their national and provincial organizations.

In general, where leadership was highly personalized, internal dissensions were liable to occur between the top leaders and those elements who sought to resist excessive centralization. Thus, the vice-president of the Abako, Daniel Kanza, bitterly criticized Kasa-Vubu for his "dictatorial" attitude during the Brussels Round Table, and, in particular, for his failure to consult the other members of the Abako delegations. The controversy unleashed by Kanza led to his exclusion from the party on February 1, 1960, by a decision of the *comité restreint* of the Central Committee of the Abako, and shortly thereafter, on March 4, Kanza announced the formation of a dissident wing, which became known as the Abako Aile-Kanza. A few weeks later, on March 24, the MNC-Lumumba underwent a similar split when its national vice-president, Victor Nendaka, publicly accused Lumumba of "extreme left-wing tendencies" and subsequently resigned from his post to set up his own moderate wing, the MNC-Nendaka. Then, in April, 1960, the secretary general of the Cerea, Jean Chrysostome Weregemere, publicly dissociated himself from the leadership of the party and proceeded to organize a separate wing, the Cerea-Weregemere. Taking his cue from Nendaka, Weregemere accused the president and the vice-president of the Cerea of Communist leanings, pointing out that they had chosen for a technical adviser a notable personality in the Belgian Communist Party (Jean Terfve), and had taken upon themselves to visit Prague without consulting the other members of the Central Committee.[17] In each case it would seem that the split was due not only to a clash of personalities, but to a fundamental opposition to the concentration of authority in the hands of certain leaders.

Another possible source of tension lay in the presence of dominant tribal groupings in the parties' leadership. As already noted, it was precisely to avoid the charge of having unduly weighted the leadership of the association in favor of the Bantandu that Nzeza-Nlandu invited a Mayumbe, Kasa-Vubu, to join the Central Committee of the Abako. Still, the fact that six members of the Central Committee out of ten were of Muntandu extraction aroused the suspicion of the other Bakongo subgroups. Far more dangerous, potentially, was the overrepresenation of a particular tribe, or group of tribes, in the directing organs of a party which otherwise claimed a tribally heterogeneous following. Thus, one factor that has contributed to the secession of the Bayaka from the PSA was that they were virtually excluded from the Central Committee. Although the vice-presidency of the party was at one time entrusted to a Muyaka, Pierre Masikita, the Central Committee of the PSA remained almost entirely composed of elements who belonged to the tribes of the Kwilu—Bambala, Bapende, Babunda, Lampuku, and Badjinga.[18] Anxious to find a way out of this situation, a group of Bayaka, under the leadership of André Peti-Peti, took the initiative, in late 1959, in organizing the Union Kwangolaise pour l'Indépendance et la Liberté, better known as Luka. For the same motive, a few weeks later, the Bayanzi withdrew their support from the PSA and decided to set up the Alliance des Bayanzi (Abazi). While this did not lead to major defections among their supporters, equally noteworthy was the predominant position held by the Bashi tribes in the leadership of the Cerea, of the Ngombe in the Puna, and the Lunda in the Conakat.

Decision-making processes have also been affected by the sporadic involvement of European elements in party activities. Until the Brussels Round Table, their influence was generally confined to the presence of technical advisers. An exception was the Conakat, which, from the beginning of its collaboration with the Union Katangaise, abdicated a large measure of its autonomy to European settlers. At first, this self-imposed restriction seemed amply compensated by the material help which the Conakat could reasonably expect from settler interests. As time went on, however, their tutelage became increasingly burdensome, and by March, 1960, the Conakat leaders had decided to regain their freedom of action. On March 10 Tshombe declared before the Central Committee of the Conakat: "Ces Messieurs [les colons] ont recolté beaucoup d'argent au nom de la Conakat. ... Ils se sont fait propriétaires de notre argent. ... La rupture doit être nette, et même brusque." [19]

Tshombe's proposal was vigorously countered by Evariste Kimba. Cautioning the president of the Conakat against the disastrous consequences that might result from a sharp break with the settlers, Kimba observed: "Si on se séparait des colons brusquement ils pourraient être une arme destructrice pour la Conaka. ... Il ne faut pas que la rupture avec les colons soit une bombe atomique [*sic*] pour la Conakat. ... La rupture doit être progressive et justifiée." [20]

At any rate, by the end of April, 1960, the Conakat had successfully disengaged itself from the hold of the colonat. In a communiqué published in the issue of April 30 of *Conakat*, the Ucol-Katanga—now standing for Union pour la Collaboration des Classes Moyennes au Katanga—declared: ". . . In response to the wishes of different political leaders, our association has decided to restrict its activities to the study of economic questions and the defense of the professional interests of independent workers." Despite this announcement, prominent settler personalities like J. Humblé, G. Thyssens, and A. Belina continued to exercise considerable influence upon the leadership of the Conakat.

Meanwhile, at the Round Table a number of influential metropolitan personalities engaged in "brokerage activities" between Belgian vested interests and Congolese politicians. And insofar as they succeeded in providing financial assistance to otherwise insignificant groups, they decisively altered the balance of forces among parties. This brings us to an examination of the different sources of financial support available to political parties.

In the Congo, as elsewhere in Africa, the collection of membership dues and the sale of party cards provided a major source of financial assistance. This source of revenue proved especially useful to more extremist groups, not only because they claimed a mass membership, but also because the ownership of a party card often served as a safe-conduct for those elements—black or white—who otherwise would never have become party members. However, an accurate assessment of the proceeds from the sale of party cards is well-nigh impossible, as their price varied markedly from one region to the next, and from one "client" to the other. For example, the Abako cards were sold for 30 BF in the Mayumbe area, and for twice as much in the Madimba territory.[21] In addition, the Abako received important sums from coöperative organizations such as the Cooperative Cobakwa, whose director, Edmond Nzeza-Nlandu, was the founder of the association. Finally, in some areas, in the Lower Congo and Kwilu districts in particular, party officials sometimes acted as tax collectors, adding the taxpayers' contribution to the party funds, in defiance of the administration. Thus, shortly before the general elections, PSA officials canvassed the Kwilu District to collect *l'impôt de l'indépendance,* consisting of the *centimes additionnels* destined for the *caisses de chefferies.*[22] The use of this money-raising technique was not limited to the areas mentioned; it was also employed by the Cerea in some parts of the Kivu, and by the MNC-Lumumba in the Orientale Province.[23]

Even more important, perhaps, was the financial backing given to political parties by business groups and settler interests. The two main beneficiaries of these funds, though by no means the only ones, were the PNP (derisively referred to as *le parti des nègres payés* by its opponents) and the Conakat. Just how much "help" the Conakat received from European settlers is difficult to say; but there can be little doubt that their contribution was far from piddling. On January 20, 1960, Bonaventure Makonga flatly stated before the spokesmen of the colonat, Messrs. Thyssens and Onckelynckx: "Il faut que ces Messieurs nous donnent de l'argent —5 millions [$100,000] ou plus, pour activer notre propagande à l'intérieur ... car les intérêts que nous défendons sont les intérêts du Katanga, sans distinction de race ou de couleur." [24] Even more substantial were the contributions of the Union Minière du Haut-Katanga (UMHK) to the campaign funds of the Conakat. A rough indicator of the amount of assistance given by the UMHK to Katangese political groups is found in the annual report of the company for 1960. According to this report, "exceptional expenditures"—"incurred through the political events in the Congo in July, 1960, and composed mainly of expenses of evacuating members of our personnel and their families, expenses for their return to the Katanga, and various allowances"—amounted to $2.5 million. Yet, as Smith Hempstone correctly observed, "since mining-company personnel were evacuated by road (a distance of less than 200 miles) and most of them were back at work within three or four days, it is obvious that the entire $2.5 million could not possibly have been spent for this purpose." [25] True, the UMHK "covered its bet" by dispensing funds to other groups besides the Conakat; the latter, however, was clearly the main recipient of these donations.

Finally, one of the most valuable sources of financial support enjoyed by the MNC-Lumumba, and, to a lesser extent, the PSA, the Parti du Peuple, and the Cerea, was subsidies received from Moscow, Prague, and such neutralist states as Ghana, Guinea, and Egypt. If the global sum of 140 million BF, cited by Pierre Houart,[26] may sound like a gross overestimation of the aid received by the MNC-Lumumba from Communist states and Belgian fellow travelers, the campaign machinery utilized by the party propagandists in the Orientale Province testifies to the fact that their contribution was far from negligible. But this aid should not be regarded as a sign of doctrinal affinities between Lumumba's party, or Lumumba himself, and international communism.

In general, however, the comparatively loose internal structuring of Congolese parties, and the personalized character of their leadership, have served to enhance the influence of metropolitan and foreign pressure groups and personalities. For example, the names of A. J. J. Van Bilsen, Arthur Doucy, Serge Michel, and Madame Blouin became associated at one time or another, respectively, with the Abako, the Balubakat, the MNC-Lumumba, and the PSA. One will probably never know the exact role played by these personalities; but there is little question that, insofar as they became identified with particular ideological undercurrents, these connections have significantly added to intergroup tensions.

## Associated Organizations

Most parties have functioned in conjunction with one or several other groups identified with particular social categories—youth groups, women's organizations, syndicates, and so forth. Some of these, like the Front Patriotique de la Jeunesse—founded in May, 1960, to "provide the Congolese youth with a civic and patriotic formation" [27]—or the Mouvement des Femmes Nationalistes Congolaises—founded in February, 1960, to "promote the political education of Congolese women and assist the men in their struggle for the liberation of the Congolese people" [28]—did not attach themselves to any particular party. Others, like the Jeunesse Banunu Bobangi, the Jeunesse Lukunga, or the Fédération des Jeunes Budja, addressed themselves to specific tribal groupings, regardless of their political affinities. Beginning in 1960, however, there has been a universal tendency for parties to extend and solidify their bases of support by forging associational links with special interest groups.

In some cases this was accomplished by incorporating the membership of preëxisting associations into the party structure. As early as 1955, for example, the Abako had established close connections with a number of mutual-aid societies, youth organizations, and sports associations, such as the Mutuelle du Mayumbe, the Aurore Jeunesse Ngidienne, the Association Sportive Beerschoot, and others.[29] Likewise, the consumers' co-operative of Kikwit became organically linked to the PSA. More often, however, these specialized bodies stemmed from within the parties themselves. They were consciously organized by the parties' leadership to mobilize a wide array of potential supporters.

To the best of my knowledge, the MNC-Lumumba was the only party that ever attempted to set up an affiliate labor organization. This occurred in early 1960 with the creation of the Union Nationale des Travailleurs Congolais, an organization affiliated to the World Federation of Trade Unions (WFTU) and the Conakry-based Union Générale des Travailleurs d'Afrique Noire (UGTAN), and led by Antoine Tshimanga, spokesman of the pro-Lumumba youth group Alliance de la Jeunesse Congolaise.[30] Despite these efforts, the linkage between organized labor and the MNC-Lumumba remained extremely tenuous, not only because it was established at a relatively late date, but also because the field of trade-union activity had already been preëmpted by the Union des Travailleurs Congolais (UTC) and the Fédération Générale des Travailleurs Congolais (FGTK), identified respectively with Christian Democratic and Socialist tendencies.

On the other hand, most parties inspired the creation of youth organizations. Thus, in March, 1960, the Leopoldville branch of the MNC-Lumumba announced the creation of the Jeunesse du Mouvement

National Congolais (JMNC) for the purpose of "mobilizing and regrouping the young into a vast national movement, providing the young with a
civic and patriotic formation, creating and organizing cultural and artistic
sections, and providing its members with scholarships." [31] On May 13,
the Leopoldville section of the JMNC merged with the Jeunesse Atetela
and the Jeunesse Lulua-Frères to form the Confédération des Jeunes
Congolais (also known as the Alliance de la Jeunesse Congolaise), led
by the late Emmanuel Nzouzzi.[32] Meanwhile, the MNC-Kalondji organized the Mouvement National des Jeunesses Congolaises (MNJC), the
Abako the Jeunesse Abako (Jabako), the PSA the Jeunesse PSA (JPSA),
and so forth.

In Leopoldville, as in most other urban centers, these groups were
associated with their parent parties through horizontal links at the communal level; but they nevertheless formed distinct organizational entities. For example, the Jabako, though operating in close liaison with
the Abako, came under the control of a separate leadership structure
and printed its own newspaper, the bimonthly *Vigilance,* and its members
usually wore a distinctive uniform. And, as elsewhere in Africa, this organizational autonomy frequently expressed itself through independent
action.

Sometimes, as in the case of the JMNC, youth organizations were
given a free hand by the party to "verify and control" the activities of
the party "at the local level." [33] But where they did not enjoy such freedom of action they simply took the initiative in formulating demands
intended to support or criticize the parent organizations. For example,
when Kanza was expelled from the Abako, the spokesmen of the Jabako
gave their full support to the decision of the Central Committee; at the
same time, however, they urged the Central Committee to take appropriate steps to remove Kanza from the *collège exécutif provincial:* "Kanza
révoqué par le très honorable Comité Central de l'Abako ne peut en
aucun cas occuper le siège important qui vient de lui être attribué par
l'administration colonialiste." [34] A few weeks later, on April 12, the
Jabako unilaterally rejected the nomination of a certain Ndebo Mantezolo
to the *collège exécutif territorial,* on the grounds that he did not have the
support of the population. To add weight to their demand, the spokesmen of the organization specified that "the payment of taxes will be
refused if the nominee remains in office." [35] In short, while they undoubtedly played a significant role in indoctrinating the young and
converting them into party activists, youth organizations generally operated as semi-independent pressure groups.

However, the nature of the relationships between youth organizations and political parties underwent a radical transformation in the
weeks following independence. Thus, from a semiautonomous pressure

group, the Jabako suddenly transformed itself into an organ of criticism directed against the party's parliamentary representatives. In a motion issued in the early days of August, the Kintambo section of the Jabako bitterly attacked the *élus nationaux et provinciaux* for their failure to fulfill their promise of an independent and sovereign Kongo state. Threatening to destroy the Abako unless the party representatives lived up to their promise, the Jabako leaders bluntly declared: "Cet Etat souverain nous l'attendons, ou bien nous serons obligés de saccager l'Abako—les biens, les dirigeants aussi et les élus enfin." [36] Similarly, the youth organization of the MNC-Kalondji continually pressed for the division of the Kasai into two different provinces. In a motion to the president of the Senate, Joseph Ileo, the MNJC stated in July, 1960: "Pour nous une solution équitable n'est autre que la division du Kasai en deux provinces, comme l'a exprimé clairement la lettre que le Mouvement Solidaire Muluba a adressé au Premier Ministre." [37] In the Orientale Province, the opposition of the JMNC to the *élus* led its spokesmen to adopt a firm stand in favor of a dictatorial regime. Thus, in an article entitled "Vive la dictature pour mettre fin au sabotage," Yvon Thompson Yakusu wrote in August, 1960: "En notre qualité de membres fanatiques de la JMNC, et au nom de tous les jeunes nationalistes soucieux de l'avenir de notre beau pays ... nous réclamons la dictature." [38] In the Katanga the Jeunesse Balubakat asserted its complete independence from the party leadership and soon transformed itself into a terroristic organization, inaugurating a reign of terror and anarchy in many parts of the northern districts.[39] On the whole, therefore, as Thomas Hodgkin points out, "youth organizations have shown a fairly consistent tendency to independent action and radicalism," [40] to the point where they finally supplanted the parent parties.

That this tendency was even more pronounced in the Congo than elsewhere in Africa is in itself indicative of the organizational weakness of Congolese parties. While youth groups naturally tended to become potential centers of opposition once independence had become a reality, no effort was made by the parties to control these organizations, for they simply did not have means or opportunity to do so.

THE PRESS

The growth of the nationalist press since the latter part of 1959 is illustrative of the variety of interests competing for political control on the eve of independence. As shown by table 18, about twenty newspapers, representing almost as many different tendencies, circulated among the Congolese in the early part of 1960. More than half of these, however, were published in Leopoldville and hence did not achieve a very wide circulation among the populations of the other provinces.

Moreover, like the parties with which they were associated, most of these newspapers had only an ephemeral existence. In addition to the lack of available capital, the same reasons that inhibited the growth of political activity also prevented the development of party newspapers. Thus, until

TABLE 18

SELECTIVE LIST OF PARTY NEWSPAPERS PUBLISHED IN 1960

| Name | Place of publication | Frequency | Political group |
|---|---|---|---|
| *Notre Kongo* | Leopoldville | Weekly | Abako–Kasa-Vubu |
| *Kongo Dieto* | Leopoldville | Weekly | Abako–Kasa-Vubu |
| *Kongo Dia Ngunga* | Leopoldville | Weekly | Abako–Kasa-Vubu |
| *Vigilance* | Leopoldville | Bimonthly | Jabako |
| *Congo* | Leopoldville | Weekly | Abako-Kanza |
| *La Voix du Peuple* | Leopoldville | Weekly | MNC-Kalondji |
| *Emancipation* | Leopoldville | Bimonthly | Parti du Peuple |
| *Solidarité Africaine* | Leopoldville | Weekly | PSA |
| *La Nation Congolaise* | Leopoldville | Weekly | PUNA |
| *La Liberté* | Leopoldville | Weekly | PNP |
| *L'Indépendance* | Leopoldville | Weekly | MNC-Lumumba |
| *La Vérité* | Leopoldville | Irregular | Cerea |
| *Congo Libre* | Leopoldville | Irregular | Interfédérale |
| *Uhuru* | Stanleyville | Weekly | MNC-Lumumba |
| *Rédemption* | Stanleyville | Irregular | MNC-Lumumba |
| *La Lumière* | Lulaubourg | Weekly | PNP |
| *Franchise* | Luluabourg | Weekly | Lulua-Frères |
| *L'Abeille* | Luluabourg | Weekly | MSM |
| *Le National* | Elisabethville | Irregular | Cartel |
| *Congo d'Abord* | Elisabethville | Irregular | Balubakat |
| *La Voix du Katanga* | Elisabethville | Irregular | Conakat |
| *Conakat* | Elisabethville | Weekly | Conakat |
| *Le Phare* | Coquilhatville | Weekly | Unimo |

1959, about the only newspapers available to the Congolese were those published under the auspices of missionary societies and the administration.

One notable exception was the *Kongo Dia Ngunga,* founded by Nzeza-Nlandu in 1952 to assist the Abako in the "unification, preservation, and expansion of the Kikongo language." Although the statutes of the association specified that *Kongo Dia Ngunga* was "une société de presse autonome de l'Abako quant à sa direction, son administration et ses ressources," [41] its objectives were in fact inseparable from those of the Abako. Moreover, the Executive Committee of the association and the Comité de Direction of the "press section" were interchangeable. Indeed, the statutes of the "press section" clearly suggest that *Kongo Dia Ngunga* was not to be administered like an ordinary newspaper. "Le Directeur-

Fondateur," said the statutes, "organise, dirige et gouverne le journal." [42] In other words, the journal provided the starting point for the organizational development of the Abako.

In 1955 appeared the bimonthly *Conscience Africaine*, edited by Ileo and Ngalula. While the journal achieved a wide renown after the publication of the Manifesto of July, 1956, it remained otherwise highly deferential toward the administration. It was not until 1957, with the publication of *Congo*, that the Congolese press began to assert its nationalist vocation. By 1959 a number of nationalist press organs were suddenly flourishing in Leopoldville and Luluabourg, each seeking to build up a popular following. An official report describes the effect of this new journalism on the attitude of the évolués:

On constate une défaveur générale à l'égard de la presse officielle. Seuls les journaux politiques ont obtenu une audience auprès du public. Les journaux édités dans la province [Kasai] par les Congolais ont suivi le mouvement. *La Lumière* est devenu l'organe du PNP; *Franchise,* édité par l'Association Lulua-Frères, défend uniquement la politique de l'ethnie Lulua. *L'Abeille* est devenu le journal officiel du Mouvement Solidaire Muluba, créé en 1959. D'autres journaux de Léo ont également obtenu une large audience dans la province, principalement *Présence Congolaise,* organe du MNC-Kalondji.[43]

By this time several European newspapers had begun to trim their sails to the "winds of change." In Stanleyville, for example, *L'Echo de Stan,* under the editorship of Dr. Barlowatz, became a staunch supporter of Lumumba. In Bukavu, *L'Echo du Kivu* threw its weight behind moderate parties like the ARP, Reco, and Union des Bashi. In Elisabethville, *L'Essor du Congo* wholeheartedly endorsed the ideas of the Conakat, while the editor of *L'Echo du Katanga* sat on the fence, his wetted finger to the wind. In Leopoldville, the *Courrier d'Afrique* provided a platform where Congolese leaders of different tendencies could express their own particular viewpoints.

While the involvement of European-sponsored newspapers in political activities has undoubtedly heightened tensions among competing groups, even more significant in this respect was the part played by Congolese newspapers. First of all, most nationalist newspapers, including those organs whose appellations would suggest that they were entirely printed in French, carried articles in the vernacular—either because they wished to enlarge their readership, or because in so doing they hoped to stimulate the cultural awareness of their following. This indeed was the main objective of newspapers like *Kongo Dia Ngunga* and *Kongo Dieto,* both equally notable for the impassioned, lyrical overtones of their editorials. *Kongo Dieto,* in particular, with a circulation of about 40,000,[44] was followed with keen interest by Bakongo intellectuals. Like many similar publications, it provided a major platform for the expression of ideas based on the intrinsic worth of the Bakongo culture. In short, by drawing attention to the cultural distinctiveness of the group, through the use of traditional symbols and categories of explanation, the vernacular press made the Congolese all the more aware of their differences and thus intensified cultural antagonisms.

Another characteristic feature of Congolese newspapers was their general tendency to emphasize local issues. This tendency was perhaps least evident among newspapers that sought to attract a nationwide audience. But even then, a large amount of space was devoted to issues of a purely local or regional interest. Finally, one must note the highly personalized character of the messages conveyed by the party organs, a tendency which became especially noticeable after the Brussels Round Table, when a campaign of invectives no longer held the risk of retarding independence. From then on the attacks of party newspapers against their opponents were usually centered upon specific leaders, not their programs. Thus, while Lumumba was depicted by the editor of *Conakat* as a red-tinted agitator and a spreader of sedition, Kamitatu was branded as a "hypocrite" and an "opportunist" by *La Voix du Peuple,* and Tshombe, Kalondji, and Kasa-Vubu were all condemned as "traitors" by *L'Indépendance.* The net result of this campaign of abuse and slander was to exacerbate antagonisms among political leaders, and to render all the more distant the prospects of a rapprochement at the national level.

In sum, the development of the African-owned press has affected the organization of political parties in quite different ways. As noted earlier, the growth of a vernacular press among the Bakongo was largely responsible for the early success encountered by the Abako in mobilizing popular support for its ideals. The fact that it was sent virtually unchecked by the monitoring services of the Sûreté,* together with the comparatively high percentage of literacy claimed by the Bakongo (37 per cent in the Cataracts and Bas-Congo districts, and 54 per cent in the Leopoldville area), made it possible for the Abako to enlist the support of a mass following long before it transformed itself into a political party. In this connection, there is a striking parallel between the development of Bakongo nationalism and the spread of the Mau-Mau movement in

---

* This fact was confirmed to me by Father Van Wing. After the unrest provoked by the emergence of Kimbanguism, a strict censorship was established by the Belgian government through a decree of 1922, which enabled the governor general to take such measures as he deemed fit to "prevent the circulation or introduction in the Congo of any item likely to lead the Congolese to engage in subversive activities." Partly because of his personal antipathy toward Governor Lippens, whose liberal convictions were viewed with considerable distaste by most Catholics, Father Van Wing refused to comply with these directives, and continued to refuse even after Lippens had handed in his resignation. Thus such early publications as *Ntetembo Eto,* printed under the auspices of the Catholic mission of Kisantu, and, more recently, *Kongo Dia Ngunga,* were apparently never checked by the Sûreté.

Kenya. However different in their external manifestations, both movements derived their initial impetus from a vernacular press which in a large measure escaped the censorship of the colonial authorities.

Unlike the Bakongo press, most other nationalist organs came into being only a few months before the elections, when independence ceased to be a major issue. Consequently, they tended to look more like electoral pamphlets, or tracts, directed against their immediate opponents. Instead of serving as instruments of political mobilization—communicating directives to the militants, keeping them informed of major decisions and day-to-day activities—they merely undermined what was left of the parties' organization.

In summary, Congolese parties share many structural characteristics with other African parties. From the standpoint of their morphology, leadership, and internal organization, they reveal the same basic features as parties elsewhere in Africa, the same complexity, the same flexibility. In regard to the scope of their activities, however, they are altogether different institutions. Except for the Abako, few parties engaged in social, educational, and recreational activities of the type sponsored by the Convention People's Party in Ghana, the Parti Démocratique de Guinée, or the Parti Démocratique de la Côte d'Ivoire. The dominant characteristic of Congolese parties was their rudimentary organizational framework. With a few exceptions, Congolese parties tended to look more like jerry-built organizations than effective political organisms, a fact which is as much a reflection on the recency of their development as on the natural handicaps imposed by the very size of the Congolese territory, and the absence of adequate communications facilities. Under the circumstances, it is not surprising that so few Congolese leaders managed to extend their organization beyond the confines of the major towns. Nor is it surprising, in view of their structural weakness and limited geographical extension, that so few parties survived the turmoil which followed independence.

# XIII. INTERGROUP RELATIONSHIPS

Owing in part to the sheer number and mutability of the groups involved, the political alignments that have taken place in the Congo between January, 1959, and June, 1960, tend to convey an impression of extreme complexity. Part of the difficulty lies in the fact that the political options and priorities of Congolese leaders have been influenced by entirely different factors, depending on the period considered.

Thus, before the Brussels Round Table, intergroup relationships had been largely conditioned by tactical maneuverings vis-à-vis the metropolitan government. The principal aim of Congolese leaders during this period was to organize common fronts designed to bring to an end the policy of *attentisme* pursued by the Belgian government, and to reach agreement on the timing and the method of political transfer. At the same time, however, the main lines of cleavage tended to reflect fundamental differences of opinion concerning the timing of emancipation, and the nature of the future political institutions.

In the period which followed the Brussels Round Table, the immediate objective of Congolese parties was no longer the attainment of self-government, which was soon to become a reality, but the mobilization of political support. From then on they functioned not only as the instruments of various brands of nationalism but as electoral machines as well. Consequently, Congolese leaders became increasingly responsive to local issues; previous coalitions suddenly collapsed, to give way to a flurry of local alliances, often based on the exploitation of ethnic antagonisms.

While the following discussion is primarily centered upon the pattern of intergroup relationships that emerged before and after the Brussels Round Table, something must be said of the agreements reached at the Round Table between specific parties. Even though these agreements amounted to little more than conciliatory gestures, they nevertheless cast a revealing light on the attitude of certain leaders at this particular juncture of the Congo's political evolution.

BEFORE THE BRUSSELS ROUND TABLE

The first and by far the most significant of all interparty congresses to be held in the Congo was the Luluabourg Congress, which met April 7–12, 1959, in a town where tribal warfare was already brewing. The two

272

major participants, the MNC and the Union Congolaise, were joined in their deliberations by a host of minor parties which, as the president of the Union Congolaise, Alphonse Ilunga, stated, "recognized the vocation of the Congo to self-government and the need to preserve the national unity of the Congo." *

If the choice of Luluabourg was essentially designed to impress upon the local populations the necessity "of maintaining the geographical unity of the Congo," the main purpose of the gathering was to set the political objectives of the participant parties in the perspective of the constitutional changes announced by the declaration of January 13, 1959. Thus, in a resolution which was apparently urged upon the congress by Lumumba, the delegates unanimously endorsed a proposal for the establishment of a Congolese government in January, 1961. "The congress," said the resolution, "demands the installation in January, 1961, of a government to determine at what date the Congo will accede to independence." [1]

However, shortly before the congress adjourned on April 13, 1959, a counterdeclaration was issued by a group of moderate parties which brought important reservations to the initial position taken up by the delegates. Arguing that "in many African countries which are now members of the Commonwealth, an autonomous government existed prior to the granting of full independence," they specified that the election of an autonomous government in January, 1961, was in no way synonymous with independence. Commenting on the implications of this development, the Leopoldville newspaper, *L'Avenir,* noted: "It cannot be said that the chips are down, far from it, but the break could not be more clear between those who look at Accra and elsewhere for guidance, and those who desperately turn toward Belgium." [2]

Although this deviationist move carried within itself the portent of a regroupment of moderate parties, this tendency did not actually crystallize until the Coquilhatville Congress, held in this town November 11–16, 1959, under the aegis of the Interfédérale. On this occasion, four of the participants in the Luluabourg Congress—the Parti Démocrate Congolais, the Parti de l'Unité Congolaise, the Union Progressiste Congolaise, and the Union Congolaise—joined a group of newly born moderates to form the Parti National du Progrès (PNP). [3] Unlike the Luluabourg Congress, therefore, which was little more than an *ad hoc* meeting of unitarist parties, the Coquilhatville Congress paved the way for an organic union of moderate parties. While in practice this merger took on different

---

* These minor parties were the Parti Démocrate Congolais (PDC), the Parti de l'Unité Congolaise, the Parti du Progrès National Congolais, the Union Progressiste Congolaise (Upeco), the Union Economique Congolaise (Uneco), and the Mouvement National pour la Protection des Milieux Ruraux.

forms depending on the groups concerned,* they all shared a deep commitment to "moderation," "reasonableness," and "honesty." In other words, they were in no mood to accept the "dictatorial and exclusive leadership" [4] of a man like Lumumba, and, for the time being at least, this attitude gave them a sense of unity.

About the same time, the position of the Belgian government on the question of a federal versus a unitary structure brought about a regroupment of federalist parties. A decisive element behind this new coalition was the "telex" message addressed by the vice-governor general, André Schoeller, to the Minister, on September 2, 1959, in which he urged the metropolitan authorities to maintain a unitary structure in the Congo.[5] This message, which was subsequently published in the press through an indiscretion, led the Abako leaders to believe that the only way in which the issue could be effectively forced was through the formation of a "united front" of federalist parties.

As early as July, 1959, a close rapprochement had occurred between the Abako and PSA leaders, motivated in part by their common desire to consolidate their position against the administration. By November of the same year, as the need for unity seemed all the more pressing, the MNC-Kalondji and the Parti du Peuple decided to throw their weight behind the alliance. The result was the so-called Cartel-Abako, a front organization committed to the attainment of "immediate independence" and the "creation of autonomous provincial states . . . federated under a central government named Congo Federal Government." [6]

Despite its motto—"S'unir pour triompher!"—the Cartel-Abako was essentially an amalgam of autonomous political groups held together by their common urge to activate "the struggle against colonialism." As the statutes of the organization stated: "While forming a single corporation, the parties composing the cartel retain their autonomy and present field of action. . . . Their goal is to achieve the immediate liberation of the country." [7] But even in the absence of a tightly knit political machinery, and, indeed, long before its statutes were elaborated, the Cartel-Abako concentrated a heavy fire on the administration. During the months of November and December its leaders issued a flood of communiqués, letters, and memoranda, each bringing additional pressure to bear upon the Belgian government, until the latter finally accepted the idea of a negotiated settlement on the terms advocated by the cartel.

As the time for great decisions drew near, the cartel leaders took the initiative in organizing a congress of federalist parties at Kisantu, near

---

* For example, while some parties were completely absorbed by the PNP, others, such as the Luka and the Mederco—and later the ARP, the Reco, and the Mouvement Social du Maniema—though technically affiliated with the PNP, insisted on retaining their local autonomy and original appellations.

Leopoldville. The Kisantu Congress, held December 24–27, 1959, was attended by delegations from three other parties besides the Cartel-Abako: the Abazi, the Parti de la Défense du Peuple Lulua, and the Fédération Générale du Congo, all of which presumably shared the conviction that federalism was best for the Congo. The resolutions adopted at Kisantu dealt with a variety of problems, ranging from the liberation of political prisoners to the measures that should be taken to stop the aggravation of the Lulua-Baluba conflict; but the main emphasis was on the need for "immediate and total independence," and the recognition of federalism as "the only form of government which can assure the harmonious development and the normal flowering of all the people." [8] The fourth resolution, dealing with "Tribalism and Regionalism," condemned both manifestations as "a factor of social, political, economic and cultural regression"—a statement which, incidentally, did not accord precisely with the leanings of some delegations. In effect, it would seem that the main purpose for which the Kisantu Congress was organized was to allow the Cartel-Abako to strengthen its position before the Brussels Round Table, so as to apply maximum pressure upon the government once the negotiations would get under way.

Not unexpectedly, the MNC-Lumumba responded to this move by organizing the so-called "Congrès des Unitaristes," held in Bukavu January 6–8, 1960. The congress was attended by the Union Congolaise (which had just seceded from the PNP after a dispute over party funds), the Assoreco, the Front d'Unité Bangala (FUB), the Cerea, and a delegation of Basonge and Bena Samba chiefs,[9] all of whom shared the MNC's position on the federal versus unitary issue. That this was about the only area of agreement among the participants is clearly borne out by the content of the eleven resolutions adopted by the congress: all of these but two sought to demonstrate the necessity of maintaining the unity of the Congo. After condemning federalism as "the source of the Balkanization of the Congolese territory," the delegates gave their full support to "unitarism," which they described as "the political system which is most likely to defend and reconcile all the rights guaranteed by the Universal Declaration of Human Rights." [10] This consensus, however, masked widely different motivations: just as the PSA endorsed the idea of federalism to satisfy the exigencies of a particular situation, the commitment of the FUB leaders to a unitary structure was essentially due to their apprehension that any other system might place them under permanent Bakongo domination.

In sum, the main lines of cleavage behind the processes of regroupment which took place before the Brussels Round Table were determined to a large extent by the position of Congolese leaders on two major issues: (1) the timing of emancipation, and (2) the future character of the

Congolese polity. We have seen how Lumumba's stand on the first question caused a number of moderate leaders to dissociate themselves from the MNC, and, at a later stage, to seek greater unity by entering a broad coalition front. Similarly, the insistence of the Belgian government on maintaining a unitary structure in the Congo was the catalytic agent behind the emergence of a federalist front under the leadership of the Abako, a move which the MNC promptly countered by calling a congress of unitarian parties. The convening of the Brussels Round Table Conference was to give these leaders an opportunity to establish new relationships among themselves, and to redefine their position on a number of critical issues.

DURING THE BRUSSELS ROUND TABLE

Realizing that the success of the Round Table would depend on their ability to reach a consensus on the issues of major importance, the Congolese delegations decided at the outset to organize a common front. According to the statement issued by the delegates, the purpose of the front was "to promote the accession of the Congo to immediate independence . . . by defending the same positions on all the questions placed on the agenda [of the conference]." [11] While there can be little doubt that the Common Front served the purpose for which it was brought into being, the internal unity which once prevailed among the delegates rapidly evaporated once agreement was reached on a target date for independence. As shown by the voting records of the party delegations, from this point on it was a moribund organization.

One of the more significant aspects of the voting patterns at the Round Table lies in the sharp contrast between the position of the "moderates" on key procedural issues, and that of the "radicals." Thus, the PNP, the Conakat, the ARP, and the customary chiefs voted as a bloc (1) to reject universal suffrage for elections to the lower chamber; (2) to assign as many seats as possible in the upper chamber to customary authorities; (3) to adopt the Congolese Constitution after a mere approval by the provincial assemblies instead of by way of a referendum; (4) to recognize the king of Belgium as head of state during the interim period preceding the ratification of the constitution; (5) to grant eligibility to all Belgian citizens; (6) and to adopt an indirect system of election to the provincial assemblies. On the other hand, the stand of the "radicals" on most of the foregoing issues was just the opposite: the MNC-Lumumba, MNC-Kalondji, Abako, PSA, and Parti du Peuple voted as a bloc to advocate universal suffrage at all levels, to deny eligibility to Belgian citizens, and to refuse to recognize the king of Belgium as head of state. A minor but otherwise insignificant deviation occurred on the issue of the representation of traditional authorities in the upper chamber; while the Cerea and the MNC-Lumumba tried to minimize the weight of such interests, the Cartel-Abako settled for a fixed number of customary chiefs. In other words, the efforts of the moderates to enhance the position of traditional authorities and European settlers were paralled by an equal determination on the part of the radicals to curb the influence of all such vested interests.

Other delegations assumed a middle-of-the-road position, apparently unable to resolve the conflicting aspirations of their leadership. The Unimo and the Union Congolaise, for example, favored universal suffrage for the elections to the lower chamber and the provincial assemblies, and denied eligibility to Belgian citizens. On the other hand, they both favored the recognition of the king of Belgium as head of state, and the adoption of a constitution by a two-thirds majority of the Constituent Assembly. Furthermore, the Unimo advocated as high a proportion as possible of traditional chiefs in the upper chamber, but abstained on the question of their designation.

True, the voting record of the delegations does not provide a very reliable index of the parties' ultimate objectives. Aside from the fact that it does not reflect the parties' position on the crucial issue of federal versus unitary structure, the role of European advisers in influencing the vote, though admittedly difficult to ascertain, cannot be ignored. Nonetheless, it provides a partial insight into the range of attitudinal differences which separated the moderates from the radicals.

Another set of relationships which needs to be mentioned has to do with specific agreements among parties on issues which they considered to be of mutual concern. The most important of these were the agreements concluded between the Parti de la Défense du Peuple Lulua (formerly the Lulua-Frères) and the Mouvement Solidaire Muluba (MSM) on the one hand, and the Conakat and the Cartel-Balubakat on the other.

According to the terms of the compromise adopted by the Conakat and the Cartel-Balubakat on February 9, 1960, the primary objective of the parties was "to achieve an *entente* among the principal political forces of the Katanga"[12]—or, to put it more crudely, to stop the recurrent fighting between the Baluba and the southern tribes. The core of the agreement lay in the provision whereby the Conakat and the Balubakat would each receive half of the posts of bourgmestre available in Elisabethville (i.e., two each), while the Fedeka agreed "not to claim any leadership post," be it that of bourgmestre or provincial minister. The same parity was to be observed in the composition of the "commissions set up in Belgium or the Congo to implement the decisions made at the Brussels Round Table." A *comité de contact* made up of representatives from each of the two parties was "to examine all questions concerning the constitution and functioning of present and future public institutions, at the communal, provincial, and national levels," and "to settle all litigations that might arise among the parties to the convention." If this failed, the matter was to be referred to a commission of arbitration whose main function was "to resolve all conflicts, of any nature, related to the political activity of the parties and their members." Finally, the signatories, "while maintaining their own political doctrine and principles . . . [proclaimed] their willingness to take concerted action whenever the general interest [would] so require." In sum, there seemed to be a manifest determination on both sides to attempt to ease the tensions which continued to permeate the Katangese scene.

A few days later, on February 27, a somewhat similar agreement was reached between the Mouvement Solidaire Muluba and the Parti de la Défense du Peuple Lulua, this time at the insistence of Minister de Schrijver. Since Luluabourg was soon to become the seat of the Constituent Assembly, it was of the utmost importance that peace and order be restored before June 30, the date on which the Congolese Chambers were to convene to draft the new constitution. As a first step toward the achievement of a settlement, the zone annexe of Luluabourg was to be organized into three or four communes, in the hope that it would thus eliminate the possibility of a controversy over proprietary rights. According to Article 3 of the convention, "any Congolese, regardless of his ethnic origins, who wished to settle in the Lulua communes could do so within the framework of urban regulations." [13] In addition, the number of Baluba allowed to settle in these communes was to be regulated in such a way as "to avoid all unfavorable social repercussions." The implementation of this convention was entrusted to a special commission composed of three Baluba and three Lulua, all designated by the Collège Exécutif Provincial.

Despite their promising implications, however, neither one of these conventions proved to be worth the paper on which it was written. Exactly a month after the signature of the Lulua-Baluba agreement, new incidents broke out in the Ndesha commune in Luluabourg, and rapidly spread to other quarters. Meanwhile, on March 13, violent clashes were reported in Elisabethville, Jadotville, and Kolwezi between the militants of the Conakat and those of the Balubakat. In subsequent weeks the fighting continued off and on, not only in the towns but in the countryside as well. By then the Brussels agreements had long been forgotten.

There are several reasons for the failure of the Congolese leaders to honor their commitments. One is that such commitments would probably not have been contemplated if it had not been for the pressure exercised upon the parties by certain European personalities—by Minister de

Schrijver on one side, and by Messrs. Grévisse and Doucy on the other.*
Secondly, admitting that the parties concerned earnestly intended to
live up to their obligations, there is no certainty that they could do so.
It is indeed doubtful that the personal authority of men like Moise
Tshombe and Jason Sendwe in the Katanga, or Albert Kalondji and
Emery Wafwana in the Kasai, could possibly hold up against the tremendous pressure generated by ethnic rivalries. The key to this situation
is not to be found in what some Belgian observers call the "Bantu conception of authority," which would presumably make the leader a captive
of his following, much like the customary chief in regard to his subjects,
but, rather, in the very nature of the issues involved, as well as in the
climate of extreme tension ushered in by the electoral campaign. This in
turn suggests a third explanation, namely, that the factors which once
made it necessary, or advisable, for parties to establish certain types of
relationships among themselves ceased to be operative after the Brussels
Round Table. As we shall presently see, from then on political alignments
shifted into an entirely different pattern.

AFTER THE BRUSSELS ROUND TABLE

With independence in sight, the most important factor of cohesion disappeared from the scene of Congolese politics. The ties of solidarity
which had once existed among the members of different factions became
increasingly tenuous as each party sought to consolidate its position at
the local or provincial level. This change in the direction and location
of the lines of political cleavage is best illustrated by the sudden disintegration of the Cartel-Abako: almost overnight each of its constituent
members reasserted its independence, with the PSA loudly proclaiming
that it never intended to become a satellite of the Abako. Interviewed by
the *Libre Belgique,* Cléophas Kamitatu bluntly stated: "Quand l'Abako
aura lavé son linge sale, nous verrons s'il est blanc. Le PSA n'est pas un
parti satellite de l'Abako. En fait, nous sommes le plus grand parti de la
province." [14] Thus, in the general reshuffle of party relationships, many
former allies became enemies.

For the sake of analysis, a distinction must be drawn at the outset
between those alliances which were essentially motivated by electoral
circumstances, and those which were intended to assume a more permanent character. The former are perhaps best illustrated by Bolikango's

---

* Arthur Doucy, who is presently director of the Institut de Sociologie in
Brussels, acted as adviser to the Balubakat during the Brussels Round Table, while
Fernand Grévisse at one time held the post of district commissioner in the Katanga
before he became director of social affairs for the Union Minière. If their initiative
stemmed from different motives, they both had some interests at stake in the
Katanga which they sought to preserve as best they could.

Front Commun, created in Leopoldville in May, 1960, which included among its several components such odd bedfellows as the dissident wing of the Abako, led by Daniel Kanza, the Leopoldville section of the Unimo, and the Puna. Similarly, the list-coupling arrangements concluded between the PSA and the Kalondji wing of the MNC in the Leopoldville Province, the PNP and the Puna in the Equator, and the Coaka and the MNC-Lumumba in the Kasai, were all intended to maximize the electoral chances of those parties which only had a marginal following in these provinces.

Aside from such ephemeral coalitions, however, other alignments occurred at the regional level, which took the form of an organic union of the groups concerned. The most notable were (1) the FUB-Assoreco-Fedunec merger, which led to the creation of the Parti de l'Unité Nationale at the Lisala Congress, (2) the Reco-ARP-PNP "cartel," formed at the Bagira Congress, and (3) the alliance concluded between the MNC-Lumumba and various Bakusu and Batetela tribal associations at the Lodja Congress. Each of these coalitions involved an effort on the part of specific parties to build up nationwide support through local alliances based on ethnic and/or sectional affinities.

The Lisala Congress, which lasted from March 24 to April 3, 1960, was organized by the FUB leader, Jean Bolikango, for the purpose of grouping together a number of political formations of the Equateur which, for the most part, found themselves in the same predicament as Bolikango's own party: they lacked the support necessary to score a significant victory at the polls. For Bolikango, in particular, who was ambitious for a position of national prominence, the support of his "grande ethnie Bangala" seemed clearly insufficient to realize this objective. His primary concern, therefore, was to organize a broadly based political movement that would incorporate the Mongo, Ngombe, Ngwaka, and other minor ethnic groupings of the Equateur. This task, in Bolikango's view, could best be accomplished through an alliance with such parties as the Unimo, Fedunec, Unilac, and Assoreco, and those customary chiefs who had not yet cast their lot with the PNP.[15]

In his opening address to the delegates, Bolikango emphasized at the outset that "parties based on ethnic foundations" were only the first step toward a unified Congo, that the "national interest" of the country demanded a "unity of will"; this, he added, "does not mean that each ethnic group must abandon its own characteristics but that through these differences one must endeavor to form a harmonious ensemble."[16] Mainly because of his ethnic origins, Bolikango's overtures found a highly receptive audience among the Ngombe delegates, who tended to look upon him as a "favorite son." On the other hand, the Mongo delegation reacted with a great deal of skepticism to the prospect of a fusion with the Puna. Speaking on behalf of the Unimo, Louis Ekamba pointed out that, although "the Mongo's only wish [was] to collaborate with the Bangala," for the time being, at least, "the efforts of the Unimo must be for the benefit of the Equateur." [17] Furthermore, added Ekamba, his delegation had no authority to commit the Unimo to the fusion wished by the Puna. Clearly, the Mongo leaders were in no mood to accept Bolikango's proposal, partly because of his political stand on a united Congo, and partly because they felt that it would subordinate their group to the fiat of a Ngombe personality. Nonetheless, Bolikango could now count on the support of the Ngombe, of some Ngwaka and Bangala elements, and of the customary chiefs of the Lisala, Bongandanga, and Bumba regions.

The different leadership positions assumed by Bolikango provide the best illustration of the effect of ethnic polarities on political alignments. Once the leader of an ethnic association based in Leopoldville (Liboke Lya Bangala), Bolikango then decided to organize a federation of regional and ethnic associations (Interfédérale) which was to form the basis of a "vast political movement" called Parti de l'Unité Congolaise (PUC). However, no sooner had the party been constituted than it virtually disintegrated under the centrifugal pull of its ethnic components. At this point Bolikango, like most other leaders, turned to his own group of origin for the support which led to the creation of the Front d'Unité Bangala. Yet, as he rapidly discovered, whatever degree of internal unity existed among the Bangala was largely restricted to the Leopoldville area, a situation which was hardly compatible with his immediate political aims. With the creation of the Puna, Bolikango shifted his bases of support from Leopoldville to the Equateur. But here again, historical and cultural differences between the Ngombe and Ngwaka populations on the one hand, and the Mongo on the other, stood in the way of an effective consolidation. The result was that the Puna remained a primarily Ngombe-centered movement, with only a marginal following in Leopoldville.

Meanwhile, a somewhat similar move was made by the PNP at the Bagira Congress, held in the vicinity of Bukavu from March 20 to 22, 1960. The aim of the congress was to bring under the roof of the PNP a group of minor parties of the Kivu—essentially the ARP and the Reco, together with such smaller parties as the Mouvement Social du Maniema (MSM), Concorde Congolaise, Action Civique du Nord, and so forth— in the hope that it would extend the territorial spread of the party to a province where it had not yet penetrated. At the same time, for the leaders of the ARP and Reco, who were closely associated with the Bashi chiefs of the Kabare, Ngweshe, Rutshuru, and Maisi regions,* an alliance with the PNP seemed logical enough, as long as it did not deprive them of their local autonomy. Thus, while the resolutions adopted at the Bagira Congress recognized the PNP as the party "from which will emanate all political directives," the affiliate organizations were to "remain the masters of their respective zones." To add further cohesion to the "cartel," an attempt was made to elaborate a common platform, which dealt with such questions as the land problem, the exploitation of mineral resources, unemployment, wages, salaries, and so forth.[18] In essence, therefore, the Bagira Congress was a continuation of the policy inaugurated at the Coquilhatville Congress, with perhaps less emphasis on "honesty" and "moderation," and more stress on local autonomy.

Far more significant, from the standpoint of its implications, was the initiative taken by the MNC-Lumumba at the Lodja Congress. The congress, held March 9–12, 1960, was attended by 297 delegates who represented the Bakusu (or Bakutshu) and Batetela tribal associations of some fourteen different localities. While the avowed purpose of the gathering was "the reconstitution of the unity of the Bakusu, Batetela, and related tribes," † the head of the Leopoldville delegation emphasized at the outset that this goal was in no way synonymous with "tribalism": "A ceux qui nous accuseront de tribalisme," he stated, "nous disons que nous sommes les adversaires acharnés du tribalisme, mais avec cette petite différence que nous reconnaissons être d'abord des Bakusu et des Batetela avant d'être des Congolais." [19] Despite this official disclaimer, however, the real motive for the congress was to use Lumumba's ethnic origins to sensitize the Bakusu and Batetela populations to the appeals of the MNC.

More specifically, the objectives of the MNC were to awaken a sense of group consciousness among the delegates, to make them aware of the social, economic, and educational needs of the Bakusu and Batetela populations, and to relate these needs to the political goals of the MNC. Thus,

---

* A "rally of the great customary chiefs of the Kivu" was held on March 6, 1960, at the residence of the Mwami of Kabare, Alexandre Rugema, for the purpose of unifying the Bashi populations behind a new party, the Union des Bashi. Although the evidence is lacking, it seems that the party never developed beyond this stage mainly because of a disagreement between the chiefs who were already associated with the ARP (André Kalinda, of Sake Maisi; Kamirogoza, of Kalehe; Ndeze, of Rutshuru, whose son-in-law, Gervais Bahizi, was président sectionnaire of the ARP for Rutshuru) and those who favored the idea of a merger (Alexandre Rugema, Mwami of Kabare; and Abraham Lwanwa, coregent of the chefferie of Ngweshe with his mother, the Mwamikaze Astrid. It was after this meeting that the Reco came into being: founded by Abraham Lwanwa, with the blessing of a prominent settler personality, the Reco then aggregated the interests of the Bashi populations of Ngweshe.

† Asongomeno, Bangengele, Bakongolameno, Bahamba, etc.

after agreement was finally reached on a common ethnic denomination,* the delegates promptly recognized the identity of interests between the MNC and the populations represented at the congress. In the words of the report of the political commission: "On the question whether the Akutshu-Anamongo must create a political party, the political commission decided against it. . . . But, on the other hand, it favors the idea of entrusting the defense of the Akutshu-Anamongo interests to a party that has a majority [*un parti majoritaire*] in this region, possibly to the MNC." [20] With regard to the position of the customary authorities in the future political order, the consensus was that appointed chiefs (*chefs de secteurs imposés*) should not hold office unless they had been democratically elected, and that only the real customary chiefs should be given recognition. Finally, special emphasis was placed on the need for "seriously prospecting the subsoil resources of the Anamongo regions," opening new means of communications, building new and better schools, medical centers and hospitals, housing complexes, and so forth.

As the foregoing tends to suggest, there was an obvious lack of consistency between the professed doctrine of the MNC leader and the way in which he gave it its application. Lumumba saw little or no contradiction between a public castigation of tribalism and a style of action based on the exploitation of tribal affinities. But this is not necessarily indicative of an erratic behavior. In essence, what the Lodja Congress sought to accomplish was to give some sense of unity to a group of tribes which had virtually no tradition of previous political unity. As one resolution put it, its declared objective was to "minimize, and, if at all possible, destroy tribal tendencies." In a sense, therefore, the process of consolidation commenced at Lodja may well be regarded as a first step toward the goal of national unification; while seeking to infuse a sense of inner unity into a group of tribally diverse but culturally related people, the MNC also aimed at the construction of a national community out of a group of different cultural entities.

In summary, behind the extraordinary fluidity of political alignments established before independence, one can nevertheless discern a certain inner coherence. Until the Brussels Round Table the development of nationalist activities involved two recognizable patterns of interaction: one, centered on the issue of federalism versus unitarism, opposed ethnic and regional parties to panterritorial movements; another, centered upon the issue of a timing for independence, opposed the more moderate to

---

* Although the majority of the delegates favored the appellation "Ana-Mongo," a group of customary chiefs from the Maniema threatened "to go home immediately and sever all fraternal ties" unless the name "Akutshu" was adopted. In an effort to please everybody, the congress finally settled for the name "Akutshu-Anamongo."

the more radical parties. To be sure, these cleavages were largely incompatible with each other, for if the attainment of independence presupposed a substantial measure of agreement on the priority of this objective, the evidence shows that this was far from being the case. The paradox is, however, that in spite of fundamental differences over the timing and the methods to be employed, Congolese leaders nonetheless managed to wrest their independence from Belgium. It may be that if the conflict between the forces of nationalism and the colonial power had become more fully developed, it would have lessened, perhaps eliminated, these incompatibilities. As the Congo moved toward self-government, however, the issue of independence rapidly lost its relevance, and therefore lost its capacity to maintain a measure of solidarity among the leaders of different factions.

The displacement and multiplication of conflicts engendered by the approach of independence are familiar aspects of the dynamics of colonial nationalism at this stage of its evolution. In their efforts to build a modern nation-state, most African leaders have been faced at one time or another with the task of suppressing or mitigating ethnic and sectional disunities. In the Congo, however, this task was rendered especially difficult by the rather unique circumstances under which it was given its independence. For while the pursuit of self-government was indeed the primary goal of Congolese nationalists, immediate passage from colonial rule to self-government considerably lessened the chances of a genuine and lasting political integration. This is not meant to suggest that Belgium's precipitate surrender of authority was intended to demonstrate the incapacity of the Congolese for self-government, as the more severe critics of Belgian colonialism have hinted, but, rather, that the sudden collapse of Belgian authority destroyed at the same time the unifying urge which only the struggle for independence could sustain.

# CONCLUSION

Granting that the predominance of parochial loyalties constitutes a formidable obstacle to national unification, how should one account for the failure of Congolese nationalists to transcend regional and ethnic particularisms? To what extent is this failure the consequence of environmental factors inherent in the Congolese situation? How far is it a reflection of Belgian colonial policies and practices? In what ways has this affected the dynamic of Congolese nationalism? Since some of these questions have already been explored in the preceding chapters, here one needs only to summarize the arguments presented earlier, and relate the concluding hypotheses to probable future political trends.

One point that should be reëmphasized at the outset is that the circumstances which have prompted the growth of nationalism in other colonial areas have also been present in the Congolese situation; as elsewhere in Africa, the social and economic changes introduced by Belgian colonization provided the background elements, the predisposing circumstances for the rise of nationalist sentiment and activity. Among the conditions which Professor Deutsch considers essential to the process of nation building in general, and which also obtain in the Congo, one may cite the "shift from subsistence agriculture to exchange economies," the "social mobilization of rural populations in core areas of denser settlement and more extensive exchange," the "growth of towns and the growth of social mobility within them, and between town and country," and the "growth of basic communication grids linking important rivers, towns and trade routes." [1] Inasmuch as these various forces of social change were operative in the Congo, the efforts of Congolese nationalists to overthrow the colonial superstructure were the product of a "colonial situation" which, to paraphrase Marx, contained within itself the seeds of its own destruction.

Yet, the incidence of such transformations has also produced a situation which in many respects differs from that which is found in other African territories. One must note, in the first place, the eccentric position of two major "core areas" around which processes of social mobilization have been the most intensive. Though considerably more "advanced," industrially and commercially, than other regions, the Elisabethville and Leopoldville areas occupy a tangential position on the map of the Congo which made further integration all the more difficult. True, virtually all

285

capital cities in West Africa occupy a similar position in relation to the hinterland; in view of the sheer size of the Congolese territory, however, this factor acquires a much greater significance. Briefly stated, it meant that the populations of the vast central basin remained largely insulated from the "social updraft" generated by urban acculturative influences.

Second, the degree of social mobility between the towns and the countryside varied markedly from town to town, and from one segment of the urban population to the other. In the case of Leopoldville, for instance, the contiguity of this town to the Mukongo traditional habitat made it relatively easy for the Bakongo urban population to keep in close touch with their rural kinsmen. This is not so for the Bangala, whose rural homelands were miles away from their urban residence. In Elisabethville and other urban centers of the Haut-Katanga, the degree of social mobility of the urban population was minimal, largely because of the policy of labor stabilization pursued by European enterprises. The same is true of such industrial centers as Manono in the north of the Katanga, Bakwanga and Tshikapa in the Kasai, where every effort was made to stabilize the African population in the labor camps installed near the towns. On the whole, whatever degree of mobility actually took place between town and country affected particular tribes to the exclusion of others, which in some cases had the effect of reinforcing primary group ties among the people concerned. The example of the Bakongo clearly shows how new community ties can be substituted for old ones and still provide a source of solidarity for the group as a whole. In point of fact, it was largely from this feeling of group cohesion that the Bakongo nationalists derived the collective strength which sustained their drive toward emancipation.

Third, one may wonder if the discontinuities evidenced by these patterns of social mobility are not due in part to the limited extension of communication facilities offered to the African population. The basic communication grid of the Congo is shaped in the form of the capital letter Y placed horizontally, in which the top and bottom strokes are represented in the north by the Congo River, and in the south by the Chemin de Fer du Bas-Congo au Katanga, which links Port Francqui to Sakania. Thus, the two major axes of communication which link the capital city to the interior tended to limit processes of social mobilization to the "rimland," and hence made it extremely difficult for the populations of the central basin to intermingle with the peoples of other regions. All these discontinuous features have seriously complicated the process of nation building in the Congo.

What made this task even more arduous was the essentially static character of Belgian colonial policy, evidenced by the total absence of integrative governmental structures at the local and central levels. No effort was made to institutionalize social changes through meaningful representative organs, to activate the African communities toward the attainment of common goals, to revitalize traditional social structures for administrative purposes. Thus, when the Africans finally seized the levers of power they were faced with the phenomenal job of developing a suitable governmental machinery where none previously existed.

There are other compelling reasons for Belgium's failure to impart a sense of nationhood to the Congolese masses. One must remember, first of all, that the duration of Belgian colonial rule was exceedingly short compared to that of France or England in other parts of Africa. But even if the Belgian presence could have maintained itself in power for more than fifty-two years, there is no certainty that it could have produced a "more effective union" of the Congolese tribes. Aside from the difficulties arising from the nature of Belgian colonial policy, the heterogeneous character of Belgian national culture fostered a situation where "national" symbols were generally identified with a subculture (Flemish or Walloon) rather than with the larger national culture. Quite obviously, a nation lacking a strong national group awareness, such as Belgium, can hardly be expected to kindle strong national loyalties among other peoples. Thus, as one Belgian authority observed, "from this contact between two countries, none of which was a 'nation' [*pays*], resulted a total absence of [national] political structuring."[2] Another element which tended to inhibit the flow of loyalty toward the larger territory has to do with the several media through which Belgian acculturative influences have been projected onto the Congolese scene, that is, business interests, Christian missions, administrators, and so forth. In essence, the multiplicity of agencies involved in colonial control processes has produced a widespread ambivalence in the attitude of the Congolese masses toward the locus and nature of civil authority, as well as a tendency to conceptualize the very notion of self-government in purely negative terms. As we already mentioned, independence meant the eviction of Belgian "vested" interests rather than a common striving toward the construction of a viable nation-state.

The foregoing considerations, coupled with other situational factors, throw into relief three major disabilities suffered by centrally minded nationalists in their quest for national unity. One is that Congolese nationalism received its initial impetus from a narrow-based political movement which asserted itself as the vehicle of an *ethnic* brand of nationalism. We have seen how, from the very beginning, the vanguard role played by the Abako in spearheading the fight against Belgian colonialism enabled its members to pose as the real champions of independence. And since the Abako could reasonably claim most of the credit for initiating the first important changes in Belgian policy, it endowed its leaders with the aura of legitimacy and respectability desired by territorial nationalists.

To be sure, this particular aspect of Congolese nationalism has been paralleled by similar situations in other African territories. One only needs to recall here the predominant role played by the Kikuyu in Kenya, the Ewe in Togo, the Baganda in Uganda, or the Ibo in Nigeria. By and large, however, the "separatist" implications of such narrow-based movements were in many cases attenuated by the counterattraction of a unified territorial movement. This was especially the case in Nigeria, where the prospects of attaining national unity had a restraining influence on the impatience of southern nationalists. To quote Professor Coleman: "The vision of the prestige and power that a united Nigeria would bring was highly seductive, and therefore sobering. As a result, self-government was postponed for a few years, the north drastically revised its timetable, and a new unity was achieved." [3] In contrast, the Bakongo nationalists never consented to delay the advent of independence for the sake of national unity. Not only did they lack the patience to do so, but prior to independence they simply refused to accommodate their ultimate political objective (the revival of a Bakongo state) to the idea of a united Congo.

Another handicap suffered by territorial nationalists lay in the ever-increasing competition engendered by the Abako's bid for "immediate independence." Compelled as they were to emulate the claims of the Abako in order to meet the expectations of their followers, they became, in a sense, the victims of a situation which they had consciously created. For if the pursuit of self-government as a primary objective was a political necessity, it destroyed at the same time the chances of maintaining a modicum of national unity.

A third factor which diminished the relative political influence of territorial nationalists relates to their stand on the issue of federalism versus unitarism. They necessarily shared with the Belgian administration a strong commitment to the principles of a *Congo unitaire* as a fundamental premise for the establishment of a modern nation-state. They argued, with the Belgian government, that "federalist tendencies [represent] the past convulsions of the old spirit of tribal particularism which for many centuries prevented the emergence of a national consciousness in Africa." But this political imperative, however understandable, inevitably aroused the anxieties of ethnic minorities. Hence their repeated efforts to escape what they considered to be a "neocolonialist" venture, and to assert the legitimacy of their own special claims at the expense of an overriding national interest.

In view of the extremely fluid situation which still characterizes the Congolese political scene, any attempt to delineate with precision the properties of the emergent Congolese polity is at best a hazardous enterprise. Nonetheless, the main lines of political development have already been drawn, and are likely to remain so for some time to come.

First of all, attention must be paid to some of the internal changes brought in the wake of independence. No sooner had the Congo crossed the threshold of independence than the rapport which previously existed between the Congolese leaders and their following underwent a radical transformation. The party cadres became disillusioned by the seemingly indifferent attitude of their leaders toward the future of the parties as autonomous political units. Among the rank and file of the parties, those who had been vainly awaiting the jobs which they had been promised in the heyday of the nationalist crusade had already grown disenchanted. As they added their unhappy voice to the growing mass of unemployed workers, social unrest developed in the urban areas. Meanwhile, the confusion engendered by the revolt of the force publique confronted the party leaders with a range of demands on their energies which could be satisfied only at the expense of party activities.

The wholesale and abrupt Africanization of the civil service also had major political ramifications. Aside from the fact that the number of posts to be filled could hardly be expected to meet the demand, the situation prevailing in the upper reaches of the civil service soon became one of institutionalized nepotism. A number of permanent secretaries, deputy secretaries, and undersecretaries were appointed on the basis of merit, but this was exceptional rather than typical. In most instances, a minister not only selected his chef de cabinet from his friends and relatives within his own tribe, but his administrative staff as well. Party members denied these favors grew bitter. Erratic promotions in the lower echelons of the administrative hierarchy also created jealousies. As a result of the uneven distribution of Congolese personnel in the various services under Belgian rule, the rate of promotions in a given service inevitably depended on the number of aspirants in that service. A commis chef might find himself catapulted overnight to a top position in one department, while a *rédacteur principal* would be granted only marginal advancement in another. But perhaps the most consequential aspect of the Africanization of the civil service is that it caused a rapid absorption of the parties' leadership into the administrative superstructure. Under the circumstances, the chances of reactivating the party structures became rather slim.

Another source of tension lay in the failure of deputies and provincial councilors to communicate with their constituents. The latter, who had vested high hopes in their elected officials, were bitterly disappointed by what they considered to be total indifference to their own desiderata. Thus, shortly after independence, the président sectionnaire of the Walikale section of the MNC, in the Kivu, wrote the party chairman deploring that the local representatives, elected on an MNC ticket, "never visited the people of Walikale to inquire about their needs and grievances," [4] and further noted that "the whole population of Walikale laments that it never has a chance to meet its provincial councilors." In other words, many Africans felt that the parties which they once supported were nothing but the instruments through which Congolese politicians reaped the fruits of their sinecure.

What seems to have emerged since independence is a system where the bureaucracy clearly plays the predominant role. Indeed, just as the administration was the guiding political force during the colonial era, so today the single most important source of power lies in the civil service. With very few exceptions, party activities have lapsed into a state of limbo, even though administrative appointments are usually made on the basis of party affiliations. As Crawford Young reported, in May, 1962, "politics and politicians have become terms of blasphemy; one finds no trace whatsoever of party activity *per se* either in the Bas-Congo or the Kwilu. . . . The three figures in the local power structures are the territorial administrator, the police commissioner, and the commander of the local army detachment. The latter are not always under the control of the territorial administrator, but for the moment have no political pretensions or policies of their own." [5] Under the circumstances, therefore, the functioning of local institutions remains largely isolated from the sphere of party politics. An indigenous *fonctionnariat* has been substituted for the colonial administration, but the former continues to operate along the lines established by its predecessor. At the central and provincial levels, party alignments remain an important feature of the political life of the assemblies; but their deliberations have practically no effect on decision-making processes. On the whole, parliamentary debates give the outside observer an impression of extreme confusion, and seldom reveal anything approaching a recognizable pattern of consensus and dissensus on major issues of public policy.

In the absence of alternative integrating structures, is there any hope that the Congolese parties will ever play the unifying role which they have been assigned in other independent African states? In a recent article, Crawford Young contends that "Congolese parties are dead and there is no early prospect for their revival. . . . The one thing which might give a new *raison d'être* for parties would be elections; yet elections held now, without viable political parties to structure and channel the electoral competition would merely exacerbate beyond endurance the many ethnic conflicts now in varying degrees of latency." [6] This statement is perhaps too categorical, and is partly disproved by the author's own description of the "areas of strength" and "present situation" of

Congolese parties. But it accurately sums up the essence of the dilemma involved in contemporary Congolese politics. It seems clear that a long-term solution to the Congo's political problems will not be found in the lingering structures of an amorphous, tribally oriented party system. What, then, are the alternatives?

Many observers, and not the least qualified, have expressed the fear that the Congolese masses will in last resort turn to communism for an answer to their problems. Thus, in an article that appeared in the *New Leader* of March 27, 1961, Immanuel Wallerstein argued that conditions seemed ripe for "the emergence of a revolutionary movement Yenan-style." "Lacking a strong party on the Tunisia-Guinea model," wrote Wallerstein, "the Congo will see semi-anarchy and stagnation and may begin to turn to an organized peasant Communist movement as its only long-term nationalist solution."

At the time these lines were written, the chances of Communist penetration were further enhanced by the secession of the Katanga Province, which made it possible for the Soviet bloc to pose as the true champion of Congolese unity, not only against Tshombe's regime but against those Western powers upon which it became so heavily dependent, politically, economically, and militarily. Another factor which also strengthened the appeal of communism among some nationalists was the support accorded by the Soviet Union to the short-lived Gizenga regime in Stanleyville, then regarded by the Casablanca group, that is, Ghana, Guinea, Mali, Morocco, and the United Arab Republic, as the sole legitimate successor to Lumumba's government. Since the collapse of the Stanleyville regime and the reintegration of the Katanga into the fold of the central government, the concurrence of interests between Communist states and radical nationalist elements has tended to evaporate. In other words, the removal of Congolese politics from the global East-West struggle has tended to reduce the sources of Communist influence in the Congo.

Nonetheless, social and economic conditions still provide a very fertile environment for the implantation of Communist ideology. In fact, recent developments in the Kwilu region tend to confirm Wallerstein's pessimistic diagnosis. Under the leadership of Pierre Mulele, minister of education in Lumumba's government and at one time a key figure in the PSA, a guerrilla movement has come into being which has already spread chaos and sedition throughout the province. There can be little doubt about Mulele's commitment to the Chinese brand of communism, but for the time being the outward manifestations of the rebellion suggest a closer connection with the nativistic revolts that have recurrently swept across the Kwilu than with a full-fledged Yenan-style Communist movement. A conscious effort has been made to channel the frustrations and grievances of the African peasants into a terroristic, nativistic organization directed against the central government authorities. The available evidence suggests that the movement has gained steadily increasing support among the local populations, partly through intimidation and partly through seduction. A similar pattern of antigovernmental violence is now developing in the Kivu region, where a group of Communist-backed rebels is reported to have gained control over a considerable stretch of territory on the eastern bank of Lake Tanganyika. As in the Kwilu area, ethnic antagonisms are skillfully manipulated by the rebel leaders to spread the insurrection into the countryside, with the result that insurrectionary activities inevitably tend to reactivate tribal animosities. The situation is still too fluid to permit a final judgment, but at the time of this writing killing, looting, and burning have reached such alarming proportions that it is questionable if the central government will have the capacity to deal effectively with the rebels, or maintain a degree of order and political stability if and when the revolt is quelled. Meanwhile, the extreme poverty and hopelessness of the African rural masses are likely to make them increasingly receptive to the appeals of communism, if only because they now feel that any change would be for the better.

A second alternative lies in the possibility of a military coup d'état by the officers of the force publique. Like the Sudan, where the multiplicity of political parties played into the hands of the military, the Congo may again become the scene of military upheaval. The recent mutiny of the Leopoldville police force, officially described as the consequence of a "political conspiracy,"[7] suggests that the army will continue to be a major determinant of political development. The force publique is still very much a "rabble," with little discipline or political consciousness, but the present situation greatly enhances its potential influence. Speaking of the "characteristic desire [of Africans] for a strong man who will be powerful and pure, leading the nation to harmony and achievement," David Apter notes that "this is particularly true when bitter rivalry between parties divides the public. The greater the rivalry, the more people with passionate political attachments wish for an end of party conflict; but they are less willing to accept the dominance of a party other than their own. Hence they may look for an outside force (army, civil service) to save them from themselves."[8] Moreover, in the context of the present situation many Congolese would be willing to accept the rule of the military in order to prevent a further trend to the left.

A third alternative is suggested by the current efforts of some Congolese leaders to resuscitate a broad nationalist front, bearing the posthumous stamp of Lumumba's ideals and personality. Their immediate objective can best be described as "Lumumbism without Lumumba." Accordingly, they wish to create a strong central government, depending on the existence of a single party; they favor a neutralist, Pan-African foreign policy of the "Casablanca" variety; and they show a marked preference for a domestic policy inspired by "African socialism." However, in the absence of a political leader of Lumumba's stature, this initiative is, for the time being at least, more like a tribute to Lumumba's memory than a constructive step toward national integration. Meanwhile, from the strategic positions which they have created for themselves, the ruling elites will try to forestall the development of any such collective action. In brief, as long as the administration retains control over the army, the civil service will be the only outside force capable of infusing a sense of national unity into the Congolese masses.

"To be attached to the subdivision," wrote Edmund Burke in his *Reflections on the Revolution in France,* "to love the little platoon we belong to in society is the first principle (the germ as it were) of public affections. It is the first link in a series by which we proceed toward a love to our country and to mankind." [9] This kind of an argument, of course, is anathema to all self-respecting Jacobins, and therefore to many African nationalists as well. Yet, what Burke meant by the attachment to the subdivision is likely to remain for a long time the most conspicuous feature of Congolese society. Whatever else the future may hold, Burke's statement should serve as a reminder that a love for one's tribe is not necessarily exclusive of a love of one's country. If nothing else, then, Burke's wisdom may still provide a source of optimism for those Congolese who seek in their past an answer to the future.

# APPENDIXES

# APPENDIX I

## Selective Listing of Major Congolese Parties (1960)

The following list is intended to provide a brief and highly selective nomenclature of Congolese parties, in the hope that it will help the reader to find his way through the maze of political movements and associations in existence on the eve of independence. Those groups marked with an asterisk became affiliated at one time or another with the Parti National du Progrès (PNP); double asterisks refer to groups that entered into electoral alliance with the Mouvement National Congolais–Lumumba (MNC-Lumumba). Territorial parties—those having branch organizations in two or more provinces—have been listed under the name of the province where they enjoyed maximum support. Finally, it must be remembered that most of these political movements have now ceased to exist, and that many of their leaders have either disappeared from the Congolese political scene or have been replaced by new personalities.

I. LEOPOLDVILLE PROVINCE

ABAKO (Alliance des Bakongo): Ethnic party originating from a Bakongo cultural association founded in 1951 by Edmond Nzeza-Nlandu. President: Joseph Kasa-Vubu. After the Brussels Round Table a dissident wing emerged under the leadership of Daniel Kanza, which came to be known as the Abako–Aile Kanza; since independence two other splinter groups have come into being: the Rafeco (Rassemblement des Fédéralistes du Congo), led by Edmond Nzeza-Nlandu, and the Udaco (Udaco Manianga Mayumbe), led by Toto Kinkhela. In the 1960 parliamentary elections the Abako won 12 seats in the Chamber of Representatives and 33 in the Provincial Assembly.

ABAZI (Alliance des Bayanzi): Ethnic party founded late in 1959 by Gaston Midu, with main support among the Bayanzi people. President: Gaston Midu. Won 1 seat in the Chamber and 2 in the Provincial Assembly.

* LUKA (Union Kwangolaise pour l'Indépendance et la Liberté): Ethnic party founded late in 1959 by André Peti-Peti, with main support among the Bayaka people of the Kwango region. President: Arthur Delvaux. Won 3 seats in the Chamber and 9 in the Provincial Assembly.

PSA (Parti de la Solidarité Africaine): Regional party founded in April, 1959, by Gabriel Yumbu, with its main area of strength in the Kwilu region. National president: Antoine Gizenga; provincial president: Cléophas Kamitatu. Since independence the party has split into two irreducible factions, headed respectively by Antoine Gizenga and

297

Cléophas Kamitatu. The Gizenga wing, by far the most radical, joined the Fronaco (Front des Nationalistes Congolais) in 1961; since then it has launched a guerrilla movement which operates in the Kwilu region under the leadership of Pierre Mulele, at one time vice-president of the National Council of the PSA. Won 13 seats in the Chamber and 35 in the Provincial Assembly.

PARTI DU PEUPLE : Local party founded in Leopoldville in January, 1958. Evolved from a left-wing association (Action Socialiste) founded in 1957 by a group of Congolese syndicalists. President: Alphonse Nguvulu. Won 1 seat in the Provincial Assembly.

° PNP (Parti National du Progrès) : Territorial party founded in November, 1959, at the Coquilhatville Congress by a fusion of 27 minor political groupings of moderate leanings. Its main areas of strength are in Leopoldville and Equateur provinces. President: Paul Bolya. Thanks to its electoral alliances, the PNP managed to control 11 seats in the Chamber, 11 in Leopoldville Province, 10 in the Equateur, 5 in the Kivu, and 4 in the Kasai.

RDLK (Rassemblement Démocratique du Lac Léopold et du Kwango) : Regional party founded in January, 1960, by Jacques Massa, with main support in the Lac Léopold region. President: Jacques Massa. Won 1 seat in the Chamber and 2 in the Provincial Assembly.

## II. EQUATEUR PROVINCE

° MEDERCO (Mouvement de l'Evolution et du Développement Economique Social du Congo) : Regional party founded in 1959 in Gemena (Equateur) by André Anekonzapa. Developed from an ethnic association known as the Association des Ressortissants des Peuples Soudanais. Aggregates the interests of the Ngwandi, Mbubu, Mbanja, and other tribes of Sudanic origins. President: André Anekonzapa. Won 5 seats in the Provincial Assembly.

PUNA (Parti de l'Unité Nationale) : Territorial party founded in March, 1960, at the Lisala Congress by a fusion of the FUB (Front d'Unité Bangala), the Assoreco (Association des Ressortissants du Congo), and other minor groupings. Derived most of its support from the Ngombe population of the Equateur. President: Jean Bolikango. Won 7 seats in the Chamber and 9 in the Provincial Assembly.

UNIMO (Union Mongo) : Ethnic party founded in January, 1960, by Justin Bomboko, with main support among the Mongo population of the Equateur. National president: Justin Bomboko. Won 1 seat in the Chamber and 8 in the Provincial Assembly.

## III. ORIENTALE PROVINCE

°° MNC (Mouvement National Congolais) : Territorial party founded in November, 1956, by a group of Congolese intellectuals of Leopoldville associated with the journal, *Conscience Africaine*. Under the leadership of the late Patrice Lumumba the MNC became a Congowide movement. In July, 1959, a dissident wing emerged under the leadership of Albert Kalondji, with its main influence among the Baluba population of Kasai Province. Another break occurred after the Brussels Round Table, when the vice-president of the MNC, Victor

Nendaka, decided to organize his own moderate wing. After the death of its national president, Patrice Lumumba, in 1961, the leadership of the party went to Alphonse Kiwewa and Christian Gbenye. The party scored its greatest victory in Orientale Province, where it swept 58 seats out of a total of 70. Won 33 seats in the Chamber.

## IV. KIVU PROVINCE

CEREA (Centre du Regroupement Africain): Regional party founded in July, 1958, by Philippe Nkubiri. President: Anicet Kashamura. A major split occurred in March, 1960, when the secretary-general of the Cerea, Jean-Chrysostome Weregemere, organized his own moderate wing. Won 10 seats in the Chamber and 25 in the Provincial Assembly.

* RECO (Rassemblement des Habitants de l'Est du Congo): Local party founded in Ngweshe (Kivu) in March, 1960, by Abraham Lwanwa, with its main support among the Bashi population of Ngweshe. President: Donat Kalimbiriro. Won 1 seat in the Chamber and 6 in the Provincial Assembly.

* ARP (Alliance Rurale Progressiste): Local party founded in Bukavu in July, 1959, with the assistance of a Belgian settler, Raoul Piron. President: Marc Banazi. Won 1 seat in the Chamber.

** UNEBAFI (Union des Bazembo de Fizi): Ethnic party founded in Fizi (Kivu) in 1959. Evolved from a Bazembo mutual-aid association. President: Albert Kingoma. Won 3 seats in the Provincial Assembly.

## V. KATANGA PROVINCE

CONAKAT (Confédération des Associations Tribales du Katanga): Regional party founded late in 1958 by Godefroid Munongo, Moise Tshombe, and Bonaventure Makonga. Received most of its support from certain tribes indigenous to the Katanga—essentially the Lunda, the Bayeke, and the Batabwa—and from European settlers. President: Moise Tshombe. It underwent a major crisis in November, 1959, when one of its main constituent units, the Balubakat (Association des Baluba du Katanga), seceded. Won 8 seats in the Chamber and 25 in the Provincial Assembly.

** BALUBAKAT (Association des Baluba du Katanga): Ethnic party originating from a Baluba cultural association founded in 1957 by Jason Sendwe. President: Jason Sendwe. After withdrawing its support from the Conakat, the Balubakat formed an alliance with the Atcar (Association des Tshokwe du Congo, de l'Angola et de la Rhodésie) and the Fedeka (Fédération Kasaïenne), which led to the creation of the Cartel Katangais. Won 7 seats in the Chamber and 22 in the Provincial Assembly.

FEDEKA (Fédération Kasaïenne): Ethnic party originating from a tribal association (Fédération Générale des Baluba Centraux du Katanga) founded in 1957 by André Kadima. Derives most of its support from Kasaian immigrants, for the most part of Baluba origins. President: Isaac Kalondji. Won 3 seats in the Provincial Assembly.

ATCAR (Association des Tshokwe du Congo, de l'Angola et de la Rhodésie): Ethnic party founded by Ambroise Muhunga in 1959, with main support among the Tshokwe population of the Katanga. President: Ambroise Muhunga. Won 2 seats in the Provincial Assembly.

* UNION CONGOLAISE: Local party founded in Elisabethville in 1957 by a Belgian lawyer, Antoine Rubbens. President: Gabriel Kitenge. Won 1 seat in the Provincial Assembly.


### VI. KASAI PROVINCE

MSM (Mouvement Solidaire Muluba): Ethnic party founded in 1959 in Luluabourg by Evariste Kalondji and Albert Nyembwe. President: Evariste Kalondji. After forming an electoral alliance with the MNC-Kalondji, the MSM shifted its activities to Leopoldville. In Kasai Province MSM candidates in the 1960 elections ran on an MNC-Kalondji ticket.

MNC-KALONDJI (Mouvement Nationale Congolais–Kalondji): Dissident wing of the MNC founded in Leopoldville in July, 1959, by Joseph Ileo and Joseph Ngalula, with its main influence in the Kasai, among the Baluba population. Also received marginal support from Baluba intellectuals in Leopoldville and Elisabethville. President: Albert Kalondji. Won 8 seats in the Chamber and 21 in the Provincial Assembly.

** PDPL (Parti de la Défense du Peuple Lulua): Ethnic party originating from a Lulua cultural association (Association Lulua-Frères) founded in 1956 by a Lulua chief, Sylvestre Kalamba. President: Alphonse Ilunga. Subsequently the party changed its name to Union Nationale Congolaise. On the eve of the polling date the PDPL entered into an electoral coalition with the MNC-Lumumba, which led to the formation of the Cartel MNC. Won 3 seats in the Chamber and 10 in the Provincial Assembly.

** COAKA (Coalition Kasaïenne): Regional party founded in 1959 by Grégoire Kamanga, with its main influence among the smaller tribes of Kasai Province—Babindji, Basala Mpasu, Bena Mputu, and so forth. President: Grégoire Kamanga. Won 3 seats in the Chamber and 5 in the Provincial Assembly.

# APPENDIX II

The following report illustrates better than any other document the kind of activities carried out by ethnic associations in the years preceding Congolese independence. It shows, among other things, the variety and complexity of functions (administrative, judicial, educational, and recreational) devolved upon these associations. It also testifies to the persistence of ethnic-group loyalties among urbanized Africans. Like other similar groupings, the Association Lulua-Frères served as a matrix within which traditional and modern bureaucratic forms combined to give its members a sense of solidarity.

ASSOCIATION LULUA-FRÈRES

AVENUE BUKAMA

B.P. 4033
*Elisabethville*

RAPPORT DU SECRÉTARIAT SUR L'ACTIVITÉ DE L'ASSOCIATION
LULUA-FRÈRES:
EXERCICE DU 1 JANVIER AU 31 DÉCEMBRE 1956.

Comme chaque maison de commerce, pour connaitre le mouvement général et la marche de ses affaires, fait l'inventaire et établit un rapport sur les activités de son commerce, il est logique et nécessaire qu'une association comme Lulua-Frères, qui groupe un nombre assez considèrable de membres, doive présenter son rapport annuel, afin de faire constater si, au cours de l'année, elle a fait des progrès, ou elle est restée stationnaire ou bien elle a tout simplement dégénéré.

CHAPITRE I: MEMBRES EFFECTIFS
Le rapport sur la situation des membres étant du ressort du Trésorier-Adjoint, Mr. Symphorien Tshiandamu, qui s'y étendra plus largement, je me bornerai simplement à vous dire que notre Cercle, qui comptait 540 membres au 31 décembre 1955, groupe actuellement, au 31 décembre 1956, 676 têtes inscrites dont presque la moitié en règle de cotisations mensuelles.

CHAPITRE II: OCCUPATION ET SITUATION DES MEMBRES DU COMITÉ
A. PRÉSIDENCE: Pour le mandat 1956, ce poste de haute importance fut confié à Monsieur Denis-Samuel Munda, qui remplissait précédemment la fonction de Vice-Président, trois ans durant.
Ce Président dynamique, brave et laborieux, a su conduire notre Cercle avec toute compétence. Sa sagesse et sa simplicité, son courage et son autorité,

301

sa patience et sa charité font en lui un homme sincère et dévoué qui fait tout pour l'amour et le progrès de sa tribu.

Dans tous les domaines le précité fut secondé par ses deux Vice-Présidents fidèles et consciencieux; ce sont: Messieurs Jacques Tshifunda et Jean Tshimanga. Chargé de la mission du règlement des affaires avec l'Administration Publique et les milieux sociaux, Mr. Tshifuma donna entière satisfaction dans l'accomplissement de sa tâche, tandis que son collègue, Mr. Tshimanga, qui lui s'occupait de la gestion des finances de l'Association, des relations et entente entre les membres ainsi que de la réception des membres d'autres sections, de leur assurer nourriture et logement, ne rendit pas moins service à la Société.

B. Secrétariat: Vu l'augmentation des membres et la surabondance des besognes, les travaux du secrétariat furent cette fois exécutés par trois secrétaires, qui ont eu à leur tête le Secrétaire Principal, Mr. Francois-Albert Mukendi, qui remplissait précédemment depuis deux ans les fonctions de Secrétaire-Adjoint.

Ci-dessous je me permets de vous citer le rôle de chaque Secrétaire dans ce departement:

*François-Albert* Mukendi: *Secrétaire*
—Rédiger des correspondances concernant l'administration générale de l'Association; des correspondances avec l'Administration de la Colonie; avec la siège de Lulua-Frères à Luluabourg ainsi que toutes celles traitant des questions délicates et importantes.
—Rédiger des procès verbaux dans des réunions et des discours de toutes circonstances.
—Etablir des rapports annuels et autres; élaboration du plan sur l'étude des modifications de statuts.
—Contrôle général des travaux exécutés au Secrétariat.
—Assumer la responsabilité de tous les objets appartenant à l'Association.

*Louis* Tshimwanga: *Secrétaire-Adjoint*
—Rédaction des correspondances avec l'extérieur et différents sièges de l'Association.
—Établissement des procès verbaux des jugements rendus au Conseil Clanique.
—Rédaction des lettres de transmission des affaires litigieuses au Tribunal compétent.
—Seconder le Secrétaire dans l'établissement des procès verbaux des réunions en cas d'absence ou d'empêchement de celui-ci.
—Dactylographie des documents précités.

*Crispin* Tshisungu: *Secrétaire-Adjoint*
—Rédiger des correspondances avec l'extérieur et entre diverses sections.
—Dactylographie et classement de toutes les pièces du Secrétariat.
*Jerôme* Ntumba: *Secrétaire-Adjoint*
—Rédaction des correspondances concernant les affaires de l'équipe "Lulua-Sport."
—Dactylographie et classement général de toutes les pièces du Secrétariat.
—Assister aux matches disputés par nos équipes.

Ces travaux marchèrent d'une façon satisfaisante. Cependant, pour des raisons que nous ignorons totalement, deux de nos Secrétaires-Adjoints se trouvèrent dans l'impossibilité de continuer leurs fonctions, ce qui pesa lourd sur les épaules des restants, empêchant ainsi l'accomplissement harmonieux de leurs devoirs, notamment le classement, qui resta presque toujours en souffrance.

Enfin, malgré ces inconvénients, les grosses difficultés furent surmontées et le Secrétariat se redresse d'une manière vigoureuse, grâce à l'effort conjugué et surtout à la bonne volonté du travailleur assidu et laborieux qui est Louis TSHIMWANGA. En effet, de sincères remerciements adressés à ce jeune homme ne seraient jamais superflus.

### C. COMPTABILITÉ

Le mouvement de l'Association devenu important, la création du département Comptabilité s'impose et le comité en confia la direction a Mr. David KABASELE (Chef Comptable), qui organisa le système de comptabilité en partie double, suivant les conseils donnés en son temps par Mr. d'Hondt Camille, Administrateur, Ancien Chef du Centre Extra-Coutumier.

Grâce à une tenue de comptabilité impeccable et irréprochable, nous nous réjouissons de la bonne marche des affaires financières, car l'existence ou la dissolution de l'Association en dépend. Comme dans tous les domaines, le Comptable est assisté de deux Aide-Comptables, qui sont: Messieurs David MUKENDI et Barthélémy TSHIMANGA. Le transfert de ce dernier pour Kolwezi, causa certainement du préjudice à la Comptabilité. Il convient sincèrement de remercier Mr. KABASELE et ses Adjoints, qui nous ont fourni du travail soigné.

### D. TRÉSORERIE

Ce poste délicat et de haute confiance, fut confié depuis l'existence du Cercle Lulua-Frères, à Monsieur Samuel LUSHIKU. Le précité eut comme Trésorier-Adjoint, son fidèle et dévoué Monsieur Symphorien TSHIANDAMU. Nous devons aussi les remercier de tout coeur, de ce qu'ils ont fait la bonne garde auprès de la Caisse de l'Association.

S'il faut absolument changer de membres au Département Trésorerie, il est nécessaire qu'il soit fait une étude approfondie sur le choix d'un élément dont la conduite est irréprochable, et que dans tous les cas un des Trésoriers existants continue à la Trésorerie, ceci afin d'éviter tout risque possible.

### E. CONSEILLERS ET NOTABLES CONGOLAIS

Malgré la diminution progressive dans l'affiliation de nouveaux membres, nos conseillers et notables ne se decouragèrent pas, mais au contraire ils doublèrent leurs efforts pour en recruter un bon nombre au fur et à mesure des possibilités.

Certains parmi eux, chargés de la mission de juge au Conseil Clanique, règlèrent aimablement bien des affaires entre pas mal de Lulua, affaires qui pouvaient coûter cher et aux uns et aux autres si jamais ils devaient s'assigner par devant le Tribunal.

### F. POLICE DE L'ASSOCIATION

Notre Cercle dispose de . . . Commissaires, qui ont à leur tête le Commissaire en Chef, Mr. Jean TSHIBWABWA. Ce dernier s'occupa aussi de l'établissement des invitations qu'il passe à chaque occasion aux Commissaires pour être distribuées aux membres.

Ces Commissaires, chargés du maintien de l'ordre au sein de l'Association, montrèrent leur bonne volonté dans l'accomplissement de leur devoir, sans toutefois tenir compte de quelques uns qui ne marquèrent jamais leur présence aux réunions. Ils portèrent toutes commissions à n'importe quelle destination d'Elisabethville. Certains d'entre eux assistèrent régulièrement au Conseil Clanique du soir. Enfin, il n'est pas mal d'augmenter le nombre des commissaires afin d'alléger leur tâche.

### G. Conseillers Européens

L'adhésion de ces personnages en qualité de Conseillers Sociaux auprès de notre Association, et ce depuis mars 1955, nous a rendu et nous rendra encore toujours de nobles et précieux services.

Leur collaboration et leur dévouement, leurs idées et leur esprit constructif vivifie notre groupement et fixe sa position au sein de la Communauté. Qu'ils daignent trouver ici l'expression de notre sincère gratitude.

### H. Nombre et Lieux des Réunions

Nos réunions furent toujours tenues dans la Maison des Associations et pour chacune d'elles, un procès fut chaque fois établi par le Secrétaire ou un de ses Adjoints et transcrit ensuite dans le Registre des Procès Verbaux.

Il resulte que sur 64 membres du Comité, un peu plus que la moitié, soit 38 membres environ, assistèrent régulierement aux réunions; tandis que sur le nombre brut de . . . membres, 400 seulement marquerent leur présence aux assemblées.

### I. Candidats Membres du Comité pour l'Année 1957

Etant donné que son mandat penchait vers son expiration, le Comité a jugé utile de proposer un nombre de candidats parmi les quels on pourra élire les membres pour le nouveau Comité. Cette proposition fut décidée sur place au cours de la réunion du Comité du 24 novembre 1956, et, après l'étude assez approfondie l'on établit ensuite une liste des candidats proposés.

Dès lors, ces candidats furent invités à collaborer avec le Comité existant afin de se familiariser avec les différentes fonctions qu'ils seraient appelés à remplir.

### Chapitre III: Comité Sortant

Les membres du Comité sortant montrèrent leur effort en travaillant main dans la main, pour l'avancement de notre Association. Voici quelques unes des réalisations qu'ils ont faites au cours de l'année qui vient de s'écouler:

### A. Activités

#### 1. Conseil Clanique

Ils organisèrent mieux que jamais le Conseil Clanique dont le mouvement est devenu plus pompeux.

#### 2. Construction Cercle Lufres

Ils prirent l'initiative et le courage d'entreprendre un travail gigantesque qu'est la construction du Bâtiment "Cercle Lulua-Frères," qui sera sous peu achevé. Il convient à cette occasion, de remercier très chaleureusement les entrepreneurs Lulua, tous les Maçons et tous les membres en général qui se sont dévoués pour construire gracieusement le Home Lulua.

### 3. Création du Comité Restreint

Suivant l'avis de nos Conseillers Européens nous avons trouvé bon de former un Comité Directeur où l'on aurait le loisir d'étudier des idées à soumettre au Comité Général qui les étudiera à son tour, et les soumettra ensuite à l'approbation de l'Assemblée Générale.

Ce Comité est composé uniquement des Présidents, Secrétaires, Comptables et Trésoriers qui sont normalement des gens instruits et capables de trouver des idées intéressantes ou de faire une réflexion intelligente sur l'un ou l'autre problème qui se pose.

### B. De la Propagande

### 1. Offre des Prix aux Élèves

En nous basant sur l'un des buts poursuivis par notre Association et pour faire connaitre son existence et sa politique, nous avons offert une somme de mille francs aux dirigeants de l'Ecole Officielle, avec instructions de les distribuer comme prix aux élèves Lulua qui auraient obtenu de meilleurs résultats aux examens, ceci pour les encourager à bien étudier.

Il serait très intéressant d'envisager la possibilité de mettre à la disposition des établissements scolaires frequentés par nos enfants des cadeaux semblables, qui seraient distribués à ces enfants moyennant leurs mérites aux examens.

### 2. Impression Calendrier Lufres

Selon l'idée de notre cher Président, nous avons fait imprimer pour la première fois un calendrier Lufres pour l'année 1957. Par la beauté de ses images et par sa légende, qui reflète nos activités et nos occupations au sein de l'Association, ce calendrier aura réussi, j'espère, à gagner l'entière satisfaction non seulement des membres mais aussi de tous ceux qui songent à notre cause.

### C. Distractions des Membres

### 1. Lulua-Sport

Il est à remarquer que cette équipe, qui nous a toujours fait dépenser énormément d'argent dès sa création, ne nous avance à rien; surtout au cours de la dernière saison sportive où elle n'a fait que perdre plusieurs matches, et en plus, tous ses matches ont été supprimés pour la saison 1957 sous prétexte que les joueurs se sont méconduits sur le terrain.

Si tout ceci s'est produit, c'est surtout par manque de Représentants Européens qui pouvaient défendre loyalement les intérêts du club, car nos joueurs prétendent avoir assez souvent constaté de l'injustice de la part de l'arbitre et des joueurs de l'équipe adverse, qui trichaient continuellement et n'écoutaient aucune plainte de leur part. Fâchés des mauvais agissements manifestés de part et d'autre, nous avons été obligés de suspendre nos équipes jusqu'à nouvel ordre.

### 2. Lulua-Danse

Ce groupe fonctionne toujours très bien et réussit avec satisfaction au concours de danses folkloriques organisé à l'occasion des fêtes du cinquantenaire de l'Union Minière du Haut Katanga, B.C.K. et Forminière. A la demande des autorités du Centre Extra-Coutumier il exécuta ses danses au camp de police au quartier Albert. Presque tous les mois notre club folklorique est invité à présenter ses danses dans chacun des quartiers du Centre Extra-Coutumier, et ceci pour l'agrément de la population.

### 3. Lulua-Toilette

N'étant pas encore satisfait de ces inventions, le Comité sortant créa encore une section de beauté, connue sous le nom de "Lulua-Toilette," et sous la direction de Mr. Alphonse BATA.

Le but de la création de ce mouvement est d'apprendre, d'une facon pratique, à tous les Bena Lulua d'être propres, apprendre comment s'habiller convenablement et selon la mode, etc., et en consequence les exalter à acquérir l'habitude d'économiser de l'argent, non seulement pour se procurer des vêtements, mais aussi et surtout pour subvenir aux besoins de leur famille et pour les sauver dans leurs vieux jours.

Les jeunes gens s'intéressent plus à ce mouvement, et nous croyous encore pouvoir l'intensifier au moment où l'Association aura son propre local.

### Chapitre IV: Conclusion

Si ce Cercle donné l'espoir à un avenir heureux, c'est grâce à la ténacité et l'assiduité de son Comité et surtout à la bonne volonté des membres qui se soucient sans cesse de verser leur quote-part mensuelle, la quelle permet favorablement l'administration de cette Association.

Tout en les félicitant du grand effort déployé je leur souhaite à tous un bon courage et une bonne continuation.

Il est à noter que la présence d'Européens au sein de notre Groupement est chose très nécessaire, sinon indispensable, si nous voulons former l'élite Lulua et donner à sa masse des armes utiles qui les serviront dans la vie.

D'autre part, il serait très souhaitable que nos Civilisateurs tâchent de prendre l'habitude de nous fréquenter. C'est par contacts d'homme à homme, contacts aussi réguliers que familiers, que nous parvièndrons à acquérir leurs belles manières et leurs conceptions d'idées, ce qui nous aidera efficacement à assimiler petit à petit leur civilisation.

Enfin, quant au nouveau comité, une sélection sérieuse s'impose: il conviendrait d'éliminer les éléments paresseux, nuisibles et dangereux, de peur qu'ils ne contaminent des arbres sains et vigoureux qui ont l'envie de produire des fruits délicieux.

Aussi ne faudra-t-il pas tellement augmenter le nombre, mais veiller à tout prix à la qualité.

Chers successeurs, vous êtes appelés à accomplir une tâche lourde, ingrate et sans salaire—vous êtes les pionniers du progrès du peuple Lulua! Sentez-le et prenez donc votre courage à deux mains. Nous ne vous délaisserons pas, mais collaboreront toujours avec vous pour assurer la bonne marche de notre Oeuvre.

Fait à Elisabethville, le 20 Janvier 1957,
Le Secrétaire, François-Albert MUKENDI

# APPENDIX III

## Letter of the Vice-Governor General André Schoeller to the Provincial Governors, August 4, 1959.

The following document is illustrative of the rigorous surveillance exercised by the colonial administration over all forms of public expression deemed incompatible with the aims of Belgian policy. The character of the sanctions stipulated in this letter, and the fact that they remained enforceable during the ultimate stages of the Congo's political evolution, will give the reader an idea of the disabilities suffered by Congolese nationalists during the colonial period. It also casts a revealing light on the general expectations of Belgian authorities. Even at this late date, and in spite of his initial disclaimer, Vice-Governor Schoeller suggests in this letter that the political evolution of the Congo would indeed occur in the fashion of a "controlled experiment," regulated at every stage by the colonial administration.

PERSONNEL ET SECRET                    Léopoldville, le 4 Août 1959
                                       no. 1050/CAB

Monsieur le Gouverneur,

J'aurai l'honneur de vous entretenir dans la présente lettre, de la ligne de conduite à adopter à l'égard des mouvements politiques au cours de la période qui mènera le Congo aux élections de décembre prochain.

Cet exposé confirmera les directives qui vous furent données lors de la dernière réunion des Gouverneurs et précisera certaines initiatives à prendre.

Le Congo, dont l'évolution passée fut surtout économique et sociale, est entré depuis quelques années dans la phase de son évolution politique. Les populations des centres réclament cette évolution, celles des campagnes la souhaitent mais à un rythme plus lent. La déclaration gouvernementale du 13 janvier 1959 l'a solennellement promise, elle en a défini le but, précisé l'allure et organisé les premières étapes.

Vouloir que les choses s'accomplissent dans une sérénité de laboratoire relèverait de l'utopie. Les populations dont le pays se prépare à l'autodétermination sont immanquablement ébranlées par le travail qui s'accomplit en elles. Aussi est-il normal que jusqu'au terme de cette évolution le pays vive dans une atmosphère d'effervescence plus ou moins marquée selon les régions. Ceci ne doit pas alarmer.

Cependant, l'autorité chargée de conduire le processus risque à de nombreux moments, sous la pression de ces forces frémissantes, de se sentir débordée. Il est inéluctable en effet que des individus ou des mouvements extrémistes tentent d'exciter les foules en leur proposant des revendications outrancières. Or, la Belgique continue d'exercer la souveraineté sur ce pays. Elle en assume les devoirs. Un des plus importants est de veiller à ce que l'évolution s'accomplisse, non pas dans l'anarchie, mais dans l'ordre.

307

A cet égard, je traiterai successivement de l'attitude à adopter:
1) à l'égard de ceux qui feraient campagne pour des idées subversives
2) à l'égard de ceux qui troubleraient l'ordre dans les lieux publics.

## I. Action Politique Fondée sur des Thèmes Subversifs

Chacun peut évidemment, dans l'intimité de sa conscience et même dans ses conversations privées, nourrir ou formuler les idées politiques de son choix. Mais il n'est pas permis d'admettre qu'une personne, ou un groupe de personnes cherchent à rallier les foules, par une action militante publique, à des idées politiques susceptibles de mettre en péril la politique fondamentale que la Belgique a arrêtée pour conduire le Congo au point où il aura une démocratie capable d'exercer les prérogatives de la souveraineté et de décider de son indépendance. De telles actions politiques seraient en effet contraires au bien supérieur des populations du Congo, dont la Belgique assume, sans partage, l'entière responsabilité.

Dès lors, la double question qui se pose est de savoir:

1) quels thèmes doivent être considèrés comme subversifs
2) quelles mesures doivent être prises à l'égard de ceux qui fonderaient leur action politique sur ces thèmes.

*1. Thèmes subversifs au regard de la politique fondamentale arrêtée par la Belgique.*

Je vous communique en annexe le texte intégral de la note dont il vous fut donné connaissance lors de la réunion des Gouverneurs, tenue à l'occasion du dernier Conseil de Gouvernement.

Cette note devra être lue et commentée au cours des réunions de contacts avec les partis politiques dont il sera question plus loin. Un échange de vues suivra, car il est bon que les partis se sentent associés à la mise au point de cet important problème, et peut-être certaines suggestions ou positions intéressantes sortiront-elles de ces conversations. Vous me rendrez immédiatement compte des réactions enrégistrées. Je prendrai mes décisions quant au contenu définitif de la note, qui sera aussitôt diffusée le plus largement possible (radio, presse, causeries). Cette phase doit être très rapide; la diffusion sur grande échelle devra commencer fin août.

*2. Mesures à prendre à l'égard de ceux qui fonderaient leur action politique sur des thèmes subversifs*

Il faut pour agir, j'y insiste, que vous vous trouviez en présence d'une action militante publique comportant le développement régulier d'un ou de plusieurs thèmes subversifs.

Dans ce cas, il y a lieu de procéder comme suit:
a) Un fonctionnaire sera officiellement chargé des relations avec les mouvements politiques. Ce fonctionnaire:
   —recevra les responsables de l'action politique subversive,
   —leur expliquera en quoi elle est répréhensible,
   —les invitera, courtoisement mais fermement, à modifier leur attitude;
b) Vous confirmerez immédiatement par écrit (le ton de votre lettre sera, lui aussi, ferme et courtois);
c) Si les responsables persistent vous prendrez les mesures suivantes:
   —s'il s'agit d'un autochtone, vous provoquerez l'expulsion immédiate;
   —s'il s'agit d'un autochtone, vous prononcerez la mise en résidence sur-

veillée. Celle-ci sera limitée dans le temps, et, sauf dans les cas particulièrement graves, suffisament courte pour que vous ne puissiez être suspectés d'avoir voulu écarter ces éléments turbulents jusqu'après les élections; la résidence ne pourra être fixée dans un camp de rélègués; si plusieurs personnes font en même temps l'objet de cette mesure, une résidence distincte devra être designée à chacune d'elles; il faudra veiller à ce que, pendant la durée de cet éloignement, les intéréssés disposent de moyens suffisants d'existence et soient traités avec une correction parfaite par les autorités locales;
—s'il s'agit d'associations, outre les mesures prises contre les responsables, comme dit ci-dessus, vous apprécierez s'il y a lieu de suspendre ou de dissoudre l'association.

Les mesures énumérées au c) doivent intervenir rapidement, mais l'opinion doit y être préparée: dès qu'un groupement ou un individu développe publiquement un thème subversif, la radio provinciale doit y faire allusion, sans prendre cependant les responsables à partie et sans donner une publicité excessive à leur comportement: elle signalera que depuis quelques temps on assiste à la diffusion de telle idée, que cette idée va, pour telle raison, à l'encontre de la politique fondamentale de la Belgique au Congo, que la réalisation de cette idée aurait telle et telle conséquence néfaste. Cela suffira pour que le public comprenne.

N.B. Il va de soi que dans les cas suffisament graves, vous pouvez dès à présent agir comme il vient d'être exposé, sans attendre que les groupements politiques et le public aient été complètement informés des thèmes que le gouvernement considère comme subversif. Mais dès que cette information aura été assurée, votre action devra s'exercer systématiquement.

## II. Maintien de l'Ordre dans les Lieux Publics

Celui qui trouble l'ordre dans les lieux publics est, bien entendu, passible de mesures normalement prévues pour le maintien de l'ordre: il peut être obligé de circuler, emmené au poste de police s'il persiste, poursuivi pour le délit de droit commun qu'il aurait commis, relègué si sa présence compromet gravement l'ordre et la tranquillité publiques.

Je profite de cet exposé pour appeler votre attention sur un aspect important du problème du maintien de l'ordre. Les nouveaux décrets sur les libertés publiques supprimeront, vous le savez, toute autorisation préalable, sauf pour les réunions en plein air. L'abandon des mesures préventives doit entrainer comme corollaire une activité accrue des forces de l'ordre. Comme dans tous les pays qui connaissent ces libertés les forces de l'ordre ne doivent pas hésiter à se montrer dans la rue et se tenir ostensiblement à proximité des lieux où se tiennent des réunions publiques: la protection des personnes et des biens est une des conditions fondamentales de la démocratie.

Les dispositions qui précèdent ont pour but de conserver à l'autorité la maitrise de la situation au cours des mois difficiles que le Congo a devant lui.

Leur application n'aurait cependant que peu d'effets, si, en même temps, l'autorité ne menait une action en profondeur pour inciter les groupements politiques à agir—quelle que soit la vivacité de leur action—dans le sens réel du bien commun. Souvent encore ils sont dépourvus de doctrine et mettent leur dynamisme au service de slogans purement démagogiques; il arrive aussi qu'ils se fassent une fausse idée des initiatives du Gouvernement, et qu'ils formulent, avec outrance, des griefs sans aucun fondement; certaines notions ou certains concepts sont par ailleurs utilisés par eux dans un sens inexact, ce qui ajoute à la confusion des esprits; enfin, ils ont en général l'impression que les autorités refusent de reconnaitre leur importance et affecte en conséquence de les ignorer.

Pour l'ensemble de ces raisons, j'estime urgent d'organiser avec ces groupements des contacts suivis et réguliers.

Ces contacts seront à la fois collectifs et individuels.

### 1) *Contacts collectifs*

J'annoncerai incessament, dans une conférence de presse, l'inauguration à chaque chef lieu de province d'une série de réunions au cours des quelles le représentant de l'Administration entretiendra les groupements politiques de diverses questions relatives à l'évolution politique du pays.

Ces réunions doivent être conçues dans l'esprit suivant:

a) il ne s'agit pas de négotiations mais d'échanges de vues afin que les partis et l'Administration en arrivent à mieux comprendre leurs positions respectives;

b) il arrive souvent qu'un parti adopte des positions différentes de celles du Gouvernement ou de celles des Conseils Consultatifs actuels; pour autant que ces positions n'aillent pas à l'encontre de la politique fondamentale de la Belgique elles peuvent évidement figurer au programme de ce parti; c'est même pour lui la seule manière démocratique d'essayer de faire triompher ses idées que de les inscrire à son programme et d'essayer de recueillir sur ce programme de nombreux suffrages lors des élections; l'Administration ne peut évidemment donner satisfaction aux positions— souvent contradictoires d'ailleurs—de tous les partis; c'est aux assemblées élues qu'il appartiendra de dégager les positions dominantes;

c) très fréquemment, la seule divergence de vues entre les partis et le Gouvernement porte sur une question de rythme et non d'objectifs à atteindre; il est bon de le mettre en lumière. Il sera bon et prudent que les premières réunions soient consacrées à l'exposé des nouvelles institutions dans l'état actuel des projets.

Les sujets abordés pourront être tous ceux qui intéressent les groupements politiques. Les échanges de vues seront absolument libres, pourvu qu'ils se fassent en termes courtois et qu'à aucun moment ils ne prennent l'allure de négotiations.

Ces contacts étant particulièrement délicats à mener à Léopoldville, j'en ai chargé Monsieur le Secrétaire de Gouvernement, STENMANS, qui tiendra ces réunions sous l'égide de la province. Il n'aura pas le loisir de rédiger des exposés complets, mais il écrira le canevas de ses exposés, il vous en fera régulierement tenir copie, afin que vous puissiez vous rendre compte des sujets abordés et de la manière de les présenter. Je vous demande d'agir de même à son égard, afin qu'il puisse suivre l'évolution des contacts noués et m'en faire régulièrement rapport.

Monsieur STENMANS commencera ses réunions dans la première quinzaine du mois d'août; il devra en être de même dans chaque province.

### 2) *Contacts individuels*

Parallèlement, le fonctionnaire que vous chargerez de ces contacts collectifs devra veiller à maintenir des contacts individuels avec les dirigeants de chaque groupement. A titre d'exemple, lorsqu'un groupement lance un manifeste, ce fonctionnaire en parlera aux dirigeants du groupement, il leur demandera de lui expliquer leur pensée sur des points obscurs, il leur signalera l'un ou l'autre point particulièrement faible ou dangereux, il discutera avec eux certains autres points, etc. . . .

Ces contacts prouveront aux groupements politiques que l'Administration suit avec attention l'évolution de leurs activités et de leur pensée; ils rendront plus facilement [*sic*] les mises au point ou les mises en garde qui devront inévitablement être faites à certains moments. Bref, ils établiront le dialogue, corollaire indispensable d'une politique nette et vigoureuse.

Ici aussi, vous voudrez bien me tenir régulierement au courant des réactions enrégistrées.

Le problème particulier que soulèvent les revendications séparatistes de certains milieux du Bas Congo nécessitent des directives complémentaires. Celles-ci feront l'objet d'une lettre distincte, adressée au Gouverneur de la province de Léopoldville et communiquée pour leur complète information aux Gouverneurs des autres provinces.

POUR LE GOUVERNEUR GENERAL,
Le Vice-Gouverneur Général,
André Schoeller

# NOTES

INTRODUCTION

¹ Ali Al'Amin Mazrui, "Edmund Burke and Reflections on the Revolution in the Congo," *Comparative Studies in Society and History,* V (Jan., 1963), 122.

² James S. Coleman, *Nigeria: Background to Nationalism* (Berkeley and Los Angeles: University of California Press, 1958), p. 424.

³ Thomas Hodgkin, *African Political Parties* (London: Penguin Books, 1961), p. 16.

⁴ See my "Selective Bibliographical Survey for the Study of Politics in the Former Belgian Congo," *American Political Science Review,* LIV (Sept., 1960), 715–728.

I: THE PRECOLONIAL ENVIRONMENT

¹ A case in point is G. van der Kerken, "Populations africaines du Congo Belge et du Ruanda-Urundi," in *Encyclopédie du Congo Belge* (Bruxelles: Bieleveld ed., 1953), I, 81–135. Although van der Kerken provides an excellent description of the political systems prevailing among the traditional societies of the Congo, his classification of primitive political structures as "empires," "kingdoms," "sultanates," and "seigneuries" on the one hand, and as "patriarchal" societies on the other, is misleading in some respects, as few of the authority systems encountered in the Congo can be accurately described in such terms.

² See J. Vansina, "Notes sur l'origine du Royaume de Kongo," *Journal of African History,* IV, no. 1 (1963), 33–38.

³ Alan P. Merriam, "The Concept of Culture Clusters Applied to the Belgian Congo," *Southwestern Journal of Anthropology,* XV (Winter, 1959), 375.

⁴ See F. Pigafetta, *A Report of the Kingdom of Kongo and the Surrounding Countries Drawn out of the Writings of Duarte Lopez* (London, 1881); cf. T. Simar, "Le Congo au XVIème siècle d'après la relation de Lopez-Pigafetta," *La Revue Congolaise* (1913–1914), pp. 226–247. For a critical survey of the early sources of documentation on the history of the Kongo Kingdom, see E. de Jonghe and T. Simar, "Archives Congolaises," *ibid.* (1912–1913), pp. 419–439; (1913–1914), pp. 1–29, 85–99, 154–174, 207–225, 271–287. The classical works on the early history of the Kongo Kingdom are J. Cuvelier and L. Jadin, *L'Ancien Congo d'après les Archives Romaines (1518–1640),* ARSOM, Vol. XXXVI (Bruxelles, 1954), and J. Cuvelier, *L'Ancien Royaume du Congo* (Bruges, 1946).

⁵ E. Torday, "The Influence of the Kingdom of Kongo on Central Africa," *Africa,* I (April, 1928), 162.

⁶ H. M. Stanley, "The Congo: Its Past History, Present Development and Future Commercial Prospects," *Chamber of Commerce Journal* (London), Special Supplement, Sept. 19, 1884.

⁷ H. Bailleul, "Les Bayaka: Aperçu de l'evolution politique et économique de leur pays jusqu'en 1958," *Zaïre*, XIII, no. 8 (1959), 823–841.

⁸ E. Torday, "Notes on the Ethnography of the Bambala," *Journal of the Royal Anthropological Institute*, XXXV (1905), 408.

⁹ *Ibid.*

¹⁰ J. Vansina, "L'Etat Kuba dans le cadre des institutions politiques africaines," *Zaïre*, XI (1957), 485–489; E. Torday and T. A. Joyce, *Notes ethnographiques sur les peuples communément appelés Bakuba, ainsi que sur les peuplades apparentées—les Bushongo,* Annales du Musée du Congo Belge, Vol. II, Part I (Bruxelles, 1911).

¹¹ Mabika Kalanda, *Baluba et Lulua: Une Ethnie à la recherche d'un nouvel équilibre* (Bruxelles: Editions de Remarques Congolaises, 1959). Cf. E. Verhulpen, *Baluba et Balubaisés du Katanga* (Anvers: Editions de l'Avenir Belge, 1936). On the origins of Nkongolo's "empire," see Hadelin Roland, "Résumé de l'histoire ancienne du Katanga," *Problèmes Sociaux Congolais,* no. 61 (June, 1963), 3–41.

¹² J. Vansina, "A Comparison of African Kingdoms," *Africa*, XXXII (Oct., 1962), 333.

¹³ Kalanda, *op. cit.,* p. 89.

¹⁴ Merriam, *op. cit.,* p. 381.

¹⁵ M. van den Byvang, "Notice historique sur les Balunda," *Congo,* I, no. 4 (1937), 426–438; II, no. 2 (1937), 193–208.

¹⁶ Personal communication from Professor J. Vansina.

¹⁷ E. Torday, cited in Harry Johnston, *George Grenfell and the Congo* (London: Hutchinson, 1908), I, 421.

¹⁸ *Ibid.*

¹⁹ "Histoire de la sous-chefferie Kashobwe racontée par Kinki, Malyoko, Mutara et Mumbi, Bayeke témoins occulaires des faits à Monsieur l'Administrateur Territorial Principal Charpentier en présence de Kaindu Mwene Milambo, chef de la sous-chefferie Kaindu et d'autres Balunda de cette dernière sous-chefferie qui confirmèrent ce récit fait à l'occasion de l'investiture de Kashobwe Mulondera en ce 13 Février 1928" (unpublished document).

²⁰ Daniel Biebuyck and Mary Douglas, *Congo Tribes and Parties* (London: Royal Anthropological Institute, 1961), p. 21.

²¹ Le Commandant Delhaize, *Les Warega,* Albert de Wit et l'Institut International de Bibliographie, Collection de Monographies Ethnographiques (Bruxelles, 1909).

²² Merriam, *op. cit.,* p. 390.

²³ A. N. Tucker, *The Eastern Sudanic Languages* (London: Oxford University Press, 1940), I, 29. On the early history of the Azande, See E. E. Evans-Pritchard, "A Historical Introduction to the Study of the Zande Society," *African Studies,* XVII, no. 1 (1958), 1–15, and "The Origin of the Ruling Clan of the Azande," *Southwestern Journal of Anthropology,* XIII (Winter, 1957), 322–343. See also P. T. W. Baxter and Audrey Butt, *The Azande and Related Peoples of the Anglo-Egyptian Sudan and Belgian Congo* (London: International African Institute, 1953).

²⁴ G. van der Kerken, *L'Ethnie Mongo* (Bruxelles: Institut Royal Colonial Belge, 1944).

[25] Merriam, *op. cit.*, p. 376.

[26] H. Burssens, *Les Peuplades de l'Entre Congo-Ubangui,* Annales du Musée Royal du Congo Belge, Sciences de l'Homme, Monographies Ethnographiques, Vol. IV (Tervueren, 1958).

[27] *Ibid.*, p. 120.

[28] Melville J. Herskovits, *The Human Factor in Changing Africa* (New York: Knopf, 1962), pp. 83–94.

[29] Vansina, "A Comparison of African Kingdoms."

[30] Rupert Emerson, "Nationalism and Political Development," *Journal of Politics,* XXII (1960), 2–28.

[31] Bonaventure Makonga, "La Charité mal ordonnée: A bas le Tribalisme," *L'Etoile-Nyota,* Dec. 25, 1958.

[32] "The Counter Manifesto of the Abako," in Alan P. Merriam, *Congo: Background to Conflict* (Chicago: Northwestern University Press, 1961), p. 333.

[33] "The kingdom of Kongo is known since 1482. It included as its provinces Mpemba, Mbaya, Sonyo-Mbata, Nsundi, and Zombo on the left bank [of the Congo], and Vungu, Mazinga, Nsanga, and Loango on the right bank" (*Notre Kongo,* May 15, 1960).

[34] *Statuts de la République du Kongo Central,* Preamble (Leopoldville, 1960), p. 1.

[35] See "Discours prononcé le 16 novembre 1958 par Raymond Bikebu, Président de la Section Abako 'Barumbu' lors de son intronisation," in *Salut du peuple par l'Abako* (Leopoldville, n.d.).

[36] *La Voix du Peuple,* June 22, 1960.

[37] See "Kalamba Mangole Sylvain Grand Chef des Lulua en tournée d'inspection à Demba," *La Croix du Congo,* Sept. 18, 1955.

[38] Cited in *Le Monde,* March 25, 1961.

[39] "Conférence donnée le 13 Avril 1958 aux membres de la Fédération des Batetela par Monsieur Lumumba, Conseiller Permanent" (mimeographed; Leopoldville, n.d.).

[40] "King Kasa, as he deserves to be called, is really a king, applauded by all peace-loving men, for when he demanded independence for the Kongo he insisted on preserving the dignity and rights of the Kongolese people" (*Notre Kongo,* June 26, 1960).

[41] For an example of the litanies addressed to Kasa-Vubu, see *ibid.,* Feb. 14, 1960.

[42] *Kongo Dieto,* Nov. 14, 1959.

[43] *Ibid.,* Dec. 31, 1959.

[44] *Mbandaka,* Nov. 14, 1959.

[45] *Notre Kongo,* May 1, 1960.

[46] *Ibid.*

[47] "Le numéro attribué aux listes Abako laissait augurer un résultat heureux. Oui, en ce jour de la Restoration le chiffre trois était le mieux designé pour jouer un rôle vraiment digne de nous. Trois: Chiffre vraiment révélateur, car 'makakus matatu malambe Kongo,' trois termitières qui ont servi de support au pot dans le quel on a façonné le Kongo" (*ibid.,* May 29, 1960).

[48] "En 1959 le sort avait voulu que le jour des élections tomba [*sic*] un Nsona-Nsona. Pour le peuple Kongolais c'est le jour du Sabbat, le jour du Seigneur, le jour des Ancêtres" (*ibid.*).

[49] Province du Kasai, Administration de la Sûreté, Bulletin d'Information No. 05/46/42/B.1/21/XXX–47–3, p. 3.

⁵⁰ "Rémy Mwamba, membre du Collège Exécutif Général s'adresse au peuple Muluba," *Le Courrier d'Afrique*, April 14, 1960.

⁵¹ J. P. Ilunga, "Katangais authentiques," *Le Progrès*, June 17, 1959.

⁵² Thomas Hodgkin, *African Political Parties* (London: Penguin Books, 1961), p. 18.

II: HISTORICAL BACKGROUND

¹ T. Lewis, "The Ancient Kingdom of Kongo: Its Present Position and Possibilities," *Geographical Journal*, XIX (May, 1902), 541–560.

² For an excellent summary of this early phase of Portuguese colonial history, see James Duffy, *Portuguese Africa* (Cambridge: Harvard University Press, 1959), pp. 5–78.

³ *Ibid.*, p. 14.

⁴ *Ibid.*

⁵ Cited in Basil Davidson, *Black Mother* (London: Victor Gollancz, 1961), p. 141.

⁶ James Duffy, *Portugal in Africa* (London: Penguin African Library, 1962), p. 45.

⁷ Ruth Slade, *King Leopold's Congo* (London: Oxford University Press, 1962), p. 5.

⁸ *Ibid.*, p. 6; cf. *Notre Kongo*, Feb. 14, 1962: "Cinq siècles suffisent pour vous dire que le peuple Mukongo est d'une vieille civilisation non-occidentale mais que l'occident ne pouvait en rien récuser dans toutes les formes d'elle-même [*sic*]. C'est ainsi qu'après quatre vingts ans de domination dans laquelle il se sentait le plus indigne, le peuple Mukongo demanda son retour à la liberté naturelle et foula le colonisateur au pied."

⁹ Duffy, *Portugal in Africa*, p. 45.

¹⁰ Slade, *op. cit.*, p. 84.

¹¹ Roland Oliver and J. D. Fage, *A Short History of Africa* (London: Penguin African Library, 1962), p. 174.

¹² R. P. P. Ceulemans, *La Question arabe et le Congo (1883–1892)*, Académie Royale des Sciences Morales et Politiques, Vol. XXII, Part 1 (Bruxelles, 1959), p. 37.

¹³ Henry M. Stanley, *In Darkest Africa: Or the Quest, Rescue, and Retreat of Emin, Governor of Equatoria* (New York, 1890), I, 63.

¹⁴ A political report from the Uele region, dated April 9, 1909, describes the local African chiefs: "Mopoie Bangezigino, grand ami de Saza et pourri d'Islamisme, porte continuellement au cou en guise de fétiche ce qu'il appelle la 'waraga n'allah.' ... Saza, déjà âgé, épaissi, bouffi, garde encore une certaine dignité dans le costume Arabe. Il est très imbu d'Islamisme et ne quitte jamais son chapelet qu'il égrène à tout instant, avant de boire, avant de manger, avant de parler" (*Archives du Ministère des Colonies*, Bruxelles, A. I. 1372).

¹⁵ Adolphe Burdo, *Les Arabes dans l'Afrique Centrale* (Paris, 1885), p. 11.

¹⁶ Viscount Mountmorres, *The Congo Independent State* (London, 1906), p. 35.

¹⁷ Sometimes, however, the raids conducted by the Arab slave traders undoubtedly helped to exacerbate ethnic antagonisms. According to Mary Douglas, "the current antagonism between Ba-Luba and Ba-Tetela, which they tend to attribute to Batetela resentment of earlier Ba-Luba rule, probably gets some of its edge from Batetela retaliation when they were in the service

of the Arabs at the end of the century" (Daniel Biebuyck and Mary Douglas, *Congo Tribes and Parties* [London: Royal Anthropological Institute, 1961], p. 22).

[18] Henry M. Stanley, "The Congo: Its Past History, Present Development and Future Commercial Prospects," *Chamber of Commerce Journal* (London), Special Supplement, Sept. 19, 1884, p. 4.

[19] Henry M. Stanley, *The Congo and the Foundation of Its Free State* (London, 1885), I, 52.

[20] Stanley, "The Congo: Its Past History," p. 16.

[21] Slade, *op. cit.*, p. 41.

[22] See Articles 34 and 35 of the General Act of the Berlin Conference in Arthur Berriedale Keith, *The Belgian Congo and the Berlin Act* (Oxford, 1919), p. 315.

[23] A. J. Wauters, *Histoire politique du Congo Belge* (Bruxelles, 1911), p. 56.

[24] On October 18, 1884, an agreement was concluded between Tippo-Tip's son, Moniamani, and Lieutenant A. M. Wester, chief of the Stanley Falls Station, which stipulated that "never an Arab will come in the river below the seventh cataract of Stanley Falls or in any other territory belonging to the Comité d'Etudes du Haut Congo for fighting, making trade, or catching slaves, goats, or chickens; that the limits between the Arabs' dominion and that of the Comité d'Etudes will be the seventh cataract of Stanley Falls in the Congo River and therefrom a straight line to south and north, so that all natives in the mainland who are under the protection of the Comité d'Etudes may not be troubled in any way by the Arabs, and that the Arabs and the white man never will quarrel or fight with each other but will always get on as very good friends" (*Archives du Ministère des Colonies*, Bruxelles, A. I. 1377).

[25] Slade, *op. cit.*, p. 109.

[26] Sidney L. Hinde, *The Fall of the Congo Arabs* (London, 1897), p. 24.

[27] On the Luluabourg revolt, see H. Lassaux, "Les Evènements de Lulua-bourg en 1895. La Révolte des Batetela," *Congo*, I (1926), 567–583, and A. van Zandycke, "La Révolte de Luluabourg de 4 juillet 1895," *Zaïre*, IV (Nov., 1950), 931–965.

[28] Wauters, *op. cit.*, pp. 91–92.

[29] Sir Harry Johnston, *George Grenfell and the Congo* (2 vols.; London: Hutchinson, 1908), I, 367.

[30] In his report of 1907, the Inspecteur d'Etat Mahieu described the conditions imposed on the Africans of the Upper Lukenie: "Tshuembo, de Lodja, chef Ontete, travailleur de Kandololo allait faire du caoutchouc chez les Efunda, dans un groupe de 50 à 70 travailleurs. Ils mettaient environ six jours pour se rendre au campement. Le premier jour ils construisaient des huttes pour eux, et les trois capitas qui les accompagnaient avec leurs femmes. Le deuxième jour ils se mettaient au travail, les capitas restant au village, s'en allant comme ils l'entendaient. On leur disait de rapporter journellement dix boules de caoutchouc de 30 grammes, les menacant du fouet s'ils ne les rapportaient pas. Ils passaient environ deux mois dans la forêt. Après chaque voyage les travailleurs rentrent au village, où pendant deux mois ils font du portage et des plantations; leurs femmes sont employées au service de Kandololo. Le chef partage le paiement reçu à Lodja avec ses nyamparas, ses capitas, ses boys domestiques et ses femmes; il en revient peu de chose aux travailleurs" (*Archives du Ministère des Colonies*, Bruxelles, A. I. 1374).

[31] In his report of 1906 for the Lake Leopold II and Lualaba districts, Mahieu wrote: "Ce qui amène surtout des explosions de mécontentement de la part des indigènes, ce sont les exigences on pourrait dire inassouvissables des chefs de poste en matière d'imposition. Quant un village fournit regulièrement le nombre de paniers de caoutchouc demandé, on en augmente le nombre, s'il satisfait aux nouvelles exigences on augmente encore, et ainsi de suite jusqu'à ce que la corde casse. Un beau jour les indigènes ne viennent plus au poste, et il en résulte des operations de police qui entrainent des morts d'hommes et sont coûteuses par les frais qu'elles occasionnent ainsi par une cessation de paiement d'impôt qui dure parfois pendant plusieurs mois et anéantit le bénéfice qu'on avait cru pouvoir réaliser" (*ibid.*, A. I. 1375).

[32] Johnston, *op. cit.*, I, 380.

[33] A. Stenmans, *La Reprise du Congo par la Belgique* (Bruxelles, 1949), p. 419.

[34] Johnston, *op. cit.*, I, 475.

[35] Keith, *op. cit.*, p. 100.

[36] Alexandre Delcommune, *L'Avenir du Congo Belge menacé* (Bruxelles, 1919), p. 618.

[37] Pierre Ryckmans, *Dominer pour servir* (Bruxelles, 1948), p. 6.

[38] "Le paternaliste est celui qui veut tendre par delà, et une fois admis, le racisme et l'inegalité. C'est si l'on veut un racisme charitable—qui n'est pas le moins habile ni le moins rentable. Car le paternaliste généreux se cabre dès que le colonisé réclame, ses droits syndicaux par exemple. S'il relève sa paye, si sa femme soigne le colonisé, il s'agit de dons et jamais de devoirs. S'il se reconnaissait des devoirs il lui faudrait admettre que le colonisé a des droits. Or il est entendu par tout ce qui précède, qu'il n'a pas de devoirs, que le colonisé n'a pas de droits" (Albert Memmi, *Portrait du colonisé, précédé du portrait du colonisateur* [Buchet Chastel: Correa, 1957], p. 102).

[39] *Bulletin Officiel*, Etat Indépendant du Congo, 1906, p. 245.

[40] In a letter to the Governor-General, dated November 14, 1912, the minister of colonies, Jules Renkin, observed: "Il semble que les autorités territoriales du Kasai ont une tendance fâcheuse à trouver dans l'emploi de la force armée la solution à toute situation troublée ou simplement anormale. En ce qui concerne les opérations de Kole il me semble que les documents que me transmettait le Vice-Gouvernement Général ne dénotaient pas une situation si grave qu'elle rentrât dans les prévisions du décret de 1906, et nécessitait une opération militaire." Such remarks were not always welcomed by local authorities, as shown by the following excerpt from a letter written by an administrator to a member of the Catholic clergy on October 21, 1912: "Nous vivons dans une époque d'humanitarisme exagéré, sous la funeste devise 'Liberté, Egalité, Fraternité,' paradigme de la contradiction. Certains rêveurs et meneurs Socialistes tâchent d'appliquer toutes nos idées avancées aux noirs qu'ils croient ou paraissent croire avides et aptes à s'assimiler à notre civilisation" (*Archives du Ministère des Colonies*, Bruxelles, A. I. 1368).

[41] "Réalisme, continuité. La Politique coloniale belge tend à éveiller chez l'Africain le sens démocratique," *Pages Congolaises*, edition B, no. 38 (Bruxelles, 1954), p. 1.

[42] A. F. G. Marzorati, "The Political Organization and the Evolution of African Society in the Belgian Congo," *African Affairs*, LIII (April, 1954), 109.

[43] *Ibid.*

[44] In a letter of December 18, 1907, to the Governor General, Commissaire Général A. de Meulemeester wrote: "J'estime que dans les postes que

j'ai inspecté, il existe des 'messagers' qui sont absolument identiques aux gardes forestiers, les quels dans le décret du 3 juin 1906 sur les impositions directes ont reçus le nom de 'capitas' et sont formellement interdits. Ce sont presque tous des gens étrangers à la région dans la quelle ils exercent leurs fonctions ..." (*Archives du Ministère des Colonies*, Bruxelles, A. I. 1365).

⁴⁵ P. Piron and J. Devos, *Codes et lois du Congo Belge* (Bruxelles, 1924), p. 525.

⁴⁶ G. van der Kerken, "Notre politique indigène au Congo Belge," *Congo*, II (1929), 225.

⁴⁷ "Les agents du service territorial qui devraient avoir comme principale occupation l'administration des populations indigènes sont pour la plupart trop absorbés par des écritures, et il est assez compréhensible qu'ils en arrivent ainsi à négliger leur mission première et pour la quelle ils ne sont d'ailleurs en général nullement préparés" (*Archives du Ministère des Colonies*, Bruxelles, A. I. 1371).

⁴⁸ "Il est exact que dans le Katanga bien peu de choses ont été faites jusqu'à présent pour l'organisation des chefferies. Il faut cependant considérer que la responsabilité première remonte au Comité Spécial du Katanga qui a eu l'administration politique du territoire jusqu'au 1er septembre 1910" (*ibid.*).

⁴⁹ "Un autre point qu'il est indispensable de signaler, c'est que certaines chefferies dans le territoire de Kongolo—je n'ai rien appris de semblable dans les autres territoires—ont adopté le système du chef élu et soumis à réélection dès qu'une majorité estime qu'il a assez règné. Le mobile de cette politique qui est d'introduction récente est la cupidité du nègre. Est élu celui qui offre le plus de cadeaux. ... Ce système est un dissolvant inévitable des chefferies. Il faut réagir coute que coute et réinvestir les chefs" ("Rapport politique du IVème trimestre, 1913, du District Tanganyika Moero," *Archives du Ministère des Colonies*, Bruxelles, A. I. 1374).

⁵⁰ M. Moeller, "L'Adaptation des sociétés indigènes de la Province Orientale à la situation créée par la colonisation," *Bulletin de l'Institut Royal Colonial Belge*, II (1931), 55.

⁵¹ "Extrait d'une dépêche ministérielle au Gouverneur-Général exposant la politique actuelle et la politique future à suivre dans l'organisation en chefferies des populations indigènes," in *Recueil à l'usage des fonctionnaires et des agents du service territorial* (Bruxelles, 1920), p. 326.

⁵² Lucy P. Mair, *Native Policies in Africa* (London, 1936), p. 345.

⁵³ "Le pays habité par la race Baluba est actuellement divisé en un grand nombre de chefferies qui ont à leur tête un chef de sang sacré rendant hommage à Kasongo Nyembo. Mais depuis que le grand chef est deporté, la plupart on cessé de lui payer tribut et pris goût à l'indépendance; de plus, celles de ses chefferies qui ne sont pas dirigées par des chefs de sang sacré mais par des créatures des blancs, ne désirent pas s'incliner devant le chef héréditaire" (Paul Salkin in *Etudes Africaines* [Bruxelles, 1920], p. 219). On the policy of the administration toward the Tshokwe of the Katanga, see *Rapport sur l'administration du Congo Belge en 1922* (Bruxelles, 1923), p. 96.

⁵⁴ *Discours du Gouverneur Général* (Leopoldville, 1956), p. 20.

⁵⁵ *Ibid.*, p. 23.

⁵⁶ *Ibid.*, p. 21.

⁵⁷ Piron and Davos, *op. cit.*, p. 156.

⁵⁸ A. Sohier, "Le Problème des indigènes et la commission du statut des congolais civilisés," *Zaire*, III (1949), 68–89.

⁵⁹ *La Voix du Congolais*, no. 140 (Nov., 1957), 840.

[60] *Conseil Colonial, Bulletin des Séances* (1955), p. 383.

[61] *Discours du Gouverneur Général* (Leopoldville, 1952), p. 38.

[62] *Ibid.* (Leopoldville, 1954), p. 35.

[63] Cited in *Congo 1959* (Bruxelles: CRISP, 1960), p. 10.

[64] *Chambre des Représentants, Documents Parlementaires*, no. 108 (Jan. 20, 1959).

[65] This fact was brought to my attention in the course of a personal interview with Mr. Van Hemelrijck, who was minister of the Congo from November, 1958, to September, 1959.

[66] Devos and Piron, *op. cit.*, pp. 875 ff.

[67] *Conseil Colonial, Bulletin des Séances* (1959), Appendix VII, p. 1540.

[68] *Ibid.*, p. 1564.

[69] *Ibid., Appendix* III, p. 1517.

[70] *Congopresse*, Aug. 4, 1959.

[71] Letter 1050/CAB. Unpublished document transmitted to me by H. Weiss. See Appendix III.

[72] "Rapport à la Chambre de la Commission Parlementaire," *Chambre des Représentants, Documents Parlementaires*, no. 100 (1958–59).

[73] "Elements pour une sociologie d'une émeute," *Courrier Africain* (CRISP), Jan. 16, 1959, p. 3.

[74] *Abako 1950–1960* (Bruxelles: CRISP, 1962), p. 189.

[75] This fact was brought to my attention in the course of an interview with Assistant Commissaire de District R. Huberty.

[76] *Congo 1959*, p. 18.

[77] *Annales Parlementaires, Chambre des Représentants*, April 21, 1959, p. 13.

[78] *Congo 1959*, pp. 151–162.

[79] *Ibid.*, p. 166.

[80] *Le National* (Elisabethville), Dec. 12, 1959.

[81] *Annales Parlementaires, Chambre des Representants*, Nov. 5, 1959, p. 8.

[82] *Ibid.*, p. 13.

[83] *Congo 1959*, p. 205.

[84] *Ibid.*, p. 213.

[85] "La Conférence de la Table Ronde Belgo-Congolaise," *Courrier Africain* (CRISP), no. 6, p. 13.

III: THE ADMINISTRATIVE FRAMEWORK

[1] For an authoritative discussion of the Charte Coloniale see M. Halewyck de Heusch, *La Charte Coloniale: Commentaire de la loi du 18 octobre 1908* (3 vols.; Bruxelles: Weissenbruch, 1910–1914).

[2] As early as 1915 the leader of the Parti Ouvrier Belge, Emile Vandervelde, stated: "Je ne crois rien dire qui soit de nature à choquer mes collègues en affirmant que pour l'immense majorité d'entre eux le Congo n'est qu'une expression géographique, une tache sur la carte" (*Annales Parlementaires, Chambre des Représentants*, March 12, 1914, p. 1357). Again in 1931 a Belgian observer noted: "Quelle qu'en soit la cause, d'ailleurs,—le fait est patent,—le contrôle parlementaire est manifestement insuffisant et il en résulte un régime d'omnipotence administrative non-controlée dont on se plaint de toutes parts" (M. Speyer, "La Révision de la Charte Coloniale," IRCB, *Bulletin des Séances*, II [1931], 80).

[3] *Charte Coloniale*, Art. 12.

⁴ V. Devaux, "Le Problème du législateur au Congo Belge," IRCB, *Bulletin des Séances*, III (1948), 662–679; cf. Speyer, *op. cit.*

⁵ *Conseil Colonial, Compte-Rendu Analytique* (1954), p. 1015; cf. A. Dupriez, "Quelques considérations sur le rôle et l'activité du Conseil Colonial," IRCB, *Bulletin des Séances*, III (1932), 525–544.

⁶ "Rapport préparé par M. Dubois sur l'activité du Conseil Colonial au cours de ses 25 années d'existence," *Conseil Colonial, Compte-Rendu Analytique* (1933), pp. 1658 ff.

⁷ Lord Hailey, *An African Survey* (London: Oxford University Press, 1938), p. 210.

⁸ The text of the memorandum may be found in Maurice Lippens, *Notes sur le gouvernement du Congo, 1921–1922* (Bruxelles, 1923), pp. 115–151.

⁹ *Ibid.*, p. 122.

¹⁰ *Bulletin Officiel*, Aug. 15, 1922, p. 825.

¹¹ See Lippens, *op. cit.*, esp. pp. 183–196.

¹² The views contained in this paragraph are based on my interview with M. Pétillon in May, 1962.

¹³ For example, the Brussels newspaper *La Métropole* noted: "Le discours de M. Pétillon donne l'impression, vraie ou fausse, que l'eminent fonctionnaire a été jugulé dans l'expression de sa pensée, d'habitude plus originale et plus catégorique, par son chef immédiat M. Buisseret. On sait en effet que celui-ci n'a pas hesité, il y a peu de jours, et précisément en prévision de la réunion de ce conseil, à rappeler inopportunément au Gouverneur Général les limites de son mandat." The Luluabourg newspaper *Kasai* added: "Discours incomplet dans la mesure ou le Gouverneur Général, avec une rectitude à la quelle il faut rendre hommage, n'a pas évoqué le malaise qui fausse actuellement les relations entre Bruxelles et la colonie." *L'Echo du Katanga* characteristically stated: "Il est néfaste que le cabinet du Ministre se substitue aux services de l'administration, au Gouverneur Général chargé de cette tâche. ... La loi porte bien 'Le Gouverneur Général represente le Roi dans la Colonie. Il exerce le pouvoir exécutif sous réserve des exceptions prévues par les lois, les décrets et les arrêtés royaux.'" All these are cited in *Le Courrier d'Afrique* (Leopoldville), July 4, 1957; see also *Le Soir* (Bruxelles), June 21, 1957.

¹⁴ *Congo 1959* (Bruxelles: CRISP, 1960), pp. 125–129.

¹⁵ *Ibid.*, p. 127.

¹⁶ Henri Rolin, "Les Vices de l'administration du Katanga. Les Remèdes," *Revue de l'Université de Bruxelles* (1911–1912), p. 199. Referring to the royal decree of March 22, 1910, Professor Rolin added: "En fait la pratique administrative a étendu la portée de ces textes et aujourd'hui la subordination du Vice-Gouverneur Général du Katanga à l'egard du Gouverneur Général résidant a Boma est purement théorique. Elisabethville correspond directement avec le Ministre des Colonies par Capetown et des instructions ministérielles ont enjoint expressément au Gouverneur Général à Boma d'excepter le Katanga des ordonnances législatives qu'il est amené à prendre" (*ibid.*).

¹⁷ "La mesure la plus importante prise au cours de l'exercice 1910 est la création du Vice-Gouvernement du Katanga. C'est une mesure essentiellement décentralisatrice, dont le but est de favoriser le développement de la région en lui assurant le plus d'autonomie possible. ... Y aura-t-il d'autres Vice-Gouvernements Généraux comme celui du Katanga? C'est peu probable; l'organisation d'une administration autonome se justifiait au Katanga, district minier où l'industrie s'implantera facilement. Elle ne se justifierait pas ailleurs

pour le moment" (*Annales Parlementaires, Chambre des Représentants,* Feb. 1, 1919, p. 9).

[18] *Bulletin Officiel,* July 3, 1914, pp. 904 ff. Cf. *ibid.,* May 6, 1910, pp. 382 ff.

[19] *Ibid.,* July 30, 1914, p. 902.

[20] "Comme je vous l'ai dit, je délègue mes pouvoirs aux Vice-Gouverneurs Généraux dans les limites les plus étendues des délégations autorisées par la loi, me reservant de faire encore élargir ces limites si l'intérêt d'une bonne administration le conseille. ... Les Vice-Gouverneurs Généraux gouvernent et administrent leurs provinces en se conformant aux lois et règlements et suivant les directives et le programme que je leur trace, après m'être entendu avec eux. Mais agissant sous leur pleine responsabilité, ils prennent toutes les mesures d'exécution sans avoir à m'en référer" (*Recueil Mensuel des Circulaires, Instructions et Ordres de Service,* no. 1 [Jan., 1922], 3).

[21] The text of the final report of the commission may be found in *Bulletin Officiel,* Aug. 15, 1930, pp. 380–395.

[22] The functions of the inspecteurs d'état are described in more detail in the "lettre d'instructions générales" addressed by Minister Tshoffen to Governor Ryckmans in 1934 (*Bulletin Officiel,* Oct. 15, 1934, pp. 937–947).

[23] *Annales Parlementaires, Sénat,* July 26, 1933, pp. 608 ff.

[24] The text of the decree of 1947 may be found in *Bulletin Administratif,* July 2, 1947, pp. 1291–1296.

[25] *L'Etoile du Congo,* May 5, 1920. Discussing the proposals contained in the plan, a district commissioner of the Katanga remarked: "Le défaut capital du projet apparait immédiatement: C'est son 'Provincialisme.' Celui-ci a pris naissance dès la création de la première province, le Katanga. Des cette création, les Vice-Gouverneurs Généraux, chefs de province, ont supporté avec impatience la sujétion à l'autorité du Gouvernement Général du Congo. C'est tout a fait humain ... mais ce n'est guère admissible" (André van Iseghem, *A Propos d'un projet de réorganisation administrative du Congo Belge* [Elisabethville, n.d.]; cf. André van Iseghem, "Centralisation et décentralisation," *Bulletin de la Société Belge d'Etudes Coloniales* [Sept.-Oct., 1921], pp. 473–531).

[26] Referring to "le dictateur Tilkens," the author of the article stated: "Le grand destructeur de Kalina, qui n'a lui à son actif qu'une incompétence notoire et une incompréhensive suffisance, n'a pas hesité à sacrifier ces remarquables serviteurs de l'oeuvre coloniale pour le seul motif que leur valeur le gênait. Une homme de petite taille n'aime pas s'entourer d'athlètes. Lorsqu'on examine ces fameuses mesures de réorganisation, l'on s'aperçoit en effet que le vrai but de ce renversement n'a été que d'écarter de l'entourage du Gouverneur Général les hommes de valeur qui le surplombaient" ("Une Entreprise de démolition," *L'Essor du Congo,* July 3, 1933).

[27] *Propos sur le Congo politique de demain: Autonomie et fédéralisme* (Elisabethville, 1958), p. 37.

[28] Monsignor de Hemptinne, "La Politique indigène du gouvernement belge," *Congo,* II (1928), 359; cf. Circulaire 7001/AIMO, Oct. 10, 1929, *Province Orientale: Politique Indigène. Instructions* (Stanleyville, 1932), p. 95.

[29] One district commissioner wrote in 1922: "Evidemment ces vieux Commissaires de District qui connaissent toutes les ficelles du métier et qui se permettent d'avoir des idées personnelles et d'invoquer leur expérience sont parfois fort embètants. Il s'agit donc de neutraliser cet esprit d'insubordination et ces prétentions par des instructions précises et detaillées sur toute matière

et d'en prescrire l'application à la lettre. Est-il besoin de dire qu'à ce regime le chef de District se décourage et s'en fout?" (*L'Avenir Colonial Belge*, March 5, 1922).

³⁰ "Centralisation et décentralisation," p. 506.

³¹ *Le Peuple* (Bruxelles), March 13, 1931; cf. André van Iseghem, "La Réorganisation administrative coloniale," *L'Essor Colonial et Maritime*, April 5, 9, 12, 1931. The reaction of the European population of the Katanga to the proposals of the Association des Fonctionnaires et Agents de la Colonie found a graphic expression in an article entitled "Le Soviet des fonctionnaires congolais," *L'Essor du Congo*, May 1, 1931: "Croyant parler au nom du public de la province du Katanga nous protestons contre l'inertie du gouvernement métropolitain qui ne sévit pas contre cette usurpation de pouvoirs, contre le Gouverneur Général dont le manque d'énergie nous jette en pleine République des Camarades [*sic*], contre la suffisance et l'outrecuidance de l'AFAC de Léo qui pretend régenter tout le Congo."

³² Viscount Mountmorres, *The Congo Independent State* (London, 1906), p. 77.

³³ *Bulletin Officiel*, July 30, 1914, p. 894.

³⁴ *Ibid.*

³⁵ *Annales Parlementaires, Sénat,* July 25, 1933, p. 593.

³⁶ This principle was embodied in the exposé des motifs preceding the text of the colonial budget of 1932: "Les districts ont été ramenés de 21 à 15 et les territoires de 180 à 102. On a procédé aux regroupements ethniques nécessaires. Des tribus qui étaient réparties entre plusieurs circonscriptions ont retrouvé ainsi leur cohesion et leur organisation primitives, ce qui facilitera l'administration des collectivités indigènes" ("Budget de la colonie pour l'exercice 1932," *Chambre des Représentants, Document Parlementaire*, no. 14 [1932], p. 19).

³⁷ Margery Perham's introduction to Joan Wheare, *The Nigerian Legislative Council* (London, 1950), p. x, cited in James S. Coleman, *Nigeria: Background to Nationalism* (Berkeley and Los Angeles: University of California Press, 1958), p. 45.

³⁸ Excerpt from F. Kaninda's letter dated July 26, 1955, to the editor of *Le Courrier d'Afrique* (unpublished document).

³⁹ James S. Coleman, "The Emergence of African Political Parties," *Africa To-Day* (Baltimore: Johns Hopkins Press, 1955), cited in Thomas Hodgkin, *African Political Parties* (London: Penguin Books, 1961), p. 34.

⁴⁰ Thomas Hodgkin argues that "the absence until 1959 of Dr. Coleman's two preconditions is surely the main reason why only embryonic parties emerged in the former Belgian Congo" (*ibid.*). This statement is only partially true, for if the 1957 decree on the Statut des Villes provided only for "consultations," as distinct from "elections," it has, at least in some instances, stimulated the growth of parties. Moreover, the assertion that "only embryonic parties" are to be found in the Congo is certainly open to question.

⁴¹ Ordonnance 91/106, *Bulletin Administratif*, April 30, 1954, p. 557; Ordonnance 12/126, *ibid.*, May 11, 1957, pp. 990–992.

⁴² *Discours du Gouverneur Général* (Leopoldville, 1950), p. 36.

⁴³ Excerpt from Kaninda letter.

⁴⁴ *Discours du Gouverneur Général* (Leopoldville, 1953), p. 12.

⁴⁵ Cited in A. W. Southall, "Belgian and British Administration in Alurland," *Zaïre*, VIII (May, 1954), 472.

46 *Ibid.*, p. 483.

47 *Recueil à l'usage des fonctionnaires et des agents du service territorial* (Bruxelles, 1920), p. 326.

48 Circulaire 785, Feb. 22, 1922, in *Province Orientale: Politique Indigène. Instructions*, p. 19. A. Sohier later admitted that the aim of the circular was "primarily political, not judicial," as it did not seek to achieve "higher standards of justice" but rather "to reform the cadres of the administration" ("Les Juridictions indigènes congolaises," IRCB, *Bulletin des Séances*, IV [1935], 62).

49 *Bulletin Officiel*, May 15, 1926, pp. 448–488.

50 "Précisions sur le problème de la politique indigène," *Congo*, II (1929), 187–208; cf. A. J. Moeller, "Note concernant l'étude de Monseigneur de Hemptinne sur la politique indigène," *ibid.*, pp. 209–224.

51 See in particular F. Grévisse, *La Grande Pitié juridictions indigènes*, IRCB, *Bulletin des Séances*, XIX (1952).

52 For an interesting discussion of the decree of December 5, 1933, see J. Magotte, *Les Circonscriptions indigènes* (Bruxelles, 1952).

53 Southall, *op. cit.*, p. 482.

54 *Bulletin Officiel*, Dec. 15, 1931, pp. 767–785; cf. *Troisième Congrès Colonial National: Rapports* (Bruxelles, 1930), p. 49.

55 Lord Hailey, *An African Survey Revised 1956* (London: Oxford University Press, 1957), p. 557.

56 Ordonnance 170/AIMO, *Bulletin Administratif*, Aug. 10, 1945, pp. 955–957.

57 For a general discussion of the origins and functions of the *conseils de zone* of Leopoldville, see G. de Clercq,"Affaires communales" (mimeographed; Leopoldville, 1958); see also *Rapport annuel sur l'administration de la colonie en 1933* (Bruxelles, 1934), p. 130.

58 "Les conseils de zone ont vu le jour à partir de 1954, sous l'administration de M. Cordy, en prévision du Statut des Villes qui était en préparation. On voulait faire d'abord un essai en initiant des Congolais a leur futur rôle avant de les lancer officiellement" (*Présence Congolaise*, Nov. 14, 1953).

59 One administrator reported: "Le conseil [de zone] fut indiscutablement une 'présence' au sein de la zone. Un réel rayonnement a pu être constaté chez plusieurs 'capita ya balala' (chefs de rue) qui, conscients de leur mission se dépenserent pour réunir régulierement la population en vue de communiquer les projets et décisions de l'administration. ... D'autres innovations, telles que les syndicats d'initiative locaux ont également favorisé l'éclosion d'un esprit communal, ont animé les nouvelles communautés qu'il fallait préparer aux notions de vie communale, d'intérêts communaux, etc." (de Clercq, *op. cit.*, pp. 7 ff.).

60 *Bulletin Officiel*, April 1, 1957, pp. 750–871.

61 C. A. G. Wallis, "The Administration of Towns in the Belgian Congo," *Journal of African Administration*, X (April, 1958), 97.

62 *Bulletin Officiel*, April 1, 1957, p. 847.

63 Ruth Schachter, "The Development of Political Parties in French West Africa" (unpublished Ph.D. dissertation, Oxford University), cited in Hodgkin, *op. cit.*, p. 38.

64 *Conseil de Gouvernement, Compte-rendu analytique de la session budgétaire, 1958* (Leopoldville, 1958), pp. 140 ff.

65 *Ibid.*

[66] George Brausch, *Belgian Administration in the Congo* (London: Oxford University Press, 1961), p. 44.

IV: Goals and Organization of the "Colonat"

[1] *Rapport sur l'administration du Congo Belge en 1958* (Bruxelles, 1959), p. 27.

[2] *Rapport annuel sur l'activité de la colonie du Congo Belge pendant l'année 1921* (Bruxelles, 1922), p. 24.

[3] A. de Bauw, *Le Katanga* (Bruxelles, 1920), p. 49.

[4] Edmond Leplae, "La Situation de l'agriculture au Congo Belge," *Congo*, II (1920), 492.

[5] "L'Evolution constitutionnelle du Congo," *Compte-rendu des journées interuniversitaires d'Études coloniales* (Bruxelles, 1952), p. 8.

[6] Lord Hailey, *An African Survey Revised 1956* (London: Oxford University Press, 1957), p. 345.

[7] P. Piron and J. Devos, *Codes et lois du Congo Belge* (Bruxelles, 1954).

[8] In 1957 this caution amounted to 50,000 Belgian francs ($1,000) for the head of the family and for each child more than eighteen years old, and 25,000 Belgian francs for the wife and for each child between fourteen and eighteen (*Le Congo Belge* [Bruxelles: Infor-Congo, 1959], p. 382).

[9] Hailey, *op. cit.*, p. 345.

[10] T. Heyse, *Les Grandes Lignes du régime des terres au Congo Belge* (Bruxelles, 1947).

[11] L. O. J. de Wilde, "Les Possibilités de culture et de vie flamande au Congo," in *Les Problèmes des langues au Congo Belge et au Ruanda-Urundi* (Bruxelles: Stichting Lodewijk de Raet, 1958), pp. 65 ff.

[12] Cited in Pierre Davister, *Katanga enjeu du monde* (Bruxelles, 1960), p. 63.

[13] The sense of economic grievance which has always characterized the attitude of the Katanga settlers toward the metropolitan government is illustrated by the following statement, made in 1931, by the president of the Association des Colons Belges au Katanga: "Et le Katanga, vache laitière du Congo, celle qui contribue pour 100 millions, ses propres dépenses étant payées, au Budget Général, que fait-on pour elle? Rien. ... Que fait-on pour le Katangaleux, le colon du Katanga qui a investi tout ce qu'il possède dans le pays, qui est ici avec sa femme et ses enfants depuis vingt ans? Rien!" (*L'Essor du Congo*, June 25, 1931).

[14] *Le Comité Spécial du Katanga, 1900–1925* (Bruxelles, 1927), esp. Appendix III.

[15] "Speech Delivered by Field Marshal Smuts on October 12th, 1946," *Kongo-Overzee*, XII-XIII (1946–1947), 36–44.

[16] Jean Sépulchre, "Gens et choses de l'Afrique du Sud," *L'Essor du Congo*, June 17, 1944.

[17] *L'Etoile du Congo*.

[18] "Comité Regional, Katanga" (mimeographed; Elisabethville, 1925), p. 15.

[19] *Rapport de la Commission d'Elisabethville relatif aux defectuosités de la législation actuelle sur les concessions de terre au Congo* (Elisabethville: Fédération des Groupements et Associations du Congo Belge, 1936).

[20] *Statuts,* Fédération des Groupements et Associations du Congo Belge (Elisabethville, 1935).

21 *Ibid.*

22 "La première réunion publique de la Fédération des Groupements et Associations du Katanga," *L'Essor du Congo,* March 7, 1934.

23 "Fédération des Groupements et Associations du Katanga," *L'Essor du Congo,* March 2, 1934.

24 *Ibid.*

25 *Statuts,* Fédération des Groupements et Associations du Congo Belge.

26 *Ibid.*

27 By January, 1939, the federation comprised thirteen affiliate organizations, six of which had their seats in the Katanga, four in the Kivu, and three in the Orientale (*Bulletin Mensuel de la Fédération* [Jan., 1939]).

28 "Union pour la Colonisation," *L'Essor du Congo,* June 1, 1944.

29 *Statuts,* Union pour la Colonisation (Elisabethville, 1947).

30 *L'Opinion publique coloniale devant l'assimilation des indigènes* (Bruxelles, 1951).

31 "La Fédération des Classes Moyennes," *Courrier Africain* (CRISP), no. 25 (July, 1959), p. 19.

32 The record suggests that the colonat derived most of its metropolitan support from the Belgian Liberal Party (PLB); see, for example, the declarations made before the Chambers by the Liberal deputy, Lahaye, in April, 1959, in *Chambre des Représentants, Annales Parlementaires,* April 21, 1959, p. 13. The conservative daily *La Libre Belgique,* whose views reflect the opinion of the Social Christian Party (PSC), also displayed an overt sympathy for the colonat.

33 As early as 1925 the Association des Colons Belges introduced a motion before the Comité Régional du Katanga urging "the competent authorities . . . to examine the way in which they could facilitate the exercise of their political rights" ("Comité Régional, Katanga" [1926], p. 159).

34 *Procès-verbaux,* Commission du Colonat (Bruxelles, 1946), p. 30.

35 *Bulawayo Chronicle,* May 16, 1931. Anticipating the granting of home rule, the Katanga settler community selected sixteen "ministrables" whose names and qualifications appeared in *L'Essor du Congo,* May 20, 1931: "Affaires Etrangères: Lamotte (Elegance, charme à ses heures, brillantes relations dans les pays limitrophes); Intérieur: Verbeken (Sympathique, multiples talents de société, connait parfaitement son tout Potinville); Justice et Culte: Smits (Jovialement ferme, répression assurée et radicale des mouvements réactionnaires. A surveiller toutefois sa tendence à établir impitoyablement censure presse, mille fois justifiée sans doute mais peu, habile vis à vis opinion publique pendant premiers pas du nouveau régime); Transports: Feycher (Malgré nom, assurerait bon marché des transports routiers grâce relations avec grands trusts pétroliers); Ravitaillement: Wyckaert (Spécialisation dans bonne chère; créerait réputation gastronomique Katanga et attirerait grand tourisme)."

36 *Rapport sur la colonisation blanche au Congo présenté au Conseil Général de la Fédération des Groupements et Associations du Congo Belge* (Elisabethville, 1938), p. 18.

37 *Ibid.*

38 *Procès-verbaux,* Commission du Colonat, p. 28.

39 *Congrès Colonial National, IX*ème *Session* (Bruxelles, 1953), p. 140.

40 *L'Opinion publique coloniale,* p. 28.

41 "La Position de l'Union Agricole du Kivu sur la question de l'immatriculation," *Centre-Afrique* (Bukavu), Sept. 20, 1950.

[42] *L'Opinion publique coloniale*, p. 35.

[43] *Congrès Colonial National, IX^{ème} Session*, p. 146.

[44] "La Fédération des Classes Moyennes," p. 13.

[45] *Ibid.*, p. 11.

[46] *Courrier d'Afrique*, Aug. 8, 1944.

[47] *Conseil de Gouvernement, Compte-rendu analytique* (June, 1954), pp. 32 ff.

[48] *Ibid.*, p. 38.

[49] "The innumerable friends whom the whites count among the natives would otherwise be subject to the painful feeling of being abandoned. We do not have the right to betray the trust that they have placed in us" (*ibid.*, p. 13).

[50] "La Fédération des Classes Moyennes," p. 13.

[51] *Ibid.*, p. 11.

[52] "Doctrine politique de l'Ucol," *L'Essor du Congo*, April 17, 1957.

[53] "Doctrine politique," Ucol (mimeographed; Elisabethville, 1957).

[54] Arthur Doucy, "Sociologie coloniale et réformes de structure au Congo Belge," *Revue de l'Université de Bruxelles*, no. 2–3 (Jan.-April, 1957), 13.

[55] *Ibid.*, p. 14.

[56] *L'Etoile du Congo*, May 5, 1920.

[57] "Les Grandes Lignes d'un futur statut politique," *L'Essor du Congo*, May 24, 1958.

[58] *Courrier d'Afrique*, July 12, 1957.

[59] Achille Gavage, "Pour un politique spécifiquement katangaise," *L'Essor du Congo*, Feb. 19, 1958.

[60] "Union Katangaise, parti d'action politique, sociale et économique," *ibid.*, May 28, 1958.

[61] *Eurafrica* (Feb., 1959), p. 4.

[62] Alan P. Merriam, *Congo: Background to Conflict* (Chicago: Northwestern University Press, 1961), p. 34.

V: The Impact of Western Economic Forces

[1] Lord Hailey, "Nationalism in Africa," *Journal of the African Royal Society*, XXXVI (April, 1937), 134–147.

[2] *Rapport annuel sur l'administration*, 1940–45 (Bruxelles, 1946); *ibid.*, 1957 (Bruxelles, 1958).

[3] *La Voix du Congolais*, no. 96 (March, 1954), p. 96.

[4] For a general discussion of the factors that prompted the Congolese to leave their customary areas, see *ibid.*, no. 94 (Jan., 1954), pp. 34–41; no. 95 (Feb., 1954), pp. 103–114; no. 96 (March, 1954), pp. 179–184.

[5] *Ibid.*, no. 96 (March, 1954), p. 96.

[6] *Ibid.*, no. 3 (Oct.-Nov., 1945), p. 154.

[7] V. G. Pons, "L'Influence changeante de l'origine ethnique et du degré d'occidentalisation sur la répartition africaine de Stanleyville," in *Aspects de l'industrialisation et de l'urbanisation en Afrique au Sud du Sahara* (Paris: Unesco, 1956), p. 711.

[8] "The Role of Traditionalism in the Political Modernization of Ghana and Uganda," *World Politics*, XIII (Oct., 1960), 48.

[9] *Rapport sur l'administration du Congo Belge pendant l'année 1919* (Bruxelles, 1920), p. 9.

[10] H. Nicolai and J. Jacques, *La Transformation des paysages congolais par le chemin de fer* (Bruxelles, 1954), p. 82.

[11] *Ibid.*, p. 63; E. Toussaint, "L'Avenir de la population bantoue du Haut Katanga industriel," *Congrès Scientifique d'Elisabethville*, VI (1956), 35.

[12] "The Modern Evolution of the African Population in the Belgian Congo," *Africa*, IV (July, 1952), 34.

[13] Harry Johnston, *George Grenfell and the Congo* (London: Hutchinson, 1908), I, 177.

[14] Georges Balandier, "Travail non-salarié dans les Brazzaville noires," *Zaïre*, VI (July, 1952), 34.

[15] Joseph Van Wing, "Impressions du Congo," *Bulletin des Séances de l'Académie Royale des Sciences Coloniales*, II (1956), 184.

[16] Pons, *op. cit.*, p. 711.

[17] Herman Burssens, "The So-called Bangala and a Few Problems of Art-Historical and Ethnographical Order," *Kongo-Overzee*, XX, no. 3 (1954), 221.

[18] *Rapport annuel sur l'administration du Congo Belge*, 1945–46 (Bruxelles, 1947), p. 6; *ibid.*, 1939–1944 (Bruxelles, 1945), pp. 211, 190.

[19] F. Bézy, *Problèmes structurels de l'économie congolaise* (Louvain: Institut de Recherches Economiques et Sociales), p. 101.

[20] J. I. Roper, *Labour Problems in West Africa* (London: Penguin Books, 1958), p. 108.

[21] Bézy, *op. cit.*; L. Ballegeer, "Syndicalisme indigène," *Bulletin du Cepsi*, no. 8 (1947–1948), 99–109.

[22] P. Joye and R. Lewin, *Les Trusts au Congo* (Bruxelles, 1961), p. 138.

[23] *Année 1955, Statistiques et Commentaires* (Elisabethville: UMHK, Département de la Main d'Oeuvre Indigène, 1956), p. 4.

[24] *Ibid.*, pp. 17 ff.

[25] *Ibid.*, p. 16.

[26] Toussaint, *op. cit.*, p. 35.

[27] *La Situation économique du Congo Belge et du Ruanda-Urundi en 1954* (Bruxelles: Ministère des Colonies, 1955), pp. 230, 284.

[28] *Industrialization in Africa: A Report Prepared by the International African Institute for the Social Science Division of the Unesco* (London: HMSO, 1954), p. 51.

[29] *Ibid.*, p. 52.

[30] Arthur Doucy, "Le Rôle des influences coutumières sur les travailleurs indigènes du Congo Belge," *Revue de l'Institut de Sociologie Solvay*, no. 4 (1954), 824.

[31] William Watson, *Tribal Cohesion in a Money Economy* (Manchester: Manchester University Press, 1958), p. 226.

[32] James S. Coleman, "The Problem of Political Integration in Emergent Africa," *Western Political Quarterly*, VIII (March, 1955), 49.

[33] Thomas Hodgkin, *Nationalism in Colonial Africa* (London: Frederick Muller, 1956), p. 115.

[34] *The Congo Independent State: A Report on a Voyage of Enquiry* (London: Williams and Norgate, 1906), p. 6.

[35] E. D. Morel, *The Future of the Congo* (London, 1909), p. 71.

[36] *Rapport annuel sur l'administration de la colonie du Congo Belge en 1922* (Bruxelles, 1924), p. 105.

[37] Eric Hoffer, *The True Believer* (New York: Mentor Books, 1960), pp. 33, 109.

[38] *Dettes de guerre* (Elisabethville: Editions de l'Essor du Congo, 1945), pp. 29 ff.

[39] Joseph Van Wing, "Le Congo déraille," *Bulletin des Séances de l'Institut Royal Colonial Belge*, XVII, no. 1 (1951), 610.

[40] *Dettes de guerre*, pp. 128, 129.

[41] *Ibid.*, p. 39.

[42] See, for example, the declaration made by Arthur Pinzi before the General Assembly of the Association du Personnel Indigène (*Congo*, Aug. 3, 1957).

[43] *Conscience Africaine*, no. 3 (Nov.-Dec., 1956).

[44] "Motion d'un groupe d'assistants médicaux," *Congo*, Aug. 3, 1957.

[45] *Le Courrier d'Afrique*, Feb. 13, 1958.

[46] "Rapport à la Chambre de la Commission Parlementaire," *Chambre des Représentants, Documents Parlementaires*, no. 100 (1958–1959), Appendix VI, p. 95.

[47] Joye and Lewin, *op. cit.*, pp. 202–223, 235–263. The part played by charter companies in the early days of the Congo Free State is described in Raymond L. Buell, *The Native Problem in Africa* (2 vols.; New York: Macmillan, 1928), II, 445 ff. For a more recent appraisal of the economic power behind Belgian corporations in the Congo, see "The Congo Is in Business," *Fortune* (Nov., 1952), pp. 106 ff.

[48] Joye and Lewin, *op. cit.*, p. 121.

[49] *La Situation économique ... en 1954*, p. 174.

[50] *Conscience Africaine* (Feb., 1955).

[51] *Ibid.* (July-Aug., 1955).

[52] "Le Credit aux indigènes," *Commission pour l'Etude du Problème Foncier* (Leopoldville, n.d.), pp. 254 ff.

[53] *Ibid.*, p. 259.

[54] Joye and Lewin, *op. cit.*, p. 77.

[55] *Rapport annuel sur l'administration du Congo Belge en 1921* (Bruxelles, 1924), p. 111; *ibid.*, 1923 (Bruxelles, 1924), p. 35.

[56] IRCB, *Bulletin des Séances* (1932), p. 574.

[57] *Rapport de la mission sénatoriale au Congo* (Bruxelles, 1947), p. 68.

[58] *Conseil de Gouvernement, Session Générale*, 1959, p. 78.

[59] E. D. Morel, *A Memorial on Native Rights in the Land and Its Fruits in the Congo Territories Annexed by Belgium (Subject to International Recognition) in August, 1908* (London, 1909), p. 10.

[60] Cited in *Commission pour l'Etude du Problème Foncier*, p. 227.

[61] Joye and Lewin, *op. cit.*, pp. 210 ff.

[62] Lord Hailey, *An African Survey Revised 1956* (London: Oxford University Press, 1957), p. 751.

[63] *Conseil de Gouvernement, Session Générale*, 1957, p. 198.

[64] *Ibid.*, Appendix 1 and 2, p. 357.

[65] *Note sur le Comité Spécial du Katanga et le Comité National du Kivu* (Leopoldville, n.d.), p. 4.

[66] Jean-Paul Harroy, *Afrique, terre qui meurt* (Bruxelles, 1949), p. 342.

[67] *Conseil de Législation, Bulletin des Séances*, 1960, p. 558.

[68] *Commission pour l'Etude du Problème Foncier*, p. 124.

[69] *Ibid.*, p. 135.

[70] *Conseil de Législation, Bulletin des Séances*, 1960, p. 168.

[71] *Commission pour l'Etude du Problème Foncier*, p. 191.

[72] *Ibid.*, p. 189.

VI: The Influence of Christian Missions and Education

¹ L. Kandel, "Nationalism and Education," *Yearbook of Education, 1949* (London, 1950), p. 27.

² J. S. Harris, "Education in the Belgian Congo," *Journal of Negro Education,* XV (Summer, 1946), 419.

³ *Annales Parlementaires, Sénat,* June 20, 1956.

⁴ Ruth Slade, "King Leopold II and the Attitude of English and American Catholics towards the Anti-Congolese Campaign," *Zaïre,* XI (June, 1957), 595.

⁵ E. de Jonghe, "Les Missions religieuses au Congo Belge," *Congo,* I (1933), 14 ff.

⁶ *Ibid.,* p. 11.

⁷ *Rapport annuel sur l'administration du Congo Belge en 1954* (Bruxelles, 1955), p. 160.

⁸ *African Mail,* Nov. 12, 1909, cited in James S. Coleman, *Nigeria: Background to Nationalism* (Berkeley and Los Angeles: University of California Press, 1958), p. 105.

⁹ The leader of the Parti Ouvrier Belge, Emile Vandervelde, observed in 1911: "Au lieu d'agir directement sur la masse, comme le font, ou essayent de le faire les Catholiques, [les Protestants] ... préfèrent s'adresser à un nombre restreint d'individus sur les quels ils peuvent compter pour former des chefs de file qui aident les autres à avancer à leur tour" ("Les Missions au Congo Belge," *La Grande Revue,* LXV [1911], 8).

¹⁰ Lewis A. Brown in *Congo News Letter* (Jan., 1932), p. 30.

¹¹ For further details on the ferme-chapelle system, see A. Vermeersch, *Les Missions catholiques au Congo Belge: Etude critique de leur action* (Bruxelles, 1909), pp. 21 ff.

¹² Léopold Denis, *Les Jésuites belges au Kwango, 1893–1943* (Bruxelles, 1951), p. 63.

¹³ *Chambre des Représentants, Documents Parlementaires,* no. 20 (Dec. 1, 1911), esp. "Rapport Leclercq sur l'Action des RR PP Jesuites au Kwango," Appendix III.

¹⁴ *Annales Parlementaires, Chambre des Représentants,* Dec 5, 1911, pp. 153–172. The allegation made by the Belgian Socialists that the Catholic missionaries used physical compulsion to recruit their neophytes was categorically denied by Father Vermeersch, on the ground that the Church was opposed on principle to "conversion by constraint." But he implicitly admitted that, when used against "orphans" and abandoned children, such practices were not illicit (A. Vermeersch, *Sur-Nègres ou chrétiens?* [Bruxelles and Paris, 1911], p. 27).

¹⁵ Vermeersch, *Les Missions catholiques,* p. 9.

¹⁶ *Ibid.,* p. 17.

¹⁷ *Op. cit.,* p. 12.

¹⁸ *Recueil Mensuel des Circulaires, Instructions et Ordres de Service,* no. 1 (Jan., 1922), 6.

¹⁹ "Les Missions du Congo vues par un laic," *La Revue Générale,* Aug. 15, 1924, p. 255.

²⁰ *Annuaire des missions catholiques* (Bruxelles, 1954); Ruth Slade, *The Belgian Congo: Some Recent Changes* (London: Oxford University Press, 1960), p. 35.

²¹ *Christ and the Congo* (Leopoldville, 1934), p. 7.

²² Ruth Slade, *King Leopold's Congo* (London: Oxford University Press, 1962), p. 142.

²³ H. Haeck, "L'Avenir du catholicisme en Afrique belge," *Revue du Clergé Africain* (July, 1949), p. 142.

²⁴ That the Protestant missionaries were fully aware of these charges is indicated by the following item, which appeared in the January, 1927, issue of the *Congo Mission News:* "Two events in recent years have been seized upon by Roman Catholics and other interests in Belgium as occasions for violent anti-Protestant propaganda: The Kimbangu and the Mwana Lesa affairs. As to Mwana Lesa he had no connection whatever with Protestant missions. . . . As to Kimbangu, the informed public is already aware that while he had at one time been a Protestant communicant, yet his movement had no direct connection with his former faith, that he was consistently hostile to his former teachers and associates who disagreed with him, and that Protestant missions suffered more than any other from the results of his unbalanced mentality."

²⁵ Monsignor de Hemptinne, *La Politique des missions protestantes au Congo* (Elisabethville: Editions de l'Essor du Congo, 1929). "C'est sur le terrain de l'internationalisme social et politique," the author concluded, "que les missionnaires évangeliques se rapprochent et se coalisent: Tel est le caractère dominant de ces congrès et de ces organisations qui se réclament du patronage de Genève ... [Les Missions Protestantes] ambitionnent une action mondiale. Ce n'est plus par la fenêtre de la sacristie qu'il faut les surveiller mais bien du haut de la colonne de l'indépendance" (p. 12). Cf. L. Anet, *Vers l'Avenir: Rapport de la Conférence Jubilaire des Missions Protestantes du Congo et de la Conférence Missionaire de l'Afrique Occidentale* (Leopoldville, 1929).

²⁶ *Christian Action in Africa* (New York: Africa Committee of the Foreign Missions Conference of North America, 1942), p. 150.

²⁷ Among the various steps taken by the Bible Society to standardize Lingala, mention must be made of the All-Congo Lingala Conference which, meeting in October, 1932, grouped "missionaries from the [Congo] river and from the extreme north of the Belgian Congo" (*Congo Mission News* [Jan.-April, 1933], p. 7).

²⁸ *Ibid.* (July, 1934), p. 6.

²⁹ *Ibid.* The Swedish missionary K. Laman reported in 1928: "The central dialects spoken around Mukimbungu have been made known through the literary work of the Swedish mission. The eastern dialects spoken around Kisantu have become known through the literary work of the Kisantu Jesuit mission and the American Baptist mission. The western dialects in Mayumbe have become known through the literary work of the Roman Catholic mission and the American alliance" ("Languages Used in the Congo Basin," *Africa*, I [July, 1928], 374).

³⁰ "Taalenmaking in het Mongo-Gebied," *Kongo-Overzee*, XVI, no. 5 (1950), 298.

³¹ J. Van Wing, "Nota over de 'Commissie voor unificatie van het Kikongo,'" *ibid.*, XVII, no. 1 (1951), 38–40. The author reports that whenever differences of opinion arose over questions of vocabulary, as when a given word had no phonetic equivalent in either of the three vicariates, preference was given to the Matadi dialect "because it was closest to the language spoken at San Salvador, capital of the ancient Kongo Kingdom."

32 "Le Problème de la langue commune véhiculaire ou culturelle au Congo Belge," *Aequatoria*, July 7, 1939, p. 83.

33 See, for example, J. Van Wing, *Etudes Bakongo* (Bruxelles, 1921); E. Boelaert, *Nsona Lianga, L'Epopée nationale des Nkundo-Mongo* (Antwerp, 1949); E. Verhulpen, *Baluba et Balubaisés du Katanga* (Antwerp, 1936).

34 As Father Van Wing told me, "Quand je suis arrivé à Kisantu, les Bakongo se comportaient comme des esclaves; j'ai voulu leur donner un sens national, une certaine fierté de leur culture. ... On cultivait les germes du nationalisme, à travers la langue et la culture." One of the most widely read of Father Van Wing's publications was a booklet entitled *Enkeda mi Monemambu*, published in 1931, in which he recounts the feats accomplished by a legendary figure, Monemambu. In recording the adventures of Monemambu, the author drew most of his inspiration from the Flemish legend "Tyl Uilenspiegel."

35 Armand Abel, *Les Musulmans noirs du Maniema* (Bruxelles: Publications du Centre pour l'Etude des Problèmes du Monde Musulman Contemporain, 1960), p. 32.

36 *Le Mouvement Géographique*, no. 39 (1903), 507.

37 In 1958 the Belgian government decided to give the Congregation of the White Fathers full control over the schools located in the Kasongo vicariate, thereby suppressing the official schools and the Muslim schools, which had been authorized by the Buisseret-Moermans-Thompson agreement in 1956. This decision, motivated by "national and political imperatives," significantly helped to arouse the hostility of the Maniema population toward the missions (Abel, *op. cit.*, p. 13).

38 Cited in Slade, *The Belgian Congo*, p. 33.

39 *Indépendance*, Sept. 25, 1939.

40 *Ibid.*, April 30, 1959.

41 *Solidarité Africaine*, June 4, 1960.

42 Monsignor Roelens, "Esquisse psychologique de nos noirs," *Grands Lacs*, April 15, 1935, pp. 279–286.

43 *Instructions aux missionnaires des Pères Blancs du Haut Congo* (Baudoinville, 1938), p. 486.

44 See, for example, "Règlement et statut des frères auxiliaires indigènes," *ibid.*, pp. 412–413.

45 Guy Mosmans, *L'Eglise à l'heure de l'Afrique* (Paris: Casterman, 1961), pp. 89–113.

46 *Indépendance*, Sept. 25, 1959.

47 *Op. cit.*, p. 105.

48 *An African Survey Revised 1956* (London: Oxford University Press, 1957), p. 1209.

49 "Note pour M. Van Bilsen," April 19, 1955 (unpublished document). I am grateful to Professor A. A. J. Van Bilsen for permission to consult this document.

50 The recommendations of the commission may be found in E. de Jonghe, "L'Enseignement des indigènes au Congo Belge," in *L'Enseignement aux indigènes*, Institut Colonial International, XXI ème Session (Paris, 1931), pp. 86 ff.

51 Jessie Jones, "L'Education des nègres," *Congo*, II (1921), 162–175.

52 De Jonghe, "L'Enseignement des indigènes," p. 88.

[53] *Rapport sur la question de l'enseignement au Congo,* Bureau du Comité Permanent du Congrès Colonial National (Bruxelles, 1922), p. 18.

[54] *Ibid.,* p. 19.

[55] *Projet d'organisation de l'enseignement libre au Congo Belge avec le concours des missions nationales* (Bruxelles, 1924).

[56] L'Instruction publique des indigènes au Congo Belge," *Congo,* I (1940), 253.

[57] The program adopted in 1929 provided for additional courses in elocution, spelling, and composition, and a somewhat stronger emphasis on French as a foreign language (*Organisation de l'enseignement libre avec le concours des missions nationales* [Bruxelles, 1929]). The Scheutist Father A. Maus took a very dim view of this reform which, he said, will "considerably augment the number of *demi-lettrés,*" and therefore has "betrayed the purpose of [Belgian] educational policy." "N'y a-t-il pas la une espèce de démagogie scolaire," he added, "qui favorise des exigences toujours croissantes, impossibles à satisfaire et qui travaille directement à la désorganisation de la société?" (A. Maus, "Le nouveau Programme de l'enseignement libre," *Congo,* II [1938], 552).

[58] *Organisation de l'enseignement libre pour indigènes* (Bruxelles, 1948).

[59] Bernard Fall, "Education in the Republic of the Congo," *Journal of Negro Education* (Summer, 1961), p. 271.

[60] "L'Université Lovanium," *Lovania,* no. 34 (1955), 40.

[61] "Chronique: Centre Universitaire Congolais Lovanium," *ibid.,* no. 28 (1953), 64–65.

[62] "Les Examens de Lovanium: Un Succès!" *ibid.,* no. 34 (1955), 68.

[63] *Ibid.*

[64] "The Intellectuals in the Political Development of the New States," *World Politics,* XII (April, 1960), 330.

[65] *Organisation de l'enseignement libre subsidié pour indigènes avec le concours des sociétés de missions: Dispositions générales* (Bruxelles, 1953), p. 13.

[66] *Ibid.,* p. 25.

[67] "L'Enseignement aux indigènes tel que le conçoivent les missionnaires catholiques," in *L'Enseignement à dispenser aux indigènes dans les territoires non-autonomes* (Bruxelles: Les Cahiers de l'Institut de Sociologie Solvay, 1951), p. 50.

[68] *Organisation de l'enseignement libre subsidié pour indigènes,* p. 24.

[69] "Pour une histoire du Congo," *Kongo-Overzee,* XV (1949), 119.

[70] *La Réforme de l'enseignement au Congo Belge: Mission pédagogique Coulon-Deheyn-Renson* (Bruxelles: Ministère des Colonies, 1954), p. 94.

[71] "The Metropolitan Axis," *West Africa,* Jan. 9, 1954.

[72] Cited in Laman, *op. cit.,* p. 373.

[73] "La Question des langues au Congo," *La Flambeau,* Sept. 1, 1929, p. 7.

[74] "Les Langues indigènes dans l'enseignement," *Zaïre,* IV (July, 1950), 709.

[75] "La Question de l'enseignement au Congo," *Congo,* II (1924), 6.

[76] "La Langue véhiculaire de l'enseignement," *Aequatoria,* no. 3 (1939), 87.

[77] Cited in Laman, *op. cit.,* p. 379.

[78] J. Tanghe, "Le Swahili, langue de grande expansion," IRCB, *Bulletin des Séances,* XV (1944), 174–197; cf. E. de Jonghe, "Vers une Langue nationale congolaise," *ibid.,* VI (1935), 340–351.

[79] Laman, *op. cit.*, p. 376.

[80] "En fait on peut dire qu'une bonne partie des écoles subsidiées ne respectent pas la loi des quatre linguae francae officielles. On constate tout au moins en dehors des centres que l'enseignement se donne en dialecte local, ou dans un idiome lingua franca apparenté à un dialecte, ou encore dans une lingua franca que le missionnaire a introduite comme langue scolaire, même en dépit des divergences qui séparent cette lingua franca des dialectes locaux" (*Organisation de l'enseignement libre subsidié pour indigènes*, p. 35).

[81] *Ibid.*, p. 37.

[82] "Un Problème difficile de politique africaine: L'Éducation des Africains," IRCB, *Bulletin des Séances*, XXII (1951), 306.

[83] Based on information communicated to me by the secretariats of the universities of Louvain, Brussels, and Liège.

[84] The petition handed in by the Action Socialiste (Leopoldville), for example, urged: "L'intensification immédiate de l'enseignement sous toutes ses formes en quantité et en qualité; création immédiate d'écoles normales pour former des instituteurs; application du programme dit métropolitain a tout le réseau scolaire du pays; développement de l'enseignement universitaire et la possibilité pour ceux qui en bénéficient de complèter leur formation en Belgique et ailleurs."

[85] In a note communicated to the Groupe de Travail, M. Geurts, district commissioner for the Sankuru-Kasai, stated: "Ainsi dans le nord-Sankuru ou se fait jour un mouvement je dirai nationaliste Otetela il nous est reproché même par des notables des milieux les plus retirés, de n'avoir pas créé des écoles secondaires en temps opportun et en nombre suffisant. ... Bien souvent nous n'entendons que des récriminations, des critiques, mais rarement une idée constructive."

[86] *Congo Pratique* (July, 1953).

[87] *Uhuru*, Aug. 28, 1960.

[88] *Ibid.*

[89] *Indépendance*, April 30, 1960.

[90] *Ibid.*

[91] Evariste Kimba, "Ce que les Congolais attendent de l'enseignement du Français," *Revue Pédagogique* (Sept., 1957), pp. v–ix.

[92] According to René Bavassa, an évolué, "Ces pauvres Congolais ... tout en se croyant les plus civilisés du Congo, ont honte de parler la langue de leur mère. Drôle de civilisation. ... Il est très nécessaire qu'un enfant digne de ses ancêtres parle la langue qu'ils lui ont donnée en héritage, et qu'il la conserve jalousement. Honte aux familles qui perdent l'usage de la langue maternelle!" (cited in "Pour ou contre les Langues indigènes," *Aequatoria*, no. 4 [1953], 160).

[93] *Questions scolaires aux missions*, Rapports et comptes-rendus de la XXIVème semaine de missiologie de Louvain (Paris: Museum Lessianum, 1955), p. 106.

[94] A. J. Omari, "L'Avenir de la coutume," *La Voix du Congolais*, no. 84 (March, 1953), p. 153.

[95] *Congo Pratique* (Aug., 1953).

[96] *Ibid.*, July 27, 1957.

[97] "Les Écoles dans le district du Haut-Lomani," in *L'Etoile-Nyota*, Nov. 28, 1957.

[98] *Op. cit.*, p. 426.

[99] *La Réforme de l'enseignement au Congo Belge*, p. 95.

[100] Karl W. Deutsch, *Nationalism and Social Communication* (New York, 1953).

VII: EXTERNAL INFLUENCES

[1] Ruth Slade, *The Belgian Congo: Some Recent Changes* (London: Oxford University Press, 1960), p. 2.

[2] *La Revue Politique* (March, 1956), p. 7.

[3] See, for example, the petitions submitted to the Minister of Colonies by the évolués of Leopoldville, Luluabourg, Luebo, Dibaya, Coquilhatville, Bukavu, and Elisabethville in *Annales Parlementaires, Chambre des Représentants*, Dec. 7, 1954, pp. 20 ff.

[4] *Annales Parlementaires, Sénat*, June 20, 1956, p. 1473.

[5] *La Réforme de l'enseignement au Congo Belge: Mission pédagogique Coulôn-Deheyn-Renson. Rapport présenté à Monsieur le Ministre Auguste Buisseret* (Bruxelles: Ministère des Colonies, 1954).

[6] Thomas Hodgkin, "Battle of Schools in the Congo," *West Africa*, Jan. 28, 1956, p. 79.

[7] *La Réforme de l'enseignement au Congo Belge*, p. 81.

[8] *Ibid.*, p. 13.

[9] *Ibid.*, p. 210.

[10] *Ibid.*, p. 207.

[11] *Annales Parlementaires, Sénat*, June 20, 1956, p. 1471.

[12] *Ibid.*, p. 1473.

[13] The text of the Buisseret-Moermans-Thompson agreement may be found in *Annales Parlementaires, Chambre des Représentants*, April 25, 1956, p. 25.

[14] "Il ne faudrait pas que par attachement au principe de collaboration les missions soient englobées dans la réprobation qui se fait jour à l'égard des méthodes paternalistes. ... A aucun prix l'Eglise Africaine ne peut donner à penser qu'elle lie son sort à celui d'une classe déterminée" ("Les Impératifs de l'action missionnaire," *La Revue Nouvelle* [April, 1956], p. 53).

[15] Slade, *op. cit.*, p. 33.

[16] *Congo My Country* (New York: Frederick A. Praeger, 1962), p. 193.

[17] Excerpt from F. Kaninda's letter of July 26, 1955, to the editor of *Le Courrier dAfrique* (unpublished document).

[18] *L'Avenir du Congo Belge menacé* (Bruxelles, 1919), p. 123. For an interesting discussion of the historical background of linguistic problems in Belgium, see *ibid.*, Appendix II, pp. i–xv.

[19] "En réclamant l'école laïque," declared M. Buisseret, "nous voulons en tout premier lieu apporter un remède à une lacune bien connue, l'enseignement du français. Nous avons appris avec une grande satisfaction que le français sera la langue véhiculaire de l'école laïque; nous nous permettons d'y compter" (*Annales Parlementaires, Chambre des Représentants*, Dec. 7, 1954, p. 20).

[20] *Le Problème des langues au Congo* (Bruxelles: Sichting Lodewijk de Raet, 1958), pp. 80 ff.

[21] "Het Geval van Rechter Grootaert," *Rechskundig Weekblad*, no. 42 (July, 1956); cf. "La Vérité concernant l'affaire Grootaert ou la libéralisation de la justice au Congo" (mimeographed).

[22] In his letter of April 20, 1954, Governor-General Cornélis notified Grootaert: "Je suis chargé par le Ministre de vous avertir que des mesures disciplinaires seront prises à votre égard dans le cas où vous manqueriez au

respect dû aux magistrats de la cour d'appel" (unpublished document transmitted to me by M. Grootaert).

23 *Annales Parlementaires, Chambre des Représentants,* June 15, 1956, p. 34.

24 Article 3 of the Charte Coloniale stipulates: "The use of languages is optional. It will be regulated by decree in such a way as to guarantee the rights of Belgians and Congolese in judicial matters and official documents. Belgians will enjoy in the Congo guarantees similar to those they enjoy in Belgium. To this effect decrees will be promulgated within five years following the enactment of this law." For the text of the petition submitted by the *Vlaams Vriendenkring,* see *Conseil de Gouvernement, Compte-rendu analytique,* July 17–25, 1955, Appendix I, pp. 191 ff.

25 *Annales Parlementaires, Sénat,* May 29, 1957, p. 1407.

26 *Le Courrier d'Afrique,* Nov. 13, 1957.

27 *Conseil Colonial, Compte-rendu analytique,* April 25, 1958, p. 814.

28 *Le Problème des langues au Congo,* p. 85.

29 "Le Point de vue africain sur le problème linguistique," *L'Avenir,* March 23, 1957.

30 A. A. J. Van Bilsen, "Pour une nouvelle Politique de mouvement en Afrique," *La Revue Nouvelle* (Nov., 1954), pp. 395–411.

31 The French version of Van Bilsen's plan may be found in *Les Dossiers de l'Action Sociale Catholique,* no. 2 (Feb., 1956), 83–111.

32 I am grateful to Professor Van Bilsen for permission to consult his files.

33 From Van Bilsen's files.

34 Vernon MacKay, *Africa in World Politics* (New York: Harper and Row, 1962), p. 329.

35 Jules Chomé, *Indépendance congolaise: Pacifique Conquête* (Bruxelles: Editions de Remarques Congolaises, 1960), p. 18.

36 From Van Bilsen's files.

37 Georges Rhodius, "Vers l'Emancipation du Congo Belge?" *Rythmes du Monde,* V (1957), 115.

38 For the complete text of the countermanifesto of the Abako see Alan P. Merriam, *Congo: Background to Conflict* (Chicago: Northwestern University Press, 1961), pp. 330–336.

39 "L'Evolution de la société noire au Congo Belge," *Zaïre,* II (Oct., 1948), 846. Pierre Clément, "Patrice Lumumba (Stanleyville 1952–1953)," *Présence Africaine,* XII, no. 40 (1962), describes the traumatic experience undergone by the future leader of the MNC when he visited Brazzaville in 1947: "After having strolled a little in this capital, he became thirsty. He lingered in the neighborhood of a bar and finally decided to stop near a hedge which separated the avenue from this establishment. . . . A European woman invited him into the garden and told him to be seated where he pleased. Whites were seated at other tables. Patrice's throat tightened. Into what trap had he fallen? The owner of the bar served him herself. . . . Patrice was very uneasy; he managed to pay for the drink and left as quickly as possible, without having swallowed a drop of it."

40 *La Voix du Congolais,* no. 86 (May, 1953), 318.

41 *Abako 1950–1960* (Bruxelles: CRISP, 1962), p. 50.

42 *Congo,* June 1, 1957.

43 Peter Ritner, *The Death of Africa* (New York: Macmillan, 1960), p. 36.

44 M. C. C. de Backer, *Notes pour servir à l'étude des "groupements politiques" à Léopoldville* (Leopoldville: Infor-Congo, 1959), I, 25.

[45] *Ibid.*, p. 26.

[46] Slade, *op. cit.*, p. 45.

[47] *Tôt ou Tard, Ata Ndele* . . . (Bruxelles: Le Livre Africain, 1959), p. 34, cited in Merriam, *op. cit.*, p. 81.

[48] *Ibid.*

[49] De Backer, *op. cit.*, p. 54.

[50] Based on oral information communicated to me by M. C. C. de Backer.


VIII: The Genesis of Congolese Parties

[1] For a systematic discussion of the various types of manifestations associated with African nationalism, see James S. Coleman, "Nationalism in Tropical Africa," *American Political Science Review*, XLVIII (June, 1954), 406 ff.

[2] E. de Jonghe, "Formations récentes de sociétés secrètes au Congo Belge," *Africa*, IX, no. 1 (1936), 57.

[3] E. de Jonghe, "Fetiche indigène de guerre Tonga-Tonga," *Congo*, II (1921), 423 ff.

[4] *Rapport annuel sur l'activité de la colonie en 1921* (Bruxelles, 1922), pp. 91, 92, 116.

[5] *Ibid.*, p. 91.

[6] *L'Avenir Colonial Belge*, Aug. 21, 1931.

[7] Ralph Linton, "Nativistic Movements," *American Anthropologist*, XLIV (April-June, 1943), 232.

[8] Louis Jadin, "Le Congo et la secte des Antoniens," *Bulletin de L'Institut Historique Belge de Rome* (1961), p. 412.

[9] E. Andersson, *Messianic Popular Movements in the Lower Congo* (Uppsala, 1958). For an interesting discussion of the political implications of prophetic movements in Africa, see Vittorio Lanternari, *Les Mouvements religieux des peuples opprimés* (trans. from Italian) (Paris: François Maspero, 1962), esp. pp. 21–40.

[10] J. Maquet-Tombu, *Le Siècle marche: Récit historique* (Bruxelles, 1936), pp. 196 ff.; Andersson, *op. cit.*, pp. 270–286.

[11] Andersson, *op. cit.*, p. 58.

[12] *Rapport annuel sur l'activité de la colonie pendant l'année 1924* (Bruxelles, 1926), p. 32.

[13] Andersson, *op. cit.*, pp. 71 ff.

[14] *Ibid.*, pp. 117 ff.

[15] *Ibid.*, p. 100.

[16] Lanternari, *op. cit.*, p. 35.

[17] *Rapport AIMO, Léopoldville* (Leopoldville, 1956), p. 38.

[18] "Kitawala," *Bulletin des Jurisdictions Indigènes et du Droit Coutumier Congolais* (1943–44), p. 231; Jean Comhaire, "Sociétés secrètes et mouvements prophétiques au Congo belge," *Africa*, XXV, no. 1 (1955), 54–59; Ian Cunnison, "The Watchtower Assembly in Central Africa," *International Review of Missions*, XL (Oct., 1951), 456–469.

[19] Andersson, *op. cit.*, p. 247 n. 1.

[20] The statements made in this paragraph and the next are based on a Sûreté report, entitled "Watchtower-Kitawala: Synthèse no. 43" (unpublished document).

[21] D. Biebuyck, "La Société Kumu Face au Kitawala," *Zaïre*, XI (Jan., 1957), 7–40.

22 P. Raymaekers, "L'Eglise de Jésus-Christ sur Terre par le prophète Simon Kimbangu," *Zaïre*, no. 7 (1959), 682.

23 "Notice relative à l'Association Lulua-Frères" (unpublished document; Luluabourg, 1955).

24 *Ibid.*

25 Thomas Hodgkin, *Nationalism in Colonial Africa* (London, 1956), p. 84.

26 S. Ottenberg, "Improvement Associations among the Afikpo Ibo," *Africa*, XXV (Jan., 1955), 1–27; Robert I. Rotberg, "The Rise of African Nationalism: The Case of East and Central Africa," *World Politics*, XV (Oct., 1962), 75–90. Cf. José Lobeya, "L'Action subversive des associations illégales mixtes," *Congo Pratique* (Aug.–Sept., 1953).

27 F. Grévisse, "Activités sociales des indigènes dans le Centre Extra-Coutumier d'Elisabethville," *Bulletin de l'Association des Anciens Etudiants de l'Institut Universitaire des Territoires d'Outre-Mer*, no. 10 (1950), 7.

28 "Associations indigènes," Dossier A, Archives of Ministry of Interior, Elisabethville.

29 *La Voix du Congolais*, no. 128 (Nov., 1956), 825.

30 *Ibid.*, no. 94 (Jan., 1954), 61.

31 *Abako 1950–1960* (Bruxelles: CRISP, 1962), p. 18.

32 "La Liboke Lya Bangala. Ses Statuts, ses chefs," *La Croix du Congo*, Dec. 4, 1955.

33 See "Fedekaleo" (unpublished document).

34 "Notice relative à l'Association Lulua-Frères," p. 3.

35 In a letter to the provincial governor of the Katanga, the British consul of Elisabethville reported in July, 1954: "Members of a society called Lulua-Frères have approached the District Commissioner [of Kitwe] as they wish to collect money from Africans in the Kitwe area who come from the Luluabourg District of the Belgian Congo. These people have a number of membership cards printed for Northern Rhodesian members. Members are apparently requested to pay a membership fee of £2/0/9, and a monthly subscription of 3/9 d. The society has a banker who changes the funds collected into Belgian currency at Luanshya and then forwards it to the Belgian Congo authorities who in turn deposit the funds into the society bank account in Luluabourg" (unpublished document).

36 *Rapport AIMO, Katanga* (Elisabethville, 1956), p. 27.

37 Kenneth Little, "The Study of Social Change in British West Africa," *Africa*, XXIII (Oct., 1953), 278.

38 Dominique Manono, "Le Chauvinisme Clanique," *La Voix du Congolais*, no. 126 (Sept., 1956), 634.

39 Thomas Hodgkin, *African Political Parties* (Penguin African Series, 1961), p. 64.

40 *La Voix du Congolais*, no. 65 (Aug., 1951), 466.

41 J. Van Wing, "Quelques Aspects de l'état social des populations indigènes du Congo Belge," IRCB, *Bulletin des Séances*, XVIII (1947), 189.

42 "Du Véritable Rôle des associations d'évoluants," *La Voix du Congolais*, no. 88 (July, 1953), 472.

43 Rotberg, *op. cit.*, pp. 81, 82.

44 M. C. C. de Backer, *Notes pour servir à l'étude des "groupements politiques" à Léopoldville* (Leopoldville: Infor-Congo, 1959), I, 3.

45 *Ibid.*, p. 6.

[46] *Ibid.*, p. 8.

[47] R. Poupart, *Première Esquisse de l'évolution du syndicalisme au Congo* (Bruxelles: Institut de Sociologie Solvay, 1960), p. 24.

[48] *Ibid.*, p. 23.

[49] *Rapport sur l'administration de la colonie en 1956* (Bruxelles, 1957), p. 100.

[50] *International Labour Office, Legislative Series* (Sept.–Oct., 1958).

[51] According to an official report from Stanleyville, "la liberté syndicale n'a pas provoqué beaucoup de remous parmi la grande masse du centre-extra-coutumier. Bien que les syndicats prétendent surtout s'adresser à la masse, leurs quelques prises de position spectaculaires n'ont encore une fois ému qu'une minorite évoluée" (*District de Stanleyville, Rapport annuel*, 1957, p. 43).

[52] "Political and Social Problems in the Belgian Congo," *Industrial Labor Review*, LXXV (June, 1957), 540.

[53] "Les Elections Communales" (mimeographed; Leopoldville: Action Socialiste, 1958).

[54] *Quinze* (Aug., 1957), p. 6.

[55] In a letter to the editor of the pro-Socialist weekly *La Gauche,* one Congolese stated: "Ces socialistes intègrés au capitalisme et au colonialisme, à la manière de leurs confrères Européens d'Algérie, s'opposent en fait, comme de nombreuses occasions en ont déjà donné la preuve, à l'émancipation politique, économique et sociale du noir" (*La Gauche*, Sept. 27, 1958).

[56] *Quinze* (Aug., 1957), p. 8.

[57] For example, in January, 1958, when the workers at the Office des Transports Congolais (Otraco) went on strike to protest the wage policy of the management, the CSCC declared that the FGTBC "practiced a dangerous demagogy which threatens the unity of the workers," and accused its leaders of "obstructing the conciliation procedure" (*Le Courrier d'Afrique,* Jan. 24, 1958).

[58] *Congo Pratique* (Sept., 1953).

[59] The views contained in this paragraph and the next are based on a personal interview with Edmond Nzeza-Nlandu.

[60] *Le Courrier d'Afrique*, Nov. 23, 1953.

[61] *Ibid.*

[62] *La Voix du Congolais,* no. 88 (July, 1953), 455.

[63] *Ibid.*

[64] *Le Courrier d'Afrique*, March 21, 1954.

[65] Alan P. Merriam, *Congo: Background to Conflict* (Chicago: Northwestern University Press, 1961), Appendix II, p. 331.

[66] *Abako 1950–1960,* p. 111.

[67] *Ibid.*, p. 135.

[68] *Ibid.*, pp. 153–155.

[69] *Notre Kongo,* Feb. 14, 1962.

[70] *Abako 1950–1960,* p. 195.


IX: THE DISPERSION OF POLITICAL FORCES

[1] *Annales Parlementaires, Chambre des Représentants,* no. 89 (Nov. 4, 1959), p. 3; Pierre Artigue, *Qui sont les leaders Congolais?* (Bruxelles: Editions Europe-Afrique, 1960).

[2] For example, in a letter dated November 11, 1959, the *administrateur*

*de territoire* of Demba (Kasai) urged the provincial authorities to take appropriate steps to "sever all ties between the Demba branch of the Association Lulua-Frères and that of Luluabourg. . . . The sums received by the Luluabourg sections must be returned to Demba. . . . If we wish to keep the upper hand over the association we must deal a telling blow to the pride and conceitedness [da morgue et l'orgueil] of the Luluabourg section" (unpublished document).

³ *Présence Congolaise*, April 28, 1957.

⁴ The text of the address may be found in *Abako 1950–1960* (Bruxelles: CRISP, 1962), pp. 54–58.

⁵ *Congo*, April 17, 1957.

⁶ *Abako 1950–1960*, pp. 94–96.

⁷ *Congo*, April 17, 1957.

⁸ *Abako 1950–1960*, pp. 103–109.

⁹ As one Congolese journalist of Elisabethville correctly noted: "Il est vraisemblable qu'une majorité de conseillers appelés à siéger dans chacune des communes sera originaire de la province du Kasai. Ce n'est là que la reflet normal de la démographie du centre d'Elisabethville" (*L'Etoile-Nyota*, Dec. 23, 1957).

¹⁰ Upon the inauguration of the Fédération des Bangala, which in fact was the political expression of the Liboke Lya Bangala, Bolikango said: "Quelles sont nos appartenances politiques? Nous n'en avons rigoureusement aucune et nous defendons d'en avoir jamais. Notre Fédération n'est ni attachée ni favorable à aucune parti politique importé; elle n'est influencée par aucune conviction d'ordre confessionel: Nous n'avons qu'une étiquette—Bangala" ("Discours plein de bon sens prononcé par Bolikango à Léopoldville à la veille de son départ pour la Belgique," *L'Essor du Congo*, April 16, 1958).

¹¹ See M. C. C. de Backer, *Notes pour servir à l'étude des "groupements politiques" à Léopoldville* (Leopoldville: Infor-Congo, 1959), I, 46–48.

¹² Antoine Rubbens, "Political Awakening in the Belgian Congo," *Civilisations*, X, no. 1 (1960), 66.

¹³ *Kasai* (Luluabourg), Dec. 28, 1958.

¹⁴ *La Voix du Congolais*, no. 162 (Sept., 1959).

¹⁵ *Le Phare* (Coquilhatville), June 30, 1960.

¹⁶ *Ibid.*

¹⁷ *Horizons*, March 12, 1958.

¹⁸ *Le Courrier d'Afrique*, April 7, 1959.

¹⁹ *Annales Parlementaires, Chambre des Représentants*, no. 89 (Nov. 4, 1959), p. 3.

²⁰ *Présence Congolaise*, Jan. 2, 1960.

²¹ Artigue, *op. cit.*, p. 117.

²² *Congo*, April 20, 1957.

²³ See the *Conscience Africaine* manifesto in Alan P. Merriam, *Congo: Background to Conflict* (Chicago: Northwestern University Press, 1961), pp. 321–329.

²⁴ *Ibid.*, p. 328.

²⁵ *Présence Congolaise*, Oct. 18, 1958.

²⁶ This discussion of Lumumba's background and early political activities is drawn from my article, "Patrice Lumumba: A Political Post-Mortem?" *Africa Report* (Feb., 1961). See also Pierre de Vos, *La Vie et la mort de Patrice Lumumba* (Paris: Calmann-Levy, 1961).

²⁷ See, for example, P. Lumumba, "Le libre Accès des Congolais dans les

établissements publiques," *La Voix du Congolais,* no. 109 (April, 1955), 361–363; "A propos de l'accès des Congolais dans les établissements publiques pour Européens," *ibid.,* no. 115 (Oct.,1955), 803–807; "Un Exemple à citer," *ibid.,* no. 118 (Jan., 1956), 27–31.

[28] Pierre Clément, "Patrice Lumumba (Stanleyville 1952–1953)," *Présence Africaine,* XII, no. 40 (1962), pp. 84 ff.

[29] Cf. Merriam, *op. cit.,* pp. 290 ff.; M. N. Hennessy, *Congo* (London: Pall Mall Press, 1961), pp. 77 ff.

[30] P. Lumumba, *Congo My Country* (New York: Frederick Praeger, 1962), p. 173.

[31] For an illuminating discussion of the transformations undergone by the Batetela before and during the colonial period, see G. Brausch, "Political Changes in the Upper Lukenyi Area of the Congo," *African Studies* (June, 1944), pp. 65–74.

[32] *Congo My Country,* p. 42.

[33] De Backer, *op. cit.,* I, 31.

[34] *Ibid.,* p. 24.

[35] De Vos, *op. cit.,* pp. 119 ff.

[36] Jean Van Lierde, "Patrice Lumumba, leader et ami," *Présence Africaine,* no. 36 (1961), 114.

[37] José Lobeya, "Notice sur le MNC" (mimeographed; Leopoldville: Commissariat General à l'Information, June, 1960).

[38] *Mbandaka* (Coquilhatville), May 30, 1957.

[39] *Indépendance,* Oct. 9, 1959.

[40] De Backer, *op. cit.,* III, 81.

[41] *Ibid.*

[42] *Ibid.,* pp. 83–86.

[43] See *Mbandaka,* Sept. 10, 1959.

[44] Cited in Mabika Kalanda, *Baluba et Lulua: Une Ethnie à la recherche d'un nouvel équilibre* (Bruxelles: Editions de Remarques Congolaises, 1959), p. 67.

[45] Excerpt from personal communication.

[46] *Rapport de la Commission pour l'Etude du Problème Foncier* (Leopoldville, 1958), p. 192.

[47] See "Rapport de la Commission Parlementaire de la Chambre sur le Conflit Baluba-Lulua," in *Congo 1960: Annexes et Bibliographies* (Bruxelles: CRISP, 1961), pp. 45 ff.

[48] Cited in Kalanda, *op. cit.,* p. 11.

[49] For the full text of the Dequenne report see *ibid.,* pp. 21–34.

[50] For a study made by a group of Baluba students at Lovanium University see *Congo 1960,* I, 194–198.

[51] Kalanda, *op. cit.,* p. 32.

[52] Unpublished document.

[53] Rubbens, *op. cit.,* p. 70.

[54] For the text of the agreement see *Congo 1960,* I, 188–190.

[55] According to the Baluba chiefs Mobyaie and Katende, the president of the commission, Mr. Rae, conducted the debates with "de la dictature mêlée à une partialité" (*Le Courrier d'Afrique,* Jan. 14, 1960).

[56] This opinion is also expressed in Artigue, *op. cit.,* p. 39.

[57] *Présence Congolaise,* May 2, 1960.

[58] "Groupement d'action politique, sociale et économique: Projet de

programme d'action," Union Katangaise (unpublished document; Elisabeth-ville, April, 1958).

59 *L'Essor du Congo*, April 17, 1957.

60 *Europe-Afrique* (Bukavu), Feb. 13, 1959.

61 "Statuts," Alliance Rurale Progressiste (unpublished document).

62 De Backer, *op. cit.*, I, 30.

63 *Ibid.*, pp. 49 ff.

64 Ruth Schachter, "Single Party Systems in West Africa," *American Political Science Review*, LV (June, 1961), 295.

65 Artigue, *op. cit.*, p. 124.

66 *Mbandaka*, Nov. 14, 1959.

67 *La Cité*, Dec. 17, 1959.

68 See, for example, Pierre Davister, *Katanga: Enjeu du monde* (Bruxelles: Editions Europe-Afrique, 1961), pp. 17–27.


X: THE GENERAL ELECTIONS

1 For the text of the resolutions adopted at the Round Table see Alan P. Merriam, *Congo: Background to Conflict* (Chicago: Northwestern University Press, 1961), pp. 337–351. For the loi fondamentale see *Documents Parlementaires, Chambre des Représentants*, no. 489, pp. 1–44.

2 *Congo 1960* (Bruxelles: CRISP, 1961), I, 107.

3 "Loi relative aux élections legislatives," *Moniteur Congolais*, March 28, 1960, pp. 863 ff.

4 Walter J. Ganshoff van der Meersch, *Congo: Mai-Juin, 1960* (Bruxelles, 1960), p. 87.

5 *Le Courrier d'Afrique*, May 17, 1960.

6 Merriam, *op. cit.*, p. 184.

7 Unpublished document.

8 *Notre Kongo*, May 15, 1960, p. 4.

9 *Ibid.*, p. 7.

10 *Conakat*, May 5, 1960.

11 *Congo 1960*, I, 175–179.

12 *Ibid.*, pp. 179–181.

13 *Ibid.*, p. 260.

14 Based on mimeographed documents transmitted to me by the *bureaux* of the assemblies.

15 Van der Meersch, *op. cit.*

16 *Congo 1960*, I, 280 ff.

17 *Ibid.*, p. 283.

18 *Ibid.*, p. 294.

19 Van der Meersch, *op. cit.*, pp. 344 ff.


XI: THE SECESSION OF THE KATANGA

1 *La Situation économique du Congo Belge et du Ruanda-Urundi en 1958* (Bruxelles: Ministère des Colonies, 1959), p. 22.

2 *Rapport annuel sur la colonie du Congo Belge en 1924*, p. 83; *ibid.*, 1947, p. 258.

3 By 1957 the contribution of the Katanga to the total value of the Congo's mineral production (10,924 million BF) amounted to 8,764.5 million

BF (*Bulletin de la Banque Centrale du Congo Belge et du Ruanda-Urundi* [Dec., 1958], pp. 462 ff.; cf. *La Situation économique*, p. 49).

[4] For a global appraisal of the economic activities of the UMHK see Pierre Joye, *Les Trusts en Belgique* (Bruxelles, 1960), pp. 121 ff., and Pierre Joye and Rosine Lewin, *Les Trusts au Congo* (Bruxelles, 1961). Cf. "The Colonial Big Five," *Fortune* (Nov., 1952), pp. 113 ff.

[5] Elliot J. Berg, "The Economic Basis of Political Choice in French West Africa," *American Political Science Review*, LIV (June, 1960), 391–405.

[6] Unpublished document.

[7] This statement is corroborated by the views expressed by Professor J. Vansina in a letter to me.

[8] *Conakat*, April 20, 1960.

[9] According to Jean Brabon, some years earlier the Baluba had set up a tribal association presided over by Evariste Kimba, who subsequently joined the Conakat. But Kimba apparently misused the funds of the association and thus "lost the confidence" of the *présidents sectionnaires*. The association was dissolved, only to be resuscitated by Jason Sendwe in 1956 ("Bref résumé de la vie de la Balubakat depuis sa création jusqu'au 30 juin 1960" [unpublished document]).

[10] Commenting on the bankruptcy suffered by Tshombe's firm, a European journalist of Elisabethville, Y. de Boitsfort, wrote (*L'Essor du Congo*, Feb. 3, 1954): "Ces indigènes s'étaient crus capables à l'instar des frères de race blanche de se lancer dans le commerce en gros: 71 magasins en brousse et en outre une hotellerie; ils avaient meme fondé une société privée à responsabilité limitée, la Société Kapenda Tshombe. ... Ils declarent un passif de 3,700,000 francs alors que celui-ci atteint 7 millions." On February 23 Tshombe issued a statement in which he pointed out that such invidious comments were uncalled for, considering the assistance rendered by his firm to the Europeans during the war: "Pendant la guerre n'est-ce pas cette société qui assura régulièrement le service des transports publics entre Dilolo, Sandoa et Kapanga sans qu'il y ait la moindre réclamation de la part du service postal? Pendant la mutinerie de Luluabourg n'est-ce pas cette même société qui fut chargée d'une mission d'information?" (*L'Essor du Congo*, Feb. 23, 1954).

[11] "Une Manifestation d'envergure en l'honneur de Monsieur le Gouverneur et Madame Schoeller," *L'Etoile-Nyota*, Jan. 8, 1959.

[12] In an article published in *L'Essor du Congo*, and reproduced in the June 6, 1959, issue of *Présence Congolaise*, the leaders of the Conakat stated: "Si les indépendants nonindigènes qu'on appelle colons, vu les circonstances, nous tendent la main, nous avons tout intérêt à ne pas la refuser. En effet, le hasard ayant voulu qu'ils aient presque les mêmes intérêts à défendre dans ce beau et riche Katanga, nous les acceptons et collaboreront dorénavant avec eux." This statement prompted the editor of *Présence Congolaise* to comment: "Mais Messieurs les Conakatistes, le bras que vous vous foutez dans l'oeil risque de dépasser le coude."

[13] *L'Etoile-Nyota*, June 25, 1959.

[14] In a letter to Godefroid Munongo, dated June 8, 1959, a group of Katangese commerçants of various tribal origins declared: "Votre position vous a été dictée par l'Union Katangaise des colons pour nous imposer le fédéralisme qui sera après considéré comme l'apartheid et l'autonomie. Le 6 juin vous vous êtes dirigé vers les campagnes. Votre ami le grand colonialiste Gavage, Président de l'Union Congolaise des colons, se mit au volant de sa casserole

roulante et s'est dirigé en brousse chez tous les chefs coutumiers du Katanga pour les obliger, en les payant des grosses sommes, de refuser catégoriquement l'indépendance du Congo et accepter le fédéralisme maudit. Nous vous demandons, Munongo, de rentrer à l'Uganda d'où vous êtes ressortissant, et laissez-nous, Congolais, seuls à réclamer notre droit à l'indépendance immédiate. ... Nous sommes tous Kinois, Bukaviens, Kasaiens, Katangais, en un mot Congolais et Bantous" (unpublished document).

[15] *L'Essor du Congo*, May 26, 1959.

[16] *Ibid.*, July 29, 1959.

[17] *Le Phare du Katanga*, June 3, 1959.

[18] Antoine Rubbens, "Political Awakening in the Belgian Congo," *Civilisations*, X, no. 1 (1960), 68.

[19] "Réunion de Tentative de Conciliation entre Conakat et Fedeka tenue au domicile de Monsieur Musengeshi Laurent, bourgmestre de la Commune de Ruashi, Elisabethville" (unpublished document).

[20] In contrast with the Baluba of the Katanga, who speak Kiluba and are organized along patrilineal lines, the Baluba of the Kasai speak Tshiluba and conform to a matrilineal type of social organization. Despite these differences, however, there are still important cultural and historical affinities between the two groups (Mabika Kalanda, *Baluba et Lulua: Une Ethnie à la recherche d'un nouvel équilibre* [Bruxelles: Editions de Remarques Congolaises, 1959], esp. pp. 67–100).

[21] As specified by Sendwe in a letter sent to the Conakat leaders on February 5, 1959, "La Balubakat se réserve formellement le droit de garder son autonomie de direction et de gestion." In his letter of November 10, 1959, in which he notified the president of the Conakat of his decision, Sendwe stated: "La Balubakat se référant aux clauses contenues dans sa lettre en date du 5 février ... , après un examen approfondi et dans l'intérêt de tous, a jugé utile de se retirer pacifiquement de la Conakat. ... Ce retrait n'engage en rien les Baluba qui désirent continuer à titre individuel leur collaboration au sein de la Conakat, étant donné que nous concurrons tous par des voies différentes vers un même objectif" (unpublished document).

[22] After Sendwe was elected president of the Balubakat by the General Assembly of the association, on January 26, 1957, Kimba and Makonga became increasingly critical of the way in which he conducted the affairs of the association. Moreover, while Kimba was regarded with considerable distrust by the rank and file of the association for reasons already mentioned, Makonga antagonized the présidents sectionnaires by his alleged chauvinism toward the members of his clan, the Bene Samba. This state of affairs, further aggravated by his repeated criticisms of the internal organization of the Central Committee of the association (see "Allo, Balubakat?" *L'Etoile Nyota*, April 17, 1958), led him to resign from his post of secretary general of the cultural section of the Balubakat.

[23] "Bref Resumé de la vie de la Balubakat."

[24] G. Brausch, "L'Action en Afrique Belge de l'Institut de Sociologie Solvay," *Problèmes d'Afrique Centrale*, no. 41 (1958), 160–164.

[25] The fact that Fréart and Beckers, both employed by the Union Minière, regularly attended meetings of the Conakat is indicative of the company's interest in party policies.

[26] Commenting upon the financial aid extended to Katangese parties by "Belgian institutions with important moral and material stakes in the Katanga,"

Jules Gérard-Libois notes that "the paradox lies in the fact that the Belgian source remained the same," and that "only the channels were different" (*Congo 1960* [Bruxelles: CRISP, 1961], p. 239).

[27] The newly created party was presented by Makonga as a committee of conciliation between the Baluba of the Katanga and the other groups of the province. Citing the Kiluba maxim "Kibundi Kiswa na Bantu," Makonga stated in the April 30, 1960, issue of *Conakat*: "Certains croient que la Balubakat-pro-Conakat est un groupe de renégats qui ont rejeté le buluba. Si la maxime citée plus haut reflète notre attachement à l'autorité traditionelle, comment pouvons nous renier le buluba, chose matériellement impossible d'ailleurs et logiquement indémontrable [*sic*]."

[28] Gérard-Libois reports that this sudden defection was in part the result of a *quid pro quo* between Tshombe and Kalondji. The latter, anxious to obtain the support of the federal deputies of the Conakat for his candidacy for the post of prime minister of the central government, had apparently promised the leader of the Conakat to lend him the support of his own party in the provincial assembly on the condition that the Kasaian minority be given special guarantees (*Congo 1960*, p. 244).

[29] In the Elisabethville constituency, for example, where the Conakat polled 8,617 votes—exactly seven more than the Balubakat— three seats went to the Conakat, two to the Balubakat, and one to the MNC-Kalondji. In Dilolo the Balubakat won only as many seats as the Conakat, in spite of the fact that it obtained 2,947 more votes than its opponent (*ibid.*, p. 243).

[30] Jules Chome, *La Crise Congolaise* (Bruxelles: Editions de Remarques Congolaises, 1960), p. 48.

[31] See "Loi Fondamentale relative aux structures du Congo," Art. 123, in *Congo 1960*, p. 121.

[32] *Ibid.*, p. 253.

[33] *Ibid.*, p. 305.

[34] On June 25 Tshombe and Munongo secretly appointed a former Belgian functionary, Franz Scheerlinck, as "special ambassador" and provided him with an airplane ticket for New York, via Brussels. But the news leaked out and the authorities of Leopoldville euchred Tshombe out of his "coup" by arresting the special ambassador before he had a chance to carry out his mission (*ibid.*, pp. 254–256). It is interesting to note that during the Brussels Round Table Bonaventure Makonga went so far as to suggest a coup d'état if the Congo was not granted a unitary form of government. During an extraordinary session of the Executive Committee of the Conakat, held on January 20, 1960, Makonga stated: "Qui ne risque rien n'a rien. Il vaut mieux tenter un coup d'état et l'échouer que de se tenir les bras croisés et accepter un régime qui n'apporterait rien au Katanga" ("Procès-verbal de la séance du Comité Exécutif de la Conakat," Jan. 20, 1960 [unpublished document]).

[35] "Le Pourquoi de l'Affaire Katangaise," *Présence Africaine* (June-Sept., 1960), pp. 56 ff.

[36] *Ibid.*, p. 58.


XII: PARTY ORGANIZATION

[1] Thomas Hodgkin, *African Political Parties* (Penguin African Series, 1961), pp. 68–75. Readers of Hodgkin's admirable book will be aware of my debt to him in this chapter.

[2] *Ibid.*, p. 69.

[3] H. H. Gerth and G. W. Mills, eds., *From Max Weber: Essays in Sociology* (New York: Oxford University Press, 1946), p. 79.

[4] *Mbandaka* (Coquilhatville), Nov. 14, 1959.

[5] *La Libre Belgique,* Jan. 21, 1960.

[6] *L'Echo du Kivu,* March 22, 1960.

[7] Evaluating the effect of these restrictions on the growth of political parties in the Equateur Province, one Congolese journalist observed: "L'inexistence de partis ou de mouvements politiques est due au fait que la majorité des intellectuels de Coquilhatville oeuvrent dans l'administration. Or il ressort que ceux-ci, de par leur fonction d'agents de l'administration se voient frustrés une fois reconnues leurs activités politiques; ils deviennent les souffre-douleurs, les boucs émissaires du service, traqués per tous les moyens mis à la disposition des chefs de service" (*Cuvette Centrale* [Coquilhatville], May 15, 1959).

[8] "Agents mis en disponibilité pour convenance personelle," *La Voix du Congolais,* Supplement (April, 1959).

[9] *Courrier Africain* (CRISP), no. 49 (Jan. 22, 1960), p. 7.

[10] *Ibid.,* no. 60 (April 22, 1960), p. 3.

[11] *Abako 1950–1960* (Bruxelles: CRISP, 1962), p. 334.

[12] *Ibid.*

[13] *Courrier Africain,* no. 60 (April 22, 1960), p. 4.

[14] "Rapport de la délégation de la mission de discipline et de paix chargée de régler le différend Tati-Kini à Tshela" (mimeographed).

[15] *La Libre Belgique,* Jan. 21, 1960.

[16] J. H. Dumont, *La Table Ronde Belgo-Congolaise* (Bruxelles, 1961).

[17] See the letter addressed by Weregemere to the provincial governor, Mr. Borlée, in *L'Essor du Congo,* April 13, 1960.

[18] José Lobeya, "Notice sur le PSA" (mimeographed; Leopoldville: Commissariat à l'Information, June 11, 1960).

[19] "Procès-verbal du Comité Exécutif de la Conakat, Séance du 10 mars 1960" (unpublished document).

[20] *Ibid.*

[21] *Courrier Africain,* no. 60 (April 22, 1960), p. 5.

[22] Based on information obtained in an interview with René Lehman, former district commissioner in the Kwilu District.

[23] Based on the oral testimony of several présidents sectionnaires of the MNC-Lumumba during an interview conducted in August, 1960, in the Orientale Province.

[24] "Procès-verbal du Comité Exécutif de la Conakat, Séance du 20 Janvier 1960" (unpublished document).

[25] Smith Hempstone, *Rebels, Mercenaries and Dividends* (New York: Frederick Praeger, 1962), p. 98.

[26] P. Houart, *La Pénétration communiste au Congo* (Bruxelles: Centre de Documentation International, 1961), p. 12.

[27] *Le Courrier d'Afrique,* May 6, 1960.

[28] *Ibid.,* Feb. 19, 1960.

[29] *Abako 1950–1960,* p. 32.

[30] Houart, *op. cit.,* pp. 13–14.

[31] *Le Courrier d'Afrique,* March 11, 1960.

[32] *Ibid.,* May 13, 1960.

[33] *Ibid.*

[34] *Ibid.,* March 17, 1960.

[35] *Ibid.*, April 12, 1960.

[36] *La Voix du Peuple*, Aug. 4, 1960.

[37] *Ibid.*, July 27, 1960.

[38] *Uhuru*, Aug. 28, 1960.

[39] Hempstone, *op. cit.*, pp. 177 ff.

[40] Hodgkin, *op. cit.*, p. 122.

[41] *Abako 1950–1960*, pp. 18–19.

[42] *Ibid.*, p. 19 (italics added).

[43] *Rapport AIMO, Kasai* (Luluabourg, 1959), p. 49.

[44] *Courrier Africain*, no. 60 (April 22, 1960), p. 7.

XIII: INTERGROUP RELATIONSHIPS

[1] M. C. C. de Backer, *Notes pour servir à l'étude des "groupements politiques" à Léopoldville* (Leopoldville: Infor-Congo, 1959), I, 15–27.

[2] *Ibid.*, p. 23.

[3] Pierre Artigue, *Qui sont les leaders Congolais?* (Bruxelles: Editions Europe-Afrique, 1960), pp. 123–125.

[4] *Mbandaka*, Nov. 14, 1959.

[5] *Congo 1959* (Bruxelles: CRISP, 1960), p. 159.

[6] *Abako 1950–1960* (Bruxelles: CRISP, 1962), pp. 248–254.

[7] *Ibid.*, p. 256.

[8] *Ibid.*, p. 298.

[9] *Le Courrier d'Afrique*, Jan. 11, 1960.

[10] *Ibid.*

[11] *Congo 1960* (Bruxelles: CRISP, 1961), I, 22.

[12] "Accord entre les principales forces politiques du Katanga conclue à Bruxelles le 9 février 1960" (unpublished document).

[13] *Congo 1960*, p. 202.

[14] "Notice sur le Parti Solidaire Africain," Document No. 75 (mimeographed; Leopoldville: Commissariat Général a l'Information, June 11, 1960), p. 3.

[15] *Le Courrier d'Afrique*, March 30, 1960.

[16] *Ibid.*, March 25, 1960.

[17] *Ibid.*, March 31, 1960.

[18] *Ibid.*, March 19, 1960; *L'Echo du Kivu*, March 22, 1960.

[19] *Le Congrès de Lodja* (n.p., n.d.).

[20] *Ibid.*

CONCLUSION

[1] Karl W. Deutsch, "The Growth of Nations: Some Recurrent Patterns of Political and Social Integration," *World Politics*, V (Jan., 1953), 168–196.

[2] *Congo 1960* (Bruxelles: CRISP, 1961), p. 7.

[3] James S. Coleman, *Nigeria: Background to Nationalism* (Berkeley and Los Angeles: University of California Press, 1958), p. 412.

[4] Unpublished document.

[5] Personal communication.

[6] Crawford Young, "Congo Political Parties Revisited," *Africa Report* (Jan., 1963), p. 20.

7 *New York Times,* May 6, 1963.

8 David Apter, "Some Reflections on the Role of a Political Opposition in New Nations," *Comparative Studies in Society and History,* IV (Jan., 1962), 157.

9 Edmund Burke, *Reflections on the Revolution in France* (World's Classics ed.; London, 1907), p. 109.

# INDEX